Thiefing Sugar

Perverse Modernities

A series edited by
Judith Halberstam
and Lisa Lowe

Thiefing Sugar

Eroticism between Women in Caribbean Literature

Omise'eke Natasha Tinsley

Duke University Press
Durham and London   2010

Printed in the United States of America
on acid-free paper ∞
Typeset in Trinité
by Tseng Information Systems, Inc.

Library of Congress
Cataloging-in-Publication Data
appear on the last printed page
of this book.

For my very beloved great-grandmother,
Artis Phillips Stapler,
who left Good Water, Alabama,
so that she would never have to be a farmer's wife
but took her landscape knowledge to Birmingham,
where she went into the forests to find healing roots
when her family needed them

And with honor and respect for
Dr. *Barbara Christian*
Dr. *VèVè A. Clark,*
without whom it would not have been possible

Contents

Acknowledgments

As I have visited and revisited the overflowing, erotic geographies of these texts over the past seven years – waking and dreaming, in body and in imagination, tracing them in loving amazement – my gratitude to the women whose complex, brilliant work I have had the honor to live with has deepened continually. My first acknowledgments, therefore, go to them, for their generosity in giving words and silences to their desires. Gloria Wekker, whose work on the *mati* I stumbled on in a bookstore in Amsterdam and which immediately changed my intellectual life, has been unflaggingly open and generous in answering my questions over these years. Her support of my work, her transcription of *lobisingi* – beautifully, even singing them for me – and, most important, the work she has done to change the fields of Caribbean and queer studies, have been invaluable to me. Jean Faubert has greeted my work on his grandmother Ida with such luminous kindness and enthusiasm that I certainly cannot thank him enough here. His ongoing willingness to share photos, information, and encouragement has been an incredible, golden gift. Michelle Cliff and Dionne Brand remain generous about answering my inquiries, a much appreciated act for such busy writers. I thank you all abundantly.

And as I have worked to become a [better] writer about these writers, I have been graced with incredible mentors who helped make my impossible aspirations possible. First and foremost, Karl Britto, my dissertation director at the University of California, Berkeley, has been a more wonderful advisor than I ever could have imagined. From near and from far, he has read my chapters, prospecti, worries, hopes, and joys for the last eleven years and has always come back to me with calm, measure, and encouragement. Thank you, Karl; this book exists because you nurtured it. Also at Berkeley, Chana Kronfeld's insightful, beautiful readings of my work and her purple-penned comments have continued to be an inspiration, and I thank her for introducing me to the possibilities of poetics. Johan Snapper, Estelle Tarica, and Francine Masiello offered their continued support of my project and of my unconventional choice of Dutch over Spanish as my official third language in comparative literature. The brilliant VèVè Clark, who directed my undergraduate thesis, saved my undergraduate intellectual life and continued to direct me through her own illness in graduate school: everything I am as a scholar, I am because of her – I recognize her in every word I write. And Barbara Christian, for the light that she was and is, I thank her, unendingly.

Support for the research in this book has come from the Department of Comparative Literature and Dutch Studies at the University of California, Berkeley; from the Andrew Mellon Postdoctoral Fellowship in Caribbean Literature at the University of Chicago, which made more difference to this project than I can express here; and from the Department of English and the College of Liberal Arts at the University of Minnesota, Twin Cities. Special thanks to Joshua Scodel, Michael Hancher, and Paula Rabinowitz, my department chairs at the University of Chicago and the University of Minnesota, for their help in securing these funds for my work.

Many colleagues have generously read versions of this manuscript and/or its parts, pushing me to expand and contract, to move toward the lyrical and the experimental. At the University of Chicago, Jacqueline Goldsby, Joshua Scodel, and Robert von Hallberg showed their engaged support by reading early versions of my work and suggesting turns toward the unexpected; thank you for taking the time. At the University of Minnesota, Ellen Messer-Davidow and Maria Damon generously showed their support for this junior colleague by reading and commenting on the manuscript as I prepared to send it off to publishers; their thoughtfulness in doing so has helped make this publication possible. And the members of my writing group, Siobhan Craig, Shaden Tageldin, and Christophe Wall-Romana, acted as sensitive and insightful readers during the fifteen months of my final revisions; the brightness of their eyes and thoughts, and their attention to detail and inspiration, have been wonderful to me. From far across the country and far beyond the call of duty, Rosamund King, on the other side of the Great Lakes, and Matt Richardson, at the other end of the Mississippi, generously read chapter drafts in spare time that they did not have but made. As scholars who are opening groundbreaking work in black queer studies, their careful readings have been inspiring, and their great-spiritedness in taking the time has been invaluable. Thank you, humbly.

A special debt of heart appreciation goes out to those colleagues and friends who believed in the importance of this queer sea of Black Atlantic islands I went looking for, reflected that importance back, and encouraged me to go where the texts led. Thomas Glave, for generosity with advice, support, and the beauty of his prose; E. Patrick Johnson, for encouraging me to take chances; Cathy Cohen, for reaching out and supporting me; and Roderick Ferguson, for encouragement, strategy, and the great gift of academic health: to all of you, my sincere, expansive gratitude. And an endless, warm thank you to my series editor Jack Halberstam. His fierce intellectual support, his gentle yet firm push for me to make this project better than I imagined, and the continual, crystal-sharp clarity of his insight have been unexpected, wonderful gifts, and he remains my model of what it means to mentor a junior scholar with all generosity.

Much appreciation also goes to the anonymous readers of this manuscript, whose carefulness, precision, and beautiful prose left me—yes, quite seriously—with tears of gratitude for taking so much time with and paying such attention to my work. Ken Wissoker at Duke University Press has been an incredible editor to work with, and his support, generosity, and good humor have made this process a wonderful experience. Mandy Early at Duke University Press and Dale Mossestad at the University of Minnesota Libraries more than deserve my copious thanks for their patience and attentiveness with my many, many questions about preparing this manuscript: thank you for help every step along the way! And my gratitude to the editors of the groundbreaking Perverse Modernities series, Lisa Lowe and Judith Halberstam. Their work in this series has been an inspiration to me and an enormous contribution to the present and future of scholarship, and I am so very, very honored to be included in it.

My family's patience with and support for my intense, ongoing relationship with my computer-bound manuscript, and their hope that they would one day hear me talk about its results on Oprah, have bolstered me through this long process. Thank you to my mother, Helen, and my father, Jim, who have wanted to read drafts of what their daughter has done; to my stepfather Sheldon, who always asks, and my stepmother Rowena; to my sisters and brothers, Christina, Nicole, Adam, and Rabbit; my niece Sophia, who let me take breaks from playing Little Mermaid to write, my nephew Elijah, and my niece Katie. And to my grandfather John, that he may see this with pride on the other side, and my grandmother Herta—yes, as I promised as a little girl, I have become a writer as I have grown up. Dulce and Ariel, my loves, know that I never could have done this without them by my side, warmly and unconditionally. Thank you to my godmother, Imani, for seeing so much creativity waiting in the depths for me to dive into. And—with amazement—to my daughter Baía Amihan, growing beautifully, patiently, rainbowly inside me as I finished the last of the copy-edits.

And last but never, never least, Kale Bantigue Fajardo has seen me through the writing of this from the longest, brightest days of summer to the longest, bluest nights of winter, and has, with a generous Leo heart, believed in me throughout them all. To you, Kale, *salamat* for being my shipmate, always, for being my companion in scholarship and so much more, and for being the only sailor I know who still recognizes mermaids.

Introduction

The Spring of Her Look

If you are from a country, if you're born there, a natal native
as they say: well then, you have it in your eyes, your skin, your
hands, with the flowing hair of the trees, the flesh of its earth,
the bones of its rocks, the blood of its rivers, its skin, its taste,
its men and women: it is a presence in your heart, indelible,
like a girl you love, you know the spring of her look, the fruit
of her mouth, the hills of her breasts, her hands which
protect then give in, her knees without mysteries, her
strength and weakness, her voice and silence.

— Jacques Roumain, *Gouverneurs de la rosée*

I want to show homosexuality or lesbianism or gayness,
whatever you want to call it, as a whole identity, not just
a sexual preference. . . . What would it mean for a woman
to love another woman in the Caribbean?

— Michelle Cliff in Judith Raiskin, "The Art of History"

Grace. Is grace, yes. And I take it quiet, quiet,
like thiefing sugar.

— Dionne Brand, *In Another Place, Not Here*

If, on a spring morning that begins with what the Martinican poet Lucie Thé-sée calls a sea sky and an earth like sea floor,[1] you have found this book on the bookstore shelf . . . if you have opened its cover, run your fingers and eyes over the title and subtitle, flipped past the table of contents to see the opening epigraphs . . . you may come to this first paragraph with two questions. First, you may wonder along with the Jamaican lesbian novelist Michelle Cliff: what *does* it mean for a woman to love another woman in the Caribbean? Having stumblingly asked this question of women, rivers, sea floors, dreams, drums, and books from Suriname to the Seine and Brooklyn to Blanchisseuse, I have listened well enough to offer no transparent answer. Instead, this exploratory study puts into conversation West Indian poets and novelists who answer Cliff's question in slippery, opaque, indeterminate, and metaphoric ways by imagining desire between women moving obliquely – riverinely – through the uneven geographic and cultural landscapes of the Caribbean. Looking at texts from Suriname, Jamaica, Haiti, Martinique, and Trinidad, this book engages dance, songs, poems, and novels in which women writers reclaim and rework traditional landscape metaphors like Jacques Roumain offered as one of the epigraphs here.[2] As they take rushing springs and breast-hills into their own mouths, these authors perform what Jean Franco calls "struggles for interpre-tive power . . . incandescent moments when different configurations of gender and knowledge are briefly illuminated."[3] These electric struggles are initiated here with a question: What happens when the beloved/landscape and the poet/lover are *both* women? While Franco's influential study plotted women in the history of Mexico, *Thiefing Sugar* traces women's complex material and symbolic relationships with the plots of land on which they live, work, play, garden, talk politics, and engage in relationships with other women. Most simply, I engage those "incandescent moments" at which their queering of a Caribbean landscape charts a poetics and politics of decolonization. That is, I stop to look where texts take tropes like women-as-flowers, women-as-water, women-as-sugar cane, invented to justify keeping Caribbean women and territories in someone else's control, and redeploy these same tropes to imagine a landscape belonging to Caribbean women and Caribbean women belonging to each other. In this, these writers' working and reworking of intimate landscapes constitute black feminist imaginations that complicate, dismantle, and reconfigure the interlocking fictions of power that shadow the region.

You may wonder, too, at the title: what does it mean to *thief sugar*? Those words come from the graceful opening sentences of Dionne Brand's novel

In Another Place, Not Here, and they ground the metaphor that the cane cutter Elizete uses to describe her first encounter with her lover Verlia. A woman
loving a woman, she imagines, is like a cane cutter thiefing sugar. Beckoned by
this rich image, I chose my title because I see each of the women's texts I read
here as "thiefing sugar" in a number of ways. The sugar they reclaim for their
own use is the syrup of figurative language – the long-standing colonial tropes
of Caribbean women as sugar, water, and flowers that these authors take up for
their own poetic and political uses. It is the cane stock of their geographic and
cultural landscape, the sugar plantations, gardens, and rivers that they reclaim
as a space in which (post)colonial women can move in creative ways. And it is, of
course, their sexuality, the sweetness of eroticism. The metaphoric phrase *thiefing sugar* calls up the contested space of the cane field: a site of sexual violence
and exploited labor, a Caribbean landscape that was never a natural topos but
one constructed for colonial purposes. A central undertaking of my book is to
draw parallels between women of color's sexuality and this manipulated cane-
scape. Slavery's writs restrained Afro-Caribbean women's ability to dispose of
the sugar and the sexuality that their laboring bodies produced with equal
brutality. France's Code Noir made it illegal on pain of whipping for slaves
to sell sugar "for any reason or occasion whatsoever, even with their masters'
permission," while the code's declaration of slaves' status as movable property
made it legal for women's bodies – along with their productive, reproductive,
and sexual labor – to be sold, inherited, and traded from before they were born
until they died.[4] If these are the orders of slavery, then how can an imagination
of emancipation not include many ways of thiefing sugar?

Placing my work under this title, I want to open a space to think of creative ways for envisioning both female sexuality, which is not a natural "ori-
entation" but a historically constructed understanding of women's bodies, and
landscape, which is not trees, rivers, or flowers but an imagined relationship
between all these as something other than already formed entities. Instead,
both sexuality and landscape emerge as ongoing processes that can be interrupted and redirected. Like cane fields, they are sites of continuing work that
Caribbean women poets and novelists engage in complex ways. Recognizing
their literary cane-work, I argue, stands to intervene incisively in several fields
of contemporary scholarship. Plotting the sugar thiefing of Caribbean women
who love women means opening discursive space for sexuality studies to engage historically specific, previously unmapped erotic geographies, looking for
what resistant sexualities mean outside the metropole and in the (cane) field.

At the same time, it means imagining space for postcolonial studies to map the material and symbolic contributions of historically unseen, feminized, and sexualized bodies to decolonizing nations, looking for resistance in muscles tensed in Lordean revolutionary eroticism as well as Fanonian revolutionary violence.[5] Perhaps most resonantly, though, listening for stolen sugar means opening a call-and-response within black feminism: asking for dialogue that speaks with and beyond African North America's cotton-field languages, with and beyond Caribbean feminism's plotting of male-female cane field alliances, to imagine brown women keeping sweetness among themselves.

Thiefing sugar has never been easy – sharp cane stalk can cut cane cutters – and so the work that follows is neither straightforward nor simple. Moving as precariously and carefully as bench trails between critical stylistics, history, anthropology, linguistics, black feminist theory, queer theory, and postcolonial studies,[6] my readings explore the intersections of women's erotic love for women with issues of gender, colonialism, migration, labor history, violence, and revolutionary politics implicated in the literary topoi these texts reimagine. The texts' linguistic span reaches across Dutch-, English-, and French-language regions, and their time span reaches across the past century. When I began this project, I imagined working mostly with contemporary texts that spoke to current issues. In fact, however, what held my attention were their ancestors, "recovered" texts from the first half of the twentieth century. While much queer scholarship on the Global South begins by speaking about the present, I find it impossible to fully engage that present without taking stock of the erased stories of where heterogeneous sexual formations came from. With this in mind, I begin at the opening of the twentieth century, examining the period considered by most historians as that in which the modern lesbian subject emerged, and runs through its final decade to current debates on international gay and lesbian rights.

As I have conceptualized it, the book is divided into two sections. The first focuses on how recovering women-loving women's voices complicates received pictures of postcolonial cultural landscapes. Chapter 1, "Rose is my mama, *stanfaste* is my papa," analyzes the performances of Surinamese women in turn-of-the-century Paramaribo, where working-class communities normalized sexual partnerships between women, and – never hidden or marginalized – *mati* ("girlfriends") sang to female lovers in the town square on Sundays. Chapter 2, "Darkening the Lily," turns to *Luminous Isle* (1934), an autobiographical novel by Jean Rhys's friend, the white Jamaican Eliot Bliss, and explores how its representations of interracial same-sex desire "mix up" colonial geographies of whiteness. "Blue Countries, Dark Beauty," chapter 3, excavates long-buried erotic poems to women written in the 1920s by Ida Faubert, the daughter of a Haitian president, and considers why, instead of the Paris Lesbos where she lived, she chose a Haiti of her imagination as the "natural" space to sketch desire between women. The second half focuses on how centering islanders' expressions of desire disrupts the worldview of Eurocentric queer theories. "At the River of Washerwomen," my chapter 4, opens queer readings of waterside love scenes in Mayotte Capécia's I Am a Martinican Woman (1948), a novel made infamous by Frantz Fanon's shredding criticism of its sexual politics, to show how material, historical circumstances complicate universalizing theories of the emancipatory value of sexual fluidity. Chapter 5, "Transforming Sugar, Transitioning Revolution," looks at riverine intersections of race and gender in Michelle Cliff's No Telephone to Heaven (1987), looking at how the mixed-race, gender-complex, male lesbian protagonist models expansive imaginations of decolonization. Finally, "Breaking Hard against Things," chapter 6, examines how Dionne Brand maps a seaside confluence of anticolonial and sexual revolutions in her groundbreaking collection No Language Is Neutral (1990), reclaiming the beaches of Trinidad and Grenada as sites of embodied resistance.

I want to be clear, though: these are neither the only nor the "best" texts that speak of desire between Caribbean women. My choice of texts is based not solely on the commonality that each features same-sex desire but also on the key interventions that their poetics of decolonization stands to make in Caribbean, black feminist, queer, and postcolonial studies. As a case study of specific texts, this book is also a case study of the possibility of reconfiguring how we gender history and historicize sexuality: thievery and sweetness here fill in absences associated with "the Caribbean" and "woman" to imagine both differently – not as isolated islands in a sea but as a fiery sea of islands where cane and bodies burn insistently.[7]

Whatever You Want to Call It:
A Working Vocabulary for Desire

Recognizing how Cliff's question echoes like a refrain for me through the geographies and desires traced in these texts, I want to return to its specifics. For a woman to love another woman in the Caribbean: what would it mean, who would it mean, and how would it mean in this sea of islands in which names and histories multiply volcanically? Every phrase of Cliff's comment and question reverberates with the difficulties of language for African diaspora sexuality studies. Homosexuality or lesbianism or gayness – what to call it? In the past fifteen years, *queer* has gained solid theoretical preference over *gay/lesbian* among Euro-American scholars. Teresa de Lauretis made the first high-profile use of *queer theory* in her introduction to an issue of *differences* in 1991 titled "Queer Theory: Lesbian and Gay Sexualities," in which she explained that the term's importance lay in its broadening of the conventional meanings of *gay* and *lesbian* and that the theory's queerness should be understood not as a consideration of same-sex desire but as the disruption of normative gender, sexuality, and relationships: "The term 'queer,' juxtaposed to the 'lesbian and gay' of the subtitle, is intended to mark a certain critical distance from the latter, by now established and often convenient formula. . . . the term 'Queer Theory' was arrived at in the effort to avoid all of these fine distinctions in our discursive protocols, not to adhere to any one of these terms, not to assume their ideological liabilities, but instead both to transgress and to transcend them – or at the very least problematize them."[8] But in gender and sexuality studies *queer* itself has now become an established and convenient term from which scholars might mark critical distance. Emerging work on Global South sexual formations like Martin Manalansan's *Global Divas*, Megan Sinnott's *Toms and Dees*, Gayatri Gopinath's *Impossible Desires*, and Joseph Massad's *Desiring Arabs* challenges northern theorists to recognize why, in addition to positing that *queer* means many things, they must take seriously that *queer* is only one construction of nonheteronormative sexuality among many – and that listening to other languages, and others' historically specific sexual self-understandings, is crucial to broadening the field.[9]

So can a woman be *queer* in Patwa or Kreyòl or Sranan, and should she want to be? What vocabulary works for African diaspora grammars of gender and sexuality in the English-, French- and Dutch-based creoles that spread rhizomatically through the Americas' (former) slave societies? Scholars of black American sexualities have suggested many answers to this question over the past decade. In Kingston the Jamaican Forum of Lesbians, All Sexuals, and Gays (JFLAG) opts for *lesbian and gay*, and the organization's cofounder, the fiction writer and essayist Thomas Glave, notes that while he favors *queer*, this is not a term that people use for themselves in Jamaica or elsewhere in the Anglophone Caribbean.[10] Speaking from a similar situation in African North

America, E. Patrick Johnson calls for the development of "quare studies": *quare* being the black southern vernacular for *queer*, so that quare studies would be to queer studies what womanist is to feminist and what "reading is to throwing shade."[11] But while the Caribbean women's texts I look at do speak African pan-American languages, *quare* is not in them, and though some writers identify as *lesbian*, many do not. Sappho's birth island only became the spatial signifier for female same-sex sexuality in 1870 and in Europe; and in the current-crossing archipelago of Caribbean islands, other histories and words circulated before and after the invention of that noun.[12]

Like Trinidad's *jamettes*, Jamaica's *man royals*, Haiti's *madivines*, and Barbados's *wicca*, many involved in same-sex relationships here have done so openly in the context of working-class Afro-Caribbean traditions called *mati* in Suriname, *zanmi* in Grenada, and *kambrada* in Curaçao. These last terms can refer without distinction to female friends or lovers: *mi mati* is like *my girl* in African American English, maybe my friend or maybe my lover. *Mati* and *zanmi* particularly are used more frequently in verbal constructions than in nominal ones. Women do *mati* work or make *zanmi*, verbalizing sexuality not as identity but as praxis, something constantly constructed and reconstructed through daily actions. As the doubly signifying Creole vocabulary for these practices suggests, *mati* love women in a language and culture that at once leave this eroticism unnamed or undifferentiated from other sharings between women *and* bend to communicate it without separating doing *mati* work from other aspects of their lives and languages in Caribbean working-class communities. *Lesbian* markedly comes from a Mediterranean island, Lesbos; but east and south of there and sinking deeper, *mati* comes from the middle of the Atlantic Ocean. Derived from the Dutch *maat* or *mate*, *mati* also means "mate" as in "shipmate": she who survived the Middle Passage with me.[13] On these crossings captive African women created erotic bonds with other women in the sex-segregated holds, resisting the commodification of their bought and sold bodies by *feeling* and *feeling for* their co-occupants on these ships. Once arrived in the New World, women in some parts of the Caribbean continued relationships with *mati* in female friendship and kinship networks. As early as 1793 Bryan Edwards remarks: "This is a striking circumstance; the term *shipmate* is understood among [West Indian slaves] as signifying a relationship of the most endearing nature; perhaps as recalling the time when the sufferers were cut off together from their common country and kindred, and awakening reciprocal sympathy from the remembrance of mutual affliction."[14] Two hundred years later, the anthropologist Gloria Wekker traced linkages between these shipmate relationships that exist throughout the African diaspora and the sociosexual practice of *mati* in twentieth-century working-class Creole communities. And, she concludes, "slave women in other parts of the Caribbean developed comparable forms of relating to each other, pointing to the resiliency of West African cultural heritage."[15]

At the turn of the twenty-first century, *lesbian* had entered Caribbean languages as a noun, but it was not the only word and history women could call on to speak desire for females. The adoption of gay and lesbian identity and human rights vocabulary strategically links JFLAG to well-known, well-funded groups like the International Gay and Lesbian Human Rights Commission (IGLHRC). At the same time, it makes the Jamaican organization vulnerable to imperialist rhetoric that sees Caribbean lesbians as passive victims of the Global South's "underdevelopment" of sexual identity who need assistance from more advanced northern sisters. The answer to this conundrum, of course, is not to crown any one noun or adjective "most" emancipatory but to maintain productive tensions between them, and the vocabularies of the texts examined here speak to this. Some of the writers I read use European lexicons of same-sex sexuality while others use Afro-Caribbean ones; some interweave the two while others reject both. Dancing with these mobile terms and taking a cue from Creoles' verbal constructions of sexuality (that you "make" rather than "are" *zanmi*), I avoid the culturally specific nouns *lesbian*, *dyke*, *zanmi*, *madivine*, and *sodomite* to designate same-sex sexuality in general in the Caribbean and opt for a verb phrase — *women who love women* — that aims to reach beyond shortcomings of either-or identity politics.[16] To put Caribbean writers' work in conversation as the expressions of women who love women means imagining a space in which *mati* and lesbianism enter into multilingual, multigenerational dialogue that, beginning in a volcanic global Southern archipelago, destabilizes the current cultural balance of power in queer/quare theory and LGBT activism. Like Cliff's phrase "homosexuality or lesbianism or gayness, whatever you want to call it," the many vocabularies possible under the umbrella "women who love women" work to dismantle the closet by decentering it, by positioning this trope in a spectrum of constructions of sexuality in which *mati*, *zanmi*, *bull dagger*, or *lesbian* all carry their own cultural and historical weight. In so doing, they leave conceptual room for what Rinaldo Walcott calls the "whatever" of black diaspora studies: the whatever, where "the uncertainties and commonalities of blacknesses might be formulated in the face of some room

for surprise, disappointment, and pleasure without recourse to disciplinary and punishing measures . . . a whatever that can tolerate the whatever of blackness without knowing meaning – black meaning, that is – in advance of its various utterances."[17] Black meaning, or Kreyòl meaning, or queer meaning, or *mati* meaning.

Still, a noun persists both in my verb phrase and in Cliff's question: women who love women, a woman to love another woman – the problematic noun *woman* returns. It is both an easily available and uncomfortable word; I myself identify as femme rather than woman, for what I think are good reasons. Creating *Gender Trouble*, Judith Butler famously demonstrates why *woman* is a heteropatriarchal invention that feminists should no longer naively, unproblematically organize around.[18] But years before this foundational queer theory text, black feminist scholars already powerfully showed the limits of "woman" as a universal subject by arguing that slavery in fact systematically *ungendered* African females. Not only is no one born a woman, they documented, but for centuries enslaved Africans were prevented from becoming such a thing in the discursive and material universe of their captors. In this work "woman" emerges not as a universal signifier for a feminine female – *obinrin* is not the "same" as woman, as Oyèrónke Oyěwùmí, insightfully argues in her work on Yoruba gender – but as the name given to an exclusive, policed, and specifically European gender formation.[19] Hortense Spillers's chillingly insightful "Mama's Baby, Papa's Maybe: An American Grammar Book" (1987) and Rhoda Reddock's precise, pioneering "Women and Slavery in the Caribbean: A Feminist Perspective" (1985) set the standard on blacks' unwomaning in African North America and the Caribbean, respectively. Perhaps because of this history and as an example of a *Caribbean* "grammar book," Creole languages speak gender in the region as more complex than any naturalized masculine-feminine duality. The absence of grammatical gender for Creole nouns (Sranan *wan* instead of Spanish *uno/una*) and pronouns (Haitian *li* instead of French *il/elle*) suggests a culturally specific grammar of gender that differs from Europe's compulsory binary. This absence is accompanied by rich vocabulary to express female masculinity and male femininity. *Mannengre meid, man royal, masisi, makoumè* name masculine females and feminine males, and all – like *fanm* (woman) or *man* — are spoken of in the third person using gender-neutral pronous *li* and *im*.[20] Yet despite these Creole gender complexities – though not all the authors I engage with call themselves *lesbian* or *mati* and though some might also call themselves *mannengre meid* or *man royal* – all identify as *women*. Indeed, part of what engages me in their work is an ongoing wrestling with and refusal to release this word that is, like the continual revision of *shipmate*, a legacy of slavery and resistance.

To make historical sense of these writers' continual struggle with womanness, consider more closely how unwomaning did and did *not* work under chattel slavery. Slave ships and cane fields, Spillers and Reddock document, constituted critical sites in which colonial machinery systematized Africans' violent ungendering in the eyes of their captors. Plans for slave galleys calculated the difference between kidnapped females and males *only* as one of volume occupied onboard: five females were allotted the same cargo area as four males. From this chilling detail, Spillers underscores how the passage's radical "unmaking" of identities – names, nationalities, religions, languages – also included forced gender undifferentiation, so that "the slave ship, its crew, and its human-as-cargo stand for a wild and unclaimed richness of possibility that is not interrupted, not 'counted'/'accounted' or differentiated, until its movement gains the land thousands of miles away from the point of departure. Under these conditions, one is neither female, nor male, as both subjects are taken into 'account' as *quantities*. The female in 'Middle Passage,' as the apparently smaller physical mass, occupies 'less room' in a directly translatable money economy. But she is, nevertheless, quantifiable by the same rules of accounting as her male counterpart."[21] Once ships landed in the Caribbean, cane fields continued the dehumanization and/as unwomaning begun at sea. Caribbean plantations, Reddock details, leveled labor distinctions between the sexes even more severely than those in North America. For one, females were employed in cane gangs in equal or higher numbers than males, performing the same tasks but living up to five years longer. But West Indian planters' strategy of "buying rather than breeding" – working slaves to death and replacing them with new kidnapees rather than allowing slowed work for gestation, birth, or breast-feeding – also meant that pregnant workers received no differential treatment, and slave motherhood was not (as Spillers finds in North America) a way for females to become women. Conscripted to cut cane even in the ninth month of pregnancy, more than half of enslaved females never gave birth at all due to miscarriages, amenorrhea, and abortions.[22] To justify this treatment of kidnapped Africans as neuter work units, imperial narratives insisted that ungendering preceded slavery and that, in fact, no significant markers ever distinguished black females from males – that something in the race's physical makeup made its members' animal sexual differences incapable of adding up to desirable, recognizable femininity. Traveling to West Africa in 1555, William Towerson proclaimed that "men and women go so alike that one cannot know a man from a woman but by their breasts which in the most part be very foule and long, hanging down low like the udder of a goat"; Richard Burton saw African females not only as beasts but as beasts of burden, noting that their "masculine physique" matched males' in "enduring toil, hardships, and privations" – proving the sexes equally fit for slavery.[23]

While this machinery of violent unwomaning was never abandoned, it became increasingly insufficient to regulate power spirals between capitalism, slavery, sexuality, and reproduction as both the plantation system and organized slave resistance expanded in the eighteenth century. Their plantations ringed by waves of maroon wars and rebellions, colonizers experimented with promoting the birth of Creole blacks, whom they assumed less likely than Africans to revolt. So colonizers legislated social distinctions not only between males and females but also between females who participated in reproductive heterosexuality and those who did not. Tobago laws of 1798, for example, awarded the former a house, livestock, and clothing when married, spared them from five weeks' work after childbirth, and granted total work exemption to mothers of six children.[24] But this push to gender through reproduction fell flat in the cane. Not only did the enslaved continue to resist bearing new chattel for their owners, so that birth rates never significantly increased, planters also vociferously refused to obey the laws, loudly arguing that the masculine, aggressive, and unruly nature of black females made any concessions to them unnecessary, foolish, and dangerous. When Britain outlawed whipping female slaves (a frequent cause of miscarriage), Mr. Hamden proclaimed to the Barbados legislature: "Our black ladies have rather a tendency to the Amazonian cast of character; and I believe that their husbands would be very sorry to hear that they were placed beyond the reach of chastisement."[25] Ridiculing the feminine gender "black ladies," Hamden's counterassertion of "a tendency to the Amazonian" suggests more than it admits about the complex workings of gender, sexuality, and resistance that planters were attempting and failing to control. By the eighteenth century, *Amazonian* connoted female masculinity, female same-sex sexuality, and female warriors; and in an era that resented female slaves both as failed heterosexual reproducers and as potential rebels, this adjective intimates that planters saw black females' resistant genders and sexualities, their stubborn unwifeness, enmeshed with the armed resistance threatening plantations, their stubborn unslaveness.[26] Hamden's statement also insinuates that Caribbean planters' supposed solution to dangerous Amazonianness was not *compulsory motherhood*, as in North America, but *compulsory heterosexuality*: slave husbands, without actual patriarchal power, are evoked less as real people than as symbols of a heterosexual domination that could keep enslaved females properly docile. Caribbean slavery would compel black females to become women not so that they could be bred, but so that they could be hetero-fucked.

And they were, often by white men. In this archipelago where few European women settled, the presence of housekeepers, *ménagères* or *huishoudsters* — females of color in ongoing relationships with white males — at once institutionalized interracial heterosexuality and domesticized slavery's social imbalances, embedding them in the realm of the intimate in ways that partnerships between slaves could not. But these relationships also caught planters in a bind: the forced unwomaning of African females that had migrated so supply from slave ship to cane field stumbled when invited into the bedroom. White males sharing beds with brown females did not want to see their sexual consorts as almost-men, making their sex sodomy; nor did they want to equate them absolutely with animals, which would make their encounters bestiality. To navigate this bind, especially in cases of long-term concubines, colonial imaginations experimented with the idea that some females of African descent could be humanized *and so feminized* by relationships with white men. Exceptional specimens could become dark versions of *women*, that is, legitimate objects of white male heterosexual desire. This idea informs the imagination of Isaac Teale's famous "Sable Venus," which exclaims:

> O sable queen! Thy mild domain
> I seek, and court thy gentle reign
> So soothing, soft and sweet;
> Where mounting love, sincere delight
> Fond pleasure, ready joys invite
> And unbought raptures meet.[27]

What makes sable beauties into women is how naturally, how sincerely they express interracial heterosexual desire, "mounting love" and "unbought raptures" for European male partners. Such love, planters rationalized, not only elevated interracial sex above the bestial but also mitigated slavery's inhumanity. "Love," writes M. de Chanvalon of Martinique, "the child of nature . . . inspires and invigorates all the thoughts and purposes of the Negro, and lightens the yoke of ... slavery."[28] Increasingly, though, this love slipped from the yoke of slavery altogether, as housekeepers and their progeny were among those most frequently manumitted. Brown women first gendered, then freed through hetero-sex became increasingly visible presences in Caribbean colonies: Haiti's free colored population skyrocketed from 500 in 1700 to 28,000 in 1789, and Cuba's increased from 36,000 in 1774 to 153,000 in 1841.[29] On many islands free women of color quickly outnumbered white men, white women, and free men of color, standing Amazonianly as heads of their own households.

So how to manage this treacherous heterosexualization, which both justified keeping women of color under white men and emancipated them from the cane fields' ungendering and unfreedom? Colonists responded by putting pen furiously to paper, writing checks on women of color's freedom as well as on their womanness. Legal strictures – which, unlike laws favoring slave pregnancies, planters upheld – mounted a backlash against Afro-Creoles. Trinidad, Suriname, and Haiti were among the colonies to pass laws that limited mulattos' right to own property and testify, and – in an attempt to limit dark beauties' "refinements of voluptuousness" and "their influence over the men, and the fortunes lavished on them," as the contemporary visitor Leonora Sansay writes of Haiti – forbade mulattas to be called *madame*, wear silks or jewelry, or appear in public with uncovered hair.[30] These sex-specific strictures not only aimed to keep women of color from being classed too closely to white ladies but also legally restricted their ability to be gendered like them, ensuring that the latter's femininity never looked or sounded like the former's (even if they attracted the same sexual partners). Colonial chronicles bolstered this unwomaning by imagining new paths to old stereotypes. They carefully mythologized a split between the luminous attraction of white ladyhood's receptive femininity and the glittering seduction of brown womanhood's aggressive voluptuousness – which, by ensnaring partners indiscriminately, proved a kind of forceful masculine libido in drag. Edwards cites Teale's and Chanvalon's assessments of sable Venuses' prodigious love and then goes on to strongly object to any possible humanization or distinction of the female through eroticism. Noting the "licentious and dissolute manners" of both sexes of "Negroes in the West Indies," he retorts: "That passion therefore to which (dignified by the name of Love) is ascribed the power of softening all the miseries of slavery, is mere animal desire. . . . This the Negroes, without doubt, possess in common with the rest of the animal creation, and they indulge it, as inclination prompts, in an almost promiscuous intercourse with the other sex."[31] Under patriarchs' pens, a *so very feeling*, Oshun-like eroticism was at once an avenue to the female of color's humanization and proof of its impossibility; it at once promised to elevate her to womanness and returned her to unevolved femaleness.[32]

And so Cliff's question continues to echo louder and louder for me: *what does it mean* for a brown woman to love another woman in the Caribbean, when both the verb *love* and the noun *woman* have been such volatile, policed concepts in the ships, cane, and beds of the region's history? Slavery's overlapping, conflicting, violent mythologies trace historically specific reasons why heterosexuality becomes a dense site of power transfer in the Afro-Caribbean, as well as what remains at stake in resisting its compulsions. They also trace why *womanness* is such fraught, contested terrain in the archipelago: volcanic terrain whose destructive potential does not – especially in the years just after emancipation – dissuade Caribbeans from claiming their right to inhabit it, asserting their need to decolonize it. Tracing the poetics of this Amazonian decolonization, I insistently background the copious imperial writs that hypersexualized and unwomaned females of African descent and instead foreground imaginary landscapes in which the enslaved and their descendants gender and eroticize their own kind: an imagination that often survives, as Brand writes, in fire-ravaged "triangles, scraps, prisons of purpled cloth" asking to be read with special care.[33] Such scraps insist that while conscription into white womanhood was always already a trap, the legal denial of brown womanness was always already part of material bondage; so for writers to proclaim that females did not have to become women would not be new in the African Americas, would not be in and of itself emancipatory. In using the phrase *women who love women*, then, and in respecting that the masculine, feminine, and androgynous cultural workers whose texts I analyze all return to this term, I remain painfully attuned to the historical reverberations of a contested noun, a problematic marker of humanity.

At the same time – just as to assume that *mati* means the same thing as *mate* would be to miss Creolization altogether – to assume that calling oneself woman, *uma*, or *fanm* means accepting colonial masculine-feminine, human-animal divisions is also to miss the difference that Creolization makes. Not despite but partly because of histories of enslavement, the Afro-Caribbean *woman* seems poised to be rescripted as what we might in another language call black queer or quare gender. Exclusionary, "pure" womanness was as much an invention of white supremacy as of heteropatriarchy; and to undercut the power of this invention, Caribbeans stretched, hybridized, recolored, reshaped, redressed and reformulated this category so that it no longer remains the same flattening, oppressive one that queer theorists critique. Systematically denied slaves in the cane fields, it is sugar that they continuously thiefed, broke, melted, burned, fermented, and reconstituted to meet their needs: insisting on being both/and, either/neither, endlessly shifting combinations of black ladies and Amazons, women and not-women, *obinrin* and *machas*,[34] making this strategically unstable composite mean *otherly* than what colonists ever imagined. Like the fair-skinned, haloed images of Santa Barbara that Cubans and Brazilians transculturated into representations of the Yoruba *orishá* Shango (Kawo Kabiosile) – Shango, the protector of female masculinity and female same-sex desire; Shango, energy of revolution and social justice – *woman, uma,* and *fanm* will be transculturated to mean radically, explosively, electrically differently.[35] When a woman loves a woman in the Caribbean, none of these words will mean the same as they do in the Global North.

The Spring of Her Look:
Landscapes of Work, Landscapes of Desire

"What would it mean for a woman to love another woman in the Caribbean?," Cliff asks, then going on to clarify, "not in a room in the Mediterranean, not in a Paris bar, not on an estate in England."[36] And the specificity of place, *in the Caribbean,* is much more than a backdrop for eroticism in the texts of Caribbean women who love women. Like the African bodies claimed and altered by colonialism, the region's waterways, flora, and earth constitute concrete, contested sites whose manipulated materiality matters complexly. Sugar islands, islands planted with tamarind, mangoes, star apples, bougainvillea, breadfruit, and palm trees, full of aluminum mines, oil fields, resorts, communal yards, and *hounforts*:[37] if anything in the archipelago has been as constantly, systematically transformed, exploited, contested, and subverted as the colonial invention called Caribbean womanhood, it is the colonial invention called Caribbean landscape. Since shortly after Columbus's arrival, Europeans have worked to "fix" this topos for cultivation and exploitation. Beginning in the sixteenth century, ships transplanted African, Asian, and Pacific cash crop (sugar cane) and food (breadfruit) plants in the same vessels that carried slaves and indentured laborers; and – in a constant war with rain forests' unruly, unprofitable biodiversity – planters conscripted those workers to create monocultural plantations that would fulfill European nations' capitalist and imperial desires. Since Columbus's very logbooks, European observers have also worked to fix this topos on paper, simultaneously recording and inventing West Indian "nature" through obsessive travelers' descriptions, landscape painting, and encyclopedic natural histories (including those of Bryan Edwards). In these texts, colonialist logic – the logic that drives enterprises from the plantation to the free-trade zone or the all-inclusive hotel – imagines the landscape in which enslaved, indentured, or underpaid laborers work as a natural given, a passive, preexisting totality that the plantation owner charts and "develops." But landscape – which is not trees, rivers, or flowers, but *an imaginary way of organizing these into a "whole"* – in fact appears not as a preexisting entity but as a continual practice: one that, like the invention of womanhood, proves subject to constant disruption and rerouting.

One early European landscape artist who covertly experimented with such rerouting was Agostino Brunias. Commissioned to paint for the colonial elite, Brunias produced very few "pure" landscapes. Instead, he peopled idealized outdoor scenes with colorful, active figures – notably women of color of various skin tones and occupations – dancing, smoking, returning from market, washing, selling fruit, or enjoying the smell of flowers. One such humanized landscape, *Three Caribbean Washerwomen by a River* (c. 1770–80), features two mulattas and a black woman literally *in* the landscape, submerged to the ankles in a stream bordered by a cliff and hanging foliage while gracefully wringing, beating, and laying out white clothes and talking to each other (figure 1). In the painting's interweaving of blues, greens, and browns, the diversity of the Caribbean landscape appears not as a space of feminized passivity but as a space of active, ongoing work – and in fact, active *women's* work. Not only the site of work, landscape also *constitutes* work here. *Three Caribbean Washerwomen* traces parallels between the women's work in the landscape (ordered, we imagine, by colonial planters) and Brunias's work in producing landscapes (contracted, in fact, by colonial planters). The clothing wrung by the central mulatta recreates the curving form of the vines hanging above her, while the cloth beaten by the black woman carves an outline similar to the mountains over her shoulder. These visual echoes remind us that Brunias's hand shaped these supposedly natural features in the same way that the washerwomen's hands shape clothes. It also emphasizes that creating a stylized relationship between supposedly empty, passive land forms and savage, self-offering tropical flora that colonists could justify exploiting is intellectual *labor* that, like the manual labor of

Agostino Brunias, *Three Caribbean Washerwomen by a River.*
Painting, oil on canvas, 30.5 × 22.9 cm, c. 1770–80

bleaching stains on white clothing, erases much to produce the desired effect. The whiteness of the clothes also recall the painter's blank canvas, intimating that the conceptual work of producing landscape is not a flat reproduction but, like the working over of that other cloth, a process of manipulating, twisting, bleaching, and reshaping material to suit colonialists' needs.

While landscaping, like laundry, is ostensibly done here in the service of local whites, that women of color are performing work paralleling the painter's also has another implication. Washing out the Caribbean, reshaping its landscape, is the kind of work that women of color have always done and can, in fact, do on their own account. Or, as Jill Cassid puts it in her fine study of colonial landscaping: "'Landscape' [should] be understood not merely as a European genre of painting and gardening or technique for the production of imperial power but also as a vital but overlooked medium and ground of contention for countercolonial strategies."[38] Working not only as physical laborers on Caribbean lands, female field hands and their descendants also took on that other intellectual land work of inventing landscape. Washerwomen and their zanmi continually imagined their own, anticolonial topographies, talking out relationships to surrounding rivers, mountains, and trees over laundry and leisure. In this book, I seek out the submerged epistemologies plotted in their fields. The Caribbean reinvented in these women's landscapes will be an interactive ecology in which the colonized struggle for interpretive power by asserting the right to imagine a geography in which they can live, wash, talk, work, and rest safely. Like the women themselves, roses, everlasting, jasmine, oranges, and cane—all transplanted to the region by European colonists— perform another move to enter this ecology. They travel from the position of commodity to that of living being and interlocutor, talking to the women as the once thingified women talk to each other in the river. This move is not simply a "cultural difference" in viewing landscape but a challenge to the empiricism of empire. As these imaginary mappings refuse the passivity and stasis of nature morte (still life) and nature à l'état brut ("unimproved" nature), they— like the constant migration of rivers—reshape land that conquistadors hoped would stand still under their feet. At the same time, they question whether any of the living matter that the colonizer's model of the world posited as (socially) dead and empty—brute nature or brute humans in need of civilization—really were such. They assert, instead, that vines and waters, mountains and trees, women and slaves interact in complex ecological systems in which their agency is continually both undercut and reestablished, drowned and dredged up.

If landscape and work run together in *Three Caribbean Washerwomen*, so do work and sexuality. These water-soaked women's poses evoke a brown female sexual availability that washes through the West Indian terrain as "naturally" as their riverine work—whose nature, as seen in the manipulated shapes of laundry and land, is figured as ongoing artifice that female artisans stand to intervene in. All three women are beautiful and bare-chested in the river, breasts thrust together by the work of washing. The standing mulatta wears a tellingly scarlet cloth tied loosely around her waist to reveal the length of her left thigh, whose fullness seems at once a product of hard work and a promise of abundant sexuality. From breasts to thighs, the suggestive ways in which work and eroticism intermingle in these laundresses' bodies intimate how inextricably sexual and manual labor were woven together in slavery. They trace how, like harvesting cane or washing clothes, sexual activity formed part of the unpaid *work* slaves were legally bound to perform for owners—work they performed so regularly that their sexualization became a standard element of Caribbean tableaux. Since Brunias's paintings were sold to male owners of great houses and mansions, this brown female sexuality initially seems to run as effortlessly as the river toward white masculine viewers who could enjoyably fantasize about claiming heterosexual connections with the same entitlement with which they claimed Caribbean lands, and vice versa.

But these round-thighed brown women crouching before one another, standing open-legged toward each other, suggest another possible "natural" direction for Caribbean female eroticism in these constantly replanted, reconfigured tropics. The subjects are actually not looking out at the (putatively white male) viewer at all. Instead, the washerwomen gaze intently at each other; and their pleasurable engagement, their graceful leaning together at once humanize their work and homo-eroticize their lovely coworkers. This electric shared gaze turns the washerwomen's river into a space that (reappropriating Roumain's phrase) I call "the spring of her look": somewhere women keep fresh water and fresh eyes for each other, refusing to imagine them as commodifiable natural resources for someone else to survey or claim. The painting's most intriguing figure is, for me, the seated mulatta whose back faces us. This washerwoman has completely stopped working—and completely turned her bare breasts and (laughing, I imagine) eyes away from viewers, toward the black and brown laundresses in front of her. An alternative landscape and womanscape could be gathering in these eyes: the spring of *her* look, which contemplates river, trees, mountains, breasts, thighs, and open mouths in ways that cannot be intercepted by the landowner who buys this Brunias landscape and its cleverly posed washerwomen. The imaginary space of the mulatta's gaze, working over three Caribbean women by a river, suggests to me one of the most important connections between land and female beloved that I explore. Like landscape, female sexuality has never been passive ground for fulfilling imperial desires, but rather, as Arjun Appadurai writes of the former, "an organised field of 'social practices,' a form of work . . . and a form of negotiation between sites of agency" that women of African descent have always taken on for themselves.³⁹ Just as they reorganized the field of social practices that created landscape, so too did women of color workers reorganize those that invented female sexuality, carving out creative space to imagine eroticism working for them. Recent studies, including Hilary McD. Beckles's *Centering Woman*, illustrate how housekeepers used sex with white landowners to receive benefits ranging from manumission to cash with which to buy property.⁴⁰ In this project, I focuse on how enslaved women and their descendants used *sex with each other* to effect a different kind of erotic autonomy, on how same-sex eroticism enters into the history of sexual labor in the Caribbean as a practice by which women take control of sexuality as a resource they share with each other.

What does it mean not only for women to love women in the Caribbean but also for us to engage these lovers as activists in their erotic and sexual practices? The following chapters chart women's reclaiming of *eroticism* as a wellspring of resistance to colonial symbolic and economic orders. I mean this term in the sense explored by Audre Lorde in her landmark essay "The Uses of the Erotic: The Erotic as Power": as a sharing of deep, possibly but not necessarily sexual feeling that emerges as a resource with the power to motivate individual and collective change.⁴¹ The chapters also trace an intersecting stream of resistance that runs through taking back *sexuality* as a powerful "commodity" (to rework a phrase from Luce Irigaray) that women keep for themselves.⁴² Some recent queer scholarship has chosen to downplay the centrality of same-sex sexual activity as a category of analysis, privileging myriad forms of queering gender and sexual norms including erotic friendships, spinsterhood, and masturbation. However, I maintain that both the erotic *and* the specifically sexual reclaiming of women of color's bodies remain crucial points of consideration in a West Indian context. It examines the importance of women of color's mutual sharing of eroticism – their shipmate-like *feeling for* each other when, as (possible descendants of) reified, enslaved, *unwomanly* workers, they were not supposed to feel. But it also highlights the importance of their mutual sharing of sexuality – their *feeling* each other's breasts, thighs, and waists when their (ancestresses') bodies, as working and sexual commodities, were supposed to be the exclusive property of white men.

In Haiti, *tè* (land) is another word for vagina; in Trinidad, *wuk* (work) is another word for sex.[43] My interest concerns how women of color reclaim *tè* and *wuk* for themselves – in both senses of both words – and how this reappropriation works and falls short as a strategy for resisting the imperial logic that naturalizes the exploitation of territories and bodies alike. The reclaiming of sexuality as alienated labor emerges most clearly in chapter 1's discussion of the practice of *matiwroko* (or *mati* work) in Suriname, where Creole women engage in a system of relationships that views sexuality neither as a natural given nor as an identificatory marking. Instead, like other work, it emerges as a series of activities that these women can perform or refuse, accept or transform, enact or rescript. The linkage of sexuality and work continues in chapter 2, where a white woman's refusal to embrace the roles of wife and mother is simultaneously imagined as a sexual and a career choice – a decision to love women and to pursue a career she loves. In chapters 4 and 6, the site of work is consistently imagined as the site of same-sex eroticism in the texts of Capécia and Brand, whose characters' working and sexual bodies are reclaimed through parallel reimaginations. Moreover, providing a counterpoint, it is the lack of working bodies in chapter 3 that ultimately emerges as one of the chief rifts in the utopian gynoerotic vision of Faubert's poetry. In the geographies and sexualities of these texts, the link between woman-to-woman eroticism and landscape is not simply that both are (mistakenly) assumed as natural, but that the cultural production of both depends on their erased connection to a third term, *work*. After all, nothing is natural in the fabricated tropical paradise of the West Indies because it has always already been under workers' hands.

Patronized by planters and governors, Brunias's insufficiently colonial landscapes were quickly reappropriated by the enslaved and their allies. In campaigns for emancipation mounted during eighteenth-century revolutions, abolitionists used these paintings as propaganda to prove the humanity of the Africans that slave owners had likened to apes and tropical fruit.[44] Toussaint L'Ouverture, the brilliant leader of the Haitian revolution that toppled slavery in the region's richest colony in 1791, wore a coat decorated with buttons featuring miniature Brunias landscapes. One on display at the Smithsonian Institution sports sumptuously dressed mulatta and black women standing tall in a landscape of beautiful palm trees. For Toussaint, too, these images of ennobled black women in dignified landscapes must have looked like freedom. What might the revolutionary impact of such humanized land and woman images be, then, when the work of revisioning the social construction of Caribbean terrains and bodies is taken on by women of color themselves? What would it mean to the postcolonial Caribbean imagination if Brunias's washerwomen could describe the building of landscape and desire in their own terms? In the following chapters, I answer these questions by turning, literally, to texts penned by Caribbean washerwomen. Their writings, along with those of Afro-Creole domestic workers, brown ladies of leisure, and female revolutionaries, paint a "spring of her look" that washes out, blurs, mourns, electrifies, and sweetens the imperial lay of Caribbean lands in unscripted ways. When the washerwoman turns to face us, flora and female sexuality cease to lie still like *so many things* and begin to turn insistently like *so many actions* – like ongoing choreography that can always be interrupted and redirected.

Like Thiefing Sugar: (Mati) Working Creole Metaphorics

One of these dance-like actions will be putting together sentences, the daily, lifelong reworking of words and images. Something as simple as a figurative phrase – like *thiefing sugar* – can mean a lot, poetically and politically. In an archipelago in which what empire charted as "physical reality" – flowers, trees, land forms, sexed bodies, sexual natures – has been constantly, tactically remade by both colonialists and countercolonialists, the elasticity of figurative language becomes a vital tool for reconfiguring those fields of social practice that make *Caribbean* and *woman* what they "are." As Alejo Carpentier famously put it, a "return to the real" cannot be sufficient to challenge the empiricism of empire: for "what is the history of America if not a chronicle of the marvelous in the real?"[45] Challenges to the linearity of the literal punctuate Caribbean literary and oral cultures, in which a command of Anansi stories, proverbs, extended metaphors, and double-entendres flourishingly prove speakerly skill. Certainly, this "feeling for language, for imagery, and for the expression of abstract ideas through compressed and allusive phraseology" is, as the Jamaican linguist Velma Pollard notes, a West African inheritance.[46] But just as certainly this language play constitutes a practice that, like imaginations of Oshun and Shango, Creoles transculturated to serve their countercolonial conceptual needs in the Americas.

In Suriname, for example, the enslaved crafted *odo* – (traditionally) women's sayings or proverbs – that voiced their understanding of the power of feminine gender and sexuality as work, not as artless nature. "Ya na wan uma: yu pata smara, ma yu safu ala meti!" (You're a woman: you have a small pot, but you soften all meat!), quips one, speaking the feminized labor of cooking and "giving sweetness" as something far from subjection.[47] And what may be the nation's most popular *odo* imagines tropical flora and women sharing an ability to take strength from adversity rather than succumbing passively to outside pressure. "Mi na banabon, a moro doti y'e trowe, a moro mi tya' bana" (I'm a banana tree: the more dirt you throw on me, the more bananas I bear), women say, multiplying sweetness under duress.[48] These metaphors refuse the pseudo-science of colonial chronicles that chart the properties of banana trees and black females in very different ways. Their figures of comparison (metaphor, simile, analogy) speak back to an imperial obsession with separation and categorization that divides human from slave, female from woman, man from nature. Instead, they *make sense through connection* – through a constant negotiation between "unalike" terms in which only relationality can make meaning happen. From its title onward, then, *Thiefing Sugar* centers on metaphors of landscape and sexuality because these have long proven central to Caribbean women's poetics of erotic decolonization. I approach their metaphors not as rarified literary tropes but as *everyday praxes of black feminism*.

I engage these imaginative comparisons because such metaphors make relational, black feminist sense of a history in which sugar, water, womanness, sex have been contested, explosive terrains. At the same time, it makes just that kind of sense to read their metaphors as points for opening dialogue not only with complex history making but with contemporary theory making. The intellectual work of enunciating regionality and sexuality (perhaps) no longer passes through travelogues or planter-commissioned landscape paintings. But it does, often, still pass through mappings of imaginative geographies, as writers and scholars speak back to imperial and heteropatriarchal world orders by contesting their lay of the land. As far-reaching as their banana trees, the metaphoric lands and waters of Caribbean women who love women stand to revise these recent theoretical landscapes in provocative ways. Not unlike the poems and novels of Surinamese *mati* and Jamaican lesbians, Caribbean and queer theories are saturated with spatial metaphors. Unlike these, however, such theory often misses intersections between nationality, race, gender, and sexuality also in need of decolonization. In the case of West Indian scholarship, spatial figures are drawn largely from the so-called natural world, which, writers contend, is not a passive thing but a crucial actor in regional histories and imaginations. Beginning with the groundbreaking work of Jean Bernabé, Patrick Chamoiseau, and Raphaël Confiant, Caribbean theorists of *créolité* moved from a search for African "roots" to the imagination of "mangroves of virtualities," an image that employs the rhizomatic mangrove swamp as a standard vehicle for conceiving the Caribbean as a space of constant cultural intergrowth and interaction between blacks, browns, yellows, and whites.[49] Another influential work, Édouard Glissant's *Caribbean Discourse*, explores the abyss of the sea as a metaphor for the turbulence and opacity of Caribbean histories.[50] Yet neither the *créolistes* nor Glissant address these landscapes' gendering. Does the mangrove retain the swamp's dangerous, sticky femininity? Does Glissant's frightening sea keep its conventional motherliness? Nor do the *créolistes* move to imagine interlocking mangrove vines as a space for viewing a multiplicity of desires like those that crisscross in the spring of her look, any more than Glissant makes account for the sexual and gender fluidity of the watery Martinican folkloric figure *manman dlo* or the Cuban ocean *orishá* Olokun.

While Glissant's *Poetics of Relation* includes a diatribe against feminism, the surface gender blindness of Bernabé et al's *In Praise of Creoleness* poses its own problems.[51] Take, for example, the passage in which the now famous mangrove metaphor first appears: "Creoleness is our primitive soup and our continuation, our primeval chaos and our mangrove swamp of virtualities. We bend toward it [*vers elle*], enriched by all kinds of mistakes and confident in the necessity of accepting ourselves as complex."[52] The authors' commitment to a poetics of complexity finds expression in the initial metaphors, whose vehicles – from the biological diversity of primitive soup to that of the mangrove – express *créolité*'s irreducible multiplicity. Ostensibly, this praise of the fantastically, diversely (re)productive landscape remains gender neutral. Nonetheless, the grammatical gender of the invented noun *créolité* enables a persistent, conventional feminization of the fertile topoi associated with it: the moist, evergrowing mangrove swamp, the primitive *soup* that images primal birth and, in the double meaning of soup, women's reproductive labor of cooking. This feminization is heightened by the immediately following reference to *créolité* as *elle* (she). In this reference, gendering quickly blends into sexualization and *hetero*sexualization as the male poets imagine themselves leaning into this *elle*. One the one hand, gender and sexuality problematically remain nonissues here in that they are not addressed. The passage goes on to enumerate cultural expressions that the authors feel *créolité* should embrace – architecture, culinary arts, painting, economics – but it never brings up (un)gender, (coerced) sexuality, or even family.[53] Yet on the other hand, gender and sexuality remain fundamental issues in the authors' imagination of *créolité* in that the feminization of Caribbean topoi (echoing the colonial vision of Brunias's era of landscape portraiture) is coded as so natural that they see no need to render it explicit or problematic. Nor do they see a need to explicate or problematize their male desire for these feminized topoi, which also appears so natural as to be beyond bearing note. In short, the most renowned theorists of inclusive Creoleness often do not recognize how their very neocolonial rootedness in binary gender and sexual identities undercuts the complexity that they express as fundamental to their project. Countering these blocks to a would-be porous regional imagination, in this work I ask: How might the flowers coloring the songs of Surinamese *mati* fit into *créolité*'s mangrove of virtualities, and are the seas where Cliff's or Brand's female characters embrace women related to Glissant's somber waters? How does reading these *mati*-worked metaphors reformulate Caribbeanness as a space that diffracts and recomposes both race and ethnicity *as well as* gender and sexuality?

[margin note:] limits of language as system of expression?

The metaphorical ground for women who love women in the Global South is no more decolonized in canonical queer theory. While postcolonial queer theorists like Manalansan, Sinott, and Gopinath have recently and crucially pushed for new queer cartographies, this push comes in response to sexuality studies' longtime provincialism. Also emerging in the past century's final decade, queer studies' foundational spatial metaphors were set up to map the (generally urban) contours of the Global North – a geographic bias that helps explain why black queer studies can quite acceptably take African North America as its ground zero. Inspired by Eve Kosofsky Sedgwick's landmark study *The Epistemology of the Closet*, too many northern studies of same-sex sexuality stay out of springs or swamps and close to bedrooms.[54] Their cartographies often rely on standard metaphors of interior and exterior space, of the closet and of "coming out." This division reflects an Enlightenment-inspired bifurcation between the invisible and the visible, between private and public expressions of desire in which invisibility and privacy are linked to oppression, while access to visibility and publicity is aligned with empowerment.[55]

[margin note:] ✳

Never questioning the colonial implications of this Enlightenment vision – which relegated entire continents to darkness and subhumanity – Sedgwick synthesizes the near universality soon ascribed to this visible-invisible binary as she explains: "A lot of the energy of attention and demarcation that has swirled around issues of homosexuality since the beginning of the nineteenth century, in Europe and the United States, has been impelled by the distinctively indicative relation of homosexuality to wider mappings of secrecy and disclosure, and of the private and the public . . . oppressively, durably condensed in certain figures of homosexuality. 'The closet' and 'coming out,' now verging on all-purpose phrases for the potent crossing and recrossing of almost any politically charged lines of representation, have been the gravest and most magnetic of those figures. The closet is the defining structure for gay oppression in this century."[56] The passage's too-smooth move from the specific to the totalizing draws a queer map in which, once again, Europe and North America occupy center stage, generating the "rule" to which all other geographies can only provide proof or exception. Initially, Sedgwick proposes to discuss the closet as the figure of a particular time and place, nineteenth- and twentieth-century Europe and North America. But by the end of the paragraph, this northern block has once again come to stand for the universal as its spatial signifier of queer sexuality – the closet – is named "the defining structure for gay oppression in this century," a claim whose validity is bounded by no geographic markers. As with the heterosexualization of the mangrove, the universalization of the Euro-American closet appears so natural as to need no explanation.

In fact, "the closet" seems to work not (only) as the space that confines queers but also as the space that confines queer studies, whose closed-off perspective – closed off, too often, to the world outside the Global North – speaks to the field's early myopia. Since Sedgwick's landmark text, several queer of color writers have wisely seen fit to signify on the closet, drawing attention to what it would mean to map other culturally specific sexual formations. Jason King's consideration of black and Latino MSMs (Men who have Sex with Men) and homothugs in "Remixing the Closet: The Down-Low Way of Knowledge" is one of the most often cited of these.[57] Reclassed and recolored, though, closets and other queer mappings often continue to take Global Northernness for granted. Stuck between the closet and its remixes, canonical and queer of color theorists alike can fail to open ground to consider how an obsession with inside versus outside, closet versus street, is or is not relevant to field and yard cultures like those of the Caribbean, where home life is generally lived outdoors and the division between interior and exterior space does not hold the same cultural anxiety. Is being "out"/doors a mark of privilege for cane field workers or washerwomen? And for how many Caribbeans is a closet a standard feature of houses?[58] Unintentionally and unfortunately, theorists of the closet keep their interior doors closed to the erotic geographies of these "outside" African diaspora cultures – to thiefable cane fields, washerwomen's unruly rivers, and insistent banana trees, among other possibilities. The work of this book is thus also to ask: Can Bliss's mountain or Faubert's tropical garden join and challenge the closet as a culturally specific imagination of same-gender loving space? How can mapping othered, postcolonial spaces not only queer but fundamentally destabilize emerging geographies of sexuality? In reading their landscapes this way, we position ourselves to see not only that Caribbean women have long imagined ground on which to challenge colonialism and heterocentrism but also that their texts provide ground from which to challenge narrow conceptions of Caribbean and queer studies.

To plot these landscapes and their ramifications, I read the texts of Caribbean women who love women closely – intimately, in my way – taking time and care with their nouns, verbs, metaphors, and images. I consider this critical praxis part of the African diaspora epistemology that the texts enter into, a recognition of what orishá devotees call ofo ashe: the power of every word uttered or traced to reshape the "real" world. I also consider it a strategy for leveling the academic field, giving women of color's words the weight usually reserved for literary and theoretical masters. For despite my critique of some foundational assumptions of Caribbean and queer theory, I am hopeful for the dynamism of both fields. In the twenty years since the work of Butler and Sedgwick put gender studies on the academic map, queer theory has found itself increasingly faced with an impetus to change still imperial assumptions about the superior advances of Euro-American thinking on gender and sexuality. At the same time, African diaspora and Caribbean studies are faced with an imperative to recognize sexuality as a crucial category of analysis. The joyous and energetic scholarship gathered by E. Patrick Johnson and Mae Henderson in the groundbreaking Black Queer Studies makes this lightning clear.[59] The question that looms is not if queer and African diaspora scholarship will be diversified, but how: which voices will be called on and/or tokenized to join the most prominent scholars in the field? Or, to paraphrase the Trinidadian writer-activist Colin Robinson: the challenge is not simply to imagine the same-sex loving Caribbean but to imagine it imaginatively.[60]

This book stems from the belief that literature – with its room for ambiguity, for the creative redrawing of slave ships, cane fields, and "the spring of her look" – remains particularly fertile territory for such imaginative imagination. Choosing to engage women's work of (re)plotting landscape as theorizing and countertheorizing, I look to rigorously apply the reading methodology outlined by the black feminist critic Barbara Christian. In her watershed "The Race for Theory," Christian forcefully argues that in the writings of people of color, "theory" may not be a discrete genre. Rather, it emerges as a way of knowing and illuminating configurations of race, class, gender, and sexuality that is inscribed in literary texts themselves.[61] As I consider the women whose words I study not only as literary figures but as theorists of race, gender, and sexuality, dissolving divides between theorizing and imagining becomes one of the chief interventions my work looks to offer postcolonial and queer studies. While it is of paramount importance that we have theorists who engage with, deconstruct, and reconstruct now canonical cultural and gender theory, a real restructuring of postcolonial and sexuality studies will only take place when the academy *listens to other kinds of theorists*. In establishing space for Caribbean woman-loving theory in particular and global queer theories in general, we must search for foundations not only in the work of theorists like the *créolistes* or Sedgwick but also in the subversive and silenced ways of knowing gender and sexuality embedded in colonial subjects' texts. It is by dialoguing with concepts of decolonization, queerness, and theory in this way that queer and postcolonial theory will not only come in different colors and genders but will also come to be decolonized; that we will see not only different flora planted here but also a different organization to the field.

What would it mean for a woman to love another woman in the Caribbean, and to plot her bodily and imaginative work of womanness, eroticism, and decolonization nowhere stable, nowhere fixed, nowhere conventional . . . but in the malleable, explosive, volcanic force of the so often buried words she puts together to speak her body, her desires, her work, her island?

one

"Rose is my mama, stanfaste is my papa"

Hybrid Landscapes and Sexualities
in Surinamese Women's Oral Poetry

And when, Bible in hand, my grandmother responded to my love
by sitting me down, at the age of twenty-seven, to quote Genesis. . . .
When she pointed out that "this was a white people ting" . . . it was
a strong denial of many ordinary Black working-class women
she knew.

— Makeda Silvera, "Man Royals and Sodomites:
   Some Thoughts on the Invisibility of Afro-Caribbean Lesbians"

In 2004, the cinnamon-skinned, wavy-haired Aruban native Charlene Oduber-Lamers moved to Oranjestad with her white Dutch wife, Esther, and their baby daughter, Elisa. When they passed through immigration at Queen Beatrix International Airport, Esther may have looked to the official stamping her passport like one of hundreds of thousands of sunblock-armed European and North American vacationers who flock to this Antillean outpost of the Kingdom of the Netherlands, where tourism dominates the small island to such an extent that the government once put a moratorium on hotel building. And, at first glance, light brown Charlene may have looked much like another arrival in the overwhelming wave of mostly female immigrants who relocate continuously from neighboring countries like the Dominican Republic, Suriname, Venezuela, and Colombia to work in the tourist-driven service industry. By 2004, one third of Aruban residents were born abroad; and this newly transnational "small place" was electrically charged with tensions that pitched native Arubans against others come to take "their" jobs, affordable housing, and potential sexual partners (since foreign women were rumored to have magical powers of seduction).[1] Once Charlene began working for the Aruban government, she went to register her marriage, so that Esther could remain in the country, be covered by her insurance, and have custody of Elisa in the event of her death. When the public registry flatly refused although the couple had wed when the Netherlands legalized same-sex marriage in 2001, the Oduber-Lamers filed a lawsuit for discrimination. Public outrage ensued. Protesters threw rocks at the couple, slashed their tires, and picketed against same-sex unions outside the parliament until the family finally returned to Holland to await the trial's outcome.[2]

Both the Aruban government and international media framed the event as a culture clash between European liberalism and (invented) Caribbean tradition. The government spokesman Ruben Trapenberg proclaimed: "If we accept gay marriage, would we next have to accept Holland's marijuana bars and euthanasia? They have their culture, we have ours."[3] The press repeatedly quoted this statement, and in an article titled "Aruba, Holland Miles Apart on Gay Marriages," the journalist Peter Prengaman explained Trapenberg's words this way: "The strong emotions ignited by their legal fight seeking to force Aruba's government to recognize their marriage has underlined a deep cultural rift between liberal Holland and its conservative former colony."[4] No print source framed this as a conflict fueled by the contradictions of globalization, the neocolonial cycle that keeps Aruba flooded with tourists from the Global North and workers from the Global South to serve their food and clean their hotel rooms. No one stopped to ask whether the situation would have been different if both women had been Arubans living on the island all their lives, rather than one of many recent arrivals. Nor did anyone attempt to parse out what part of public reaction was fueled by homophobia and what part by anticolonial sentiment – by resentment that Aruba was bound to recognize the Netherlands' laws despite its autonomous status, and that Dutch travelers and Dutch legislature alike continued to dictate the day-to-day realities of this place, right down to its intimate partnerships. After three years and two major court rulings, the Oduber-Lamers emerged victorious. On 13 April 2007, the Netherlands Supreme Court declared that same-sex marriages registered in the Netherlands or elsewhere carried the "same force of law" in Aruba, making this the first Caribbean territory to legally recognize such unions.[5] The moral of the story, as reported by the international gay press, seemed to be that globalization brings social progress: see how continued colonial presence helped this Caribbean nation modernize not only its infrastructure but also its sexual politics?

To arrive at so simple a moral, commentators had to turn a blind eye to the complexities of globalization in contemporary Aruba. They also had to remain ignorant of the rich history of sexuality – and particularly female same-sex sexuality – that marks (former) Dutch Caribbean colonies. *Cachapera, kambrada, mati*: Papiamentu (the Creole of Aruba, Bonaire, and Curaçao) and Sranan (Surinamese Creole) contain many words for women who love women, vocabulary that speaks to long traditions of female relationships that are perhaps stronger in these territories than in any other in the region. *Kambrada* and *mati* relationships were common for much of the nineteenth and twentieth centuries, but no one thought to register these partnerships by law. As the Surinamese writer Astrid Roemer puts it: "In the community from which I come, there is not so much talk about the phenomenon of women having relations with other women. There are, after all, things which aren't to be given names – giving them names kills them. But we do have age-old rituals originating from Africa by which women can make quite clear that special relations exist between them. For instance, birthday rituals can be recognized by anyone and are quite obvious. . . . Why then is it necessary to declare oneself a lesbian? It is usual there."[6] Perhaps, then, the problem with the Oduber-Lamers' union was partly a culture clash of a different kind: their self-naming as *lesbian* rather than as *kambrada*, their recourse to Dutch law rather than Afro-Caribbean ritual to formalize partnership. In fact, the advent of gay rights politics in the style of the Global North in no way represents a "step forward" from the early twentieth century, perverse modernity of Dutch Caribbean women's once prevalent relationships. The poet-activist Guillermo Rosario, born in Curaçao at the turn of the twentieth century, remarks: "Things have changed for the homosexual or the lesbian here in Curaçao. . . . In the old times, you could hear people say: Talitha and Malita are *kambradas*. . . . There were a lot in our society, out in the open."[7] These memories of *kambrada* tell another, countercolonial story of globalization: a history of sexual formations that circulate throughout the African diaspora, providing alternatives to heterosexuality and official partnerships of all kinds. Far from standing outside a "real Aruban" lifestyle, these same-sex relationships could also be called on as historically specific Creole formations exemplifying the cultural complexity and transculturating inventiveness of Caribbeanness. What if the Aruban government and the gay press were challenged by the memory of *these* Creole traditions?

This chapter calls on this complex, buried history through a reading of the rituals evoked by Roemer. Here I engage the performance poetry produced by Surinamese *mati* at the turn of the twentieth century as an active theorizing of African diaspora sexuality, one that predates discussions of both gay rights and *créolité* by a century. Linguistically and conceptually, these texts are Creole. Sung at parties and in town squares, they deploy Creole poetics and Caribbean metaphoric systems to theorize gender and sexuality, making serious (and playful) business of telling their stories in a public setting very different from a courtroom. Through the rhythms of repeating and shifting constellations of Sranan vocabulary and imagery — moving through words that carry layered memories of forced transport, enslavement, emancipation, colonialism, and resistance — these working-class women speak their history of sexuality between the global and the local, between legacies of dislocation and reinvention. They call listeners to take seriously Makeda Silvera's statement that silencing same-sex eroticism means denying the reality of black working-class women, and they chart paths for a different kind of arrival for women lovers in a Dutch Caribbean capital.

Where journalists reporting on the Oduber-Lamers repeatedly cited the same few sources and/as facts, this chapter looks to multiply the kind of texts that can be brought together to tell the always necessarily partial stories of Afro-Caribbean sexualities. Patching together narratives from natural histories, garden books, folklore collections, bureaucrats' reports, proverbs, ethnographies, and novels, I want to pressure and expand what (literary) intertextuality can comprise and enable in reading the complexity of "love in the Third World."[8] In particular, my discussion of *mati* oral poetry builds interdisciplinarily on close literary readings of songs recorded in, and as, renowned anthropological texts. I turn to ethnographies by Melville and Frances Herskovits and Gloria Wekker as both literary narratives and literary archives, embedding Surinamese women's imaginative texts – descriptions of their dancing bodies, transcripts of their singing words – in anthropological accounts. And I approach these palimpsestic texts not as documenting "realities" of Caribbean women's sexual "culture," but as examples of how Creole bodies and sexualities emerge as complex artifacts continually constructed, deconstructed, and contested through language and other meaningful expressions. The English- and Dutch-language anthropological texts are inlaid with fragments of *mati* languages – both Afro-Surinamese Creole and Afro-Surinamese grammars of gender and sexuality – but they do not *contain* these languages, and my interest lies as much with what makes such writings *différents* as what they report. At the same time (as my unmarked reference to Jacques Derrida prefigures), this chapter's intertextuality is also intentional in the texts it backgrounds – namely, canonical literary, Caribbean, and queer theories. Instead of reifying such theory, my work on *mati* work attempts to *do theorizing* – that is, to analyze a set of narratives in relation to each other – in conversation with many unconventional ways of knowledge production.[9] Or, as Roemer says of how Surinamese women love each other, the point of this look at *mati* work is not to post a well-known name or a theory on Caribbean erotic doings, but to follow along with their performance, with their song and dance.

Pleinen, Dyari, and the Capital of Women

The reporters on the Oduber-Lamers case were not the first generation of arrivals to mistakenly take the Caribbean as a simple extension of Dutch space, or to miss the Afro-Creole women's history present behind the scenes. Traveling in "Netherlands America" in the early twentieth century, Philip H. Hiss described the street scene in Paramaribo as "recognizably Dutch in its character." Alongside canals, he cited as evidence of Dutchness well-ordered flowering trees lining streets and landscaped public squares that government officials enjoyed on the way to their offices, "always at the same hour . . . their white suits freshly starched and gleaming in the sunlight."[10] These were city spaces in which the colonial government and its white (suited) male officials had visibly rational-ized nature's excess: tropical trees manicured out of improper fullness, time consistently measured, clothing untouched by dirt underfoot, even the sun "gleaming" rather than blazing. Contrast this to the anthropologists Melville and Frances Herskovits, doing fieldwork in Paramaribo in the 1920s, who color and gender the urban landscape differently. Backgrounding Dutch influence, their *Suriname Folk-Lore* of 1936 records a recognizably Afro-American city and locates the center of Creole culture in the yards of its working-class, colorfully kerchiefed women, where "such Africanisms as have been retained are almost wholly in the custody of women, and through the women are passed on to the succeeding generations."[11] This Afro-Surinamese culture was passed on in the backgrounded, circular, female spaces behind Paramaribo's white, linear, land-scaped, and "recognizably Dutch" streets: in lots in which in the eighteenth century slaves and free people of color began grouping houses to open into common *dyari* (yards). By 1821 the number of yard dwellings was three times that of Dutch-style houses, and after the 1863 abolition of slavery, these num-bers increased steeply as Afro-Surinamese migrated away from cane fields to Paramaribo to become four-fifths of the city's population.[12]

When the Herskovitses arrived in 1928, *dyari* typically included several female-headed households in which mothers lived with biological and adopted children. These female heads of house were market women, washerwomen, and domestics whose pay often did not suffice to provide for their families. Consequently, yard dwellers made architectural and social connections that pooled resources. *Dyari* acted as crossroads of networks formed and contested, where neighbors crossed from individual dwellings into communal space to cook, gossip, tell stories, fight, sing, and hold religious ceremonies. Lucky *dyari* were marked by the growth of a flowering tree that served as a carrier of the Afro-Atlantic spirit Leba who, in Surinamese cosmology, shifts from her/his male African counterpart to most often appear – like the yard's inhabitants – as female.[13] Indeed, the yard maps the quintessential space of this spirit of the crossroads: a pathfinder who bridges inside and outside, here and there, self and other, Leba represents the divine principle of transversal connection – a meeting of many roads, realities, and possibilities.

In view of this tree and its network of branches, many *dyari* women en-gaged in the sexual and social networking they called *matiwroko* (mati work). Well before 1900 this sociocentric tradition of women's erotic relationships had been integrated into working-class Paramaribo. While Creole women often had sexual relationships with men, they also engaged in societally recognized relationships with women.[14] Wekker's ongoing, multidecade study of this practice highlights that in working-class Suriname, both female and male relationships gathered material resources for women who gained access to shared income by forging kinship networks. But same-sex relationships served the additional purpose of shoring up emotional resources, as female partners ensured companionship, moral support, and help with household management that men were not always expected to provide. Women called their female partners by a broad, metaphorical lexicon of nouns including *mi skin* (my body), *mi sma* (my someone), *mi spiri* (my neighbor), *mi eygi gebruik* (my own use), and *mi kompe* (my companion).[15] But the most common name for a same-sex lover was *mati*, a creolization of Dutch *maatje* or *maat* meaning "mate," "helpmate," "friend."[16] As discussed in the introduction, this term dates to the Middle Passage. *Mati* is a mate as in "shipmate," she who survived forced transport and enslavement with me. Shipmate relationships were in fact a widespread response to this first venture in European globalization, the triangle trade. "In various parts of the Diaspora relationships between people who came over to the 'New World' on the same ship had been and remained a special one," Sidney Mintz and Richard Price explain in *The Birth of Afro-American Culture*. "Brazilian *malungo* ['shipmate'], Trinidadian *malongue*, Haitian *batiment* [the word for a large sailing vessel], and Surinamese *sippi* [from 'ship'] and *mati* are all examples of this special, non biological, symbolical connection between two people of the same gender."[17] Unlike males, females were often packed onto slave ships unchained, a state that left them more vulnerable to systematic rapes. However, this unchaining also left them more mobility to interact in the holds and so to form *feeling* connections to each other—when, as chained property, they were not supposed to feel at all—as a resource for survival. In his *Caribbean Discourse*, Édouard Glissant muses that sexual assault by Europeans gave the enslaved female an "incalculable advantage" over her male counterpart: "When she disembarks in this new land, she already knows the master."[18] But the *mati*'s story suggests that when enslaved women arrived on the Other American shores, their advantage was *already knowing each other*.

Maroon oral histories date *mati* back to the seventeenth century, and the word *maatje* (used to mean "friend") appeared in Surinamese writings throughout the nineteenth century. In a letter written by the Moravian missionary Sister Hartmann around 1850, Wekker notes a "tantalizingly short" reference to *mati* relationships that suggests they were ruffling colonial feathers just after emancipation. Reporting the many complaints that converted men have about their too sexually liberal female partners, Hartmann writes: "The wife of Gottlieb is a mati (female friend) of another woman. Gottlieb does not want it, but he cannot do anything about it."[19] But despite pregnant comments like these, colonial accounts did not explicitly register mati-speak as sexual language until after the turn of the twentieth century. In 1900 Paramaribo, police temporarily stopped all lobisingi (songs women performed for female lovers, discussed in depth later in the chapter) in public squares, citing them as neighborhood disruptions.[20] In 1912, mati's erotic relationships entered written colonial records as a social ill needing immediate redress in the high-ranking official A. J. Schimmelpennick's memorandum to his report on urban poverty. Deploring the conditions of the working class, he listed as causes of local women's physical weakness unhealthy food and "sexual communion [gemeenschap] between women (mati play)."[21] The following year, J. G. Spalburg's popular novel Bruine Mina depicted this "play" as a fashion that the heroine eschews out of loyalty to her absent male lover. Both Schimmelpennick and Bruine Mina explain matisma's prevalence by the predominance of women in Paramaribo. In the 1890s rubber and gold mining drew city-dwelling Afro-Surinamese men back to the interior to bleed trees and to mine, leaving women the overwhelming majority of the black population of Paramaribo. Paramaribo suddenly was, as the Herskovits noted, a city of women.

Though mati work was not established in response to the rubber or gold exodus, these circumstances help explain why it came to Dutch attention around 1900. Certainly the fact that black women formed a larger proportion of the urban population increased mati's visibility to officials, but this new visibility appears more politically than numerically motivated. The turn of the century witnessed a crisis in Suriname's colonial machine. While declines in sugar and cocoa markets rapidly sapped the plantocracy's economic base, the discovery of rubber and gold attracted Dutch, German, and North American investors – a second wave of globalization – who immediately manifested a keen awareness of the need to "tame" Suriname's "virgin" forests. This taming partly took the form of new legal ownership, as the colonial government prodigally doled out gold concessions and let the rubber industry take possession of forests without intervention. It also took the form of new scientific "ownership," as botanical and zoological studies undertook to document the "contents" of this previously undervalued Caribbean colony. The principal achievement of these new studies of flora, fauna, and mineral resources, as Stuart McCook writes, "was, for better or worse, a physical and cognitive reorganization of tropical nature . . . on the basis of modern scientific principles – the commodification of nature."[22] At the same time, Suriname's new investors also showed a keen awareness of the need to conscript the evasive Creole male workforce – reluctant to labor outside Paramaribo since emancipation – to assemble enough workers to tap trees and mine gold. Creole women were deemed crucial to meeting this second need. Schimmelpennick deplored that *mati* was practiced not only by single women who might live together due to poverty but by women with male partners to support them, labeling this "immorality." His judgment may be colored by the fact that, like later colonial observers, he misunderstood the dual sexual system and assumed that sharing partners with women would nullify men's patriarchal "moral" obligation to earn the higher wages that the mining companies promised.[23] His consistent translation of *matiwroko* into *matispelen* – unproductive "play" – underscores that one of his chief concerns was the impact of this "weakness" on the labor pool.

The threat that Schimmelpennick saw in *matispelen*'s prevalence among women engaged in relationships with men may be symbolic as well as economic. Its enunciation of sexuality denaturalized a colonial system of socioeconomic organization erected to fulfill investors' first need, to "rightfully" claim and exploit "virgin" lands. The dual sexual system established a complex system of *kamra prekti* or "bedroom obligations," which Wekker details as unwritten, communally recognized codes of behavior understood to be *eerlijk* (fair or honest) in sexual partnerships. These codes diverged widely from the husbandly and wifely duties propounded by contemporary Dutch household manuals distributed to European arrivals in the colonies.[24] Instead, the cooperative ecology of erotic relationships paralleled the cooperative ecology of the *dyari*. Whether relationships were between a man and woman or between two women, Surinamese Creole partners were expected to bring equal resources to the association. Sex (satisfying sexual performance was the duty of both men and women), housework, and money all counted toward fulfilling *kamra prekti*. "Ef i tek' a sensi, dan i ab'verplicting, dan na wan wroko" (If you take money, then you take on obligations, then you have to work):[25] whenever a woman takes money from a sexual partner, she understands that she is not his or her dependent but a worker in an equal partnership and must match the monetary contribution with equally valued contributions of sex, domestic labor, and money she earns herself. The more money she brings in, the less she will perform sexually solely to please her partner; the more often a male partner is impotent and cannot please her in return, the less housework she must do. At any time she can choose to take other work or other lovers to fulfill unmet needs, since sexual integrity is understood not as exclusivity but as a woman's assurance that she gives what she can and receives what she needs in any partnership. When men accept their female lovers' *mati*, they recognize that the economically and socially dominant partner in a relationship is *not* entitled to exclusive possession of the "natural" physical and emotional resources of his or her significant other.

The Dutch government, in turn, maintained a complex system of what might be termed "colonial obligations," which were, of course, neither mutual nor egalitarian. Suriname itself never significantly profited from the gold or rubber industries. The environment became rapidly depleted: land stripped for mines, trees bled dry by 1917, deforestation a growing problem. And while individual Surinamese obtained jobs as miners and bleeders, industry profits went entirely to the Dutch, British, or U.S. companies that owned the enterprises and The Hague never required them to make financial or environmental contributions (reforestation, for example) to local governments. Instead, the Dutch forced local governments to pay for a railroad the Netherlands initiated to facilitate mining even after the gold industry collapsed. The underlying logic of Creole bedroom obligations and that of Dutch colonial obligations stood in fundamental contradiction. Suriname was providing overseas companies with resources – unregulated amounts of raw materials – and getting no money and little else in exchange. Applying the guidelines of *kamra prekti* to the colonial relationship, Suriname had none of the obligations of political and economic subordination that the Dutch government insisted were its due. No money, no obligations, no work. As it involved both men and women, *mati* was not only a non-European sexual configuration but an anticolonial model of societal ecology: a community of limited resources that exacted an environmental and economic accountability that Dutch colonists had no interest in accepting. Schimmelpennick's description of *matisma* as *gemeenschap*, which evokes economic as well as sexual commerce and indicates a relation to *gemeente* (the local political unit), suggests that he perceived potentially symbolic – and threatening – linkages between sexual, economic, and environmental systems of "community" established in Paramaribo *dyari*.

Creole women continued to speak in defiance of Dutch policing, carrying on parties and *lobisingi* in their yards without the government-required written permission. "Law!" (Craziness!), the contemporary *mati* worker Juliette Cummings exclaimed to Wekker when told of Schimmelpennick's report.[26] Performed in public while colonial reports lay in State House drawers, the communal texts produced for these gatherings call for Creole women's control over the bodies and terrains that colonial governments sought to discipline and exploit. These short songs, dances, and ritual exchanges are imagistically dense, spun in a metaphoric language whose codes let women recognize *mati* by their double-entendres. My discussion of *mati* performances focuses on one of many highly developed metaphoric domains that mark their poetics, namely, flowers as vehicles for Creole women's sexuality. Unlike rubber or cane, the *fayalobi*, roses, and *stanfaste* (*gomphrena globosa*) that color *mati* poetry are "unproductive" contributions to the Surinamese landscape, flora cultivated for pleasure. And like female sexuality, they constitute a form of pleasure that has a long, intricate history of manipulation, regulation, and reappropriation in the colonial making of the Caribbean world. Before turning to a close reading of these images as deployed by Creole women, I want to look more in depth at this imperial history of disciplining floral and sexual profusion. This history tells the back story of why the police were right to imagine *mati* songs as doublespeak that ruffled not only the women of the community but also the colonial order and to try to shut them down as public disturbances to the tree-lined quiet of the squares through which government officials strolled.

Tropical Gardens, Changeable Roses: Unnatural Histories of Floral and Sexual Landscapes

African women and men were not the only, now emblematically Caribbean living beings forcibly transported to the region via European ships. *Fayalobi* (*ixora*), the national flower of Suriname, is a transplant from Southeast Asia and Africa; *choublak* (*hibiscus rosa sinesis*), the national flower of Haiti, came from Southeast Asia and India. Indeed, from its emergence, Caribbean flora has been a product of constant, violent migration. The volcanic islands' first plants blew in as seeds on Atlantic trade winds, and Columbus's arrival aggressively accelerated this transoceanic floral exchange. Globalization became botanical too, as colonists systematically replanted West Indian landscapes at such a speed that it soon became difficult to distinguish pre- from postconquest flora.[27] Hernán Cortés's first letter to the king requested that no vessel be allowed to sail to New Spain without seeds aboard; subsequent slave ships carried fruit trees to feed

their cargo, while missionaries and colonists transported bougainvillea, hibiscus, flamboyant, bird of paradise, poinsettia, plumeria, frangipani, oleander,
and jasmine to decorate altars, salons, and grounds.[28] By the late eighteenth
century, the manicured exotic garden became a luxury item that was, in fact,
a necessary prop in the colonial landscape. Decorative flora was not valuable to
the colony per se but in its manipulation, which simultaneously reflected and
justified the power of colonial gardeners. Where *dyari* arranged a landscape of
cooperation, exotic gardens plotted a landscape of domination – settlers' domination of the supposedly lower orders of nature. Ostentatious grounds served
as markers of Europeans' evolution above brute survival, manifesting what
Méderic Moreau de St. Méry sees in his *Description topographique, physique, civile,
politique et historique de la partie française de l'Isle Saint Domingue* (1797) as "the contrast between nature abandoned to herself or seconded by man's industry."[29]
Elaborate private gardens landscaped in the style of the mother country in Port
of Spain, Kingston, and Willemstad proved such a source of colonial pride that
he directed all good citizens to vow to build a nursery.[30] Crown treasuries also
subsidized lavish public gardens to buttress this pride. By 1779 the English had
catalogued imported flora in botanical gardens in Kingstown, St. Vincent, and
St. Thomas, Jamaica. In 1788 M. Nectoux, the director of Port-au-Prince's fledgling Jardin Royal des Plantes, carried seedlings from Jamaica's botanical garden
to add to his ailing charge, while a floral shipment from India later that year
attempted to salvage the crown's substantial investment in the project.[31]

These painfully ordered gardens provided a crucial countertopos to daily
violence in the colonies. They acted as what Peter Hulme calls a "magic tech-
nology": a European invention or tool that, like maps, compasses, and mirrors,
enabled colonizers to ward off the psychic perils of occupying the New World.[32]
The garden was ordered space that "magically" pushed back the savagery of
hills and woods, maroon topoi in which cycles of rebellion destabilized plantations throughout the century. In the 1730s, rebellions erupted in Bermuda, St.
John, the Bahamas, St. Kitts, St. Bartholomew, St. Martin, Anguilla, Martinique,
Guadeloupe, Jamaica, and Suriname, with ongoing maroon wars in the mountains and the bush of the two latter colonies presenting continuous threats to
occupiers. In the 1760s, Tacky and Cubah's Revolt in Jamaica initiated a new
cycle of resistance in Bermuda, Nevis, Suriname, British Honduras, Grenada,
Montserrat, St. Vincent, St. Kitts, and Guadeloupe. It seems no coincidence
that colonial governments sponsored natural histories and botanical gardens
in the same years that they spent substantial funds on soldiers and weapons

to fight these revolts. Tropical gardens, too, formed a strategy of symbolic warfare. Landscaped, catalogued grounds marked territory claimed for Europe; the
colony where maroon rebels were quashed, John Gabriel Stedman metaphor-
ized in his *Narrative of a Five Years' Expedition against the Revolted Negroes of Suriname* (1796), would be a "large and beautiful garden, stocked with everything
art and nature could produce," where colonists' "persons and effects [would be]
in perfect security."[33] Disrupting this garden, maroons were not only associated
with bush, jungle, and hill but, according to Edward Long, showed remarkable
"repugnance to the labour of tilling the earth."[34] As a countertopos, rational-
ized exotic gardens served as visual symbols of colonists' will to reexert control
over the wildly multicolored Caribbean landscape, demarcating space in which
colonists lived in luxury and that no maroons could penetrate or savage.

But the propagation of flowers was not the only breeding that planters carefully manipulated. As they did for their floral arrangements, colonists exerted
continual efforts to control the sugar islands' sexual arrangements. Inevitably,
just as it produced gardens mixing blooms from Europe, Africa, and Asia, the
imperial experiment produced new forms of sexual contact and erotic partnership. Some – like shipmates' – were (terribly, literally) horizontal connections.
But others were built around the radically unequal racial and gendered dynamics of plantocracy, where northern masculinity sexually and socially dominated tropical femininity. Such sexual relations included coerced sex work that
the enslaved were legally bound to perform for masters. They also included
consensual liaisons like "Surinamese marriages," long-term, legally unrecog-
nized partnerships between single or married Euro-Creole men and enslaved
or free women of (frequently mixed) African descent. Routinely heterosexual
but physically nonreproductive – since most enslaved females never gave birth
in the Caribbean, where "buy not breed" remained the standard – this sexual
labor was set up in ways that repeated slavery's racialized power relations. As
the Caribbean historian Barbara Bush writes, it "represented a natural extension of the general power of white over black, the sex act becoming, in Win-
throp Jordan's words, 'a ritualistic reenactment of the daily pattern of social
dominance.'"[35] While individuals obtained sexual pleasure or social privilege
from sex work, that owners could and did require sex acts as part of slaves'
duties – and that freed women had few legal and economic alternatives to con-
cubinage – made coerced sex work a continual reminder that, despite rebels'
challenges, Afro-Caribbeans were there to be "fucked figuratively as well as
literally," as Maryse Condé puts it.[36]

Rape of the enslaved was routinely, violently justified by natural histories'
equations between Africans and beasts in heat, including Long's chilling hesi-
tation to distinguish the uncontrollable sexuality of black women from that
of orangutans.[37] But the more sustained intimacies of Surinamese marriages
necessitated different rhetorical and metaphoric manipulations in which the
marker of dehumanization moved from the bestial to the floral. Of course, not
just any flora would do: rather than raiding cane fields for metaphors, colonial
chroniclers turned to gardens and their decorative growth. When they describe
long-term "loverships" and want to make them look like what Bush calls "the
natural extension" of white power, the trope of women as tropical flowers fits
their rhetorical needs because they, like flora, are imagined as exotic sources of
pleasure whose taming proves Europeans' dominance. In contrast to breadfruit
and cane, the cultivated flower is a luxury item par excellence, a pure pleasure
of excess; and the Afro-Creole lover is drawn as a woman of luxury par excellence, in both senses of the word. Stedman recalls his profound arousal when
he first saw his Surinamese "wife," the mulatta Joanna, "ornamented with
flowers" whose open beauty she echoed, standing in contrast to those indomi-
table maroons and offering herself for pleasurable plucking. Moreau takes the
trope a step further when he imagines mulatta mistresses as creatures "who
love flowers passionately, who adorn themselves with them, who stuff their
beds and armoires full with them and, knowing that their perfume awakes
sensuality, take great pleasure in arranging bouquets for the object of their
affection."[38] Here flowers vehicle a racialized and subordinate hyperheterosexuality deeply rooted in the brown woman, that being utterly "devoted to
sensuality" and equipped with the same ability to "charm all the senses, deliver
them to the most delicious ecstasies" that Moreau attributes to the tropical
blooms that "awaken the sensuality" of Europeans.[39] Women of color's flowers
are their sexuality in Moreau's imperial eyes, willingly and pleasurably handed
over to white colonists — just as all products of land and Afro-Creole labor must
be to maintain the plantocratic order.

Stedman and Moreau infer identity from similarity between the terms
linked by their figures of speech, painting the brown woman's bouquets as
the same as the brown woman's sexuality. By understanding the natural properties of the first term, they suggest, colonialists can understand the second
as natural property. This conflation is discursive violence, flattening terms.
And its dehumanization enables physical violence, justifying the systematized
rape and sex work deployed or required by slave owners. The repressive force

of Stedman's and Moreau's images lies not in the "carrying" work of metaphor itself, as Paul de Man's classic work might suggest, but arises as this carrying is inscribed in the violent, hierarchical relations that exist between its terms in colonial histories.[40] The tropical flower-woman trope implicates three terms embroiled in complex power relationships: brown woman, land, and (absentee) land-/woman-owner, the imagined sameness of the first two creating the privileged difference of the third. Like the blending of plants in botanical gardens, the blending of human and vegetable, female and flower signifies the elevation of the colonial landowner above the level of the savage (read earth/slave). In *The Repeating Island*, Antonio Benítez-Rojo argues that Caribbean nature was tamed by a succession of European machines – the fleet, the mine, the plantation – each repeating a historico-economic assemblage of power generated by the previous machine. The woman-as-flora metaphor reads as an *aesthetic machine*, whose terms repeat power relationships "mechanically" produced by the workings of colonialism, not those of metaphor.[41] Like the garden, the relationship between terms is not an ahistorical configuration but an arrangement that reflects and serves specific regimes of power.

But like *systemae natura*, systems of metaphor leak, confusing boundaries. The problem with Port-au-Prince's gardens, Moreau reported, was the insects flying over hedges into surrounding neighborhoods.[42] And the problem with these metaphorical taxonomies of race and racialized gender was the excessive, overfeeling body of the woman of African descent, a tropical flower always threatening to "color" what was supposed to remain clear and distinct. Sexuality, with its links to *feeling*, was an ambiguous attribute for the brown mistress, one that threatened the invented identity between Afro-Caribbean woman and flora. In *Haiti, History, and the Gods*, Joan Dayan argues that to maintain the system of slavery, colonialists at once needed to prove that Africans were not evolved or human enough to experience emotion *and* to maintain that they *could* experience emotion in the form of attachment to their masters, an emotive capacity necessary to prevent further rebellion. Yet under no circumstances could this attachment constitute *love* between evolutionary equals. In the triangulation of the floral metaphor, the woman of color must stay at the level of the earth, not approach that of the landowner. In colonial chroniclers' portraits of interracial heterosexual loverships, as Dayan puts it, "the word *love* takes on bizarre connotations: in its most intense manifestations, the idea of love depends on a relation of domination that is enacted best in bondage. . . . Love is made better when what you love is what you own, whether slave or wife."[43] The tropical flower-woman was a necessary invention because she could be both slave and "wife" or mistress, just as she could be both woman and flower. But by the late eighteenth century, she had also become a danger-ous one because she could refuse to be either. If the ability to feel more strongly than white lovers was a quality Moreau found dangerous in the mulatta, this was perhaps because if she chose to refuse – to not feel like performing – her role as unpaid sex worker with the same intensity with which (he imagined) she experienced sexual pleasure, her equally insatiable desire to own her body would strike at the very foundations of plantation power dynamics.[44]

Indeed, the image of the hyperheterosexual flower is another magic tech-nology that colonists created to mask the very real social and sexual "disorders" that women of African descent fomented. Not merely passive blossoms, they were too often, as Mr. Hamden complained to the Barbados legislature, "Ama-zonian."[45] Resisting the role of Surinamese wife or mistress, numerous women described in Stedman's Narrative received "the most cruel tortures" for "refusing to submit to the [desire] of a libidinous master, and more frequently a rascally overseer."[46] At the same time, women like Cubah and Nanny headed rebellions in Jamaica while Cécile Fatiman and Ma Cato provided spiritual leadership to rebels in Haiti and Suriname. But not only Amazonian in the sense of warrior-like, Afro-Creoles were also Amazonian in the sense of same-sex sexually active. In Haiti, Moreau notes the frequency of what he believes to be male "women" among African slaves, whose sexual practices he finds a crime too unspeakable to name outright: "Already unlucky in their weak complexion, many are even more so as the result of a revolting practice (which other Africans sometimes also display on the islands) which strips them of the title of man while leaving them their lives."[47] He also notes same-sex eroticism among female slaves, but in contrast to the sickness and shame attributed to feminine males, female women's eroticism is recorded as a scene of celebration: "They immensely enjoy what they call 'matching up' [assortiment]: that is at certain formal parties, sev-eral dress exactly alike to go out walking or dancing. One most often 'matches' with a good friend who is a confidante, the woman she cannot do without. This attachment [is] extremely intense."[48] Moreau fails to remark on any sexual component or other threatening aspect to these relationships. He seems to read them as romantic friendships, intense affective connections between European women widely socially accepted in the eighteenth century.[49] Yet direct parallels between the coupling, dress, and party rituals of kambrada in Curaçao and mati in Suriname strongly suggest that assortiments were, like kambrada and mati, a system of sexual relationships among Afro-Creole women. But if recognized as such, what would the intense bonds and "remarkable . . . loyalty" that Moreau notes between black and mulatta women – loyalty to each other, rather than to white male owners – mean to the "large and beautiful garden," rich with planters' "persons and effects in perfect security," that Stedman hoped the colonies would become?[50] What if these "good friends" were keeping flowers from the plantocracy's garden for each other?

Records of colonists' punishment for warrior Amazonianness – for maroonage, the destruction of plantations – are copious and deeply disturbing, including frequent hanging, quartering, and burning alive.[51] In contrast, records of punishment for sexual Amazonianness are scant but suggestive. One documented, gruesome case involved Matthijs de Goyer, the son of a former governor of Suriname, accused of anal and manual sex with several men. Among these and the trial's chief witness was the enslaved overseer of a neighboring plantation, Govert, suspected of mutual masturbation with the accused (which he denied). Despite Govert's uncooperative testimony, De Goyer was convicted of sodomy in 1731. Governor Karel De Cheusses – also the first governor to lead a military expedition against the maroons – feared that if the crime were left unpunished, God's wrath might destroy the already embattled colony. Accordingly he ordered De Goyer burned alive, his remains tied to a hundred-pound weight and thrown into the ocean so that the land would not be contaminated and rendered unfruitful by his sin.[52] What is at once striking and horrific in this story is not only that government tortures for maroons and sodomites were pioneered in the same years by the same governor but also that they took the same form – burning alive. Exacting symbolic as well as physical destruction, this execution method literally sent threats to the colony up in smoke, erasing every possible trace of their anti(re)productivness from the blighted garden that Suriname had become. If De Goyer had penetrated Govert and so enabled the court to continue the fiction that penetration was domination and that white males were dominating the "lower orders" of nature, perhaps his punishment would have been less harsh. But massaging a slave to orgasm as if he were at the planter's level was "loving" in a way that violated the sociosexual hierarchy of the white man over the slave and wife, of the landowner over woman and nature.

As maroons and same-sex lovers received the same treatment from De Cheusses's executioners, so they did from Moreau's pen. In a kind of literary burning alive, both are backgrounded and dismissed until their influence on the colony seems to dissipate like ash. Omission of all forms of the Amazonian also formed part of the *Description*'s project of reasserting threatened colonial hierarchies between landowner and property: *his* plantation and garden, *his* slave and wife. Written on the eve of the Haitian revolution, Moreau's three volumes, almost unbelievably, make no direct reference to slave resistance. And while the author makes brief mention of same-sex sexual and affective connections between Africans, he introduces these only to minimize their impact. Sexuality between males, he quickly concludes, leads to incurable weakness, making these slaves completely unthreatening and un-maroonlike to his readers. And though he describes intense bonds and loyalties between black and mulatta women, he insists that all women of color are propelled by an innate, overpowering heterosexuality that necessitates their finally becoming the erotic property of male superiors. In years in which sumptuary laws looked to clothing to establish visible social barriers, the identical dresses sewn by "matched-up" (z)amies visualized the possibility of constructing outfits and relationships based on fundamental equality, a possibility that had to be erased or rewritten as the frivolous amusements of heterosexual women. Perhaps even more than De Goyer's forsaking of husbandhood for homo-sex, enslaved women acting as each others' "wives" would have been the ultimate violation of the mandate that "what you love is made better when it is what you own, whether slave or wife."[53] Women of color could not be their own gardeners; exotic flowers could not exist without (European, male) masters.

But before and after Moreau, the prestige of the colonial garden and the power of its regulatory systems have been constantly undercut by the mutability of Caribbean physical and cultural landscapes. What colonists attempted to fix in parterres refused to stay in place. Not only were plants constantly uprooted and rerooted, but even those flowers that appeared settled into their surroundings still underwent continual, disruptive shifts. Returning to the twentieth-century Caribbean – and to the kind of transatlantic travel that continues to bring Dutch adventurers to the immigration lines in which Esther Oduber-Lamers began her stay in Curaçao – witness the colorful photo essay *Flowers of the Caribbean*, in which Jeanne Garrard narrates one tourist's encounter with such a surprising flower:

> Arising early, she looked out on the Caribbean landscape and particularly admired a large, pure white flowering bush right by her window. Returning after shopping, a glance up to the window-view made her grab up her packages. She thought she was in the wrong room . . . for the

bush outside *this* window was covered, not with white, but with showy rose-pink flowers! . . . She decided she'd been mistaken about the flower color that morning. Surprise took over late that afternoon. She returned to dress for dinner. She couldn't believe her eyes.

The bush outside her window had changed again. Now it had dull RED Blossoms!

Mysterious? Not in the tropics. She had just met her first Hibiscus Mutabilis—the Changeable Rose. Like so many of the unusual tropical flowers and chameleon-like trees, this lovely flower changes color all during the day.[54]

This "lovely" flower's journey away from whiteness warps the colonial fantasy it was planted to create. The changeable rose confuses the space that the tourist thought she could occupy unproblematically, the agency these flowers demonstrate making her temporarily believe she is in the wrong room. It also disrupts the traveler's sense of time, in which people move while nature remains unmoved; it interrupts her economic praxes of conspicuous consumption (shopping and eating); and finally it disrupts her sense of reality, the imperialist epistemology normalizing the unchangeable natural world and its static color divisions.

Like the changeable rose, Caribbean flowers can be used for botanical, literary, and political effects the original gardeners never foresaw, and for centuries women of color have drawn on flowers and sexuality for their own purposes. They, too, have taken what first looked "pure white" and recolored it darker and darker—redder and redder, browner and browner—to unsettle the hegemony of imperial eyes. In colonial Suriname and Haiti, slaves reappropriated the European invention of the garden by growing flowers on provision grounds. These flowers were sold at market and used in Afro-Caribbean religious ceremonies, providing enslaved women with a measure of economic, spiritual, and social autonomy that prompted the Surinamese governor Jan Nepveau to denounce such "freedom" in 1770.[55] Women of color, forbidden by law in Dutch and French colonies to wear jewelry or to leave their houses without their heads covered, circumvented sumptuary laws by adding flowers to their dress; in so doing, they asserted a control over their bodies that colonists never anticipated. The elaborate floral adornments that struck Moreau were not the transparent heterosexual coquetry he assumed, but resistance to legislated restrictions on women of color's bodies.

It is this tradition of uprooting and reappropriating flowers and their mythologies of race, gender, and sexuality that I follow as I explore reworkings of floral metaphors in the poetry of Surinamese *mati*. In the next pages, I look to read floral metaphors in their texts much in the same way in which an observer might read flowers on Afro-Caribbean altars. Describing the Winti altar of a Paramaribo Creole woman, Wekker registered surprise at seeing a photograph of Queen Juliana at its center.[56] Usually hung in the schools, government buildings, and bourgeois living rooms of Suriname, this portrait acted as an *imperial fetish*: imperial power allowed this photograph to signify *and* was what it signified.[57] This changed, however, when it was set on the altar. There, Juliana's regal image was emptied of its power to represent Surinamese subjection to Dutch political and gender systems. It now vehicled gender-shifting, continent-hopping Winti honored by the offerings placed before (no longer) her picture. The "altaring" of this photograph interrupted the fetishistic intention of the photographer, disrupting a representation of the Dutch sovereign that assumed the image of Juliana to represent Dutch power. Instead, it moved to another metaphorical representation, one that assumed the image of Juliana also to represent *other(s') power*. The image "is" at once Juliana and Winti; European, African, and Creole; female, male, and gender shifting. Like this altar, *mati* poetry reclaims colonial images to make them *act differently*. These images become objets trouvés pieced together to vehicle Creole concepts of gender born in the Middle Passage and elaborated in *dyari*, according, as Daniel Cosentino writes of Haitian altars, "to an aesthetic they carried in their heads, their hearts, their entire bodies."[58]

Playing with *Fayalobi*: The Birthday Party

A dance party is another kind of journey from the tourist's or the explorer's, another, fluid-bodied way of imagining meaningful movement through the Caribbean landscape. And while colonial representatives from De Cheusses to Schimmelpennick pathologized same-sex eroticism as a cause of widespread contamination, for over a century, Afro-Caribbean women themselves expressed it as a cause for celebration played out in the dancing, singing, gift-giving, drinking, and fighting of the birthday party: that celebration of another year of individual and community life that symbolically recognized erotic connections between women. The historians Wim Hoogbergen and Marjo de Theye suggest that these traditions originated during slavery, and the earliest description of such a ceremony may be Moreau's record of *assortiments* at parties in eighteenth-century Haiti, where pairs of *bonnes amies* or *zanmi* dressed identically and danced together. But it was in the early twentieth century that they reached their peak in various parts of the region including Curaçao, Trinidad, and—most elaborately—Suriname. In Curaçao, Guillermo Rosario remembers that in the early 1900s *kambradas* ritually revealed sexual relationships by appearing in twin clothing at celebratory masses, wakes, and parties.[59] In Trinidad, informants told the Herskovitses that erotic relationships between black women were celebrated by parties that the elder partner threw for the younger, and they themselves witnessed songs women composed and sang for each other.[60] And in Suriname, as numerous anthropologists and folklorists recorded, every year the elder partner in a *mati* relationship threw a birthday party for the younger in her *dyari*. Not at all "closeted" events, birthday parties were loudly fêted affairs. On the birthday morning, flowers and gifts were delivered to the doorstep of the woman celebrated. After dark, yard dwellers and neighbors gathered in her *dyari* to dance, drink, and party, and finally—near midnight, as the festivities reached their height—the lover arrived at the doorstep and partygoers moved to the threshold to watch her dance for her *mati*.

The Herskovitses, doing fieldwork in Paramaribo in 1928, sketch a detailed account of this scene:

> It is customary for the special "friend" of the person who is celebrating her birthday to come late, and to bring flowers for her *mati*. These she carries on her head, and, as she approaches the door of her friend's cabin, she stops some paces away, and calls out, "*Mis-misi, mi ka ko na ini? Nowa doti na de na pasi? Nowa maka? Nowa sneki? Nowa storm no sa wai mi fadon?*—Miss-missi, may I come in? Is there no dirt on the path? No thorns? No snakes? No storm to blow me over?"
>
> The answer comes from her friend, who dances toward her, "*No, no, misi, yu ka ko doro.*—No, no Miss, you can come in."
>
> The first asks again, "*Nanga baka?*—Backwards?"
>
> "*Ya.*—Yes."
>
> "*Nanga fesi?*—Forward?"
>
> "*Ya.*—Yes."
>
> "*Nanga sei? Fa mi 'e kanti de, mi no sa fadon?*—Sideways? As I lean over, I won't fall down?"
>
> "*No, yu no se fadon.*—No, you won't fall down."

This colloquy is accompanied by dancing steps, with the participants moving toward each other and away from each other. When the last phrase has been spoken, the woman whose birthday is being celebrated brings wine to steady the visitor, who is still outside the door. The music begins to play, and the people who are gathered shout, "Hip, hip, hura! *Sopi no de, ma kuku de.* — Hip, hip, hooray! There is no rum, but there are cakes." A chorus of laughter is heard. . . . and the special "friend" bearing her flowers enters the house of her *mati*.[61]

Wekker, in communications recounting interactions with older *mati*, fills in some gaps left by the Herskovitses' text. The birthday bouquet was made up of flowers grown in the friend's yard—making the *mati* attending the party not victims of the fields but active, creative gardeners. Red *fayalobi* (literally, "fire love"), whose name and brilliant color reflected the intensity of the eroticism they vehicled, figured prominently in these bouquets.[62] These flowers were known for their erotic expressiveness: "I am a *fayalobi*: you see what's on my face, you see what's in my heart," runs an *odo* (proverb).[63]

Despite these accounts, the birthday ritual remains an inevitably incomplete text. The embodied text of the dance, which I can only imagine, is condensed and translated into an anthropological one—the only one I can read, pieced together from two accounts. Such a lacunary archive offers a pointed reminder that understandings of the sexualized body and its desiring movements are *always* mediated and deferred through language, and any fantasies of transparency must fall away before thinking through the doorway dance. But the constantly blurry, unfinished character of the birthday text is due not only to its palimpsestic nature but also to how its guiding metaphoric terms— flowers and *mati* bodies—literally and figuratively keep in constant motion. Each time the dance is performed the flowers and the women's bodies change, and the mutability of the bouquets and women celebrated is part of what gives meaning and resists closure here. What seems more significant than any particular floral arrangement or dancer is the mobile relationship choreographed between flower and woman: one that sways with a very different imagination than the imperial gardening of women of color and so suggests a very different model of women's relationships to sexuality, to each other, and to the colony. Women and flowers enter together, touch each other, dance together—but they never become *the same*; the woman of color's body is not passively and involuntarily floralized as in the colonial woman-flora equation. Instead, as the flower bearer dances with, but "some paces away" from her *mati*, the sexualized body signifies with — but also independently of — her flowers to actively and playfully create Creolized, eroticized meanings. The dancers' steps trace an interactional model of nature and desire that trips up the top-down "love" naturalized by slavery — since at the party, the total domination of one term or lover by the other would spoil the game.

Neither the exotic specimen that Moreau fantasizes nor the site of disease that Schimmelpennick pathologizes, the woman of color's (homo)sexualized body greets the *dyari* as an actor who knows and communicates a lot. In *On the Postcolony*, Achille Mbembe posits that West African social reality is constituted by daily practices that are "not simply matters of discourse and language" but embodied activities — seeing, hearing, moving, feeling, touching — that constitute "*meaningful human expressions . . . meaningful acts.*"[64] The birthday party's exchanges dance diasporic examples of such meaningful acts. At the doorway, the Creole woman's body deliberately signifies through its movement. The dance steps between flower carrier and the woman celebrating her birthday publicize the dancers' sexual relationship and eroticize the *dyari*'s communal space (*baka, fesi, sei* — backwards, forwards, to the side). Like *dyari* and their *fayalobi*, the sexualized body is activated not as some "thing" privately owned but as a site-in-motion that Creole women actively, and sometimes contentiously, share with other women in their community. At the same time, the *mati*'s body signifies through sound patterns. In a verbal exchange dominated by playful repetitions, the constant return of nasal sounds (*mis-misi, mi, nowa, maka, sneki, fadon, nanga*) — where air vibrates through the nose and mouth — physicalizes the pleasurable connection between the body's inside and its outside, while repeated plosives physicalize the power of this connection by forceful expiration. Speaking as well as dancing, the body locates itself *at* a crossroads (between path and house) and *as* a crossroads: a space that bridges the individual (the arriving *mati*) and the collective (the party), the inside and the outside, with *nyan-prey* — pleasure (*prey*) as powerful and necessary as food (*nyan*). The presence of the verbal text, like the presence of other dancers, does not diminish the importance of what the flower bearer's body *means*. Its very wordlessness (since it is never described) has value in communicating the erotic, which Creole women call *tiri sani* (something silent): something for which, as Wekker interprets this saying, "words are too hard, too angular."[65]

On a warm night in the *dyari*, why dance with fiery flowers on your head? Just as the dancing body plays with intersections, so does the piece of landscape —

the flowers – carried to the door. *Fayalobi* "mean" here in Creole, as *In Praise of Creoleness*'s "interactional or transactional aggregate."[66] Their signifying force lies in a crossroads of associations that their contiguity makes available to the flower bearer's sexualized body: a meeting of Euro- and Afro-Caribbean, dominant and resistant models of the woman of color's sexuality literally attached to her signifying body. When they choose to arrange their backyard blooms in the European form of the bouquet, *dyari* dwellers usurp an image of colonial sexuality never meant to be a gift for them. The bouquet-bearing dancer marks the eroticism associated with decorative flowers as property that working-class black women manipulate, circulate, and celebrate among themselves, rather than handing it over to white men (as Moreau imagined of mulattas' bouquets). But standing a bouquet on a *mati*'s head creates meaning in another way too, in an Afro-Surinamese way. Its flowers – like references to crossroads – evoke the power of spirits who, like Leba, are honored with fresh flowers and *swit watri* (sweet water) made from flower petals. Most directly, red "fire love" summon a Creole model of powerful female sexuality, Motyo Ingi: the lavishly erotic spirit who protects many *mati* and whose sacred color, red, is the favored color of offerings to her.

If gender-shifting, crossroad-drawing Leba seems the quintessential spirit of the yard, graceful, scarlet-loving Motyo Ingi might step in as the quintessential spirit of the *mati* party. In the syncretic religion Winti, all Ingi spirits are breathtaking dancers; and Motyo in particular loves parties, celebration, and pleasure in all forms, demonstrating the divinity of *feeling good*. Like other Afro-Caribbean religions, Winti celebrates meaningful connections between Caribbeans and their physical and cultural landscapes by honoring air, water, earth, and forest *winti* (spirits). Part of an Ingi pantheon including water, earth, and forest spirits, Motyo Ingi celebrates cultural and geographic crossings as sites of power. Ingi means "Indian" (Native American); and as a group of spirits in an Afro-Caribbean religion, these *winti* remember alliances between two ecological and political traditions – Native and African – that colonists sought to dominate and efface. In her specific role in this pantheon, Motyo Ingi celebrates sexual crossings as sites of divine knowledge. Motyo literally means "whore," and like the Haitian Ezili and the Cuban Oshun, her deification honors the creative force of eroticism. But in Winti as in Vodoun or Santería, this force is not primarily procreative. Afro-Caribbean religions map conceptual landscapes in which neither male nor female, hetero- nor same-sex sexuality are normative or clearly defined. Ezili marries female as well as male spirits, and candles to her often burn on the altars of those involved in same-sex relationships; Oshun and Motyo Ingi play similarly protective roles. Other spirits shift genders from story to story, island to island, emanation to emanation, leaving the gender composition of marriages to them equally shiftable. These include spirits of crossroads (Leba), air (Obatala and Danbalah), and water (Olokun and Inle).[67]

So the ground mati walk, the air they breathe, and the water they drink is all understood as "naturally" gender and sexually complex. In this kinetic landscape gender and sexuality are not binaries (man/woman, hetero/homo) but also crossroads, multiple and intersecting paths that spirits travel. Not surprisingly, practitioners and priests at Afro-Caribbean religious ceremonies are often same-sex loving, and some women go to these ceremonies expressly to meet other women.[68] Conversely, mati may come to birthday parties both to celebrate women loving women and to recognize the spirits that support them. Commenting on the Herskovitses' account, Ineke van Wetering notes that the anthropologists overlooked the religious elements of this event meant to strengthen the soul and protective winti of the woman celebrating her birthday for another year. Van Wetering demonstrates how the hybrid social-spiritual space of the birthday party becomes a charged site of religious syncretism, one in which spirits from various traditions (African, European, Native) are honored in more "mixed" ways than at formal religious ceremonies.[69] The flowers that the arriving mati brings, then, both mark an appropriation of the European tradition of giving bouquets to the beloved and serve as a reminder of the flowers placed on altars during ceremonies during which women come to dance with women. The mati arriving at her lover's doorstep steps into a crossroads between house and yard, landscape (flowers) and body, Euro-, Afro-, and Native Surinamese womanhood, ritual, and seduction—all rendered even more complex by staying in motion at the party's threshold. The performer well earns the cheers and wine that meet her at the door.

Yet the crowd cheers not only that the mati carries flowers but also how. The mock offering to Motyo Ingi on the dancer's head also plays on Winti epistemologies of the body, in which the crown—along with eyes, mouth, and vagina—serves as a connective point for powerful spiritual energies flowing between overlapping human and spirit realms, between women and Motyo Ingi. In ecologically based Winti, human, natural, and spiritual realms are neither separated nor hierarchized; the Suriname River, the river spirit Motyo Ingi, and Motyo Ingi's human children are all assumed intimately connected, made of the same stuff. This overlap becomes clear in Robert Farris Thompson's description of forked vessel altars. Calling on the power of the meeting of earth and flora, Afro-Surinamese worshipers turn trees into altars as they place sacred vessels in their branches. In ceremonies, a priest takes such a vessel from the tree and places it on her or his head. Miming the tree's verticality, the human worshiper *becomes* the altar as "the priestess or priest dances as a living pillar, supporting a sacred vessel on his or her head."[70] In this dance, brown bodies resemble the natural world not as twin resources to be exploited but as twin gateways to a realm of powerful knowledge close enough to touch their heads/branches. The birthday party's flower-carrying *mati* echoes the meaningful acts of this ceremonial dance not only by balancing a meaning-bearing object on her dancing head but also by visualizing a link to the natural world that represents knowledge of the body, of sexuality, of social organization, and of artistic expression. All these realms form part of the epistemic-social organizing force of Winti, a force that – like landscape and sexuality – became a continuous source of struggle between Afro-Surinamese and Dutch colonists. That the Dutch quickly understood this force as a threat becomes clear in reports like those of Sergeant J. Dorig, the head of a military operation to recover Paramaribo runaways, who destroyed a Winti altar during his 1758 charge. This altar, he recognized, was "lifting up" (Latin *altare*) knowledge that had been systematically subjugated as part of the colonial enterprise.[71] In many ways, the breaking up of such altars reads as the model for the breaking up of *mati* gatherings begun in 1900: both police Creole ways of knowing "natures" (spiritual and embodied) that undermine the naturalized order of Dutch colonial machines.

But let us not forget where we are. Neither an anticolonial protest nor a religious ceremony, the birthday party loudly, unmistakably happens *for fun*. A very different kind of Surinamese movement from Dorig's charge, the *mati*'s danced approach is also motion that is not a journey at all: the creative, open-ended, happy-to-have-no-destination movement of play. The birthday party dances out a playful relationship between *mati*, their bodies, and their yards that, contrary to male chroniclers' reports, is both productive and erotic on its own terms. As the arriving lover sways her skirts back and forth for the woman celebrating her birthday, she is making an art of multiple levels of play – and a whole yard of women are enjoying it. "Crazy" though it may be, the birthday ritual is indeed play in the sense Schimmelpennick fears, namely, a refusal of Dutch ideas of work. The position of the fiery bouquet on the head, swaying in the back-and-forth of the dance, signifies on the traditional female work of head portage. The hands that are weekday tools of labor remain empty here, and instead of transporting goods to market, the black woman's head carries flowers with which she dances and seduces her lover. At the party, mati not only play instruments but also with what a working woman's body looks like, making flowers an extension of the flower-bearer's head; and they play with what bouquets look like, taking them out of the context of the elite salons that these women often cleaned. The workings of the colonial economy are interrupted by another movement, one celebrating relationships that are not financially productive or reproductive, not functional to Dutch capitalism. Paraded for fun rather than for sale, the gift of faylobi shows mati's relationship not only to spirits who possess them but to a landscape they were not supposed to possess: these transplanted tropical flowers were considered representative of Suriname, and after independence, they became the national flower. Setting these red blossoms on mati heads, having the flower of Suriname serve to entertain black women rather than to contribute to colonial gardens and parlors, was matispelen that played outside dominant symbolic and economic orders. Schimmelpennick's report assumed that not to perform wage labor was to be weak, sickly, and inactive, but this play – not the "opposite" of work – in fact reverses passivity, creating something other than goods and services for the Dutch: namely, recognition and celebration for women whose wage labor was not intended to provide them much of either.

Of course, night is not only when women do not work but also when they go to bed together; and the mati-flower interaction at the birthday party also acts out play in the sense of foreplay. The enjoyment of the danced greeting is based in observers' understanding that the flower-bearing mati is not just asking to enter her lover's house; she is dramatizing a request to enter her lover. Nothing is short-circuited in this performance: dancers take their time to move through the door with the underlying suggestion that the arriving mati will also take her time with her celebrating lover after the party. The words that the dancers exchange "sound like" sex, encoding a Creole ars erotica. When the arriving mati asks "mi kan ko na ini?" (can I come inside), she echoes the words in which the mati worker Jet described the beginning of mati sex: "Come na trawan. En wi di fienga wie srefie" (One woman comes into the other. And we finger each other).[72] When this mati poses questions about snakes, dirt, thorns, or storms on the path, she is asking if anyone else has staked a rival claim to postparty sex: if something or someone else has come to penetrate her lover (snakes/ thorns) or to get her aroused and wet (like a storm). And when the flower-bearer asks if she is safe to move backward, forward, and side to side and dances with her partner to accompany these words, the couple recalls the back-and-forth and around motion of hips during sex. "Dan wie die grietie wie srefie" (Then we grind/roll our hips against each other), continues Jet's description.[73] Will you – the dance and exchange teasingly ask – let me enjoy your body tonight, just as I am letting you enjoy the flowers of my *dyari*? Can our open bodies play together like these open, thornless flowers? The flowers of Motyo Ingi and Suriname, *ixora*, are known for something else too: their juice tastes sugary, and women bite buds open and suck them when they want some sweetness in the yard. The flower-bearer's offer of this bloom and her playful request, in return, for a storm-free eroticism "dance back" to imperial imaginations of women of color as eternally passive parts of the cane field, picked at will and unable to taste their own sweetness – and instead publicize her ability to freely pick who she sleeps with. The birthday party marks a space in which flowers can move playfully if Creole women want them to and in which brown women's bodies can mean mutual pleasure if they want them to.

Mati play, then, is not the opposite of productivity and activity. However, neither is it the idyllic, rosy, community-healing activity playfulness is sometimes imagined to be; it does not shut out the possible conflicts and tensions brewing in the small space of the *dyari*. Like sex, the play of the birthday party does not escape to somewhere outside societal power dynamics, but rather is choreographed through them, and these dynamics also become part of the birthday dance. The Herskovitses go on to sketch the slippage from seduction to aggression that can happen when the flower-bearer passes through the door:

> It happens at times that when the ceremony we have just described is concluded, and the special "friend" bearing her flowers enters the house of her *mati*, she discovers that there are other flowers already in the room. The one just arrived thereupon seizes these flowers, crushes them, and throws them out, for they are the symbol of a rival claimant to the affection of her *mati*. If she knows the identity of this rival she will, in addition, slap her, to show before the assembled guests that she will not have her rights disputed. If she does not know who brought these flowers, she goes from one woman to the next to find out who it was. This byplay adds to the zest of the party . . . for while it is not uncommon for a woman to have more than one *mati*, neither will tolerate the presence of the other, nor yield her place if the challenge is thus made public.[74]

In this landscape of intersection and diversity, why does this particular multiplicity – the common practice of having more than one *mati* – elicit a fist fight? In his *Poetics of Relation*, Glissant reminds us that the interstitial spaces (yards, ghettoes, street gatherings) in which Creolization occurs most rapidly are often violent, pressured, economically and socially unstable topoi and that the recognition of their cultural productivity should not idealize these tensions away.[75] Mati – often domestic workers for Paramaribo's elite – are desperately poor women working in homes steeped in excess, workers who desire something or someone exclusively their own. The fight for the lover at the birthday party dramatizes this desire. On the one hand, the patriarchal colonial economy places working-class women in a space (the *dyari*) in which they must share resources to survive. At the same time, this patriarchal colonial system pushes working-class women to compete within the space of the yard: to act out their hunger for at least one prized possession, for some to win something they really want in a colonial landscape in which *dyari* conditions had not changed much since slavery. Desiring their own piece of land, their own *fayalobi*, *mati* act out this wish at the birthday party. As they fight for the birthday girl and dispute the other bouquet-bearers, these women claim "their own" even if the colonial machine refuses to recognize their right to it, even if they know that their shouts for possession will soon give way to the communal, messy, overlapping relationships of the *dyari*.

But perhaps this makes for too serious an interpretation for such a playful situation. In fact, Wekker's interviews with participants old enough to recall this ceremony suggest that many of its scenes of jealous rage were staged, precisely as entertainment that added "to the zest of the party." If the colonial woman-flora equation justified the real violence of the cane fields, this metaphor generated play violence: an activity that broke down concepts of ownership and sexuality that the colonial government took quite seriously, doing so with "a chorus of laughter" and a mounting of desire. Saskia Wieringa's cautions against misunderstanding butch performances of masculine possessiveness also apply to the performances of violence here: "A major reversal is actually taking place in f/b cultures: the fact that it is an all-women's game radically dislocates the patterns [of power]."[76] The "zest" that these fights provide is not only excitement at the show of Creole women's (mock) ownership of a sexualized woman's body but also an expression of eroticism in its own right, a display of passion and powerful arms that become part of foreplay. *Look how much I want you, look how strong my arms are, look how forcefully I open firelove*, the fight tells the lover. The erotic charge of the fight arises in imitating violence while making it, like flowers, something that working-class Creole women can play with. Both interpretations of these fights are viable. The birthday party taps the violent and the nonviolent, the playful and the sacred; it tells a history of sexuality and yet is not a history of sexuality at all. It is, first and foremost, a party.

Who's Your Mama, Who's Your Papa?:
Lobisingi and Hybrid Genders

The Herskovitses describe one other event that publicizes "relationships between woman and woman": the lobisingi.[77] The word lobisingi literally translates as "love song" but, like birthday parties' staged fights, they are not what they seem at first glance. These musical compositions sing social criticisms that women level against mati who violate kamra prekti between lovers. "Self-composed lobisingi – often grudge poetry about the rival of a woman scorned in love – were once sung outdoors, where ladies declaimed their lesbian love with the great fanfare of a brass wind orchestra," the folklorist Julian Neijhorst reports.[78] Like those of the birthday party, lobisingi's origins date to slavery and specifically to du, outlawed theatrical societies of people of color who composed and performed satirical dances, songs, and musical comedies. Before emancipation, competing planters hired these societies to perform sketches aimed at rival families, but when the plantocracy's economic fortunes declined, so did its interest in staging such costly spectacles. By the turn of the century, Creole women had appropriated the discarded form for their own use: instead of singing colonists' grievances, they began to sing those against their mati.

Paramaribo's mati had one day a year to shower a lover in flowers at her birthday party, but they could blast her with a lobisingi any week. Performances took place Sunday afternoons between four and seven on Saramaccastraat, in a lot bordering the Suriname River that the trader Abraham de Vries rented for three guilders during hours when no ships were docking.[79] For these hours, a plot of Paramaribo land was reclaimed from its use in the export of rubber and gold; instead, quite unprofitably, (ship)mates publicized their loves and grievances in a space where paid shipmates worked every other day of the week. The performance began with the gathering of a crowd of same-sex loving women – both female lovers sporting par weri (matching dresses) and male mati wearing koto-yaki and angisa (traditional Creole dress and head scarf).[80] At the best-funded affairs, *mati* were served food and drink, then walked to Saramac-castraat in a musical procession to witness the opening *langasingi*: an often improvised, lyrical song composed of three-line verses. But after 1900 *langa-singi* began to be omitted because, as original compositions, they could bring slander charges if Paramaribo police arrived on the scene. Instead, many *lobi-singi* were made up entirely of *kot'singi*: shorter, more fixed texts, whose words the lead singer would alter slightly between choruses to speak to the wronged lover's situation. These songs were, according to the Dutch musicologist Th. A. C. Comvalius, "a crossover genre [*overgangsvorm*] of the Negro song . . . which, in form, lies between African and European songs,"[81] combining African-style three-line verses and imagistic language with European instrumentation and popular Dutch melodies. The *lobisingi* were sung as call-and-response, the chorus ending with dance steps in which women danced in pairs, lifting their skirts in the back and shouting "Ha! Ha!"

One of the oldest and most popular *kot'singi* proudly shames neglectful lovers by proclaiming singers' "flowerness":

> Fa yu kan taki mi no moy? (3x)
> Na tu bromtji meki mi.
> Rosekunop na mi mama,
> Stanfaste na mi papa.
> Fa yu kan taki mi no moy, no moy?
> Na tu bromtji meki mi.
>
> [How can you say I'm not fine? (3x)
> It's two flowers that made me.
> Rosebud that's my mama,
> *Stanfaste* that's my papa.
> How can you say I'm not fine, not fine?
> It's two flowers that made me.][82]

This song is rhythmed by two words that echo and are used to explain each other: *mi* and *bromtji*, speaker and flower. The word *bromtji* draws immediate attention by its position in the middle of the song's first trochaic line, a mo-ment of accelerating rhythm; by its appearance directly following the metri-cally free, thrice-repeated first line; and by its inclusion in a string of allitera-tions. This meter and alliteration link *bromtji* rhythmically and phonetically, as well as semantically, to the stressed *mi* ending the line. The strong relationship between woman and flower is consistently inscribed not only in the meaning of the song's words but also in their form. In fact, the last word of each line (the most powerful position in a line) refers to the speaker and her kin, while two lines begin (the second most powerful position) with the name of flowers, metrically balancing the power of the woman and her mother and father flowers. What does it mean for this *mi*, this Caribbean woman, to tell her lover she is made from two flowers: the quintessentially European rose and the tropical *stanfaste* (*gomphrena globosa*, or globe amaranth)?

Half rose, half *stanfaste*, and every kind of attractive, this *mati* singer proclaims herself to be like no kind of flower *or* woman colonial chronicles ever imagined. Rose and *stanfaste* appear frequently in *mati* songs to vehicle two different models of womanhood negotiated in the *dyari*. The rose images a pretty young woman possessing physical qualities – paleness (the pink, white, and yellow of roses) and softness of skin – that *mati* understand to be valuable in Euro-Surinamese gender systems. Roseness is the kind of colonially, hetero-patriarchally invented womanhood that females of African descent were never supposed to have access to, either as identity or as object of desire. But here working-class Creole women imagine the right to claim roseness for themselves too; here *mati* sing that they are also born of and deserve beauty, desirability, softness. *Dyari* inhabitants who were domestic workers, dusting employers' flower vases, worked under the supervision of white women whose roselike status gave them access to the most privileged woman's work in colonial Suriname – that of elite wife. But while imagined in dialogue with this hegemonic flowery femininity, Creole women also understand their roseness as different from that other, domesticated kind. Their eroticism, their sweetness does not look for white masculinity or anyone else to protect it, and anyone arrogant enough to try to possess it, beware: "I'm a rose: I smell sweet, but my thorns prick hard," runs an *odo*.[83] In this *lobisingi* as in the proverb, feminized (*mama*) decorativeness (*moy*) is no longer the too-delicate, exclusive property of elite drawing rooms. Sung outdoors, it stays metrically, phonetically, and semantically linked to the woman speaker and to another flower, *stanfaste*.

Stanfaste was imported from Central America and Southeast Asia to flesh out the borders of exotic gardens and to color them with brilliant purples, pinks, blues, oranges, and yellows so distinctive that it was one suggestion for Suriname's national flower. Noted for growing in difficult conditions, it is especially valued for its flower heads that, if dried early, can be displayed for years. Chosen both for these physical properties and for associations tied to its name, the *stanfaste* vehicles qualities valued in the resource-sharing economy of the working class. *Stanfaste*-ness is steadfastness, loyalty to lovers, family, friends, community; is stand-upness, staying together, not falling apart; it is *ori stan*, the ability to stand ground, persist, take care of business. This collection of traits speaks to an Afro-Creole alternative to hegemonic Euro-Surinamese womanhood, a gender that often has more currency in working-class yards than the rose: the *dyadya uma* (standup woman), "a woman," Wekker explains, "who knows how to take care of business, is a psychological and economical broker; she has a network that importantly includes female relatives, but also her lovers, male and female; she has command of spiritual and cultural knowledge."[84] Many *odo* speak to the value accorded such self-possession: one praises, "You're a *stanfaste*: no one can part your petals but God."[85] Flora and women are alike in the *dyari* because neither can be dominated or manipulated without consequences. Like Leba's tree, both are engaged as living forces to interact with horizontally—at eye level—and responsibly.

A longtime couple, these two flowers often appear together in Creole women's oral literature. One *odo* promises that a rose can also be a *stanfaste*—that the lover who starts as a rose on her tabletop can become the *stanfaste* in her heart.[86] Another popular *kot'singi* asserts that a rose needs a *stanfaste* because a "rose is weak, it falls down, but [a] *stanfaste* stays upright."[87] In drawing the woman of color as a distinct species of tropical flora with exotic sexuality, colonial chroniclers never imagined such activity and interplay in Afro-Creole womannesses. Singing that she is part rose, part *stanfaste*, a *mati* recognizes that in Creole society, *blaka uma* (black women) are doubly made rather than born. Their gendered as well as racial identities are made from rule-defying miscegenation among flowers, among Euro- and Afro-, hegemonic and resistant gender models that both compete and overlap in colonial Paramaribo. Here difference resides not only *between* identities, between women and men or white, brown, and black women as in colonial chronicles. It is also *internal* to Creole gender, which produces crossovers between the rose and the *stanfaste* that upset and reorder European and tropical ideals of flowers and femininity.

When it was sung by the Suriname River in the early twentieth century, this song's imagery disrupted (not only the Sunday quiet but also) studies contracted in government buildings down the street, as well as by imperial investors throughout the region. Pan-Caribbean botanical studies researching the decline of sugar output cited cane's noncompliance with "natural" heterosexual reproduction as one of the causes of its decreased productivity. "According to the planters, the degeneration of a variety [of cane] was the logical consequence of asexual reproduction," Stuart McCook notes.[88] Rubber and gold industries, however, by bringing "virgin" forests into compliance with colonial penetration, would suitably reheterosexualize the landscape and so restore productivity. Schimmelpennick's study echoes those of botanists in its move to blame the sexuality of the object of study – here working-class women – for their own material decline. A refusal to comply with compulsory heterosexuality, rather than the economic slump caused by the resource drain of the rubber and gold industries, appears as the cause of ill health and poverty; exclusive heterosexual partnering appears as the solution. *Lobisingi*, texts by which *dyadya uma* evaluated the world, countered these studies with anticolonial, feminist readings of the feminized sexuality of nature. Rather than a commodity that produces capital for investors when properly sold or partnered off, flora is a lover of its own kind (flowers) whose lovership produces a sentient, erotic being. Namely, it creates the confidently singing *mati* who, playing in this lot on Saramaccastraat when no wages or biomen are to be found there, stays outside the economy of European-style trade or marriage. The mandate that Creole women and flora choose heterosexuality to reproduce colonial landscapes explodes in the chorus. "Tu bromtji meki mi": the singer *meki* (makes) her identity through a floral metaphor that humanizes the feminized natural world, rather than through one that botanizes and pathologizes Creole women's world.

But listen: singing of the two flowers that made her, the *mati* performer evokes more than one kind of complexity. She proclaims that she is made of flowers, the pale *roos* and the brilliant *stanfaste*, and flowers consistently vehicle womanness in *mati* symbolic language; but here the two mixing flora are differently gendered, as mama and papa. *Mama* and *papa* are not only nouns that suggest feminine-masculine differentiation but they are also sometimes used as suffixes to create gender markings in Sranan, which, like other Creoles, does not otherwise gender nouns and pronouns. So in the same couplet, temperate/tropical, feminine/masculine flowers miscegenate and transgender. Echoing the playful quare questions "Who's your mama? Who's your daddy?," the metaphor of the *roos* and *stanfaste* as mother and father evokes the "woman" and "man" roles that *mati* distinguish in sexual relationships. "When two people *mati*, then one plays the man," explains the *mati* worker Jet.[89] The man is the partner who approaches the woman to express sexual interest; helps with the woman's rent, food, and clothing, if possible; has a right to keep other *mati* while the woman must have only one female lover or risk anger or *lobisingi*; and lays on top during sex or tells the woman to. (Yes, the *odo* that brags that no one parts the *stanfaste*'s petals but God also suggests such a *mati*'s firm control over the possibility of her penetration.) All this is understood as robustly healthy sex play and, as Wekker reports, *mati* consider it "natural" to have a man and a woman in *mati* relationships.[90] In their yards, a *stanfaste*-like black female masculinity that is not pathological but socially and erotically productive is as necessary as reclaimed, rosy black female femininity to "breeding" the *mati* who sings her community. So in this symbolic system – in contradistinction to Dutch botany – it becomes ridiculous to deny that the rose/*stanfaste*, feminine female / masculine female coupling produces *moy* offspring. How can you say I am not *moy*?: *moy*, a signifier of attractiveness that can be either pretty or handsome, pointing to feminine or masculine beauty.

Like this image, *mati* communities are made up of identifications with multiple genders. These include female femininity, female masculinity, and male femininity: as routinely as they are female roses, *mati* are also males who are women or females who are men. Yet just as Creoles can be both African and European and Leba can be both male and female, *mati* can claim to be both men and women. While the late twentieth century saw more gendered variety in *mati* dress, in the early 1900s most attendees at a *lobisingi* or birthday party – mama, papa, male, female – dressed in what were seen as women's clothes: *mati* men as well as women often dressed in *par weri* with female lovers to indicate partnership.[91] In fact, all *mati* interviewed by the Herskovitses, Wekker, or the Surinamese anthropologist Rudolf van Lier insist that *lobisingi* are purely women's affairs and call themselves and other people in attendance *women*, whether or not they are also men. "This *mati* is something only for women (oema-soema)," a Creole named Wilhelmina declares in van Lier's study, and *matiwroko* is alternatively called *uma wroko* or "women's work."[92] What Wilhelmina calls *oema-soema* – literally, woman-someone – becomes a term more internally complex than *woman* or *vrouw* in colonial discourses. It does not just mean *female*, since it includes male *mati*; and it certainly does not just mean *feminine*, since it includes *mati* men. Rather, as Kara Keeling posits for African Americans, for *mati* it "cannot be assumed that 'black woman' appears within the dictates of 'femininity,' even though common sense posits a relationship between the female body and femininity that is often organized through the category 'woman.'"[93] Instead, in statements like Wilhelmina's, *uma-soema* becomes an umbrella term claimable by all those whose genders lie outside heteronormative masculine privilege, including *mannengre meiden* (*mati* men), roses who love *stan-*

faste, and males looking for husbands. Under slavery, Afro-Caribbeans were told they could have no gender; in *mati work*, Afro-Caribbeans can claim both reimagined womanhood *and* reimagined manhood, and refuse to relinquish either.

The "normality" of this gender complexity speaks to the overall complexity of the subject in Afro-Caribbean epistemology. The metaphor that compares *mati* to flowers conveys something more layered and charged than European associations between femininity and decorative frailty. In the *dyari* flowers are not inert matter but themselves have multiple levels of consciousness—a life cycle, a life force, and the possibility of reincarnation; so when one picks them for ceremonies, one must ask their permission. Flowers here resemble brown female bodies as something(s) that Europe imagined as dumb matter but that Creoles imagine as wonderfully, electrically, and multiply sentient. *Bromtji*/flower is a collective noun whose grammatical singularity signals plurality: the many petals that make a rose or *stanfaste*, the many roses or *stanfaste* that make up a bush, the many lives of each bush. Similarly, what European epistemologies conceive as a single individual is a collective proposition in Sranan. Wekker's insightful discussion of the Surinamese "self' outlines how, to reference the first person—where English would use I or Dutch *ik*—Sranan speakers use not only *mi* but, metonymically, my body, my soul, my ancestors, my ghost—all composite parts of "me."[94] This speakerly convention reflects that what in Europe would be understood as *the* consciousness is internally multiple. Working together are the *yeye* or soul, made up of a specific manifestation of *srama* (life force); the *dyodyo*, ancestral spirits passed from parent to child; and the *yorka*, the part of individual consciousness that remains after death and reincarnates. The phonetically reduplicating *yeye* and *dyodyo* are themselves a duality composed of a feminine and a masculine part: a spiritual mother and father—mama and papa—one feminine and one masculine guiding force.[95] Everyone, then, is understood to have two gendered "possibilities" for each (part) of themselves, a feminine and a masculine one; and everyone understands themselves in a lifelong process of negotiating and embodying these possibilities. In particular, some spirit guardians—those very sexual and/or masculine—influence females to take female partners or express masculinity throughout their lives. This is why Juliette Cummings, a beauty who became one of Wekker's oldest interviewees, explains her desire this way: "My soul wouldn't want to be under a man. . . . Some women are like that. . . . It's your soul that makes you that way. My soul wanted to be with a woman."[96]

And she calls herself and her lovers *women*, though one of them was also always the man; because in the hybrid flower that is *yeye*, *dyodyo*, and *yorka*, this complexity makes sense.

Beside its embedding in (pro)nouns, the complex work of *mati* gender also comes through in the use of *na* in the *lobisingi's* metaphors: "Stanfaste na mi papa." This copula corresponds only roughly to the English *is*. Like other Creoles, Sranan often elides copulas ("mi no moy"); but when speakers use them, they have two possibilities. *De* comes from the adverb *de* or *there* ("kuku de," women say at the birthday party, literally, "cake there") and is used in locative constructions – to indicate the subject's position, literally and figuratively. But the word in this song, *na*, comes from the relative pronoun *da* or *that* and is employed in equative constructions – to indicate that one subject "acts like that" other one. Strictly speaking, then, no *is* exists in Sranan.[97] Where European languages posit essence (Latin *essere*), Creoles mark the relationality of locative and relative *there* and *that*. *Na*, specifically, speaks of the subject entering into a relationship with another term, rather than manifesting a fundamental property of being. Understood is both that such relationships are unstable, that *uma*-ness does not have an unalterable link to roseness, and multiple, that different *lobi* singers can be like, follow, desire different combinations of rose, *stanfaste*, mama, papa, *yeye*, and *dyodyo* and still take (speaking) part in *mati* work and play. Saying "na tu bromtji meki mi," the *lobisingi* does not bring *uma* together around a politics of identity by celebrating that they "are" *mati*, a grammatical impossibility in Sranan. Rather, it metaphorizes ways of acting out gender as intersectional as the crossover form of the songs themselves, imagining the singer at a complex crossroads of cultures, genders, and flowers that make *mati* through varied relationships to these terms. Difference within and between *mati* is not the cause of drama here, is not why one lover sings critically of another; not knowing how to interact with this difference – not treating your rose or *stanfaste*, your female *uma* or *man* right – is. In the literal cross-traffic of a shipyard, *lobisingi* publicize the tensions and erotics of these complex relationships weekly. Reanimating a quieted Saramaccastraat, they sing out the multiple Creole nouns, verbs, genders, relationships, and cross-bred flora that Afro-Surinamese *uma* miscegenate, transgender, homosexualize, and reinvent to navigate their route out of narrow ways of being through which colonial gardens wanted to pin brown-skinned, female-sexed yard dwellers. *Fu yu kan taki fu mi no moy*: how *could* anyone in that shipyard not say that this is a fine specimen of colonial Suriname's *dyari*?

*   *   *

In city gardens grow no roses as we know them.
So the people took the name and bestowed it
generic, on all flowers, called them roses.
— Lorna Goodison, "In City Gardens Grow No Roses
    as We Know Them"

In June 2007, less than two months after the islands in the Kingdom of Netherlands became the first Caribbean territories to legalize same-sex marriage, I
arrived in Paramaribo with a tourist visa sprouting brilliant, geometric orange
and blue flowers. My first afternoon, I followed the Suriname River from my
hotel to Saramaccastraat. This thoroughfare no longer has an open view of the
river, that rushing, powerful route that brought in ships and that slaves used to
escape to maroonage. Its lots are built up with warehouses, abandoned buildings, or casinos catering to tourists. At the busy intersection with Waterkant
where the street begins now stands — not the lot that Abraham de Vries rented
for lobisingi — but the business venture of another De Vries: HJ De Vries Travel
and Tours, which promises customers the best fares to Amsterdam. The street
teems with people crossing the city and crossing paths with each other in cars,
minibuses, and on foot, and the diversity of races and genders is easy to see. I
pass masculine-presenting females of African and South Asian descent, feminine males of Javanese descent, and wonder how each of these informs the
urban space for the others. Lining the streets are older Afro-Creole women in
koto-yaki sitting on the pavement selling bananas (or other fruit that grows
in yards) for one Surinamese dollar. Like most working-class women of their
generation, many can tell of relatives who have migrated to the Netherlands
because while there is so much of world here in Suriname, there is too little of
world capital, and a dyadya uma needs to make a living. This continual stream of
migration following Surinamese independence means that mati move to Holland, where their presence begins to Creolize the lesbian community and les-
bianize the mati community.[98] It also means that those Surinamese working-
class women who stay in Paramaribo without remittances have less community
as well as economic power here — no space or money to rent a piece of Saramaccastraat.

Watching women in traditional Creole dress selling bananas in front of HJ
de Vries Travel and Tours crystallizes many complexities of theorizing female

desires in the Caribbean. Surinamese women's sexuality has been intimately entangled with processes of globalization for a very long time: first those of the slave trade that fostered sexual violence and *mati*, then direct colonialism that enabled police intervention and *dyari* partnerships, and now the unequal flows of global capital and labor that necessitate new dominant and resistant sexual formations. In all these imperial moments, part of the force of globalization has been its pressure to standardize sexual and erotic interactions, privileging northern over local formations to naturalize keeping Suriname open only to sanctioned forms of penetration. Promoting lesbianism and European-style gay marriage as the most "advanced" same-sex relationships forms part of this larger trend, whose antihomophobic turn does not in and of itself make it anticolonial. Dialogue around the current state of same-sex relationships falls very short, politically and culturally, when local histories are elided in favor of international gay rights discourse: so this chapter has offered one attempt to *remember the Caribbean* not as a generality but as a complicated specificity. Speaking of sexuality in the region must mean speaking of Creole, the particularity of *kambrada* and *mati*, as well as of lesbianism; and speaking of Creoleness must mean speaking of sexuality, the grammar of gender and desire, as well as of race. In Suriname, *mati* insist, a rose is not always a rose; and it behooves queer studies and Caribbean discourse to listen to what else it might be.

two

Darkening the Lily

The Erotics of Self-Making
in Eliot Bliss's *Luminous Isle*

Two women gonna hock up inna bed
That's two Sodomites dat fi dead.

—Elephant Man, "A Nuh Fi Wi Fault"

Yeh man, mi know she mek yu sick man . . .
Mi nuh wha nuh Man Royal gal, gal.

—Beenie Man, "Man Royal"

Jamaicans have to begin to accept that there are people who are gay
in their families, in their homes, children, mothers, fathers, sisters,
cousins. If I had an American accent and came out and said, "I am a
lesbian" people would be like, "hahahah, like Ellen. . . . When I open
my mouth people think "it's great that she is Jamaican." And then I
come out and say lesbian and people are shocked. What shocks them?
. . . The level of surprise and shock brings up the argument that being
Jamaican and lesbian are mutually exclusive states of being. It speaks
to the homophobia that is embedded so deeply into the music.

—Staceyann Chin, interview, 2004

Now, another kind of song. In March 2007, OutRage's Stop Murder Music campaign began urging reggae-dancehall artists to sign the Reggae Compassionate Act, a petition denouncing the homophobic lyrics that had become a lightning rod in globally marketed dancehall music. While Beenie Man (under threat of exclusion from concerts) was among prominent artists who signed, others denounced it as an attack on regional self-expression. Elephant Man's Patwa statement brandished violent homophobia as the mark of a literally incandescent Creole consciousness: "We [Jamaicans] know that this thing is not right and we are not going to uphold it. The Jamaican heritage is deep, we love God and we are not involve in certain things. From the time I was growing up, I learned that chi-chi man fi get bun. Until we dead pon earth, the fire nah come off dem. A just straight fire a bun dem out."[1] This inflammatory statement marks another refrain in a fifteen-year debate centering dancehall's unsettling parallels to *lobisingi*, the former establishing a new corpus of songs thematizing the (non)place of same-sex sexuality in the Caribbean. These songs' violent lyrics first came to international attention in the controversy around Buju Banton's threat in "Boom Bye Bye" (1992):

> Anytime Buju Banton come
> Batty boy get up and run
> ah gunshot in ah head man . . .
> Boom bye bye, in a batty boy head.[2]

When the song hit North American airwaves, GMAD (Gay Men of African Descent) and GLAAD (Gay and Lesbian Alliance against Defamation) came together, in the words of the *Village Voice*, to "decode Buju Banton's bullet-ridden patois" and launch a media campaign to have "Boom Bye Bye" removed from playlists.[3] Far from quashing this musical trend, Banton's notoriety became a marketing asset; the year "Boom Bye Bye" was released, he broke Bob Marley's record for most number one singles. And for over a decade songs by Beenie Man, Shabba Ranks, TOK, and Elephant Man have generated international profits by imagining violence toward *battymen*, *chi chi men*, sodomites, and *man royals*. While protests continue, so does fan support, escalating to the point at which international audiences welcome these songs with special enthusiasm as "authentically" Jamaican.[4] "This is not a fad," an activist states; "something is not a fad when it is seen as a national discourse to cleanse the island. It is not a fad when it's almost like a public service announcement."[5]

Crowds and artists have not stood as the trend's only defenders. Radio hosts,

music critics, and Caribbean scholars have joined in to insist that the problem with North American and European critiques is one of cultural imperialism. Clueless about the Creole poetics of Banton's gunshot-punctuated Patwa,
protesters (these respondents posit) misunderstand the Caribbean's culture of
metaphoricity. Carolyn Cooper argues that Banton's gun is "lyrical," a symbolic (specifically heterosexual?) penis that speaks to "the function of metaphor
and role play in contemporary Jamaican dancehall culture."[6] The declaration
"all bati-man fi ded" becomes a figurative celebration of heterosexuality in her
reading, not a literal death threat to same-sex-loving Jamaicans. Jamaican gay
rights' activists agree that these lyrics are metaphorical and insist that charged
Creole metaphoricity may constitute part of their danger. As Staceyann Chin
puts it: "Bob Marley created a revolution in Jamaica. How do movements get
started? Something as simple as 'pon de river' or 'signal the plane.' You get
people to act on those things as easy as saying it. What makes them think that
any other thing in the lyrics will not inspire them to action. . . . What makes
them think that saying, 'boom bye bye in a batty bwoy head,' will not inspire somebody to put a gun to a homosexual man's head and kill him?"[7] The
underlying metaphor justifying such violence is that queer equals freakish and
foreign, the corruption of the colonizer. Homo-sex and imperialism are both
imagined as relationships of domination and forms of unwanted penetration
that West Indians must arm themselves against. Like Chin, the activist Julian
Powell sees Jamaican rejection of homosexuality undergirded by the fiction that
"it is a foreign import. Because we have been colonized, homosexuality wasn't
in our society at all until colonization."[8] "I'm dreaming of a new Jamaica, come
to execute all the gays": Beenie Man, too, imagines a version of sexual decolonization, one proven internationally marketable in a way that *mati* songs have
never been.[9]

The proliferation of this queer-equals-foreign metaphor and the violence
that it rationalizes initially led me to leave Euro-Caribbean women outside
my project. Insisting on looking at representations of relationships between
women of African descent on Caribbean soil, I wanted to focus on figures "beyond" accusations of foreignness or sexual imperialism. As I wrote out the
white queer, I hoped to avoid adding more ink to something already discussed
too much. Elephant Man's voice and the imagination of gay foreignness had
circulated enough (I felt), generating profits from the idea that the Caribbean
is inherently homophobic (while the Global North is not). I wanted to redress
the imbalance by circulating the voice of *mati*, countering with attention to

where Caribbean culture has long been porously open to sexual diversity as part of its regional complexity. But eventually I wondered if avoiding the figure of the white lesbian and her metaphorics of queer imperialism might prove counterproductive. The white woman already constituted a shadow presence in my work, looming in the margins as I evoked white femininity as a model that excluded black females or discussed rose and *stanfaste* in contradistinction to Euro-Caribbean gender models. Like flowers, like rose and *stanfaste*, Euro- and Afro-womanhood have always been constructed relationally in the Caribbean; and it began to seem impossible to thoroughly think through a poetics of the latter without discussing the former. But more important, leaving the white woman as a shadow presence in my exploration of erotic decolonization seemed not to disempower the mythological predatory European lesbian but, in fact, to reinforce her power. It seemed to strengthen the idea that if same-sex sexuality were practiced by Euro-Caribbeans then Elephant Man would be right, then same-sex eroticism *would* be imperialist – and any Afro-Caribbean woman involved with a white woman thus sexually colonized. As Laura Chrisman argues, when imaginary imperial images like the predatory lesbian are excluded from postcolonial study, they remain "paradoxically, frozen in power, and repressed, an absent 'centre,' a hidden referent."[10] So I began thinking about the uses of uncovering this referent, looking for complications in her construction that might fissure the monolithic figure lurking both behind my discussions of Caribbean women who love women and behind Elephant Man's lyrics.

With this in mind I began a reading of *Luminous Isle* (1934), the second novel of the white Jamaican Eliot Bliss. Bliss was born Eileen Nora Lees Bliss in 1903 to an officer's family, raised on the island, and, after attending boarding school in England, returned to Jamaica where her family hoped to marry her into the local elite. Their plan failed. After two years Bliss returned to London, where she moved in with a female companion and established herself in the lesbian literary scene. She befriended Vita Sackville-West and Dorothy Richardson and later entered an intimate relationship with Anna Wickham (a poet and the rejected suitor of Natalie Barney). But in the autobiographical *Luminous Isle*, Bliss imagines the originary topos of gynoeroticism not in London salons but in Jamaican mountains: here the protagonist Em explores roving desires for many women but returns over and over to Rebekkah, the independent black woman she at once wants to *be like* and *be with*. Same-sex desire is not something the white woman lords over the woman of color here; on the contrary, Rebekkah becomes the mountain lily always beyond Em's reach. Rather than the Anglo woman "converting" this native flower to an othered sexuality, the dark lily converts her admirer to identify with an othered race: desiring Afro- rather than Euro-Caribbean womanhood, Em remakes herself as a symbolic mulatta. The slippery, complex connections between black and white women, between Em's hatred of colonial society and her desire for Rebekkah, point to contradictions in colonial ideologies of white womanhood, as well as in easy understandings of same-sex desire as colonizing or colonized. The metaphorics of interracial same-sex desire here are not that homosexuality resembles imperialism, but that desiring a black Jamaican woman resembles desiring cultural hybridity. White women's desire, Em's disruptive escapades suggest, can also break down imperial order from within, darkening the summit of the social pyramid. Thwarting the reproductive labor of elite wifehood, Em's attraction to a black Jamaican may not be liberating for the hardworking Rebekkah; but neither is it a metaphor for colonial domination. It may just be *something else.* And in being something else, the desiring imagination of this white Caribbean woman may become, if not decolonizing, then anticolonial.

Mountain Hearts: White Creole Women and the Erotics of Self-Making

Breastlike, volcanic, and distant, Caribbean mountains have long shadowed Afro-Caribbean songs and sayings. Here, these towering presences inspire humility: the Jamaican traditional "Hill and Gully Rider" sings of the precariousness of riding slopes populated by ghosts, while the Haitian proverb "behind the mountains are more mountains" vehicles rolling peaks as images of everlurking troubles. For white women arriving on the islands' shores, mountains have also loomed mesmerizingly. But these more privileged viewers identify differently with hills' cool elevation, seeing them as models and protectors of their aspirations for ascent in the colonies. In *Women Writing the West Indies, 1804–1939*, Evelyn O' Callaghan's extensive archival research shows how, like their better-known male counterparts, women travelers to the Caribbean developed standardized landscape poetics around "conventional set-pieces, the scribal equivalent of postcards."[11] Lighting on Caribbean landscapes as disembodied gazes, their imperial eyes – dominant as colonists,' subordinate as women's – consistently peered upward at sunsets, moonlight, and majestic mountains.[12] O'Callaghan documents the mountain mystique inspiring a number of white women in turn-of-the-century Jamaica, typified by E. M. Symmonnett's question about the Blue Mountains in *Jamaica: Queen of the Carib Sea*: "Which eyes of an admirer of nature, would not fain be centred thereon, on this elysium of earth! on this El Dorado of the 'Queen of the Carib Sea?'"[13] Elite women poets, organizing poetry circles and publishing for the first time at the turn of the century, echo this fascination. "Misty wreaths of love caress you . . . / Mountain passes, may God bless you / For your gifts to mine and me!," Albinia Catherine Hutton exclaims in "Up among the Mountain Passes."[14] And Mary Adela Wolcott, marveling at "fadeless mountains" with "morning mist around them like wreaths of Alpine snow," proclaims: "And the true heart of Jamaica with proud affection fills / For the Island's greatest glory – her guard of noble hills."[15]

The intrigue that mountains held for white women is verbalized and visualized in the travel guide *Jamaica*, published in 1906, which includes text by John Henderson and paintings by A. S. Forrest. This gilt-embossed tome comprising twenty-three chapters and twenty-four color plates features two descriptions of Jamaican hill stations that read as narrative twins. Both gush fascination with the lush ascent to the stations, where the traveler "experiences many climates in climbing to them, and the beauty of the country which separates them from the hot plains is magnificent beyond description. One passes forest land and dense scrub, rushing rivulets and the dry beds of larger rivers. One experiences every colour the imagination can conceive, and sees all the fruits, and flowers, and timber trees to be found in all the world."[16] But the country found on arrival is too notably English for this writer's taste. These are landscapes of "English trees fenced round by groves of tall pines, and feather bamboos, and wavy banana clumps – England growing calmly with a green freshness in the midst of the yellow tropics."[17] The peculiar Englishness of Jamaican mountain beauty is illustrated by color plates that interrupt each narrative just as the description of the charming ascent is in full force. In a text colored by illustrations of madras-coiffed, brightly clothed market women, maids, and field-workers, these sections contain the only paintings of white Jamaican women. Slender, shining, and fairylike, the women in these plates pose in high-collared white dresses and hats. They stand on white walkways that clear light-filled space in a tamed, English-looking landscape, framed by impressionistic pink and white flowers and gracefully slim palm trees (see figure 2).

The fascination in the chapter titled "The Hill Stations" with flowers and rushing waters, and its accompanying images of rose-cheeked ladies in flowing

A. S. Forrest, *A Bungalow in the Hills*. Color plate in John Henderson's travel guide *Jamaica*, 1906

skirts, underscore the mountain as a feminized topos. And its summit, where pale beauties stroll, is particularly associated with white femininity. Clichéd, this verbal and visual picture of white mountains and white women none-theless proves a complex, internally contradictory one. On the one hand, this fresh England in the middle of the tropics – pine trees spilling into banana clumps – creates a metonymic connection between tropical and European, "na-tive" and white landscapes of imperial desire. What this British traveler wants from the West Indian resort and the English garden, from black and white women, shows points of overlap concretized in the landscape here, where (ac-cording to Henderson) all the world's flowers and fruits grow. But if this land-scape's metonymics suggest common ground for all flowers and "every colour" of woman, its metaphorics – its imagination of (non)similarities – undercut this suggestion. No matter that English trees stand near flamboyants or white women near (pictures of) black market women. The greens still *are* English, not Jamaican; the brim-shaded ladies *are* white women, not the Afro-Creoles of other pages. Roses may grow next to ginger lilies here, but they are not like them. White women may live next to black women, but they never resemble them.

Yet the color plates suggest a parallel between black and white women that, given the centuries-old colonial belief that white women were unfit for work, the authors doubtless had not considered. All but one of the color plates of Afro-Jamaican women show them with baskets on their heads, wares in hand, girded for fieldwork; and in effect, the two pictures of Euro-Jamaican women also show them dressed for work. Arriving on very different ships, white and black women were both, as the anthropologist Jean Besson notes, brought to the Caribbean to perform unpaid labor for plantation owners. In the case of white women, this labor was primarily sexual and reproductive.[18] Their new world task was to reproduce whiteness – that is, to bear and socialize children phenotypically and socially equipped for reproducing Euro-Creole elites. The primacy of this work in imagining a social identity for the white West Indian woman is unintentionally underscored by the clothing in Forrest's pictures: both women's flowing white dresses and white hats recall bridal attire. In the case of the white Creole, the whiteness of her wedding gown implies a double purity – sexual and racial – that qualifies her for her reproductive labor. The dress's color suggests not only that she has no sexual contact with men but also, by blending seamlessly with the color of her skin, that she has no genetic contact with blacks.

The work of reproducing whiteness does not end with the biological capacity to bear white children but, as the dress-for-show of these gowns suggests, extends to the creation of social personae. Like sunsets and mountainscapes, white Creole ladyhood is discursively regulated through standardized images. One reason the mountain provides an apt metaphor for the white woman's "place" is that it spatializes the social structure that the Jamaican anthropologist Fernando Henriques describes as a pyramidal formation: an order inherited from slavery in which whites occupy the tiny, privileged position at the pyramid's tip, the mountain's summit.[19] Like the images of Queen Juliana mentioned in the previous chapter, paintings of these white ladies on a mountaintop act as imperial fetishes; the social ascendancy of the white colonial elite is both what allows these images to signify and what they signify. But Henriques's observations suggest that this position of social superiority is not fixed. It is property that must constantly be reclaimed, especially in the early 1900s, as the arrival of North American investors challenged the dominance of Creole elites. To maintain her family's status, an elite white wife and mother had to, among other things, give birth in a private room in an exclusive nursing home; plan birthday parties for her child attended only by guests of a certain rank and color; send her children to boarding schools; and belong to a tennis club at which she played bridge while nannies cared for her children and her husband conducted business.[20] What she needed to do to represent this summit was, like the women of Forrest's color plates, to be alone at the top of the mountain and to *be visible being alone*. That is, she must spend her time away from her children, away from fellow mothers not of her rank, and away from her husband. More important, her fellow society members needed to know that she spent her time away from these people. They must observe her in an isolation that, like a white dress, represented a mantle of privilege covering as much of her as possible, separating her from multicolored roadside flowers and leaving her alone among white and pink roses. In Forrest's picture of white Creole beauties, his subjects' high-necked, floor-length dresses visualize this stark separation as expensive cloth hermetically seals the women from dirt, sweat, and easy touch—that is, from all the economic and (imagined) reproductive praxes of the base of the social pyramid. Yet while U.S. whiteness studies argue that whiteness is "naturalized" by being neutralized or rendered invisible, the women's brightly lit figures suggest that in the case of the Jamaican white minority the opposite holds true. Whiteness must be rendered as hypervisible as it appears in this mountain sun: white dresses covering the white skins of white women on white walkways, publicizing isolation from madras-clad crowds of black market women.

The high-profile biological and social reproduction placed in Euro-Caribbean women's hands makes the smiling white lady of Forrest's paintings at once a crucial figure to the colonial enterprise and a dangerous one. As Mason Stokes posits in *The Color of Sex*, in former slave societies the white woman is "imagined as the key to whiteness' future and its weakest defense."[21] The weakness of this defense is tied to a problematic, interdependent relationship between race and sexuality, namely, the way heterosexuality acts as the "cradle of whiteness."[22] That is, it becomes the basis of a system of filiation in which white men produce legitimate heirs to white power via exclusive (on the wife's part) monoracial, heterosexual unions. As in the case of slave women, links between white womanhood and compulsory heterosexuality prove at once necessary and threatening to the colonial project. Sexuality and desire are messy, shifting, unstable quantities. Heterosexuality as the cradle of whiteness imagines that white women exclusively desire to be the wives of white men, and do so above all else: above the right to own property, enter into contracts, or have custody of children (all denied married women). But what if this single-mindedly desiring white lady – like male counterparts who fathered so many children of color – were to desire someone or something besides a white husband? This possible instability creates a fundamental contradiction in the lady's imaginary construction. The white Creole woman must be *heterosexual* to reproduce the elite; yet at the same time she must be *asexual*, an icy creature who conceives children without any autonomous desire that might lead her to choose her own partners and outside the white male elite. Recurring images of the mountain as fairyland reflect the "magic" transformation that white women's flesh imaginarily undergoes to become that of Creole ladies – sexless spirits whose skin chills into a snowy substance indistinguishable from the cloth of their dresses. Cut off from any intimacy with her husband, children, or black women, the white lady is hermetically sealed in the desireless heterosexuality of the bride awaiting an absent groom, posed amid complicit cliffs festooned with bridesmaids' flowers.

Yet the very seals that construct the white angel in the house can foster desires that frustrate the smooth reproduction of colonial racial orders. In *Making Girls into Women*, Kathryn Kent explores how disciplinary mechanisms meant to compel white girls to internalize the mandates of wife- and motherhood in post–Civil War North America end by inciting other, less normative desires.

Her discussion of Louisa May Alcott's work explores how the ideal of hetero-sexual white womanhood – embodied in the wife and mother, *Little Women*'s Marmee – is held up for girls as both a figure of intimacy and a means of gendered discipline. Because she loves her mother so much, Jo makes herself "good" like Marmee: loving mama means internalizing an ideal that trains the little woman to *self*-regulate behavior so she too can become a wife and mother. But while this disciplinary intimacy is meant to confine white female pleasure to a heteronormative matrix, the embrace of fantasized Marmeeness also pro-duces a woman-centered, solitary pleasure that Kent discusses as "an erotics of self-making." The antiheterormative byproducts of mother-daughter intima-cies are an eroticized desire for my mother and myself: for *a kind of woman*, the beloved mother whose kisses Jo craves, and *a kind of womanly self*, the pleasure of becoming like the mother she longs to kiss. So desireless heteronormativity is generated in conjunction with same-sex desire and autoeroticism; and "at the heart of disciplinary intimacy lies the erotics of self-production, an eroti-cized relationship not only to the 'other' with whom one identifies but to one's self."[23]

However, Kent is aware that this model of self-making only applies to north-ern white women; and if we consider how such a model might function in a West Indian context, the disruptive possibilities of an erotics of self-production based in an erotics of (m)other identification expand provocatively. Kent as-sumes white women's identification with only one mother and so only one model of womanhood. But in the Caribbean, the elite white child is brought up intimately disciplined by at least two mothers: the bridge-playing mother in white linen and the black *da* (nurse) she clings to while mama is at the club. While reproducing whiteness necessitates turning children over to black care-takers as a sign of status, these child-rearing relationships also become sites of disciplinary and other intimacies; and, in her preparation to stand alone at the top of the social pyramid, the white Jamaican enters interracial relationships that may incite hybrid self-makings. What happens if the white girl chooses black womanhood as the ideal she fantasizes, desires, internalizes; if the erotics of self-making makes her in the image of the black women Forrest paints in the flatlands rather than in that of the white ladies in the hills? Then the sym-metry of the twinned white ladies in Forrest's color plates might be joined by a third, where a white woman is dressed in color, her face tan without her white hat and her arms linked with brown female companions.

This erotics of self-making *in color* could represent instances in which the woman's work of reproducing mountaintop whiteness fails through its own operations. But while this failure would mark a break in the colonial family, it would not break the colony. That is, it would not magically erase power relationships in which (even brightly dressed) white daughters and (even beloved) black *das* are entrenched, would not automatically produce horizontal interracial connections. For the white woman "blackening" is always a choice for herself—a choice that draws on rather than forfeits race privilege—while for the black woman it never is; and this limitation to black-white identification cannot be underplayed. Finally, the erotics of self-making in color is an *autoeroticism* through which the white woman seeks the pleasure of producing herself differently, not an *alloeroticism* whose goal is mutual transformation.

With such complications in mind, Kent suggests strategies for reading both the resistive possibilities and limits of women's identificatory desires. Her theorizing of disciplinary intimacy stems from a search for new formulations of sexuality that tend neither toward easy analyses of sexual mores as "agents of repression" nor toward optimistic platitudes on the power of the erotic as a "utopian form of intersubjective affiliation."[24] She stipulates: "Examining the possibly resistive aspects of pleasure, centrally conceived here as relations of identification/desire, is not, however, to imagine pleasure as always already liberatory or as capable of transcending the discursive structures that produce the subject. Instead . . . I seek to understand the ways in which subjects 'make do' within overarching structures of domination by renegotiating, reinhabiting, or to use Judith Butler's terms, 'performing' with a difference what are often limiting forms of identification."[25] While a white Creole woman's erotics of self-making in the image of a black mother does not transcend racialized subject formations—the nanny-girl relationship, after all, is based in these formations—neither does it read as sexual imperialism. The black woman influences the white here, creating affective colonization in reverse.[26] To the extent that this erotics impedes white women's reproductive labor and disrupts heterosexuality as the cradle of whiteness, it becomes anticolonial—mixing, messing up the colonial elite's family structures—without necessarily becoming decolonizing. That is, it does not necessarily imagine space outside the realm of fantasy in which white and black women could interact horizontally. In effect, to imagine that the white woman *is* like the black woman is to imagine that the greens of hill towns *are* like the yellow tropics around them, or to imagine a bridge between different levels of land and society. But this imaginary bridge does not change the material conditions of mountain strata, does not raze the difference between summer villas and rural shacks. It is the erotics of colonial Jamaica performed *with a difference.*

Impossible Purities, Possible Impurities: White Creoles and/as Mulattas

Yet despite *Jamaica*'s glossy portraits, Jamaican mountains are not England – and Jamaican whites are not Europeans. "Local white," Opal Palmer Adisa explains, is "a term that suggests that while [someone] can pass for white, and even delude herself into believing that she is white, we – Jamaicans – know that she is not 'pure.'"[27] Probably not "pure" in race, but definitely not in culture. Constant, intimate bodily contact between white and black females was never limited to nanny-child dyads but continued into adulthood in the privacy of kitchens and bedrooms; it was no anomaly, but a pillar in the colonial Caribbean's economic and racial architecture. This contact began where white and black women's unpaid labor intersected in slavery, as the domestic work delegated to plantation owners' wives necessitated daily interracial interchanges. The white mistress found herself, the Jamaican governor's wife Maria Nugent noted at the turn of the nineteenth century, living "in the Creole style" with "negroes, men, women, and children, running and lying about" and slaves sleeping in passages and hallways.[28] The women not only simultaneously overlapped and hierarchized in common spaces; they also did so in common sexual and reproductive labor. Euro-Creole wives and mothers unequally shared with Afro-Creole female servants both social and biological aspects of mothering. White infants were fed by biological mothers' bodies in utero, then at black nurses' breasts after birth. White wives shared duties of sexual performance and childbearing with black and mulatta "housekeepers" who often produced parallel families for elite white men, making women of European and of African descent both comothers and cowives. Indeed, their bodies were not only physically close but also performed duties that approximated one another, feeding the same children and having sex with the same men. When the historian Barbara Bush notes how whites and blacks in the Caribbean were "'symbiotically related," both this symbiosis and this relationship were more literal than often articulated.[29]

These obligatory cowife and comother relationships, beneficial to plantation economies and therefore accommodated by them, are not my primary interest here. Instead I want to foreground *voluntary* connections between white and black women unnecessary to these economies and therefore depicted more dubiously. Among these were frequent friendships between Euro- and Afro-Caribbean women. Bush emphasizes that while these friendships did not significantly diminish social distance between the parties involved, they did occur regularly during slavery: "Cultural boundaries between black and white were constantly breached in Creole society and there is even evidence of friendship between white and black women. Mrs. Sarah Bennett, the well-to-do owner of Paradise Pen, was a close friend of Phibbah and gave her a 'negro wench named Bess . . . for life.' Maria Nugent had female 'coloured' friends from whom she received all the local gossip. In contrast to her scathing remarks about white Creole women, she admired the vivacious and poised, free coloured women whom she entertained at her 'levees.' When Mrs. Cole's son died, it was female slaves who 'sat up' with his body all night. For white women, too, black women were the main link with the 'other' culture of slave society."[30] These friendships often involved intimate address and settings. Scottish-Caribbean gentlewoman Mrs. Carmichael saw "utmost familiarity" between whites and blacks in conversation, and Nugent's journal noted the "easy manners and familiarity" between white and colored businesswomen "who all seem intimate acquaintances."[31] Even Nugent herself happily entertained "black, brown, and yellow ladies" with tea and gossip in her bedroom, the ladies all lying together in their dressing gowns.[32]

In these intimate quarters, black, brown, and white women not only entertained each other; they started to imitate each other. While darker women emulated the manners of lighter, more privileged counterparts, white women imitated Afro-Creoles with equal alacrity. My imaginary color plate of a white woman who resembled her brown servants was, in fact, not so far removed from reality during slavery. White women's emulation of nonwhites troubled many observers. Nugent enjoyed the company of brown and black women but felt repulsed by white Creoles for whom talking with people of color led to talking like people of color. She complained: "The Creole language is not confined to the negroes. Many of the ladies, who have not been educated in England, speak a sort of broken English, with an indolent drawling out of their words, that is very tiresome if not disgusting."[33] J. B. Moreton, in his eighteenth-century journal *West India Customs and Manners*, was similarly disgusted by a white woman whom he observed both speaking Creole over the dinner table and mentioning involuntary defecation caused by eating pepper pot.[34] To talk like blacks here is to interrupt plantation domesticity by talking shit.

But no criticism of white women's emulation of black companions is more venomous than Edward Long's. His *History of Jamaica* (1774) decries this influence as "infection": "Those [ladies], who have been bred up entirely in the sequestered county parts, and had no opportunity of forming themselves either by [European] example or tuition, are truly to be pitied. We may see, in some of these places, a very fine young woman awkwardly dangling her arms with the air of a Negroe-servant, lolling almost the whole day upon beds or settees, her head muffled up with two or three handkerchiefs, her dress loose, and without stays. At noon, we find her employed in gobbling pepper-pot, seated on the floor, with her sable hand-maids around her. In the afternoon, she takes her *siesto* as usual; while two of these damsels refresh her face with the gentle breathings of the fan; and a third provokes the drowsy powers of Morpheus by delicious scratchings on the sole of either foot."[35] Suffering from an absence of European tutelage, this woman falls victim to an Afro-Creole mentoring that molds her into a hybrid degenerate. With black arms grafted onto her white person, she resembles Maria Lugones' description of the purist's vision of the hybrid, a body made up of "parts that do not fit well together, parts taken for wholes, composites, composed of the parts of other beings."[36] The irony of Long's depiction is that "lolling about" gives her the air of black servants who work while she reclines. Her dress, following Creole rather than European models, becomes a kind of undress – she stays uncorseted and uncoiffed, a woman of color's head wrap sitting ridiculously on her white woman's hair. And rather than building her body up, her self-nourishment breaks it down to the level of the uncivilized "sable" women sitting on the floor with her as she gobbles pepper pot. Long's image reads as the reverse of the sealed snow fairy Forrest paints: if the white-gowned hill-station beauty represents the ideal of what the white lady should be, the luxurious, lounging Creole represents the fear of what she may become.

Instead of the white angel in the house civilizing the sable she-devils around her, the angel herself becomes bedeviled: decivilized, stripped of the white dress that marks her difference from the colored female flesh around her. In Long's text, this decivilization seems to result from two affective processes gone wrong. First, he sees a problem of misidentification. He protests vigorously the biological comothering of black wet nurses, who he fears may pass along "corruptions" (venereal diseases) in their blood; and he sees a parallel danger in the black *da*'s social comothering, which communicates "singularities, in speech or deportment," that blemish Euro-Creole ladyhood.[37] Linked to this social miscegenation, the specter of sexual miscegenation lurks tantalizingly. Details of Long's description suggest that this luxurious scene may be one in which not only white women's identification but also their desire veers off course, circulating among black women when it should go straight to white men. Long's association of black women and transgressive sexuality throughout his text – his worries that slaves' promiscuity may corrupt white women from breast-feeding onward – construct black female bodies as contaminants that infect surrounding bodies with unruly sexuality.[38] Flanked by these dark bearers of sexuality, Long's white Creole "lady" is portrayed relaxing into the luxury her servants signify. She reclines all day in bed without proper undergarments, posed and (un)dressed for an erotic encounter. The excessive hunger she satisfies too comfortably on the floor with her handmaids suggests other unseemly appetites shared with black women. And, building as the day goes on, insinuations of too-indulgent sensuality loom largest in the description of the siesta. Here the fan's gentle breathings suggest the pleasurable breath of two black mouths next to a white cheek as the "delicious scratchings" on the soles of her feet lure her to a state of unconsciousness, bringing her under the "drowsy powers" of Morpheus and the black foot scratcher.

Far from reinforcing the sexual politics of imperialism, eroticism circulating between white and black women disrupts the colonial household. After this scandalous siesta, Long goes on to make explicit how such interracial female commerce undermines the monoracial heterosexual coupling he believes necessary to the colony. If only white women were educated to converse with white men rather than black women, he contends, they would be "more desirable partners in marriage" and so "render the island more populous."[39] Black and brown female company makes white Creole women "unfit . . . to be the companions of sensible men, or the patterns of imitation of their daughters! . . . incapable of regulating their manners, enlightening their understanding, or improving their morals!"[40] The exclamation-warranting threat of interracial intimacy poses multiple dangers to Euro-Creole women's purity as the cradle of whiteness. Certainly, racial purity is at risk here. Just as certainly, sexual purity is at risk too: the lounging Creole ladies seem constantly on the brink of moving into positions in which they can no longer be read as either heterosexual or asexual, the contradictory states they must occupy in the colonial family.

But even more daunting, the very logic of purity is at risk in these white women's unsealed bodies. Their interracial dream states represent what Lugones, in her essay "Purity, Impurity, and Separation," theorizes as *mestizaje*:

not just biological or social race mixing but also a way of knowing the world that makes a mess of the concepts of purity that sanitize imperial epistemologies. "If something is neither/nor, but kind of both, not quite either . . . ambiguous, given the available classification of things," Lugones posits, then "it is mestiza," and "threatens by its very ambiguity the orderliness of the system, of schematized reality."[41] Long's Creole women are mestiza through precisely this kind of ambiguity. His History of Jamaica is obsessed with taxonomies: he pens long passages comparing blacks and primates and formulating a natural order that determines the (supposedly) precise position blacks occupy on the tree of man, midway between ape and European. But in his description of white Creole women, Long suddenly finds himself unable to classify. These madras-wrapped loungers are not quite ladies, but neither are they slaves, free mulattas, or poor whites. They are not properly heterosexualized wives, but neither are they fully homosexualized, the sexual tension of the scene never crossing into sexual contact. Always neither/nor, they resist taxonomy and one-to-one comparison by remaining open terms. The openness of the race and sexuality they represent threatens "schematized reality" not simply because these women's ambiguities undermine a particular historical order of the colonial family but also because they bring into question the empirics of empire that insist order can and must always be possible.

Colonial order proved particularly precarious when Long was obsessing over line-crossing Creoles. The Anglophone Caribbean was being aggressively Africanized to support the sugar boom: between 1780 and 1818 the British imported over one hundred thousand slaves each decade, and the average number of slaves on Jamaican plantations more than doubled.[42] This new African population took up arms against its bondage. As noted in the previous chapter, in the late eighteenth century Tacky and Cubah's Revolt in Jamaica initiated rebellions that swept through Bermuda, Dominica, Nevis, British Honduras, Grenada, Montserrat, St. Vincent, and St. Kitts, with ongoing maroon wars in the Jamaican mountains posing continuous threats to European domination. Literally and figuratively, mountains no longer constituted strongholds of the Euro-Creole elite; these years brought new luxury to the sugar plantocracy, but they also witnessed military vulnerability that undercut plantocratic security. The shockingly undefinable white woman of Long's History of Jamaica reads as an imagistic artifact of the power struggles going on around her. Fissures in English dominance are projected onto her body here, as the unlady stands in (or lounges about) as a metaphor and metonym for an Anglicized Jamaica that needs defense from encroaching Africanness. As Long watches this scene of degeneration and then offers a way to halt it – compulsory heterosexuality, the courting of suitable husbands – he models the discursive control of Jamaica's white future at a time when political control proves more elusive.

When Bliss's *Luminous Isle* imagines a racially impure erotics of self-making through the relationship between Em and Rebekkah, it resurrects the threats embodied in Long's white mulattas: an image of the inescapable messiness of the racial-sexual dynamics that shadow the mythic white-gowned lady. Her gynoeroticism echoes the ambiguous desire and identification imagined by colonial chroniclers *at* and *as* the weakest moments of British imperialism in the Caribbean. Angrily, hedonistically choosing the pleasure of *mésalliance*, Em voluntarily positions herself in the "dangerous" role of the black-identified white woman that outraged Long. But no husband comes to redirect errant eroticism and identification here; order is never restored, and attraction continues to drift as aimlessly as the lounging Creole's days. Perhaps scripted chiefly for the author's own enjoyment, Bliss's anti-imperial autoerotics produces a sprawling *mestiza* narrative whose obsessive self-focus traces a Jamaica in which the patriarchal overseer is shut out of the frame, leaving the desiring "I" and its discursive control in unsanctioned hands. This time, the drowsy, indulgent Creole herself narrates the dream state produced by sleeping among black women.

Lilies without Melancholy:
Em Hibbert and the Refusal to Choose

"The North Breeze was just beginning," *Luminous Isle* opens. "At the end of the garden the mango trees beside the fence trembled violently, and several over-ripe mangoes fell to the ground."[43] Em, the "half terrified, half fascinated" five-year-old heroine, peers into the stormy garden expecting to see spirits disturbing the night, but instead, "in the clear white moonlight were only row upon row of now colourless flowers standing erect in groups among the darkness of leaves and shrubbery" (3). So the novel opens into a bedroom intimacy that is never a calm space of domesticated white femininity. Instead it is a window into a West Indian world in which motion is as constant and powerful as the northern breeze – where established barriers like the trembling fence can fall at any moment, frightening but thrilling the young heroine. In the midst of this storm, the flowers Em identifies with remain standing, capable of sustaining and remaking themselves as darkness rids them of the constraints of color in the windy night's latently erotic explosiveness.

This exhilarated evocation of the "deeply silent West Indian night" (3) immediately situates Bliss's novel in topoi familiar to the emerging corpus of white Jamaican women's writing: poetry dominated by parades of clichéd landscapes in which whispering breezes, moonlit seas, tropical fruit, and majestic mountains become literal and figurative commonplaces.[44] But just as her opening rattles fences, her landscapes push the limits of feminine clichés even while reinscribing them. The ladylike landscapes noted above drip with speakers' emotions, but they remain consistently empty of their bodies; feeling is always affective but never physical, keeping women sealed in the bodylessness suggested by Forrest's neck-to-toe covered figures. In contrast, Em's childhood Jamaica is a landscape immediately peopled with women's bodies promising pleasure. This pleasure comes initially from physical contact between Em and black caregivers. The first paragraph ends with Em contemplating her hands in the moonlight. Suggestive of female-to-female sexuality, hands are also the body part Em associates with the good feelings only her black nanny's touch can give (9). The hope of pleasure Em sees in black female bodies grows more explicit on the next page when, tucked back in bed, she imagines what might be happening in blacks' roadside houses in the storm. She visualizes a woman nursing her baby and reflects on how she likes seeing the black breast yet not the white. Already Em imagines black breasts giving both sustenance and pleasure, here the solitary pleasure of the white girl watching and wishing she could stay attached to that maternal and sexual body. Within the racialized structure of reproductive labor in the Caribbean, the black breast was only supposed to be viewed by elite white women as part of a working body for hire—a body never trustworthy, never a source of eroticism. But Em takes this construction of the black female body to the other extreme, imagining the feeding breast *only* as producing pleasure and not as exploited labor. This wishful, naively reductive view of the black woman's corporality unwrites fictions of the white girl's "natural" asexual heterosexuality, but without understanding the material conditions of the black bodies that she gynoeroticizes in the process.

This imagination of breasts leads Em to think about differences between her white governess, Narna, and black Nanny, whose lap was "so much more comforting, softer and broader" than the white woman's (4). In the equally maternal and sexual lap, Em sees black women's bodies as capable of going beyond the reproductive labor of socializing the white girl for elite status.

They also reproduce their own eroticism, a special kind of feeling good that Em learns from their touch. In "This Body for Itself," Dionne Brand puts forth that both straight and lesbian Caribbean women learn eroticism "from other women": the laugh of women up the street, the sun on a traveler's skin, aunts hugging and singing to each other, all small "signals of sensuality, desire, and pleasure."[45] Bliss's tales of Em's childhood extend this observation, suggesting that not only women-loving *and* straight but also black *and* white Caribbean women learn sensuality from Afro-Caribbean female caregivers, comothers who mold them into both protobisexual and protobiracial subjects. For Em, the generous sensuality black women's bodies teach is paralleled by the enormity of the mountains she watches during her reverie on their bodies, breastlike peaks with "large generous forms outlined against the night sky" (5). Bliss's transgression of Jamaican feminine clichés is not just the entry of a feeling white girl's body, nor even that this feeling becomes pleasure only in contact with black women's bodies. It is her imagination that this pleasure is so intense that she identifies black Nanny rather than white mama with the mountain summit.

Bliss's break with Jamaican women's commonplaces extends beyond content to form. Espousing rigid formality, turn-of-the-century West Indian poetesses precisely controlled the meter, rhyme, and diction of their verses to demonstrate that the Caribbean and its women could produce mountain-"high" literary art. Far removed from such stylistic control, Em's visions run as wild as she does—moving slowly, circularly, and seemingly aimlessly through topoi and characters that Bliss describes with gratuitous detail. Later in the novel, Em refers to a poem that she wrote as "long, loosely constructed, immature . . . loaded with early memories of the Island," and Bliss's novel could be described the same way (355). This novel is truly sprawling, often without discernible plot or literary motivation for her character's endless, repetitive musings. Bliss seems unwilling to keep her writing within *any* confined limits, and her narrative of a female protagonist's self-making spills messily outside recognizable models.

An image of how *too-muchness* suffuses Bliss's imagination of landscape, white femininity, and form emerges later in the chapter during Em's joyful stay at a mountain summer home, where she explores the wonders of the hills and finds them "like a fairy tale—better than any fairy tale" (5). She makes friends there, not with children but with fields of flowers she discovers on morning walks—with endless ginger lilies that "grew in great numbers; [whose] full intoxicating perfume would flood the moist air" (5). One day she dodges her governess to run to a field filled with these flowers and, in an already characteristic search for pleasure, embraces them: "Alone at sunset one evening, she had embraced the ginger-lily. The flower, heavy with rain, swayed towards her as she touched it, spilling water from its leaves and its heavy head on to her light afternoon frock. The waxen-like petals, tightly curled, touched her cheek, and for a second the rich smoky scent filled her nose and head. Then it sprang back on to the bank, scattering water from its petals as it went. It had been a strange experience – almost as if the ginger-lily were alive like herself. . . . And always on their walks on the mountain-side, when they passed a group of ginger-lilies, she felt a strange exciting feeling about them as if they were her secret friends" (35). This white lily might seem an apt floral metaphor for the model of racially and sexually pristine womanhood that Jamaica's color plates visualize, but Bliss takes this image in another direction.[46] Jamaica's depictions of hill stations evoke only one sense: its description of mountain flora and paintings of lofty ladies focus on their looks, insisting on the visual pleasure they provide at a distance without coming close enough to note sounds, smells, or textures. As Mary Louise Pratt demonstrates, the creation of a disembodied colonial gaze is central to the discursive construction of imperial eyes/Is, and both male travel writers and white women poets of the period consistently reproduced this vision. But in this portrait of ginger lilies that exude scent, caress Em's cheek, and spill water, Bliss associates mountain flora with multiple sensory experiences. Em feels not only as eyes but as nose, mouth, and skin, breaking down the distance the white woman is supposed to keep from all around her; and she imagines an expansive sensuality that is not the corruption of Long's lounging Creoles but polymorphous childhood pleasure. In the presence of ginger lilies, the pale skin that is supposed to separate and elevate Em from the world around her becomes an organ of connection to an entirely different species and way of being.

While Jamaica clearly marks the summit as an unmistakably English topos, for Em it is a more indeterminate, mestiza space. The ginger lilies' features combine those that attract her in white and black women. White and waxy in color, they give off a "rich smoky scent" that Em associates with black women at market, whose "hot body smells" she finds like "rich ripe fruit" (15). Strongly attracted by this pale but exotic flower, Em seems ambiguous as to whether this attraction is identification or desire. A white girl who, like the "tightly curled" petals of this lily, is not yet in full bloom, she seems to enjoy the fusional possibilities of becoming more and more like the flower that she imagines is "alive like herself." Later in the chapter she wishes she could turn into a flower as people do in fairy stories (39). At the same time, this passage bursts with erotic suggestions making clear that Em is fantasizing a feminine image not only to be like but also to be with—one not only to imitate but also to desire. She embraces the flower as if it were a woman, and, as she does so, becomes inundated with rainwater collected on the flower's petals, its wetness making her wet. The smoothness of the flower then touches her cheek, and the scent that "fills" her suggests pleasurable penetration. The passage ends by noting the "strange exciting feeling" the clusters of these flowers arouse in her, and her imagination of a secret friendship evokes clichés of a hidden same-sex relationship. In contrast to the spectacular aloneness of Forrest's hill ladies, the ginger lily – grammatically singular – is in fact a profusion of blooms on a single stalk. And what excites Em here seems to be all the blossoms that make up the multiply blooming flower and that endless multiplication itself: their white woman's color and black woman's sensuality, their rain-washed "purity" and erotic suggestiveness, their ability to at once be herself and her other, all clustered together for her to embrace. Already Em is unwilling to imagine *one* racial-sexual model for self-making or *one* unified love object. The profusely blossoming ginger lilies offer an open metaphor and a metaphor of Em's openness – an openness that leads into a tale of a protagonist with too many mother figures, too much sensuality, too many love interests, and too many episodes to form a coherent narrative or a coherent model of white Caribbean femininity.

Following this initial childhood chapter, *Luminous Isle* jumps fifteen years ahead to a twenty-year-old Em shipboard in mid-Atlantic, returning to Jamaica after completing school in England. Shipmates suppose she is going there to undertake her proper career as an elite woman – namely, as the captain tells Em, marriage into a family of officers or planters. But as Em quickly responds, she has no interest in marriage; instead she returns to discover her own voca-tion, "what to do with her life" (50). Part of this *what*, she insists, will be the rambling eroticism she calls *love*. Love, she believes, is opposed to marriage, which she equates with falsity and death. She reflects angrily that husbands "did not want the personality of the woman to flower. But to become a still flower, drained of its honey . . . for them alone." But, she continues, "love is different . . . is the unique chemical miracle" that nurtures blossoms rather than draining them (220). Em seeks this nebulous state through a hazy diffu-sion of desires, so that every chapter becomes a chain of descriptions of people she feels attracted to. These include cousins, family friends, married men, and rakish bachelors, as well as club women, married women, women artists, and black women. For while Em has been told with disgust by a young socialite, "You know, you grow out of feeling that way about *girls*," same-sex eroticism also forms a part of Em's Jamaican past that she insists on bringing into the present (160–61). The white women she is attracted to share marked differences to her biological mother and her mountain-summit ideal of white femininity, while the black women she sighs after remind her of Nanny's soothing hands, breasts, and lap. For women as for men Em's attractions are intense, but they fade quickly: "She could never be bound . . . to any one person for long. It meant the end of one's personal life, the beginning of the unnatural life" (183). Unwilling to choose among potential lovers, she instead chooses a vacillation that keeps many roads open in her imagination while committing to none.

What Em repeatedly states she hopes to find in love is *happiness*, the joyful power of self-recreation that she experiences in the ginger lily field and that she is convinced people lose in monogamous marriage. Her quest for happiness outside heteromonogamy reads, in part, as a willful avoidance of the cultural neurosis that Judith Butler calls "heterosexual melancholy." Drawing on Sigmund Freud's exploration of melancholia as a response to loss that refuses to acknowledge or grieve that loss – that, instead, incorporates the lost love-object into the ego itself – Butler extrapolates how this process relates to gender formations. Both masculinity and femininity, she posits, are "established in part through prohibitions which *demand the loss* of certain sexual attachments, and demand as well that those losses *not* be avowed, and *not* be grieved."[47] To become a woman, a girl must transfer desire from her mother to her father and seek a lover who will be a father substitute rather than one for the mother; she must not only renounce desire for a feminine love object but also never grieve this loss or even acknowledge it. The way she deals with this loss must come through an identification with the feminine that, instead of coexisting with desire for female subjects, excludes and silences same-sex desire. Read in dialogue with Butler, Em's obstinate refusal to lose love objects – old, young, rich, poor, male, female, black, white – appears to be an attempt not only to navigate outside heterosexuality but also to plot a course away from such heterosexual melancholy. Unwilling to grow out of feeling "that way" for girls to become a wife who will "play her part . . . in the social rounds of garrison life in a Crown colony," she resists accepting a model of femininity – and of the colonial, patriarchal world – in which she must renounce loves and remain unable to speak that loss (59). Instead, she identifies with and desires at the same time; she speaks the names of all her love interests, filling the novel to bursting with their description. Keeping her hybrid identifications and desires within language, Em experiments with an *erotics of self-making* to replace the white girl's prescribed *melancholics of self-making*.

But of all these unlost love objects, one looms largest in the novel: Rebekkah, the black farmer who lives above the hills that the adult Em visits. When Rebekkah comes bearing mountain flowers, her spoken wish that Em "keep happy till Ah come agen" prompts Em to muse, "That was what a lover would say—a real lover, somebody who came not to destroy but to recreate" (281). Then, reversing the image she gives of heterosexual marriage sapping a woman's flowering, she takes "the mountain flowers and set[s] them in a glass jug in the dining room, the parched stems reaching down into the water to drink" (281). Like her water-bearing biblical namesake, Rebekkah gives love offerings that resist loss, bringing flowers that resuscitate rather than dying when passed between women; she staves off melancholy, bringing happiness instead. But Rebekkah's character begs reflection not only on heterosexual melancholy but also on how, in a West Indian context, it may intersect with Creole white melancholy. Melancholy heterosexuality is also the cradle of whiteness, and disrupting the former undermines the latter. That is, for Em to become a properly sealed heterosexual white West Indian woman, she must simultaneously reject the "impurities" of sexual and racial markedness, of same-sex and black identifications—or risk undermining a colonial social logic built on prohibitions and exclusions. As much as, and perhaps more than Em is ever supposed to grieve that she cannot be with her white mother, she is never supposed to grieve that she can never be *and* be with Rebekkah and the black caretakers that nurtured her eroticism. But Em, ever disobedient, continually imagines she can become like and become lovers with this black woman, accepting her flowers and hoping she returns with more.

Desire, Anger, and Reddened Flowers:
Rebekkah and Em on the Mountain Path

A white woman's journey to the hill stations (Em finds) can twist and turn in ways Jamaica never imagined, winding dreamily through many pleasures. Em first meets Rebekkah on a pony ride up to the hill stations—an approach that, far from a climb to sensory chilliness, becomes one of the novel's most sensual descriptions. "Washed through with continual rain and rich flower-smells," the very air Em breathes is a mixture of elements that melts into a taking in of pleasure (202). Spilling wetness across the scene, bodies of running water appear and reappear on her path. Filled with "joy" when she passes a waterfall, Em leans her head into it, watching "the rushing water pouring over the rock, the fine spray in the air mingling with the dust" in the air (197). She rejoices at the capacity this copious wetness has for mixing with elements around it – fusing with darker dirt, cascading over a purple iris. Suddenly the view brings on an intense craving for the porridge she loved as a child, for its warm creaminess in her mouth. In this mountainscape overflowing with the clitoral (wet, round stones; the hoodlike iris) and the viscous (mud, cream), hungry Em takes multisensory pleasure in all that runs together, *mestiza*-like: water mixing with petals in the stream, spray mixing with dust on her face, cream mixing with saliva in her mouth. Sensory overload lulls Em into afternoon drowsiness, from which two voices in the distance wake her. She opens her eyes to a "handsome black girl . . . tall, contemptuous, holding herself magnificently, a filled basket on her head, under her scarlet handkerchief draped like a turban . . . with eyes flashing scorn" (202). This is Rebekkah, who appears in the middle of an unexplained quarrel with a mulatta postmistress to whom she shouts haughtily: "You go to de magistrate, I go too. I speak for myself so all de world can hear" (203). Em is immediately captivated by the rebellious figure and determinedly catches up to her, asking permission to walk with her. Rebekkah agrees, her eyes now flashing a smile, and the two talk with immediate intimacy on the hill path where Forrest posed the white-gowned white lady conspicuously alone.

Em's alteration of her mountain course to pursue Rebekkah echoes her early running off the mountain path to pursue ginger lilies, and her fluid identification with and desire for the lilies is mirrored in her feelings for Rebekkah. On the one hand, Em follows Rebekkah because she imagines herself to be like her. Glowing with pride, Rebekkah makes clear that as an independent farmer she works for no one but herself and "couldn' work for anyone but meself" (205). Rebekkah's pleasure as she says this suggests that such independence paves the career path to an erotics of self-making – something Em has yet to see in the elite wife's flower-draining reproductive labor. Em believes her a kindred spirit who already possesses the completeness she searches for in herself: "She was completely happy, feeling in solid harmony with the rounded and complete personality walking beside her" (205). At the same time Em's pursuance of Rebekkah is a lover's pursuit, motivated by immediate attraction. Noting her powerful body, Em watches Rebekkah swing her hips as she carries her load on her head and marvels at the "magnificent creature with her flashing eyes, her slow, rich, powerful voice" (203). The narrator continually conflates Rebekkah's curving hips and ringing voice, and as Em's eyes slip from her mouth to her seductively dancing skirt, she grows ever more agitated: "Her desire to speak to the girl was growing stronger every moment, yet the swinging hips, the tilting skirt, seemed to get farther and farther away" (204). Slippages between speech, skirt, and desire underscore that Em's oral-sexual fixation is also a longing for an erotics of *linguistic* self-making: for women to open desiring mouths to one other in many ways, to speak desire and so keep it out of the unspoken realm of melancholy. And indeed, the promise of pleasure in women's speech is borne out as, at the climax of their conversation, Em imagines she sees "a flash of sweetness" in Rebekkah, who "softened to an almost lover-like glow" (205).

What is it in Rebekkah that Em desires to be like and be with? An answering image comes in flowers that appear for the first time on the mountain path after Rebekkah leaves: "Tall and slender pink lilies" that tremble excitedly in the breeze (207). Recoloring the ginger lily, these flowers blossom in a vision of womanhood that fuses qualities of Em and Rebekkah—their pink the fragrant whiteness Em identifies with in the other flower retinted with the red of Rebekkah's head wrap. On the one hand, these pink lilies—a flowering of the countryside that Em has never seen before, but that sprout now in the cultivator's path—offer an image of where and how Rebekkah works. When Rebekkah describes her pride in being an independent farmer, Em links this satisfaction to the blooming landscape in which she performs her work: "It was safe, this rich and holy pride, among a world of thickly-growing undergrowth, of rivers and mountains" (205). Later in the novel, Em metaphorizes the white wife as a scentless lily in a vase (228). But Rebekkah, the only female character exclusively involved in productive and never in reproductive labor, represents a differently colored alternative to the dreaded profession of wife. As utterly uninterested in the exhausting physical exertions necessary to maintain a farm as she is in the work of the nursing black breast, Em is captivated by the romanticized possibilities that Rebekkah represents for a woman owning her own land, her own labor, and her own body in a way that the white wife cannot. Through Em's rose-colored gaze, productive manual labor appears like liberation from reproductive sexual labor, a reclaiming of the working and/as erotic female body.

In fact, Rebekkah's independent work enables her to make a love offering to Em and also is that love offering. In parting, she tells Em she will visit and "bring her something from the farm as a present. 'What fruit Missus favour bes' den?" (205). Em, remembering the "magic fruit which had retained its glamour from days gone by," asks for star apples (205). Literally the fruits of Rebekkah's labor, star apples also suggest the fruits of her sexuality. Dark like Rebekkah on the outside, they are creamy on the inside, which is why Em loves them: "Star apples . . . were not disappointing like other fruits on the inside, but were heavenly to taste" (14). If only women were free to work for themselves, Em imagines, other bodily freedoms could follow. Women could have star apples — that is, both labor and eroticism — to offer each other, and fulfilling economic and sexual partnerships between them could be possible. In keeping with Em's imagination of the mountains as a fairy-tale setting, this strikingly unrealistic fantasy elides black working women's physical realities; the colonial elite has kept Em so privileged she has no idea what the work of farming entails. Yet the star apple farm does serve as an anticolonial fantasy that imagines an improved life if white and black women ceased to work in white men's houses and instead worked for each other — even without knowing how such a thing could become possible.

Sprouting from this generous landscape in which Em dreams new possibilities for Jamaican women's labor, the pink lily waves as an image through which she also fantasizes new possibilities for their race. Its blossoming somewhere between red and white (between both-and, either-or, as Lugones describes the mestiza) metaphorically suggests that on the mountain Em envisions high ground where she can become — and become partners with — a woman who is both/and, either/or, black/white. The scene opens with Rebekkah challenging the mulatta postmistress' servile, assimilatory hybridity: "You not white woman — you not nigger. What den you t'ink yourself to be?," she asks defiantly (203). Standing tall in contrast, dark-skinned Rebekkah models the reverse of such whitening. While Em guesses she has "Spanish blood," the farmer, in her "pagan hauteur" (204), seems to have Africanized the European in her. Em's vision of Rebekkah emerging from the mountains, as well as her fantasied Spanish ascendancy, aligns her with a model of mestizaje that threatened English control of Jamaica during Long's lifetime: the Afro-Spanish and Afro-Arawak creolization of the Blue Mountains' maroon strongholds. Here, capitalizing on the confusion surrounding England's seizure of Jamaica, Africans imported under Spanish rule fled to form multiethnic communities that waged devastating wars against the new occupiers. Richard Burton notes the importance of the "already partially creolized character" of this population often imagined as "purely" African, where linguistic and cultural hybridity served to unify heterogeneous African and indigenous communities.[48] The proud, mountain-dwelling, Afro-Spanish Rebekkah looks and lives like these historic maroons, inhabiting a twentieth-century maroonage in which she thrives independent of both plantocracy and patriarchy, of the lowland colonial government and a lowly husband. As a black/Spanish woman landowner who talks back to British functionaries, she performs race mixing in a way that disrupts imperial ideals of whitening. Em's attraction to the proud *mestiza* seems to stem partly from a wonder whether such a model of anticolonial *mestizaje* might be available to her too. "How would a white woman have come off in such an encounter?," she asks herself just before following Rebekkah to make an encounter happen (204).

Yet it is no concrete element of Afro-Jamaican culture that Em seeks to blend into her Creole self in Rebekkah-like *mestizaje*, not the language or dress Long saw taking over white women. Instead, just as she seems chiefly interested in the affective and erotic benefits of reimagining Jamaican women's labor—how it would *feel* to work for herself—she is fascinated by the idea of taking on elements of what she sees as Afro-Jamaican women's emotional and sexual "natures." Gazing up to her on the mountain path, Em looks to Rebekkah for an adult version of the lessons in affectivity that black nannies provided as a child. All Rebekkah's emotions—contempt, anger, impatience, happiness, tenderness—are described appearing in a "flash" or a "glow" that conveys their lightning intensity, an unmediated feelingness that Em searches for in her Jamaican self-making. "Sensitiveness, responsiveness," and the ability to move to the emotional source of life is, Em later states, "something I know that the coloured people have. It is one of the things that has always drawn me strongly to them" (342). As with her rose-tinting of the advantages of Rebekkah's work, Em seems willfully blind both to the material inequalities and to the psychic pain attached to the black female status she covets in 1920s Jamaica. Instead, she chooses to believe in a fiction in which black women's imagined emotional *difference* is romanticized as emotional *freedom*: Rebekkah, living in mountain regions Em has never penetrated, represents something beyond the emotional experiences permitted to sealed white women. In the same hills in which she once wished to give up her humanity to gain flowerness, she now dreams of giving up white socialization to gain (black) emotional intensity.

The Rebekkah-like red that retints the ginger lily may be not only that of the *redbone* (that is, the light-skinned black), though. It may also be the color of *seeing red*, of the anger that Rebekkah is so strikingly voicing when Em first hears her. Em's desire to open her mouth to star apples seems partly aroused because their offer comes just after she has heard Rebekkah open her mouth in outrage; the black woman's fiery contempt is what first makes her "magnificent" in Em's description. While Em may be responding to this as a sign of passion – the opposite of wifely frigidness – it also reads as the opposite of feminine melancholy. In the last chapter of The Psychic Life of Power, Butler maps heterosexual melancholy's relationship to anger. Such melancholy, she notes, is not only a refusal to acknowledge loss but a refusal to acknowledge the rage surrounding that loss: instead of lashing out at the losses implicit in assuming monoracial heterosexuality, the subject incorporates those losses into who she or he is. The prevalence of hetero and white melancholy in a society that continues to privilege straight and white, then, reflects the failure of anger to intervene and transform the worlds that construct subjects as singularly gendered, sexualized, and racialized. As Butler writes, "Melancholia is a rebellion that has been put down, crushed."[49] However, while Butler thoroughly considers the political possibilities of melancholy, she gives short shrift to anger, writing as if the "crushing" of the rebellion that produces melancholy were inevitable. Em, on the other hand, does not believe in this inevitability and remains starry-eyed over the possibility of finding Rebekkah in a state of rebellion not yet put down. This independent woman represents an alternative to heteromelancholy not only because she is a potential lover or because she wishes Em happiness but also because she models a melancholy-defying anger that butts against colonial hierarchies. Anger – a consciousness of inequality heightened to the point of speaking back and acting out – emerges in Rebekkah not as a bypassed stop on the way to melancholy but as an affective state capable of generating a particularly charged erotics of self-making and social remaking.[50]

In fact, throughout the romantic-sounding "Moonlight in the Mountains," Bliss thematizes the possibility of rebellions in which the rage of the oppressed might be channeled against the colonial world. Drawing on the mountains' history of slave resistance, Em's hill station hostess explains the hidden past of an abandoned great house and its barren grounds: "Round about a hundred years ago it was owned by some devil of a Lowland Scot who was supposed to practice the most diabolical cruelties on his slaves. The niggers say the place reeks of blood and that no grass will grow near the house; and the fruit trees won't bear fruit. . . . the old devil was done in, in the end, by a party of his heftiest niggers. Hauled him out of bed one night and did him in, in a particularly brutal way" (213). This stripped landscape indicates where the chapter's title comes from: moonlight in the mountains allowed the master to watch his slaves at night and to see spirits foretelling his murder. While the chapter title, like the idyllic vision of Em's mountain ascent, suggests a narrative about romance, we now learn that it is equally about revisiting a history of imperial brutality and resulting rage – a narrative path to an uncrushed past rebellion that resurfaces in the present, choking out flora. The historical attack is paralleled later in the chapter by a domestic revolt of white women that Em imagines coming in the future. Her evocation of childhood beatings intended to make her into a proper girl echoes her descriptions of blacks beaten to make them into proper slaves. While on the outside elite women learn from their beatings and adjust to prescribed roles, Em surmises that this veneer covers anger at the brutality of the "squashing of the little girls" (225). What would happen, she wonders, if this anger were expressed? Rebekkah's company seems enticing because it promises space for just such expression. Along with the possibility of joining sweetnesses, Em and Rebekkah's pink lily fusion promises the possibility of joining angers: the rage that Rebekkah expresses on the path and that Em brews quietly, the historic rebellion of black Jamaicans and the future fight for women's equality.

Yet neither the eruption of women's anger nor that of their same-sex desire ever fully break through the text. Rebekkah reappears several times in *Luminous Isle*, bearing star apples and lilies. Each time her appearance at once infuses the text with eroticism and does violence to its story line, disrupting a heterosexual marriage plot threatening to take shape. In their first meeting, Em imagines slipping a ring on Rebekkah's finger, suggesting that this connection could replace the work of racially conservative, heterosexual matrimony; and in the final chapter, Rebekkah's surfacing inspires Em to leave the man she had agreed to marry (206, 363). Yet while Em does not marry into the colonial elite, neither does she enter any form of partnership with Rebekkah. Intermittent visits, fantasies, and other characters' joking references to "Em's" Rebekkah remain the extent of their connection. Em is never explicit as to why this might be, but the text suggests that while eager to make affective transformations to be like and with a black woman, she is incapable of grasping the economic shift this would entail. Ready to give up the symbolic privileges of whiteness, she seems as unwilling to give up its economic advantages as she is to admit this limitation to herself. As her fiancé points out when she leaves him, she says she does not need his money or her father's, but in fact she does: "You have not been brought up to a mean way of living; you will certainly suffer if you have to live on small common. You are very proud; you will dislike poverty intensely" (351–52). Just before this conversation, Em met an English lesbian couple on a visit to a friend's estate, a "sporting Englishwoman on the arm of her friend's chair, possessively and arrogantly masculine," and a wealthy divorcée, their gold-rimmed monocle and silk stockings oozing class privilege (351). And while these members of the elite present a possibility of partnership in which Em could maintain her standard of living without entering the marriage profession, a lovership between a white Creole and a black farmer would certainly mean the kind of poverty her fiancé warns her against.

What undercuts the power of women's anger in the end is not the melancholy that Butler charts, but material realities – economics, not psychology. While Em fantasizes about the possibility of Afro- and Euro-Jamaican women building partnerships to work for each other, she seems to understand that she has no concrete possibilities for realizing this fantasy in 1920s Jamaica. By the end of the novel, Em is willing to admit that she stands outside Rebekkah's world and will always remain there. After breaking with her fiancé she realizes that it was Rebekkah who "had really come between herself and [him]," but she also recognizes that her relationship with the mountain woman can go no farther than it already has: "Now, much later, she saw it all and understood. . . . From the start Rebekkah had known, but in her plastic and inarticulate way she had never pressed the point. Too many things divided them. They had been equals only once – on first acquaintance; when walking up the hill together she had asked Rebekkah if she might walk with her part of the way" (354). The angry, *mestiza* pink lilies of that walk do not grow outside the fairy topos of the mountains; they are momentary, dreamy aberrations, not flora that flourish throughout the island.

Em's daydreams of erotic, angry fusion with the black farmer are not fundamentally about Rebekkah, not about pursuing practical connections with this otherly raced and classed woman. They are about Em and her desire to sever connections to the colonial patriarchy into which she was born. Caught up in fantasizing how she might be in a position more like Rebekkah's, Em never imagines a need for Rebekkah to be in a position more like hers – that is, to have access to the privileges Em lives with. Unable to envision how this farmer could be a viable partner, she returns to England, leaving Rebekkah and the mountains as guardians of her erotic memories. Looking at Maroon Mountain from her return ship's deck, she feels herself leaving behind "an episode in the past, in one's life, now held for ever in Rebekkah's strong hands, retained in the wisdom that shone out of the large, luminous eyes" (369). As she climbs aboard the ship, Em's departure is a final refusal to reproduce the colonial elite. Yet her self-recreation finds no sustainable escape route except a refusal to root herself in *any* strata of West Indian society, and her erotic experimentation hurts the colonial elite without joining in solidarity with the colonized subjects to whom she is attracted. Her rebellion is finally put down, crushed in Jamaica, and her parting hope is that she might export to England the reddened feeling of Jamaica's mountains.

* * *

> An unseen presence was replying to her in the sea breeze,
> in the strong salty air. To be sexless, creedless, classless, free.
> A soul swinging wide across the universe .
> — Eliot Bliss, *Luminous Isle*

This chapter tells the story of two failures unfolded in the pages of *Luminous Isle*. The first is that of the white lily: that is, the inability of the colonial family order to reproduce white female heterosexuality as the cradle of whiteness. Instead, the breasts and hips of black women who surround Em in her white house become the cradles to which she seeks to return and remake herself. In this slippage between disciplinary intimacy and an erotics of self-making, rigid colonial divisions between contiguity and similarity fail as, occupying the same houses and paths, white and black women both become *mestizas*. But the second failure is that of the pink lily and its imagination of white and black women's fusion, an easy and pleasurable sameness. Material and historical differences that leave Em and Rebekkah speaking different languages, living in different houses, and depending on different incomes cannot be erased by a metaphoric union that functions only in a fairy-tale topos. As both the denial of white-black similarity and fantasies of their fusion unravel over the course of *Luminous Isle*, Bliss finally leaves her readers as Em leaves Rebekkah: with nothing definitive, neither black nor white womanhood, neither heterosexual nor same-sex partnership. This constitutes a frustrating nothing, where the logic of colonial desire has been dismantled without substituting other structures of feeling in its place. But it is also the promising nothing of a future as empty and unmarked as the sea Em sails into on the novel's last pages, a space where so little is set that everything is left to the imagination. Neither villain nor hero, collaborator nor maroon, straight nor lesbian, white nor black, adult nor child, lover nor fighter, Em remains a *mestiza* whose function seems to be what Maryse Condé would later posit as the Caribbean writer's chief goal: to trouble us, always trouble us.[51]

Headed into the indeterminacy that the sea represents to her, Em is nonetheless headed somewhere: back to England, the country in which most of her readership would open the novel. In the previous chapter and the introduction I suggested that European feminism might have much to learn from (post)colonial women's challenges to gender, and Em's importation of a dream of sexless, creedless, classless existence *from* Jamaica *to* England seems to bear out this claim. The queer-equals-European sexual imperialism metaphor in fact functions in reverse in this colonial novel. Learning from (if not able to become) pink lilies, Em experiences gynoeroticism as an antipatriarchal and anticolonial way of connecting to the world around her that she discovers in the Caribbean and takes back to London. This mobile consciousness is at once promising and problematic. As Staceyann Chin makes clear, the "problem" with moving between Euro- and Afro-Creole models of same-sex desire is not sexual imperialism in the sense of white women converting black and brown counterparts to their erotic practices. Rather, it is the cultural imperialism of denying that shared sexual and economic history means a need for shared political struggle. In a poetic dialogue with white women titled "Neighbors: For Centuries," Chin writes:

> The women's movement has always made use
> of my dark body
> in the marching
> and the flag making and the taking of references when it needed it."

And with piercing anger she replies:

> The extent of our contribution demands
> that we be given some consideration
> in the distribution of wealth
> and health insurance policies that cover therapy

we would like to have someone to look at the wounds
we have been stitching
for centuries."[52]

Em sails off without looking meaningfully, but with a backward glance at the mountains whose histories trace why and how she should.

three

Blue Countries, Dark Beauty

Opaque Desires in the Poetry
of Ida Faubert

Night is luminous; night is tender and beautiful.
The sun has faded; the moon falls on the roses.

—Ida Faubert, "Soir tropical" ("Tropical Night")

Queer diasporic cultural forms . . . suggest a mode of reading and
"seeing" same-sex eroticism that challenges modern epistemologies
of visibility, revelation, and sexual subjectivity.

—Gayatri Gopinath, *Impossible Desires: Queer Diasporas
and South Asian Public Cultures*

Under a rainbow-colored logo and the bold-fonted slogan "Haitian by Birth, Gay by Nature, Proud by Choice," the "About Us" section of the Haitian Gays and Lesbians Alliance (HGLA) Web site proudly identifies the group as "the first leading community based organization which empowers the Haitian, born or identified, LGBT. . . . We support the Haitian LGBT in the various stages of the coming out process, in the creation and affirmation of positive self identities, and the promotion of human and civil rights."[1] To the right of this ocean blue text is a photo from New York's Heritage of Pride parade in 2006 with nine members posed together, smiling. Arms over shoulders in the front row stand seven Afro-Haitian American females, skin tones ranging from sand to mahogany, summer clothes blending together blues, pinks, oranges, and yellows; three women wear festive flower leis, two in the center carry rainbow flags. And also in the center, two figures appear with perfectly rounded rainbows superimposed over their faces: the same rainbows that signal outness as flags reappear as graphics to shield bearers from international outing. These doubled rainbows mirror the coexisting yet contradictory meanings that visibility takes on for the same-sex loving Haitians that HGLA represents. On the one hand, the group's leadership celebrates what the site names bilingually – in (African American) English and (Caribbean) French – as "coming out the closet/sortie du placard": "Ultimately," the section on this process assures readers, "coming out can be a very freeing experience for persons who are LGBTQ because it allows them to live a more honest life and develop more genuine relationships with others."[2] At the same time, though, HGLA's site acknowledges visually, if not in words, that the exposure of coming out does not prove empowering for all same-sex loving Haitians. The centrality of the rainbow-masked faces in this picture, and their covering with a symbol of pride every bit as brilliant as the flags below them, visualize that the desire for limited visibility is neither a fringe concern nor something to be ashamed of. Rather, its artful masks have developed crucial strategies that allow some Haitian LGBTs to self-express creatively and without backlash. Being at once brightly colored and shielded can be a good thing, the celebratory figures model.

Different from Dutch-speaking territories' long, open traditions of *kambrada* and *mati*, Francophone Caribbean histories of sexuality weave complexly between visibility and invisibility. "People hide this thing. They don't want to see it or believe it," the Guadeloupean writer Gisèle Pineau says of same-sex eroticism.[3] Yet she notes that male "roommates" and women friends sharing the same bed live as lovers without naming themselves as such, finding spaces in their communities without fixing labels. Similarly, HGLA's "Gay Haiti" section notes that same-sex sex always has been silently tolerated in both working and elite classes, but that it remains routinely unnamed; this tacit tolerance made the country a tourist destination for wealthy gays during the Duvalier era.[4] But North American LGBT activists, wedded to epistemologies of the closet, often implicitly or explicitly equate this culture of semivisibility with the Global South's lack of progress. In *Sirena Selena*, the Puerto Rican novelist Mayra Santos-Febres parodies the North's conflation of "developing" nations' electrical power outages and their lack of sexual enlightenment through the words of a Canadian tourist in Santo Domingo. He sighs, "I don't want to criticize, you know — with all the problems these islands have, it's understandable that they're less evolved. . . . You can't compare our problems with the atrocities a gay man has to face in these countries. . . . It's all hanky-panky in the dark, like in the fifties in Canada."[5]

But the "dark" or semivisibility of Caribbean same-sex sexuality can be something other than a blackout. It can also read as the "tender and beautiful" night that Ida Faubert imagines in "Tropical Night," a space of alternative vision that nurtures both eroticism and resistance. The tactically obscured has been crucial to Caribbean and North American slave societies, in which dances, ceremonies, sexual encounters, abortions, and slave revolts all took place under the cover of night. Calling on this different understanding of the half seen, Édouard Glissant exhorts scholars engaging Caribbean cultures to leave behind desires for transparency and instead approach with respect for *opacity*: a mode of seeing in which the difference of the other is neither completely visible nor completely hidden, neither overexposed nor erased.[6] The difference that Glissant asks us to (half) look at is certainly not that of sexuality (since it is never mentioned) nor of gender (since he includes in his work a diatribe against feminism). However, tactics of self-veiling like HGLA's rainbows challenge both heterocentric Caribbean critics and Eurocentric LGBT rights groups to see why opacity might necessarily be theorized as an Afro-Atlantic strategy for negotiating not only race and ethnicity but also sexuality and gender. As Byron Williams writes of the cover chosen by some same-sex loving African American men: "Ironically, it is the battle for survival that makes Down Low culture a profoundly black phenomenon. Whatever one thinks of Down Low culture, it is an attempt to define its own liberation and perceived safety. . . . Just as African slaves were forced to disavow their native religious traditions for a European brand of Christianity spawning the 'Invisible Institution,' known today as the black church, the DL community has done likewise."[7] Moreover, as Gayatri Gopinath explores in *Impossible Desires*, tactical obscurity may be a particularly *feminized* option for subverting heteronormativity. That is, Gopinath takes seriously the disruptive potential of eroticism that emerges in the supposed shelter of women's "private" domestic spaces, where "it is precisely within the cracks and fissures of rigidly homonormative arrangements that queer female desire can emerge" and flourish.[8] Or as Faubert writes, night is also when the moon covers roses — when and where feminized bodies can open in new ways.

Seeking out a predecessor to the lei-wearing, rainbow-masked women of the HGLA photo – and following up on afternoon-celebrated *stanfaste* and morning-discovered ginger lilies – this chapter plots a reading of night-blooming flowers and undercover eroticism in the poetry of Faubert (1882–1969). Like the photograph of the partying but shielded figures, Faubert's poetry celebrates women's sensuality while tantalizingly refraining from giving specifics about the sexuality she gestures toward. In an era in which ladies' literary circles created a homosocial intellectual climate allowing elite women to come to writing through the inspiration and support of other women, the most erotic expression of these connections were Faubert's dedication of a volume of poetry and several poems to women. Never "coming out" under the label "lesbian," Faubert nevertheless situates her poetry outside the stifling space of the closet; her moonlit roses and shadowy jasmine revise dominant paradigms of what Francophone Caribbean sexuality looks like. Writing from Paris, Faubert moved between French and West Indian, real and unreal landscapes to find metaphors for her erotic relationships with women. This lyrical movement transculturates Caribbean and European images of gender and sexuality to imagine love for women as at once a return to her native land and the creation of a new topos she calls a "blue country," a landscape in which flowers bloom suggestively in the dark. Navigating flower-insulated space between dark and light, public and private, open and closed, Faubert's night-gardened bodies find avenues of expression that the hypervisibility of outness cannot afford the already marked bodies of women of color in the diaspora. Through a discussion of contemporary Haitian women's literature, an examination of women of color in early twentieth-century photography, and a close reading of Faubert's poetry, I suggest how the semivisibility of her same-sex eroticism reflects both a fencing in and breaking out: both a concession to compulsory heterosexuality and a tactic of liberatory gynoeroticism. Like contemporary Francophone Caribbean LGBT activists, Faubert discovered "the meaning of the word 'visibility,'" but her meaning is both similar and different.[9] Her opaque poetics of half seenness is a flower-covered, open mask that creates visual symbols without easy explanations – flower gardens as elusive, promising, and impenetrable as mangroves.

A Legion of Flowers: Ida Faubert in Haitian Letters

In 1906, exactly a century before the HGLA photo was taken at Heritage of Pride, the former Haitian president Lysius Salomon's daughter Ida returned to Haiti after finishing her Parisian education. The same year she returned to Port-au-Prince, Haitian literary reviews registered the earliest published – but anonymous – female voices raised in protest against their second sex status, and the avid reader Ida doubtless pored over many of these. Much as the turn of the twenty-first century marked a watershed in Caribbean LGBT activism, the turn of the twentieth witnessed landmarks for Caribbean print feminism. Ida belonged to the first generation of Haitian elite women to whom formal education was widely available, and this generation pioneered a tradition of female intellectual production that professed its feminism – but did so under (flower) cover. In its tactical self-veiling, Haitian feminist expression emerged as a symbolic forerunner of Caribbean same-sex discourses, a sparse tangle of voices strategically planted between hidden and open spaces.

In the Haiti to which Ida returned, women of letters were circulating writing through two opening channels. The first of these was an intensely male-dominated space: the circuit of artistic journals flourishing as part of the literary movement known as the *génération de la Ronde*, including *La ronde* itself, as well as *Haïti littéraire et scientifique*, *Haïti littéraire et sociale*, *Le petit Haïtien*, and *Variétés*. Established by an elite, homosocial *confrérie* of poets like Etzer Vilaire, Justin Lherisson, Frédéric Marcelin, and Edmond Laforest, *rondiste* publications espoused an image-laden poetry for poetry's sake that they imagined would put Haiti on the literary map. Vilaire believed that a Parnassian-inspired aestheticism could illuminate universal truths and so produce "the arrival of a Haitian elite in the literary history of France."[10] Initially, women appeared only as transcendent images of beauty decorating male poets' work. By the movement's midpoint, though, Haitian women discreetly sought entry into Vilaire's elite as speaking subjects rather than as mute *objets d'art*. Not only did journals begin publishing frequently anonymous poems signed with floral pennames or women's first names; various nonfiction texts by women appeared here decades before the date commonly given for the beginning of the Haitian feminist movement.[11] Ann Marty documents these protofeminist publications: "Note another sign of progress in accepting local realities: that is, allowing a number of women to express themselves. . . . Miss Liane, in *La Ronde* of May 5 1898, writes a fairly ambiguous letter – a discussion at once very much in accordance with the traditional man's prejudices and modulated by accents of feminist rebellion. . . . In 1907, a lecture poses the question of whether feminism exists in Haiti (cf. *Haïti littéraire et sociale* of July 5, 1907) while the same periodical, on September 5, 1906, focused on feminist demands worldwide through the voice of Dora. . . . Finally, in *Les Variétés* of January 20, 1906, Yvette speaks of feminism associated with the rights of blacks in the United States; she evokes the solidarity of black women against white men."[12] In all Marty's examples, anonymous authors modulate tones of feminist critique by directing remarks to male readers and foreign movements. Nonetheless, they introduce the neologism *féminisme* to Haitian letters more than thirty years before the founding of the Ligue Féminine d'Action Sociale, the activist group often cited as the nation's first feminist organization.

The second channel for circulating Haitian women's writing, in contrast, was absolutely female-dominated: Primavera, Cercle Fémina, Printania, Excelsior, and other newly founded women's literary circles, which established their own homosocial intellectual space and printed their own reviews. Members of Port-au-Prince's literary Cercle Fémina, for example, collected their verse in a review of the same name in which they signed their work with floral pseudonyms – *Periwinkle, Violet, Cornflower, Lily of the Valley, Daisy, Forget-me-not, Chrysanthemum*, and *Rose*, among others. Mme. Virgile Valcin, one of the group's most prolific members, writes of the *Cercle*: "I know a 'Parterre' where admirable plants / Hide themselves to bloom, and bloom always."[13] The two meanings of *parterre* (flower bed) and *par terre* (on the ground) doubly suggest the just-aboveground location of the spaces in which women's creativity was emerging in Haiti. From their feminist flower bed, Cercle Fémina writers redeployed the flora-woman equation as a strategy of dissimulation that both reflected and tacitly protested the systematized invisibility of elite women and the danger that visibility could pose for the masked. Valcin's own volume of poetry, *Fleurs et pleurs* (*Flowers and Tears*), is the first published by a Haitian woman and preciously explores the natural world as a mirror for the speaker's profound sentiments as wife, mother, and Haitian. Her high-flown verse attests to an emerging Haitian aesthetics in the feminine mode – in dialogue with but differentiated from the male *génération de la Ronde* – in which the flower cover allows women to infiltrate a Haitian male aesthetic that had itself infiltrated French poetry. Valcin describes women's masked stance as both coquettish and soldierlike, writing elegantly in the original French: "Elles se cachent mais, leur odeur captivante / Les dénonce aux passants, chaque heure, chaque jour / Elles sont légion, ces fleurs mystérieuses" (They hide themselves, but their captivating scent / betrays them to passersby, every day, every hour / They are a legion, these mysterious flowers).[14]

Faubert's first poems, published in *Haiti littéraire et scientifique* in 1912, were among the earliest pieces signed with a female author's real name. Still, this poetry – dedicated to her daughter Jacqueline – holds to the tactic of maintaining wife and motherly respectability to allow the author entry into the literary scene. Now wed to André Faubert and a new mother, Faubert was, as her contemporary Léon Laleau describes her, "a *grande dame* of Port-au-Prince high society."[15] He remembers: "She went from a cocktail party to a tea, to a soirée. Whether on foot, her face haloed with her parasol in cheery, shifting colors, or in her car pulled by that happy horse who seemed at the height of pride when taking her out; always her mature, tropical beauty trailed behind her, like the train of a royal robe, a long, trembling wake of admiration."[16] But despite this polished exterior and visible privilege, Faubert was chronically unhappy with the social conservatism of the Haitian elite. "Ida's liberalism, her independence of character were ill-disposed to tolerate the narrowness of scope and ideas of her fatherland," the critic and biographer Madeleine Gardiner writes. She then adds suggestively, without explaining why she gives such weight to female friendship in Faubert's case, that "she felt herself a foreigner in this country where she had no true female friend [*amie*], no link."[17]

Faubert returned to Paris in 1914. Her Parisian activities had proven somewhat scandalous to her family in her school days: she had had numerous admirers, was engaged to a man her family rejected for racial reasons, and then married and divorced another man. She would become even more scandalous in her early thirties. Soon after her last move to Paris, she divorced Faubert and installed herself on the Rue Blomet, the site of the Bal Nègre – where Caribbeans came to dance on weekends – as well as of the studios of the surrealists André Desnos and Joan Miró and the famed gardens that Faubert watched from her window. Here she began a new career as a *femme de lettres*. She threw herself into the literary scene, visiting galleries and lectures and receiving poets and painters on Thursdays at her salon. Among her close artistic and personal contacts was Anna Brancovan de Noailles who, despite her illustrious marriage, continued to be called the French Sappho, both because of her poetic skill and because of her surreptitious lesbian relationships.[18] "Ida greatly admires this poetess whom she had the opportunity to frequent and whose influence is certainly notable in our heroine's work," reports Gardiner.[19] Noting the broad spectrum of Faubert's Parisian acquaintances, Gardiner and her fellow Haitian critics Ghislain Gouraige and Raphaël Berrou concur on the importance of well-known white lesbian writers – including de Noailles, Renée Vivien, and Colette – as Faubert's personal and literary influences. Gardiner also writes that Faubert engaged in a number of love affairs with her Parisian acquaintances, but she never reveals the gender (or other) identity of these lovers.

Here on the *rive gauche*, wedged between the fetishization of black Antillean culture enacted in the *bals* and an overwhelmingly white Paris Lesbos, Faubert began to write erotic poems to women. These poems are still "rainbow masked," as explicitly sexualized female bodies remain absent. But the mask slips away enough to reveal not only her family identity (no flower nom de guerre here) but the gender of the addressees inspiring her. The poems register no reaction in white lesbian circles; Haitian literary criticism systematically ignores them. Like the female bodies in her poetry, the once prize-winning Faubert became barely visible in Haitian letters. Gardiner's suggestive but vague descriptions of her female friendships and her remarks on the form – but not the content – of her female-dedicated poems stand as the most positive reactions by Haitian critics available. In the rare instances, many years following her death, in which Faubert's gynoerotic poems are commented on, they are immediately dismissed as inspired by "des petits riens," insignificant little nothings (women?).[20] Alternately, they are judged as tainted by pathological French influences, as when Gouraige notes the intertextual presence of "Renée Vivien whom Ida Faubert . . . half followed on her path of perverse and questionable loves."[21] Faubert has been excised from the emerging canon of Haitian literature, pushed to the margins where she remains virtually forgotten. Swathed in "the latest fashion, signed by famous Parisian designers and . . . jewels which . . . before starring the lobes of her ears, the gestures of her hands, or the warm complexion of her décolleté, had been in the constellation of certain store windows on the rue de la Paix," she is celebrated as an object of the male gaze, and Laleau describes her as inspiring "trembling admiration."[22] But when she verbally constructs this same body as the object of *female* gazes in her poetry, she becomes barely visible. Or, as Kara Keeling writes of the black femme (and as I will explore more in the next section), she moves to "the edge line between what commonly can be 'seen' and understood . . . and what is neither seen nor understood (the Open, or when she makes visible a problem, the outside)."[23]

In important ways, this near invisibility is imposed on Faubert by combinations of homophobia and sexism still evident in the controversies surrounding the Obdumer-Lamers' marriage and Beenie Man's lyrics. At the same time, this president's daughter's situation is more nuanced than that; and it seems crucial not to map her as merely a victim of Southern underdevelopment of queer and feminist consciousness, as Santos-Febres's traveler does vis-à-vis Dominican *locas*. As with the coquettish, soldierly positioning of Valcin's roses, Faubert's slip into the shadows is also influenced by tactical obscurity, that is, by her own choices to keep representations of desire ambiguous and opaque. In my reading of Faubert's poetry I will concentrate, precisely, on how she literally writes same-sex eroticism in half shadow and under flower cover. But before I do so, I want to explore *why* she would write desiring bodies in semiobscurity by glancing at photographs of women of color taken at the turn of the twentieth century: photos of women of African descent posed in Parisian gardens and nightclubs, whose overexposed bodies suggest why outness looks different for brown women than for their white counterparts. I stumbled on these images accidentally, in search of photographs that do not exist or that I at least never recovered – pictures of Faubert or other Caribbean writers in Parisian lesbian company. Yet what I found along the way were images that explained why the ones I wanted to view were not available, why many already hypervisible and hypersexualized women of color would be reluctant to pose themselves as *lesbians*.

Behind the Palms:
Photographing Women of Color in Paris Lesbos

Paramaribo's *mati* grew up playing out their home lives in the public space of the yard; Ida Salomon, by contrast, was raised never to be out without cover, even in her family's gardens. Born in 1882 during her father's term as the president of Haiti, Ida spent her early childhood in the new, beautifully landscaped presidential palace at Turgeau, where Gardiner imagines her shielded behind "coconut trees with long tresses combed by the wind, banana trees swaying their large fans."[24] Yet in 1888 Lysius was driven from office while seeking reelection, and the family went into exile in Paris, where Ida resided briefly with her French mother's family before being sent to an exclusive convent school. There, cloister walls enforced the distance between this elite Haitian girl and the spectacle that the black female body had become in Paris.

In the 1880s, a new entertainment was sweeping Europe: the imperial exhibition, dramatizing the strange pleasures of colonialism from morning to night. The spring after Ida's arrival, the Exposition Universelle brought 32 million people to the French capital and doubtless would have interested her father, the organizer of Haiti's first national exposition. As its title proclaims, the Paris exhibit aimed to render *all things visible* to French consumers: electronic apparatuses, weaponry, food products, and horticulture from distant lands were accumulated and catalogued on European soil for inspection and judgment by French eyes. The black female body became one of the objects made visible here, as women of African descent were hired to pose nude to authenticate colonial representations. In the Jardin Zoologique d'Acclimatation, where lush flora imported from the colonies tropicalized a section of Paris, Prince Roland Bonaparte photographed black female nudes planted as part of the exhibit. One photograph shows three women posed together in front of an island of potted banana and coconut trees, ferns, bamboo, and other foliage (figure 3).[25] The two women on the sides stand with their arms draped over the shoulder of the woman in the middle; the line of the upper arm of the woman on the left points at the second woman's breast, while the woman on the far right lays her head on the middle figure's shoulder and holds her hand close to her pubis. As the garden itself is constructed from exotic colonial species to imagine a savagery fenced off from Parisian civilization, so the women's (homo)sexualized bodies, lined up in pseudoerotic poses at an opening in the shrubbery, appear as borders and orifices marking entry into the space of the savage. These females' public outing was an act not of symbolic liberation but of symbolic dehumanization.

This is what tropical lands like Haiti *look like*, the tableau tells viewers. Posing his subjects so ferns drape their hair and graze their buttocks, Bonaparte activates the metonymy implicit in the imperial land-as-woman metaphor: the fantasy that savage (in the etymological sense of "sylvan," from Latin *silva*) landscapes are inhabited by savage (in the figurative sense of "uncivilized") women, inextricably linked to this "natural" habitat and equally in need of Europe's civilizing mission. Bonaparte deploys metonymy and photography as realist rhetorical devices that simultaneously fabricate and authenticate relationships between their subjects. They are "technologically and ideologically aiming," as

Roland Bonaparte's photograph of three unidentified women
in the Jardin Zoologique d'Acclimatation, Paris, 1889

Griselda Pollock writes of photography, "at the 'reality effect' – that is, the dis-
avowal of their rhetorical character behind the illusion of direct reproduction,
transcription, and replication."[26] Pollock goes on to discuss how photography
creates the gendered subjects it professes to represent, much as the Jardin Zoologique fabricated the savage land- and womanscapes it professed to recreate:
"The visual signifier 'woman' is potent precisely insofar as the forms of representation, especially those associated with photographic processes, naturalize
their constituents, masking their constitutedness and presenting themselves
as mere descriptions of a neutral content. Women can therefore simply be seen,
that is, in 'images of woman.'"[27] But Bonaparte's photograph not only posits
that the gender of his women subjects is as real as the (artificially arranged)
banana trees they touch. His "images of woman" are also images of race and
sexuality, which assert that blackness and same-sex desire can be read on the
surface of the body in the same way that the flora in the background can be
identified by sight. Standing at and as the entrance to a fictively naturalized
garden, the black women's bodies in Bonaparte's photograph become signifiers
that metonymically bridge fictions of *féminité*, *négritude*, and *sexualité* with the
fabricated "real" or sensual world figured by the foliage around them. Made
visible here are not only the bodies themselves but the racial and sexual *difference* – from the invisible European, male, and "modern" photographer – that
they represent. An exotic landscape of potted banana trees is set up to materialize the "natural" difference between the savage tropics and civilized Paris, one
that French viewers are cued to see as real; at the same time, an exotic human
geography of paid primitives is arranged to materialize the "natural" difference
between primal black and modern European (wo)man that viewers are cued to
accept as equally real.[28]

   Adding to the reality effect through scholarly intertexts, the women's stances
in Bonaparte's photo evoke the three classic poses (frontal, side, and rear view)
of contemporary ethnographic photography. At the same time, not only their
nakedness but also the prominence of their hips and buttocks – which attract
more light than their faces – recall ethnography's reliance on the black female
sexualized body to define race as a visible property. As Debra Willis and Carla
Williams note in *The Black Female Body*, Bonaparte's Jardin Zoologique series
references one notorious ethnographic subject in particular: Saartje Baartman,
painted in 1815 in, and as part of, the landscape of the Jardin du Roi.[29] This
mixed-race South African woman, displayed as a curiosity for English and
French audiences who paid to see her steatopygia (fatty deposits on buttocks

and hips) and extended labia minora ("Hottentot apron"), became one of the nineteenth century's most visible images of sexualized Africa. Her billing as the "Hottentot Venus" crystallized the double function of her exhibition: to invent Africa (Hottentots) through fictions of gender and sexuality (Venus), and to do so in European terms (Hottentot, the moniker bestowed on Africans by Dutch settlers; Venus, a classical European figure of womanhood and sexuality). Her reifying visibility reached its height when after her death her genitals were dissected, preserved, and referenced in scientific journals "documenting" the racial difference concretized in the excesses – the large buttocks and labia minora – of the sexualized black female body. The surfeit present in (scientists' drawing of) Africanized reproductive organs was, French researchers argued, proof of the dark race's stunted evolution. Noted case studies of Baartman, including paintings in the Jardin du Roi that Étienne Saint Hilaire and Frédéric Cuvier included in their *Histoire naturelle des mammifères*, publicly envisioned black female sexuality as a test site for determining the boundary between human and simian, civilization and barbarism.

The clasped hands-to-pubis poses of Bonaparte's image also evoke another body newly visible in Paris: the *saphiste* or *lesbienne*. In 1885, the criminal anthropology student and future colonial military leader Julien Chevalier published the first French-language medical thesis on so-called sexual inversion. In this pseudoscientific work, Chevalier creates a "reality effect" for a new sexual species using the same rhetorical strategies deployed to imagine the colonized world. Like the later work of Havelock Ellis (who cites Chevalier), his *Sexual Inversion* draws on ethnographic uses of iconography, including detailed descriptions of women's oversized sexual organs, to depict the female body as the bearer of tangible signs of "inverted" sexuality.[30] Inverted women are identified with "clitorism," an enlarged clitoris that makes their genital sex simultaneously female (vagina) and male (clitoris as small penis, inserted into lovers' vaginas). Drawing the same conclusions from this clitorism that other scholars did from the so-called Hottentot apron, Chevalier pronounces these women's bodies and sexual appetites "beyond measure."[31] In so arguing, he joined a community of European and North American scholars who implicitly and explicitly linked race and sexuality by depicting both exotics and inverts as literally, physically *too much*.

Sexology emerged at the turn of the twentieth century in the works of European and American researchers attempting to document the natural, genetically determined bases of "normal" (heterosexual, penis-vagina intercourse) and "abnormal" (same-sex, as well as clitoral, anal, or nongenital) sexual behaviors. This field of study shared with ethnology a rationalization of biological determinism and a belief in the inherent dangers of "savage" and "hysterical" biologies. Emerging sexologists systematically observed the external female genitalia of women of color and lesbians as topoi that, like tropical landscapes, exceeded and required white men's control. Drawing on French scientists' studies of Baartman's labia minora, the German gynecologist H. Hildebrant posited that the Hottentot apron led to those "excesses . . . called lesbian love." Similarly, in the findings of the American scholar Perry Lichtenstein, an "abnormally prominent clitoris" designated female homosexuality "particularly . . . in colored women."[32] The attention drawn to the prominent buttocks and well-defined pubes that occupy the exact center of Bonaparte's photograph, coupled with their association with Baartman's infamous Hottentot apron, have a striking effect. The pose of these hips materializes an imaginary contiguity not only between woman and nature but between ethnography and sexology. In purporting to discover this biology/destiny, both rhetorics in fact created anatomical and ontological difference by "excessorizing" the reproductive body of the racialized, sexualized subjects they claimed to merely represent.

The savage state of the landscape in which Bonaparte poses his subjects — fabricated *nature à l'état brut* (brute nature) literally looming over their shoulders, larger than their human presence — also visualizes sexologists' conflation of sexual inversion and racial inferiority as conditions that, like nonurban or nonagrarian landscapes, they considered primitive and regressive. Chevalier repeatedly imagines lesbians organized into sorts of exotic tribes. Marked by tattoos, gathering in parks for vigorous open-air sports, and led by "priestesses of this new cult," *lesbiennes* (he finds) are stricken with a "manie d'exotisme" that leads them to occupy savage spaces within the civilized capital.[33] In fact, he concludes, most lesbian prostitutes are foreigners, come to French soil (like the Exposition Universelle's posed primitives) to make money selling their bodies.[34] So lesbians appear foreign and foreign women appear to have a tendency toward lesbianism; the sapphist is a savage and the savage is a sapphist: this circular imagination continually relinks ethnicity and sexuality in ways made visible in the Jardin Zoologique photograph. Like the "ambiguous sphinx" Chevalier finds in the Bois de Boulougne, the *saphistes de couleur* Bonaparte creates through his lens are invented as a boundary between Parisian civilization and its other.[35] Their too large, too dark, and too visible hips and sexuality prevent these women from exiting this tightly closed garden and entering the turn-of-the-twentieth century France displayed at the exposition.

As a daughter of the elite, adolescent Ida was expected, indeed pressured, to distance herself from such spectacles of black female sexuality. Shortly after emerging from convent school, at that dangerous age when Chevalier believed many were initiated into the lesbian "cult," she was sent to Port-au-Prince to marry properly. When she returned in 1914 to live in Montparnasse as a new divorcée, the look of gynoeroticism in the City of Lights had changed dramatically. Faubert was redefining herself as an independent woman at a time when female same-sex relationships were emerging as an increasingly visible and tolerated option to compulsory heterosexuality in Paris: when, as the historian Christine Bard notes, women's literary circles, bars, and dances marked the opening of lesbian space that enjoyed a "dazzling visibility," one "that accords it a certain legitimacy – people talk of a sapphic fashion."[36] But as the adjective *dazzling* suggests – to be dazzled is, after all, to lose clear vision – lesbian subculture's visibility in fact constituted a strategic semivisibility: *garçonnes* (literally, female boys) and *femmes* in same-sex relationships shaped spaces not where they could be gazed on by all of Paris, but where they could see and recognize each other.[37] No open exposition grounds, these were the semiprivate, by-invitation spaces of living rooms, *bals*, and boudoirs.

Faubert did have access to such spaces; her time in de Noailles's salon afforded her chances to meet Colette and Lucie Delarue-Mardrus, among other women-loving women. Certainly many in her milieu were familiar with one of the most famous lesbian clubs in interwar Paris, Le Monocle. Made famous by Brassaï's nocturnal photography, this bar owned by Lulu de Montparnasse celebrated sexual inversion with song, dance, and drink. But while photographs of the club capture female subjects in an array of uniforms, ties, tuxedos, and evening gowns, they show little variation in their skin color. In contrast to Brassaï's contemporaneous, multiracial photos of the Bal Nègre, those of Le Monocle depict overwhelmingly white figures. Yet two rare photographs taken in the 1930s show a notable exception: a glamorous, lipsticked, brownskinned woman in a sheer evening gown, featured in two images on the arm of a uniformed white partner. In one shot, this subject appears surrounded by white females dressed in tuxedos, navy uniforms, and suits who sport the club's signature monocles (figure 4). From behind these glasses they look – not "straight" back, but at various oblique angles – at the camera's lens, returning and redirecting the photographer's gaze to challenge who controls visions of female gender and sexuality.

In sharp contrast to the pretense of wild nature in Bonaparte's photo, the setting here announces and elaborates its own artificiality. Clubgoers pose in

"Le Monocle," Paris. Photograph,, c. 1930

front of a trellis (a structure for redirecting natural growth) woven with syn-thetic vines and hung with framed photographs, reproductions of the natural world (of flora and humans) whose artifice backs up the subjects' forays into self-fashioning. Art is nature and art is better than nature here, offering an *alternative* reality effect. Or better, as Judith Halberstam puts it in a discussion of *Paris Is Burning*, an effect not of the real but of *realness*, which "is the way that people, minorities, excluded from the domain of the real, appropriate the real and its effects."[38] Adding to the power of the appropriated and the fabricated, clothing rather than nakedness signifies on gender and sexuality. The tuxedoed and gowned subjects model female masculinity, female femininity, and desire between the two with a sophistication that Bonaparte's naked primitives could never exemplify. Amid smiles and dancing, the gender transgression of wearing and being photographed in aristocratic masculine dress and military uniform playfully yet seriously claims power for these alternatives to hegemonic femi-ninity and dominant masculinity. The monocles looking back at the camera's lens, the one element of dress that all (but two) of the photographed share, play with reshaping not only the patriarch's gaze but also his class privilege – the monocle is, after all, a masculine and aristocratic accoutrement (famously les-bianized by Lady Una Troubridge).[39]

   Only one figure looks away from the lens here: the lone woman of color, not wearing a monocle. Cloaked in a spectacularly feminine, elegantly Euro-pean dress that outfits her as a different species from the naked females in the Jardin Zoologique, the gender transgression this *femme* seems empowered to perform is not dressing like a man but dressing like a modern Western Euro-pean woman. That is, instead of problematizing the normative relationship between (female) sex and (feminine) gender, her self-presentation problema-tizes the normative relationship between (white) race and (feminine) gender. The question her dress raises as provocatively as a skirt is not whether or not a female can be masculine, but whether a black and same-sex loving female can be feminine and desirable by European standards. In this she contests and revisions two tenets of the pseudoscientific reality effected by sexology – the universality of black unfemininity and feminine lesbian unattractiveness. Chevalier posits black femininity as a biological improbability because "the characters that mark the . . . feminine type attain complete development only in the races and classes that are most elevated and most civilized," while Ellis marks feminine lesbian attractiveness as a biological improbability because "womanly" lesbians are "not usually attractive to the average man . . . not very robust and well-developed, physically or nervously."⁴⁰ In his commentary on Le Monocle, Brassaï renders such feminine subjects invisible when he remarks that "a tornado of virility has gusted through the place and blown away all the finery, all the tricks of feminine coquetry," producing masculine females who he imagines will seem to viewers "as exotic as if they were of pygmies or Zulus."⁴¹ Yet the brown wearer of the evening gown seems alluringly posed to reverse this process – to distance herself from Zulification via the tricks of feminine coquetry. In this beautiful reversal, she performs what Keeling, in her discussion of (non)images of queer black femininity in *The Witch's Flight*, calls the *black femme function*: "Challenging affectivity to recognize the Black in the black femme, the appearance of the black femme makes visible that the set of what appears as black is problematic. Similarly, wherever and whenever she is visible, the black femme reveals that the set of what commonly appears then and there as 'woman' and the set of what commonly appears as 'lesbian' are problematic."⁴² In such a moment of visibility, Le Monocle's brown *femme* potentially stands alongside its *garçonnes* in radically undermining congealed, hegemonic versions of gendered and sexual "realities."

Yet this brown feminine disruption remains chiefly at the level of potential in this photo, since in fact this figure does not stand at all. Her position below her partner's chair and the aversion of her gaze undercut her impact in the shot, creating her absorption into a white lesbian scene. Unlike the other evening-gowned patron (whose pale dress is fully displayed blending in with her fair skin), the brown *femme* neither looks at the camera nor has her body fully in the shot. Both in face and body, she is the least visible figure. Most of the chief signifier of her racial difference – the expanse of her dark skin – remains unseeable. Her belonging to this scene appears contingent on her looking like European femininity and looking at European masculinity: that is, on her gazing up at a white partner in a faux uniform. Apparently kneeling, she clutches her partner's chair to maintain a precarious position staring at her/him while she/he stares blankly beyond. If the viewer turns her or his gaze to these off-center figures, we see a brown woman, someone who looks like a colonial subject, remaining literally beneath and unseen by a partner in uniform, someone who looks like the colonizer. Their poses suggest much about the complicated gender and racial politics of Paris Lesbos: about how French *garçonnes* and *femmes* disrupted the heteropatriarchal nature of traditional European gender without necessarily putting pressure on its colonial and white supremacist natures. At the level of the brown woman's shoulder, centered in front of the pillars, sits the subject whose gaze most directly meets the viewers' – a female in a navy uniform and monocle. While for a French lesbian such costuming bespoke the postwar sailor vogue in male and female same-sex loving venues, for a Haitian it might recall nothing so much as the uniforms of the U.S. navymen who, along with Marines, occupied Haiti for nearly twenty years (1915–34). The trappings of powerful European masculinity are not erotic for everyone, and perhaps this kind of fetishization of monocles and military uniforms makes visible something of why Faubert and other women of color are rarely seen in Paris Lesbos either desiring or embodying its alternative genders.

Neither the shots in the Jardin Zoologique nor those in Le Monocle are "really" pictures of Faubert, nor of people she ever met or even saw in Paris. Nonetheless, I have come to see them as representing her milieu in some way. Where the former makes too visible the dangers of outness in a world of overexposed black female sexuality, the latter visualizes the precarious position of the *étrange* (foreign or queer) femininity that Faubert developed to recloak and reshape a body for whom *nature à l'état brut* had become a trap. Floridly feminine and overflowing with imaginary flowers, her poetry takes up the unrealized potential of Le Monocle's brown *femme* as it elaborates a similar, pointedly artificial gender and sexuality that, like the club's vines, remake nature – and, like an evening gown, conceal more than they reveal, self-consciously shielding the speaker's vision of her beloved under flower cover. Under this cover, the woman of color can center her same-sex desire while also strategically veiling it. The poems that Faubert dedicates to women are slight, sonnets and rondels draped in creeping vines and shrouded in darkness, in which racialized gender becomes so hazy it no longer fits into any recognizable (uni)form. Like photographs taken in half light, they blur the lines intended to construct gender and race and replace the reality effect with a *poetics of the blur* in which the brown *femme* develops her own gaze.

In a Marvelous Garden: "Je Voudrais Demeurer . . ."

In 1939, the poems that Faubert had been writing and publishing since 1912 were collected in a monograph entitled *Coeur des îles* (*Island Heart*), published by Éditions René Debresse in Paris. The anthology begins with a dedication to "Madame Amy NICOLET, the incomparable interpreter 'without whom my verse would be only what it is,' with all my affection."[43] In his preface, Jean

Vignaud backhandedly praises her: "One is surprised, reading such poems . . . to learn that the author belongs to an old African race, so much grace, subtlety, and measure is there in her verse. Love, in her work, takes a form neither savage nor fierce; on the contrary, it is full of reserve, at once secret and heartbreaking."[44] Voicing this secret love, *Island Heart* contains three types of poems dedicated to female addressees: those for her daughter (collected in the section "Poems for Jacqueline"), those explicitly dedicated to women (assembled in "Rondels and Songs"), and poems unmarked by gender in which the interlocutor can credibly be interpreted as a woman. Perhaps Faubert's most complex and subtle poetics of desire appear in the last of these, poems that carefully navigate the relentless masculines and feminines of the French language to leave the gender of the addressee undetermined. Scrupulously composed with the precise rhythm, rhyme, and syntax that French form proscribes, these verses still manage to seep outside the confines of a reality effect positing that everyone must have a clear sex, gender, and race. What would happen (they ask) if bodies could mean *differently*, dramatizing island hearts rather than dark skins?

One of these shadowy portal-sonnets, "Je voudrais demeurer . . ." ("I Wish to Remain . . ."), stages its indeterminacy in an imaginary garden in which an equally imaginary interaction between a speaker and an addressee unfolds.[45] It begins:

> Je voudrais demeurer une heure auprès de vous,
> Au jardin merveilleux que mon esprit suppose . . .
> Le soleil s'éteindrait, là-bas, au couchant rose,
> Et les jasmins s'effeuilleraient sur nos genoux.
>
> [I'd like to remain an hour beside you
> In the marvelous garden my spirit imagines . . .
> The sun would extinguish itself there in a pink sunset
> And jasmine shed their petals on our knees.]

Far from posing for a photograph, this provocatively slight quatrain performs a disappearing act. The poem takes place *nowhere*, in a marvelous garden no map can locate. Yet this lyrical garden resembles somewhere described in an earlier poem: the sunset-lit, jasmine- and rose-laden Haiti of "Tropical Night," the volume's opening poem. Never effecting a "real" Haiti, however, Faubert instead conjures a nameless Haiti of the imagination—one created by a woman of color's *esprit* and words, rather silently represented by her body. In this tropical space, the presence of the woman of African descent as the imaginative creator rather than an object of study aestheticizes an other's geography, one in which nationality and race, gender and sexuality might be configured differently. Or, as Keeling writes of black femme space and time, the marvelous garden opens "a portal to a reality that does not operate according to the dictates of the visible and the epistemological, ethical, and political logics of visibility" that reify the black, the woman, and the lesbian.[46] This portal is signaled on the page by the undefined space of the ellipses, which follow (but do not conclude) the second line and the phrase "marvelous garden that my spirit imagines. . . ." Anything could happen here, hint their drips of ink.

This poem also has *no body* in it. The first line begins with *je* (I) and ends with *vous* (you), but no information is given to identify or embody either the speaker or the addressee. The sexualized woman of color's body – as codified by ethnographic and sexological markers of excess – refuses to enter the picture. The body parts referred to, particularly *genoux* (knees), are gender and racially unmarked ones symbolically (though not physically) distant from the buttocks and pubes on which Bonaparte's photography overfocused. Without grammatically or physically sexing her poetic subjects or identifying them in dedication, Faubert still obliquely feminizes I and *you*, however. The poem's speaker speaks as *to* a woman, that is, the speaker uses the formal second-person pronoun *vous* that Faubert reserves exclusively for female interlocutors (including her daughter Jacqueline). The speaker also speaks as *of* a woman: the emphasis on images of softness (flower petals, the cicada's song) and a complete absence of conventional images of virility obliquely inscribe femininity without naming it. Taken together, these elements *suggest* the addressee may be a woman while *refusing* to gender this person. The problematic (dis)location of setting and addressee come together in the stanza's final line, "And jasmine shed their petals on our knees." Beginning with a copula but obscuring the coupling that occurs here, this line writes a vanishing act: both flowers and body appear only to dissolve (as jasmine lose their petals) or to be covered over (as petals blanket the laps of both speaker and addressee). Though the addressee's body is outlined, its outline is never filled in. So while the first quatrain "seems to be" a portrait of Haiti and "seems to be" a portrait of a woman of color loving another woman, those marks that effected realities had invented as visible signifiers of places, sexes, races, and sexualities refuse to appear.

Yet this vanishing act, as if protesting the woman-loving woman of color's need to mask herself, leaves traces of her sexualized body and its erotic en-

counters. Faubert's soft, spreading flowers – bursting jasmine stripping its
petals into the speaker and the addressee's laps in the first stanza and open
roses linked to the open mouth of the addressee in the third stanza – recall
the floral-vaginal imagery abounding in the poetry of Paris Lesbos, including Gertrude Stein's roses and the roses, lilies, and violets of the poet often
cited as Faubert's influence, Vivien.[47] The suggested floral-vaginal comparison of the first stanza is evoked both via contiguity, the closeness of the stripping jasmine to the speaker and the addressee's laps, and via similarity, the
resemblance between open petals and open labia. The addressee's sexuality
is called up not only by metonym and metaphor but also by the part of the
body where the flowers fall, "on our knees." While white female nudes were
routinely painted and photographed with knees pressed together to simultaneously dissimulate and indicate sexuality, Henri Toulouse-Lautrec's series
"Les amies" draws on this cliché to signify lesbianism through the crossed and
touching knees of the embracing prostitutes he paints. More subtly, though,
the sound play suggested by *genoux* (*je/nous*) also marks Faubert's poem with
the "homo" erotics of melopoeia. As noted earlier, the sonnet's first line begins with *je* and ends with *vous*, setting up the poem as space that connects
these two. *Genoux* not only concludes this enclosed quatrain by rhyming with
vous: it repeats and alters the linked words *je* (*v*)*ous*, removing the intervening
words to phonetically create the plural subject *je-nous* (I-we).[48] The reforma-
tion of words becomes a space of erotic connection, which bridges sounds and
pronouns to concretely gesture toward knee and knee, speaker and addressee
coming together. Here, physical repetition of the *same* – whether anatomically,
in four knees touching, or phonetically, through the recurrence of [ʒə] and
[u] – creates a poetic topos in which meaning is produced not through "naturally" bounded difference but through similarities consciously arranged like
poses.

Set nowhere and describing nobody (real), this sonnet also has no speech in
it. Having obscured bodies, the second quatrain moves to obscure language:

Vous me diriez alors, en ce moment si doux,
Le secret le plus cher de votre âme morose;
Et qu'ils seraient divins, par-dessus toute chose,
Les mots qui m'apprendraient vos espoirs les plus fous!

[You'd tell me then, in that moment so sweet,
The dearest secret of your morose soul

And how divine they'd be, above all else,
The words that would tell me your maddest wishes!]

The evocation of the unspoken "dearest secret" signals that something is being masked, but it again refuses to name that something. This secret seems to have to do with "perverse" or pathologized desires, "your maddest wishes," and seems to have to do with women, as suggested by sound play in the phrase "âme morose." *Morose* phonetically combines two words that appear before and after it in the sonnet, *mots* and *roses* ("words" and "roses/pink"): a coming together that sounds out a symbolically gendered pink speech, the speech of roses. At the same time "âme morose" echoes "amoureuse" (female lover), so that the line sounds like it references the secret of a female beloved — a suggestion amplified by the use of adjectives "sweet" and "dear" to describe the unquoted speech. Phonetically and descriptively gestured toward here, this desiring feminine speech remains outside the text; the addressee *would speak* in the marvelous garden but *does not* say anything in the poem. Her unreportable pink speech reads as part of Faubert's poetics of the blur, an aesthetics working with the knowledge that for a woman of color to attempt to reduce the erotic to a single sentence or gesture — to fit it into a quote or a photograph — is to lay her body and language open for the kind of appropriation that would de-eroticize it once again.

What happens in this space that cannot be captured by either vision or words? The imagery of the first tercet shows the speaker and the addressee coming out of the sapphic savage's poses to imagine new, fluid relationships between woman and garden when both exist for women's own use:

Les roses dans l'air pur ouvriraient leurs pétales,
Et votre voix, mêlée au chant clair des cigales,
Ferait plus doux encore le soir mystérieux.

[Roses in the pure air would open their petals,
And your voice, mixed with the cicadas' clear song,
Would make mysterious night even sweeter.]

"Roses in the pure air," "your voice," and the "cicadas' clear song" all merge in these lines in a moment of the orgasmic blurring of boundaries. Cunnic flowers and vocal chords open together, punctuated by the interlocutors' and cicadas' interweaving voices whose tones seem echoed in the continuing assonance of [o] and [u]. This oblique rediscovery of the female body as pleasure is also an oblique rediscovery of the dark body as pleasure. At the moment of *jouissance*, color evaporates: neither roses nor sky, speaker nor addressee, are described by tint, refusing any codified markers of racialization. At the same time, the evocation of the increasingly sweet *night* into which the climaxing voice opens calls up darkness as a topos of erotic possibility. A suggested erotics of the dusky — an erotics of the woman *of color* in a Haiti of the imagination — enters as the mysterious evening casts its shadows on the still obscured, orgasmic bodies. The sonnet recuperates brown women's erotic bodies as it does women-loving women's erotic bodies, masking them in a darkening marvelous garden rather than illuminating them in the Jardin Zoologique.

This gynoerotic, dark erotic *jouissance* constitutes a moment at which performances of power dissolve. The roses in the pure air, the voice lifted to the skies, and the singing cicadas are all elevated to the same level, their equivalent positioning concretized by the end rhyme between "pétales" and "cigales." Interpenetrating yet still distinct — the poem acknowledging both the joining and difference of roses and sky, voice and night — their spatial relationship is not one of domination but of fluid exchange. The *no place* of these lines is *women-loving women of color space*, where vaginal roses open together in the dark; and the *no place* of these lines is *utopia*, a gynoerotic Haiti that can be rendered only through the suggestive obliqueness of figurative language. As she sidesteps any realistic description of an erotic scene in a tropical garden, her imagery simultaneously masking and evoking the speaker's and the addressee's bodies, Faubert opens a space for Haitian women's shadowy limbs to move momentarily like petals and voices in the wind. Here the imagination of *nonrealistic metonymies* — the touching of roses, sky, and voice — vehicle the new physical, linguistic, and conceptual connections of Faubert's utopia.

But the final tercet leaves this utopia shrouded in ambiguity. The sonnet concludes:

Mon coeur serait à vous en cet instant de rêve
Et vous verriez mes yeux, dans le jour qui
s'achève,
Se mourir lentement dans l'ombre de vos yeux.

[My heart would be yours in that dream moment
And in the day that draws to a close,
you'd see my eyes
Die slowly in the shadow of yours.]

Like the garden itself, the slow death of the speaker's eyes invites multiple interpretations. *Mourir* or *die* can read as a poetic euphemism for *jouir* or *climax*, continuing the orgasmic union of the previous tercet. But a more literal, less optimistic reading also presents itself. Alone in a poem composed in the conditional, the last conjugated verb is a jarring present: "the day that draws to a close," thrusting the reader into the indicative, suggests that entry into the realm of lived experience would kill this vision. The slow death that the ends sonnet may reflect an ongoing placelessness that Faubert herself experienced, somewhere and nowhere between a heteropatriarchal Haitian elite and white Paris Lesbos. In the eyes of an intimate partner was perhaps the only space where *coeur* and *corps*, body and heart "belonged" ("serait à vous"), the space where Faubert fantasized that they might live and die.

The threat of death woven into the shadow of her summery utopian vision also suggests rifts in the vision itself – boundaries that the garden leaves in place and that risk enclosing the "I"/eyes again. A dream of liberation from the Jardin Zoologique, the rose-filled, isolated garden inhabited by and centering around individual subjects – *je* and *vous*, speaker and addressee cut off from all else – remains a dream of privilege. Faubert's esprit-invented garden is a space of luxury, of those who hire gardeners to perform the physical labor of weeding the landscape while they perform the intellectual labor of conceptualizing it. This garden is marked as elite not only by its exceptional or marvelous status but by its roses, the queen of flowers that do not grow wild in Haiti and so are favored in manicured aristocratic grounds. In the poem's final lines, the isolation of elitism limits the movement not only of those women-loving women of color left out of this dream moment but also of the poetic subjects left to sink into each others' eyes with no exit from a small, two-person garden into the more expansive space of Paris or Port-au-Prince. In such a closed topos, the possibility of recognizing the woman-loving woman of color as part of not just a couple but also of a *collectivity* stays in the shadows, and the elite emphasis on creating individual subjects becomes a part of the *se mourir* (dying) folded into Faubert's poetry. Faubert's marvelous garden, which perhaps looks like the presidential gardens in which she grew up in more ways than one, hides its own blackouts under flower cover; at the end of the sonnet's day, the poetics of the blur does not erase all boundaries in which women-loving women of color can be enclosed *and* enclose themselves.

Blue Countries, Beautiful Flowers:
"Rondel à Mme. R. G."

But Faubert is no tragic mulatta, and not all *Island Heart's* poems end in such rose-colored heartbreak. In his preface, Vignaud remarks that despite the sadness of some pieces and the general downtroddenness of her race, readers should not be surprised to encounter at other moments the "sweetness and charm that emanate from poetry written – or rather dreamed – by a woman who comes from the old island of St. Domingue."[49] While Faubert favors weighty sonnets for ambiguously gendered poems like "I Wish to Remain . . . ," for more playful pieces – and for those explicitly dedicated to women – she chooses lighter songs and rondels. Like the scene in Le Monocle, these musical poems dance around and celebrate same-sex desires that sexology imagined causing only melancholy and anguish. Following the tradition of Sappho's monodic poetry, the rondels, written to be set to music, build on short, concatenated verses and repetitive rhyme schemes. According to A. J. Cuddon, "The most usual *rondel* form consisted of three stanzas working on two rhymes, thus: ABba abAB abba (B) [A and B represent repeated lines]; a thirteen line poem in which the refrain came twice in the first eight lines and the opening line was repeated as the last line."[50] When reading aloud or singing Faubert's rondels, readers mouth pleasurable connections between sounds and lines repeating, varying throughout the poem: her words and phrases play between "homo" and "hetero"-phony, between sounding alike and sounding different but always harmonious. This erotic sound play is also gender play. Rondels maintain shifting alternation between masculine and feminine rhymes (mffm mfmf mffmm) and a return of the first line – consistently a description of its feminine addressee – at the end and in the middle of the following stanzas. This schema sets up a poetic structure built on liaisons whose pleasure lies in the feminine's systematic defiance of standardized norms, patterns, and positionings.

The second of *Island Heart's* rondels, simply titled "Rondel" and dedicated to "Mme. R. G.," sings just such defiant femininity:

Avec vos yeux ensorceleurs
Dont la sombre beauté nous hante
Vous avez la grâce attirante
Du plus charmant des oiseleurs
Vous ressemblez aux belles fleurs

Des pays bleus où tout enchante
Avec vos yeux ensorceleurs
Dont la sombre beauté nous hante
Pour calmer toutes les douleurs
Votre voix se fait caressante
Et l'on vois croit compatissante . . .
Mais vous causez tant de malheurs
Avec vos yeux ensorceleurs!

[With your spellbinding eyes
Whose dark beauty haunts,
You have the enticing grace
Of the most charming of bird catchers.
You're like the beautiful flowers
Of those blue countries where all enchants
With your spellbinding eyes
Whose dark beauty haunts.
To soothe all suffering
Your voice becomes a caress
People take for compassion . . .
But you cause so much heartbreak
With your spellbinding eyes!][51]

This slight verse succinctly sings the mesmerizing power of brown *femmes* gazing, rather than being gazed on – of a look that has the magical charm of not being intercepted by a male photographer (like Bonaparte) or a masculine partner (as in the Monocle photo). One phrase opens and rhythms the rondel, "with your spellbinding eyes." Moving between these eyes and the speaker's gaze at the addressee, Haitian femininity seems locked in a stare with (unmarked) femininity here – the speakerly voice consistently feminine and self-referential in Faubert's poetry, the addressee unmistakably feminized as well through the title *Madame* and feminine adjective endings. Building on this phrase, the first, later repeated couplet holds readers' focus on the interlocutor's eyes: bewitching eyes, big eyes whose magic and largeness effect the optical illusion of standing in for the entirety of the desired body, as the description never moves below her face. Faubert outlines no lower body to either overexpose or drape clothes on, whether military uniforms or evening gowns; so while the patrons of Le Monocle were reworking very specific signifiers of gender and power in the years during which she composed her rondels, this poem sings outside any such specificity. Instead, the addressee's bewitching eyes open on a scene of female desire "bathed in an unreal light," as Pierre Dominique writes of Faubert's short stories.[52]

What kind of magical womanness bewitches the speaker? Still in the realm of spectacle, the dark-eyed beauty's gender offers more complexity than the brown woman's carefully composed *feminité* in Le Monocle. Neither completely that of the *garçonne* nor that of the femme, this charmer's look dances between masculinity and femininity. The first stanza compares the addressee to an *oiseleur*, a bird catcher, evoking Guy de Maupassant's poem of the same name in which love is personified as a man shooting phallic arrows into cunnic bushes of birds.[53] But in the next line, *oiseleur* is rhymed with *belles fleurs*—"beautiful flowers" that echo the stock floral-cunnic imagery of Paris Lesbos and Faubert's garden poems. The addressee's charm also moves between here and there, between Paris and Haiti. The evocation of flowers continues:

> You're like the beautiful flowers
> Of those blue lands where all enchants
> With your spellbinding eyes
> Whose dark beauty haunts.

Composed in Paris, the poem's vision seems to creep south in the opacity of the addressee's "dark beauty": the enchantress's round black eyes take the shape and color traditionally associated with Haiti, the black island republic. At the same time, the blue of the lands that the addressee "looks like" evokes not only the Caribbean sea but also Faubert's repeated descriptions of Haiti as a landscape encircled by compelling, even dangerous blues—"that implacable blue of hot lands," as she writes in one story.[54] The aesthetic imperative of Paris Lesbos was to evade French heteropatriarchy by looking like someone, somewhere else *European*: whether like contemporary sailors or aristocrats in Le Monocle, or like long ago, far away Sappho in the poetry and salons of Vivien and Natalie Barney. But while similarly calling on the imagination to remap female erotic possibilities, Faubert's eye-reflected Haiti calls up another island in another, *postcolonial* sea through which Caribbeans could reroute fluid desires. Yet even her Caribbean rerouting refuses straightforwardness. This bodyless feminine subject with phallic and cunnic associations, this raceless beauty with black and blueness clinging to her charm, softly blurs all edges of the "real"—blurs the edges of *woman* and *Caribbean*, making them too hazy for any exoticizing gaze to penetrate. This is Faubert's magic trick.

But Faubert was not the only same-sex loving woman of African descent in interwar Paris to sing of Haiti as a *pays bleu*, a blue country. Josephine Baker, in her famous moment in *Zouzou* (1934), sings longingly in "Haiti":

> Oh, beau pays bleu
> Bien loin, bien loin sous d'autres cieux
>
> .   .   .   .
>
> Oui! mon désir mon cri d'amour
> Haiti
>
> [Oh, beautiful blue country
> Far, far away under other skies
>
> .   .   .   .
>
> Yes! My desire, my cry of love
> Haiti].[55]

The scene mesmerized viewers by its outrageous staging: at first surrounded by beautiful women gesturing upward to her, Baker sings sexily perched in a giant cage and dressed in fluttering feathers, a caught bird offered up by seductive bird catchers. Is this what Faubert imagines her *oiseleur* can catch? Undoubtedly, la Baker was Paris's most visible, fantastic black female presence during many of Faubert's years there. While her spectacular visibility – dancing "African frenzy unfurled in the cubist décor of a nightclub," as the Martinican writer Jane Nardal describes her, and swathed in costumes like the famous Folies Bergère banana skirt – was created by staging sparklingly stylized primitivism and hyperheterosexuality, she was also one of many African American expatriates in the City of Lights involved in same-sex relationships.[56] Her famous female lovers included Colette and Bricktop (Ada Smith), the cigar-smoking African American owner of a self-named Montmartre club.[57] Famous for its African American jazz luminaries and artistic and/or wealthy white patrons, Bricktop's was a place in which elite West Indians were less likely to appear even than at Le Monocle. Certainly, many aristocratic Haitians recoiled from Baker, jazz, and other fetishes of French negrophilia out of the romantic aspiration to Europeanness that Faubert's friend Jean Price-Mars called "collective bovarysm."[58] Caribbean Parisian feminists like Nardal, however, voiced more nuanced concerns about the spectacle that Baker and other African Americans offered the City of Lights. In her discussion of Baker's feathers and bananas in the essay "Exotic Puppets," Nardal protests how the ever-desiring, ever-colonizing white male gaze swallows such performers, reinventing Bonaparte's primitivist clichés for a new century: "And the blasé artists and snobs find in them what they seek: the savorous, spicy contrast of primitive beings in an ultramodern frame."[59]

Faubert's contemporary, much more oblique reference approaches Baker's fabulous sexuality from a different angle. The poet's imagination seems piqued not by the weight of white male eyes planted in front of the stage or screen but by the possible pleasure of desiring, beautifully dark female eyes approaching more stealthily (as bird catchers will). Baker might look alluringly different to Caribbean women, Faubert's gesture toward her suggests, if they imagine that her hypersexuality is staged not (just) to titillate a white male gaze but also a brown female gaze – if they imagine that the feathers and bananas meant to turn women of African descent into objects of colonial consumption could be reappropriated for other erotic uses. While heterosexual plots dominate *Zouzou*, Faubert's evocation of the film stirs other possibilities. What if a brown feminine bird saw herself desired by a female bird catcher? Or if she found in the eyes of a female beloved the blue country that she calls her love, her only desire? This would be the kind of "out-of-field" space in which Keeling imagines black femme desire to circulate provocatively: a space of otherly framed *realness* in which bodies reified by dominant epistemologies of visibility reposition themselves in ways that cannot quite be seen by Eurocentric, heterocentric gazes yet that hover provocatively in the shadows – much as Baker's song shadows this poem without directly erupting into it. [60] Echoing but never naming *Zouzou*, Faubert's out-of-field desire hazily "enchants" readers with dark, flowery alternatives both to Le Monocle's insistent whiteness and to Caribbean feminism's unselfconscious heterocentrism; the *pays bleu* to which she dreams of rerouting Haitian female desire at once navigates a sea a continent away from Lesbos and suggests provocatively erotic points of contact with other blue(s)-singing brown women in the Americas.

Yet gazing at this arrow- and flower-decorated dark beauty, at the Haiti reflected in Paris (Noir), the speaker is not simply seduced by it. She clearly wrestles with its charm, mistrusts it from first line to last. The final stanza begins its feminine rhymes with a caress ("caressante"), but goes on to hedge that the addressee seems compassionate – "compatissante . . . ," writes Faubert, ellipses hinting at much left unsaid – "But you cause so much heartbreak / With your spellbinding eyes." Starting with locked eyes and ending in a rhyme pairing *ensorceleurs* and *fleurs* with *malheurs*, the light poem builds to a more ominous spellbinding that leaves readers to question what kind of power this *femme* is working with. "Vos yeux ensorceleurs" eventually sound related to the *sorciers* (sorcerers) haunting Faubert's short stories, Vodoun practitioners Faubert imagines engaged in fantastic witchcraft, frequent zombie making, and other *malheurs* (misfortunes). When her women characters deal in Vodoun, the spells that they combat or contract always involve struggles for sexual power. One such struggle emerges in "A Strange Story," a tale of the Haitian godsisters Mina and Lélia, raised together as best friends in the latter's family home.[61] Unbeknown to his family, Lélia's country gentleman father secretly heads a *humfort* (Vodoun temple) in which he initiates young women first as priestesses, then as lovers. Struck by Mina's budding beauty, he stages the girl's death at age ten and then turns her into a zombie, the better to hide her at the *humfort* until old enough to bed. Compulsory conscription into heteropatriarchy so emerges as a force that steals girls' souls, zombifying them by the time they reach sexual maturity. When his wife finally finds out about his actions after his death she intervenes, hiring a roots doctor to partially revive the zombie and secreting her off to a convent in Paris. Soon after she herself falls ill from remorse and charges Lélia (unapprised to this point) with finding Mina and making amends. The horrified Lélia does just that, seeking Mina out in her Parisian convent where Lélia waits, blind with anguish, until there appears before her "A young woman? No. A strange form . . . eyes sunken and without flame."[62] She passionately and lovingly throws herself at Mina's feet, bathing her hands in kisses until Mina bends down toward her and "Lélia, raising her head, found fixed on her two burning irises that extinguished themselves as quickly as they lit."[63]

Where the patriarch's violent desire turns Mina into both zombie and exile, Lélia's gaze – fresh from Haiti, in service of feminine solidarity – reanimates her for at least a life-changing moment. Read in dialogue with Faubert's rondel to spellbinding eyes meeting hers in Paris, this "Strange Story" raises charged questions. Is the addressee's gaze charming the speaker with the left-handed magic that makes a Haitian woman's body "prisoner of unknown forces" – or is it, like Lélia's, the right-handed magic that frees her?[64] More metaphorically, would being identified by her sexuality, as any particular kind of person's sexual object – no matter whose, no matter whether elite man or dashing woman, white lesbian or African American bulldagger – always seem like a *malheur* to her, a reduction and appropriation of her complexity? Or could being seen as a same-sex loving *Haïtienne* prove a reprieve from the gendered and sexual constraints she is born into as a member of the postcolonial elite, something "to soothe all suffering," to release her from her gilded cage into "beautiful flowers"? "Rondel à Mme. R. G." seems pleasurably, painfully drawn back and forth between these two possibilities, the speaker and the spellbinding addressee held in the interlocked gazes of desire and struggle that electrify the flow between them. The repetition of *spellbinding* becomes a kind of incantation that perhaps brings on the magical possession of falling into those eyes, perhaps resists it – and floats tantalizingly between the black and the blue of Faubert's always hazy, always indeterminate erotic vision.

Vodoun is not, of course, the art of zombie making. And if Faubert's stereotypically elitist, bovaryist vision of this belief system opened wider in her oeuvre (as in Price-Mars's), the powers of *yeux ensorceleurs* might look quite different.[65] They might look like the first laughing, then crying eyes of Ezili Fréda, the erotically powerful female lwa (spirit) whose "enticing grace," love of beautiful flowers and perfumes, and honeyed voice seem the reflection of the addressee's. Fréda is also a gazer at enchanting femininity, a lwa who, when possessing devotees, must be greeted with a mirror so that she can admire her image. One of many paths of the Ezili pantheon, she is also one of many whose "magic" or otherworldy power includes "making up" – that is, like a face in a mirror – the divine beauty of sexual and gender complexity. Ezili is the lover of La Baleine and other female spirits in certain emanations, especially Ezili Danto, and in other paths is androgynous.[66] These include Ezili Taureau, the Bull, whose name suggests the same connection to Dahomean Amazonian women layered into the African American term *bulldagger* – gesturing, not unlike Faubert's echo of Baker, toward overlap among Afro-Atlantic constructions of nonheteronormative female desire.[67] In spirit marriages Ezili weds women as well as men, and *Vodouisants* in same-sex relationships often burn candles to her (as same-sex lovers do for the fellow water spirit Motyo Ingi in Suriname). At once a force of nature and the patron of artifice – of powders and perfumes, art and music – Fréda in particular models an epistemology in which, as her feminine male devotees in the groundbreaking film *Of Men and Gods* express, remaking the gender and sexuality that dominant heteropatriarchy would assign to you is *natural*, not to mention lwa-like.[68] So if Faubert could reflect this spirit in the mirror of her art, Fréda's rosy beauty seems poised not only to confound the visions of the Jardin Zoologique and Le Monocle in her bejeweled gaze. More impressively, she stands provocatively placed to theorize the Caribbean power of the *étrange* (strange, foreign, queer) femininity that Faubert's poetics of the blur so florally and shadily unfolds. But again, the cage and caginess of this president's daughter's elite worldview leaves this more expansive possibility something that, like the addressee's dark beauty, only insistently haunts her blue countries, a strikingly absent presence.

* * *

> Planted with mango trees whose heavy fruit left a taste
> so strong you thought you would faint from pleasure, peopled
> with birds in shimmering colors, with its hibiscus bushes and their
> scarlet flowers . . . [it] seemed a paradise. . . . But you don't live
> long months in an island populated by legends, where mysterious
> stories circulate at night in the too heavy air . . . without one day
> realizing that they have left their impression on you.
> — Ida Faubert, "Ouanga"

The shadowy, present absence of colorful Ezili Fréda brings me back to the bright images of HGLA, to the flower-draped, rainbow-masked women posed in a manner both celebratory and secretive at Heritage of Pride. The rainbow covering their faces is of course a symbol of gay pride, as a page on the site explains. But the rainbow is also a world-making symbol in the Haitian imaginary, in Vodoun epistemology: Danbala/Ayida Wèdo, the rainbow serpent, the simultaneously masculine (extended) and feminine (coiled) symbol of the originary multicoloredness and gender multiplicity of the universe.[69] To understand the implications of the rainbow mask fully, viewers must understand both meanings; they must be able to look into the overlap and divergences in same-sex loving and Caribbean histories, the interlocking inventions of sexuality and race, to understand the problematics of visibility and the strategies of semivisibility for Haitian LGBTs. Indeed, as Byron Williams suggests, under centuries of attack, Afro-Atlantic religions' brilliantly tactical hiddenness to outsiders and expansiveness to insiders provided a powerful model for understanding the opacity of black Atlantic same-sex sexual formations. Like a *vèvè* it outlines a historically and geographically specific narrative of needing to protect embattled bodies and spirits, one that has nothing to do with the closet.[70] Yes, with decolonization and decriminalization Vodoun has become more public, but certainly not totally so — and perhaps it never needs to be to wield the cultural and epistemological power its practitioners are devoted to. The same might be the case for Caribbean blue countries in which women love each other.

At the end its French-language page of "coming out" stories, the HGLA Web site both solicits submissions and counsels in red capitals "DO NOT reveal your true identity if you are not comfortable."[71] While this page negotiates a culturally specific complexity around exposure, it also speaks to the trickiness of giving language to sexuality across a historically specific class spectrum. With tabs to coming out stories in English, French, and Kreyòl, the site notes that no one has submitted stories in the last of these. The languages of the diaspora and of an elite 10 percent are represented; the only language of 90 percent of resident Haitians is not. HGLA clearly wrestles with reaching across the class spectrum, featuring stories on cane workers and class analyses of the differences between elite, bourgeois, and poor Haitians' experiences of same-sex sexuality and what it means. But just as clearly this struggle remains unwon, and Haitian working classes are represented but do not represent themselves on the site. Why, indeed, would pride parades and cyberspace be their space, any more than Le Monocle would be blacks'? The LGBT rights model works not only from a Euro-American way of knowing visibility but also from a bourgeois construction of the empowered individual that means little to those whose dwellings have neither closets nor gardens. Faubert's marvelous gardens also hover in the background of this colorful site as a reminder of how stiflingly closed epistemologies of sexuality remain when implicit elitism remains unchallenged. To move into distant blue countries, imaginations of sexuality must not only play in the dark; they must dismantle presidential palaces and elite grounds that reinvent the colonial violence that first blacked out Afro-Caribbean bodies.

four

At the River of Washerwomen

Work, Water, and Sexual Fluidity in Mayotte Capécia's I Am a Martinican Woman

The agitation of the beaches, forgetful of all who climbed the coconut trees, once trying to reach out to Toussaint Louverture in the land of Haiti. The salt of the sea claimed them. The whites of their eyes are in the glare of our sun. We come to a halt, not certain what slows us down at that spot with a strange uneasiness. These beaches are up for grabs. The tourists say they own them. They are the ultimate frontier, visible evidence of our past wanderings and our present distress.

— Édouard Glissant, *Caribbean Discourse: Selected Essays*

Thought to be Martinique's most beautiful beach, Les Salines perches on the exposed, undeveloped sunny southern tip, near Ste-Anne. Multitudes of vendors stalk the strand in-season. To reach gay sands, park at the far end of the lot where a sign reads "Petite Anse des Salines." Plunge down the trail through thick woods and foliage to the beach. Clothing is not officially illegal in Martinique, although you wouldn't know it. Don't take shade under the machineel trees — they drop acid.

— Ed Salvato and Aefa Mulholland, "Top Ten Offbeat Gay Beaches"

Olivia, the lifestyle company for lesbians and the self-described leader in cruises and resorts for women, fêted its thirty-fifth year in 2008 with two birthday-themed Caribbean cruises. "Celebrate 35! Caribbean Dreams" and "35th Birthday Bash Caribbean" promised seven nights on warm Caribbean seas and seven days of turquoise waters, luscious beaches, and lesbians, all capped by an interlude of snorkeling and sunbathing on a private island in the Bahamas.[1] Olivia's year-long festivities celebrated not only the company's own success but the warm, watery ways in which Global Northern lesbians have become like the Caribbean Sea since the company first began sailing there in the 1990s. Like marine waters LGBs have become visibly and globally mobile, traveling on organized tours to gay-owned hotels with new confidence that the world has space for queers to move comfortably. Charting the world as an archipelago of queerness connected by a sea of new gay friendliness, Kenneth Kiesnoski proudly proclaims on Gay.com, "Grand Canary. Key West. Ibiza. Oahu. Phuket . . . a chain of gay-friendly island destinations encircles the globe"; he then happily notes that while "there has traditionally been one missing link – any Caribbean isle," this has changed dramatically since 2004.[2] In fact, in 2008 two Caribbean spots made the site's list of best offbeat beaches for gays, including Martinique's Les Salines. Underwriting this upsurge in mobility is a tide of lesbian and gay financial liquidity that has rendered queer tourism enormously profitable for Olivia and other gay tour organizers in the past fifteen years. As Jasbir Puar remarks of such travel trends, "The early 1990s are described as the golden age of the gay and lesbian tourism industry by travel providers, who ascribe this to the so-called gay marketing moment, when 'coming out' meant coming out in terms of purchasing power."[3] Kiesnoski credits the economic allure of gay tourist dollars and euros with pushing West Indians toward increasing tolerance of same-sex couples, making such travel look both financially and socially profitable. What's not to celebrate on "Caribbean Dreams"?

Olivia's Caribbean cruises luxuriously offer travelers access not only to private beaches but also to the private island of Half Moon Cay, purchased by Holland America in 1997 and billed as offering "everything you need for a day of play in paradise: a two-mile crescent of perfect beach; an interior lagoon; private beachside cabanas with butler service."[4] The "you" addressed here clearly does not include same-sex loving Caribbeans who, along with all residents, are barred from swimming, bathing, washing, fishing, sunning, or otherwise being on enclosed, privately owned beaches. On the way to such beaches, Olivia promises "you will find the comforts of home" including "24-hour room service, deluxe bathrobes, Egyptian cotton towels, salon-quality hair dryers, 24-hour front desk, laundry, pressing and dry cleaning service."[5] When passengers hand their clothes to this laundry service they add to the hundreds of thousands of tons of gray water (runoff from showers, laundry, and galleys) and toxic waste (from dry cleaning, photofinishing, and paint) that a single cruise ship dumps in the sea it travels through, continually poisoning waters, fish, and the "comforts of home" for women-loving women whose home is the region.[6] *Lesbian* and *gay* as transnational consumer identities are neither available nor attractive to millions of working-class Caribbeans who watch, wait on, and clean up after disembarking cruise passengers; like the manchineel trees that travel writers caution nudists against, resistance to northern gay consumerism stings here. At the same time, same-sex loving West Indians reclaim still uncaptured beaches and waters for their own play and profit—insisting, as Alexs Pate's characters do with the slim hundred yards of segregated beach where they swim in *West of Rehoboth*, that "they could enjoy it. Yes, Lord, the Atlantic was for them, too."[7] Carving out an erotic scene in Martinique, men cruise men at Les Salines and Fort-de-France Bay, while women throw parties for women at Rivière Salée.[8] Making money off the tourist scene in Guadeloupe, female vendors in Les Saintes arrive to offer Olivia cruisers "a good deal on a shell necklace or a delicious piece of tropical fruit!" in cleverly flirtatious-sounding ways.[9]

For West Indian women at Rivière Salée or Les Saintes, what does it mean to imagine that their sexuality is "like the Caribbean sea"—like the water around which they work, play, sell, flirt, hide, undress, haggle, and party on a daily basis? Just as tourism does not offer the same image of freedom to local *zanmi* that it does to queer cosmopolitans, the value of fluidity—the desire to be like the Caribbean—changes in islands on which, as Édouard Glissant suggests, the sea carries violent histories, present tensions, and contested futures. On beaches where tides cycle between enclosure and liberation, pollution and protest, the fluid may be less a space of physical and economic mobility than the shifting, ambivalent topos that ethnographer Kale Fajardo calls "crosscurrents." Conceptualizing the complex power dynamics of the maritime, Fajardo explains: "Oceans and seas are important sites for differently situated people—indigenous peoples, fisherpeople, seafarers, sailors, tourists, workers, and athletes. Oceans and seas are sites of inequality and exploitation—resource extraction, pollution, militarization, atomic testing, and genocide. At the same time, oceans and seas are sites of beauty and pleasure—solitude, sensuality, desire, and resistance. Oceanic and maritime realms are also spaces of transnational and diasporic communities, heterogeneous trajectories of globalizations, and other racial, gender, class, and sexual formations."[10] These crosscurrents offer an image of gender and sexual fluidity that "works" in the Caribbean: a wateriness that complicates as much as it liberates, whose myriad blues are colored as much by stark global economic realities as by individual promises of beauty and pleasure.

This chapter opens a historical perspective on such metaphoric and material blues through a reading of a novel written at an intersection of West Indian racial, economic, and sexual "fluidities": Mayotte Capécia's *Je suis Martiniquaise*, or I *Am a Martinican Woman* (1948). Sixty years before "Caribbean Dreams" set sail, Capécia became the first Afro-Caribbean woman to publish a novel in France, lucratively signing her nom de plume to a pseudoautobiography that narrates a *Martiniquaise*'s sexual and economic coming-of-age beside Caribbean waters. The protagonist Mayotte, a washerwoman who luxuriates in watching laundresses swim nude after work, explores her island's flowing waters as crosscurrents of many black female desires. Yet despite Mayotte's surface sunniness, the swells of her desire look different from, murkier than the turquoise tides advertised for cruise passengers. Capécia, herself a hotel employee, maid, and washerwoman, wrote from a class background resembling more that of Olivia's laundresses' than that of their patrons,' and she penned her novel to sell an image of female sexuality rather than buy one. So Mayotte's adolescent desire circulates among washerwomen before flowing outward in adulthood to a white French sailor, whose arrival offers Mayotte economic mobility and gifts French readers with a sexy allegory for the inevitability of colonial and heteropatriarchal seduction. Mayotte's sexuality *is* like two bodies of water, the Cambeille River and the Caribbean Sea; but this will mean less that it is free to move outside constraints and more that her Caribbean sexuality shares with these waters a complex history of flowing with and against colonial desires. As in Les Salines, sexual fluidity in Capécia's novel is neither crystal clear nor easily plunged into, as tourist brochures claim, but rather, as some tourists complain, choked in seaweed and other entanglements that render it both cloudy and rich. Reading for historically and culturally specific meanings of fluidity and/ as sexuality here brings to the surface the deep histories of tensions between Global Northern and Southern, bourgeois and working-class politics of desire, and magnifies why a tribute to lesbian liberation without "decolonial" imagination may offer little cause for celebration in the archipelago.

From *Femme de Ménage* to *Femme de Lettres*:
Naming the Martinican Woman

Mayotte Capécia was not born but made. Her self-creation as a literary figure emerges from a river of economically motivated fluid identities, names and occupations that changed throughout her life as she moved from Martinique to France, from cleaning woman to woman of letters. Capécia's lifetime of labor produced a variety of marks – black stains of manual work on white surfaces – that she afterward concealed. These range from chocolate drippings on white aprons at the factory where she had her first job (which her twin remembers her scrupulously washing off) and the dirty water of her laundry to phonetically spelled manuscripts of her novel's first draft (most of them subsequently destroyed) and grammatical exercises in which she "worked" her French (afterward discarded).[11] However, one object that consistently bore and erased the Martinican woman's labor was less tangible: her changing name. Discussing the poetics of cleanliness, Ann McClintock details the significance of boundary objects: "Domestic labor *creates* social value, segregating dirt from hygiene, order from disorder, meaning from confusion. The middle class was preoccupied with the clear demarcation of limit and anxiety about boundary confusion – in particular, between public and private – gave rise to an intense fetish for cleaning and a fetishistic preoccupation with what the anthropologist Victor Turner calls liminal, or boundary, objects. Servants spent much of their time cleaning boundary objects – doorknobs, windowsills, steps, pathways, flagstones, curtains, and banisters, not because these objects were particularly dirty, but because scrubbing and polishing them ritually maintained boundaries between private and public and gave these objects exhibition value as class markers."[12] The series of names taken by the author of *I Am a Martinican Woman* also serve as boundary markers – as signs that track her motion between the working and middle classes, between a hidden Martinican private life and the public life she would lead as a Parisian novelist. At crucial steps in Capécia's social transformations these names were, like doorknobs or curtains, ritually cleaned by their owner, purged of traces of her working past. Rather than serving to mark changes in marital status (as for a bourgeois heterosexual woman), her changing name became a Martinican woman's language of class and sexual *in-betweenness*.

On 17 February 1916, Emilie Céranus gave birth to the identical twins Lucette and Reine in Carbet, Martinique.[13] As Christiane Makward documents in her excellent biography of Céranus / Capécia, the girls were born to the market vendor Céranus and the married landowner Eugène Combette, who refused the girls his name or financial support. Following her daughters' birth, Céranus moved to Fort-de-France, and after four years of elementary education both girls left school to help her work in the market. In 1929, the mother died of a heart ailment she lacked money to treat, and the twins took on a variety of jobs to support themselves. They worked in the Didier chocolate factory, a cinema, a hotel, then took in sewing, ran a corner store, and opened a laundry in their home. The adult sisters maintained intense solidarity as they moved together between houses and jobs; they also forged support networks with female co-workers, meeting women who cared for Lucette's children on the line at Didier. Like the *mati's*, their consistent collaboration underscores how much working-class women's physical and emotional survival depends on the flexibility of female kinship and friendship networks.[14] At the same time, work in Fort-de-France allowed Lucette and Reine glimpses of a material existence outside this gynocentric economy of subsistence. In addition to providing them with working-class female friends, their status as favorites at Didier gained them entry to service jobs with local elites and wealthy visitors. Here, in a world of ostentatiously overlapping classes, they worked at the Hotel de Paix during the Fêtes du Tricentennaire du Rattachement de la Martinique à la France in 1936, participating in its lavish balls and fireworks and even catching the eye of Coco Chanel, who suggested they come to France to model.

New proximity to the wealthy also provided Lucette opportunities to ally herself sexually and financially with well-to-do men. At sixteen she became pregnant by an elite mulatto whose family financially supported its grand-child; three years later she entered a relationship with a Syrian businessman who fathered her daughter and rented the house in which she opened her laundry. In 1941, she met a French sailor named André who shipped out to Algeria just before their son's birth. In response to Lucette's unanswered requests for child support, he sent her a small sum and, in 1944, a copy of the memoirs of his stay in Martinique – dedicated "to Lucette in remembrance of our divine love" – that he had penned in transit to Algeria.[15] Following his departure Lucette began a relationship with another French seaman, the navy mechanic Albert Dupont, who proposed marriage and asked her to join him in France with the children to follow. To enter this marriage was, for Lucette, to enter another class construction of sexuality, since in the West Indies marriage is usually restricted to middle- or upper-class women.[16] Moving from

washerwoman to married woman meant a transition from the family structure that Glissant calls *l'étendue*, or extended family, to one he calls *filiation*.
The former (he theorizes) as a matrifocal network based on a plurality and the
permeability of friendship and kinship relations, while he sees the latter as a
rigid patriarchal organization particular to the bourgeois heterosexual nuclear
family and invested in the purity of family lines.[17] To "clean up" her family past
for this move, Lucette left behind both her sister and her mother's name, the
stigma of her illegitimacy. Visiting her father Combette, she convinced him to
authorize her to legally take his last name and in 1944 became Lucette Combette.

But when her ship arrived in Paris, her fiancé had disappeared without a
trace. Faced with providing for herself in foreign territory, Lucette, like the
majority of West Indian women in postwar France, found domestic work. She
used her position not only to earn her living but also to establish connections
that opened the door for another career change. Through one family who employed her, the attractive, outgoing maid made a contact at the up-and-coming
publishing house of Corréa. In 1947, she showed up at Corréa with a manuscript in hand. But it was not her own novel; what she presented to the publishers was the memoir André had composed about his time in Martinique and
subsequently sent her. Lucette was informed it would be impossible to publish
a Pétainiste's memoir in postwar France. Yet the editors stressed that they *would*
be interested in publishing the life story of a young woman from the exotic
new French overseas department of Martinique if she would undertake to write
her "own" memoirs. One editor even marked passages from André's manuscript
he found suitable to include in Lucette's rewrite.

Lucette Combette came to writing as she had come to laundry – as a job. This
new job involved whitewashing André's dirty laundry, rescripting portions of
his memoirs deemed appropriate by Corréa's editors to form the novel's second
half. For the first half, it also involved whitewashing Lucette's inconsistent
education so she could creditably straddle the divide between her working-
class past and her hopes for a bourgeois present. After long days of domestic
work, the elementary school–educated Martinican woman spent nights learning to write at the houses of more literate women friends, including her fellow Martinican Maddy Ciceron. These women worked her French, taking her
through writing and grammar exercises and helping her correct the childhood
scenes she was drafting. Of these early drafts, three fragments remain and are
reproduced by Makward: a description of her mother, a description of the vil-

lage of Carbet similar to that found in chapter 1 of I Am a Martinican Woman, and a description of fish vendors not included in the novel. These fragments' progression from run-on to standard sentence structure and from phonetic to standard spelling bears witness to the travail of writing. This memoir was not self-expression but bodily self-discipline: a job that required learning – in eighteen months – how to use pen and paper to "properly" form words and sentences and (as corrections on surviving pages attest) routinely cleaning up lapses of spelling, word choice, and sentence structure. In the end, the I Am a Martinican Woman that went to press in 1948 was a hybrid, multiauthored text. Its first part, which narrates the protagonist's childhood and adolescence, was composed by Lucette herself with the help of several ghostwriters. The second part rewrote André's manuscript almost verbatim, rescripting passages in the first person to recount the liaison between a Martinican woman and a French sailor. The fictively first-person-singular Martiniquaise's story is not a transcription of thoughts residing in an individual mind, then, but collective labor produced and marketed by a running together of Martinican and French, feminine and masculine voices. Even as Lucette's title promises to give speech to Caribbean femininity, the ensuing narrative underlines how and why a Martinican woman's work and sexuality are never completely her own story. This working-class, fluidly desiring Caribbean woman cannot speak as "a" unified subject not (only) because she is same-sex loving but (also) because she is poor.

The composite text was immediately accepted for publication. Lucette received an advance that she used to make her only return trip to Martinique to bring back her children. The pseudoautobiographical novel's cover showed a madras-coiffed, coquettish, hourglass-figured woman of color and was signed with a pen name: Mayotte Capécia. The first Francophone novel published by a Caribbean woman of African descent, it was received with overwhelming enthusiasm. "Mayotte Capécia is a Martinican woman, she has the color of one I'd say, at least the color we imagine for charming Martinican women – a very pretty café au lait," Jean Duché gushed shamelessly in an interview with the author. "This is the first time we have a woman of color novelist."[18] The novel was serialized on French radio, and the author – dubbed "the West Indian Colette" – gave a number of interviews in which the newly named Mayotte routinely fabricated stories about her own origin in a bourgeois, nuclear Capécia family; and about the origin of her autobiography, which she said she had been inspired to write one afternoon while watching snow fall in the Jardin de Luxembourg. Following positive reviews from literary figures like René Maran,

I Am a Martinican Woman was awarded the Grand Prix des Antilles, translated into German and Swedish, and slated to be made into a film starring Katherine Dunham.

I want to return to the invention of Lucette Céranus's third and final name, Mayotte Capécia, and the tactics and problems it suggests around enunciating an Afro-Caribbean female "self." Capécia was never straightforward in answering questions about the name *Mayotte*. In interviews, she vaguely responded to questions about her first name by remarking that in Martinique Mayotte was a nickname for Marie. While not explaining much (since her given name was not Marie), this trickiness does seem apt for the French Caribbean carnival figure whose name echoes hers. The Haitian novelist Edwidge Danticat describes carnival's multiply signifying lamayòt (la Mayotte):

> The lamayòt is a secret, a benign Pandora's box one willingly unveils for one's pleasure.
>
> Every Sunday afternoon during the carnival season, there would be a visit from someone whom I guess you would call a lamayòteur, usually a man walking from house to house with a box or a sack in which there was something children would pay a penny to have a look at. . . . I would watch the neighborhood children take turns peeking inside the sack or box and then listen to them describe what they had seen. Often the lamayòt was an interesting object – a large marble, a prism – but sometimes it was a small animal – a lizard, a frog, a turtle, or a snake, a marvel for city kids.
>
> Later I would notice that the word lamayòt was also used in a broader context in adult conversations. If someone tried to show you something too quickly, it was a lamayòt. If you were buying something sight unseen, you were getting a lamayòt. A too short rendezvous with one's lover was a lamayòt, as was a false personal or political promise.[19]

Capécia's prismatically colorful novel can be read not only as authored by a Mayotte, but as itself a lamayòt. Like the lamayòteur earning pennies, Lucette packages Mayotte's pleasurable "secrets" as a business strategy: she chooses writing the Caribbean woman's sexual and cultural "identity" as an alternative to other manual labor, one that earns her substantially more than most women of color in postwar Paris. While superficially submitting to norms of French grammar and French images of Caribbean women, this scribal labor allows her to simultaneously reveal the hidden realities – the inside of the box, the dirty laundry – of race, gender, and sexuality in colonial Martinique. Yet Capécia's text is also conscious that whatever look it can provide will always be "too short." Selling her novel to a heteronormative French reading public to earn the money to reunite with her children, Capécia can only offer glimpses of the fluid sexuality that must be teased out of the sea- and womanscapes her novel draws in such seductive colors. Becoming Mayotte Capécia, the author of I *Am a Martinican Woman*, she made up not only her own name but also her model of Caribbean womanhood – one more like a carnivalesque Pandora's box than a mirror of "true" identity.

Her fellow Martinican Frantz Fanon remained oblivious to this *lamayòtaj* when his scathing criticism in *Black Skin, White Masks* (1952) dealt a deadly blow to Capécia's literary career. His chapter "The Woman of Color and the White Man" discusses the second part of Capécia's novel (that is, the part rewritten from André's text). Here Fanon pens a harsh denunciation of the title character's "lactification complex," confusing her with the author and reproaching her for taking a white lover (although he himself had a white wife).[20] He interprets her choice to become a washerwoman as a symptom of her desire to bleach the race rather than as an economic strategy: "Since [Mayotte] could no longer try to blacken, or negrify the world, she was going to try, in her own body and in her own mind, to bleach it. To start, she would become a laundress."[21] How does laundry become a metaphor rather than a profession in his reading? Fanon not only overlooks the complex history of laundry in the Caribbean, where it became one of the most common and most physically debilitating ways through which women of African descent earned a living following emancipation. He never seems to have entertained the possibility of interviewing Capécia, part of a relatively small community of Martinican literati living in Paris, to determine her relationship to laundry or sexuality. (Of course, if he had, she might well have lied – Mayotte the *lamayòteuse* had an image to sell.) Fanon systematically refers to the author of I *Am a Martinican Woman* by her first and last name. When he writes such sentences as, "One day a woman named Mayotte Capécia, obeying a motivation whose elements are difficult to detect, sat down to write 202 pages – her life – in which the most ridiculous ideas proliferated at random,"[22] he takes for granted that writing constituted an occupation of leisure rather than labor, something she sat down "one day" to do. He also takes for granted that the signs *Mayotte Capécia* represent a gateway to who she really was, rather than a strategic invention.

His denunciation of this laundress's "choice" not only effectively silences

Capécia, who died penniless in 1955. It off-handedly trivializes the emerging corpus of Caribbean women's literature and stifles important questions about the sexuality of the woman of color, a subject Fanon professes to know nothing about in Black Skin, White Masks.[23] These questions arise from the contrasting foci of the novel's two parts. Fanon analyzes only the second, originally written by André and centered on his affair with Mayotte. But the longer first part narrates the protagonist's childhood and young adulthood in interwar Martinique and focuses on her relationships with a series of women who appear and disappear in her life: her girlhood crush on the laundress Loulouze, her admiration of her madras-clad mother, and her love-hate relationship with her father's beautiful lover Rènelise. The questions raised here: Why does this founding text of Caribbean women's literature begin with eroticism between *black women* that is then washed or written out? Why does sexual fluidity maintain such a tenuous position in this world of waters?

Same-sex sexuality does make one infamous, fleeting appearance in Black Skin, White Masks. Here, the West Indian "homosexual" joins the washerwoman as another historical personage that Fanon reduces to a symbolic figure. Both "mean" the alienation of the black Antillean in the doctor's seminal text. In his reading of I Am a Martinican Woman, the washerwoman is a whitewasher; conversely, in his later discussion "The Negro and Psychopathology," homosexuals are whitewashed. In a footnote to his discussion of psychosexuality and race, Fanon claims that homosexuality does not exist in the Antilles and that Caribbeans only become involved with these practices in Paris. He posits that *macommères*, Martinican males who dress and live as women, maintain a "normal" sex life; but "in Europe, on the other hand, I have known several Martinicans who became homosexuals, always passive."[24] The noun *homosexuals* can only appear without negation in conjunction with the noun *Europe* and the adjective *passive*, setting up same-sex sexuality as a symbol of West Indians' colonial relationship to France rather than an embodied, erotic practice chosen by Martinican men *and* women. The literal and material – the laboring and sexual bodies of *blanchisseuses* (washerwomen) and *macommères* – are eclipsed by the figurative, the washerwoman and the homosexual as symbols of Martinican pathology.

According to her sister Reine, Capécia died without hearing of Fanon. Since her death, Fanon has deservedly become one of the twentieth century's most recognized theorists of decolonization. I, however, want to give Capécia her due as a narrative theorist of Caribbean sexual (non)identities, one who evokes female and nonheteronormative bodies in ways that Fanon cannot. In the sections that follow, I concentrate on rereading one element that receives much play in Fanon's text: Mayotte's work as a washerwoman. Rather than reading it as biographical "fact" or as evidence of psychological alienation, I read it as *lamayòtaj*, a representation that allows Capécia at once to earn a living without literally washing clothes and to offer glimpses of the *dirt* systematically white-washed in the imaginations of Martinican women.

Women, Water, and Power:
A Literary History of the Caribbean Washerwoman

In the Caribbean, the washerwoman is a long-memoried woman.[25] Her cultural importance frames this study as the "spring of her look" imagined in Brunias's painting, and this spring flows far in Caribbean renderings of land- and womanscapes. Here I want to evoke her long memory on a literal, material level as a woman who works *in* water; and on a figurative level as a metaphor for woman *as* water. As Frances Mascia Lees and Patricia Sharpe explain: "Intertwining the metaphoric and the literal is . . . a strategy [that follows] out the implications of the use of metaphors in contemporary criticism by literalizing them, and thus exposing the hidden cultural assumptions they contain."[26] That is, the crosscurrents at which the literal meets the figurative create a lens that magnifies hidden dirt. Here *fluidity* comes into view as both a conceptual principal and a site of concrete, painful, *and* liberatory experience—as a trope that reflects the materiality of women of color's embodied experience while refusing its transparency.

The Caribbean washerwoman's waters have always been both murky and backbreaking. Glimpses of the concrete force of water and laundry on Caribbean women's bodies date back as early as the first published slave narrative by a woman; the washerwoman Mary Prince's *History* of 1831 narrates laundry as brutal work that literally ate away at her flesh. When she dictated her narrative, she, like Capécia, was attempting to reverse her estrangement from her West Indian family and seeking legal sanction to return to her husband in Antigua as a free woman. To plead her case, Prince depicted women's bodies in and as water in ways that were unrelentingly material. The chain of dislocations that brought her to England began with her sale away from her mother at age twelve, a separation that Prince narrates as a deluge, a flood of "salt water" that "[came] into my eyes" and those of the women around her.[27] The "sore crying" of Prince, her mother, and the other women slaves (a collective plaint described for three pages in a narrative less than thirty pages long) is not a metaphorical body of water but water that *is* these women's bodies, expressing their over-flowing emotional pain. Each of Prince's subsequent sales is met with tears. As she becomes used goods, more brutalized by each master, her insistent recol-lection of these tears resistantly paints her body not as a deadened commodity but as a witness to her humanity.

The saltwater of her first sale prefigures the "trials" Prince meets when moved from house slave to fieldworker in the salt ponds of Turk's Island. Here, women's immobilization in water literally eats away at their flesh. "Our feet and legs," she recounts, "from standing in the salt water for so many hours, soon became full of dreadful boils, which eat down in some cases to the very bone, afflicting the sufferers with great torment."[28] Slave owners' attempts to "fix" their property – to arrest the erosion of this woman's flesh – only reinflict pain, forcing a literal internalization of the conditions of saltwater slavery.[29] "When we were ill," Prince testifies, "let our complaint be what it might, the only medicine given to us was a great bowl of hot salt water, with salt mixed with it, which made us very sick."[30] After ten years on Turk's Island, Prince re-turned to Antigua to be put to work as a washerwoman. This work continued her physical debilitation begun in the salt pond. Crippled by rheumatism until she could no longer stand over a tub of wash, she was finally thrown out by her masters for refusing to do heavy laundry. On Turk's Island and over the washtub, the connection between woman and water is neither linguistic nor metaphoric. Instead, by literalizing enforced linkages between gendered bodies and fluidity, Prince exposes this equation's potential for imperial violence.

Further troubling the metaphor of fluid sexuality, water also appears as the site of coerced sex work in Prince's *History*. Speaking of her master Mr. D, she recounts: "He had an ugly fashion of stripping himself quite naked, and order-ing me then to wash him in a tub of water. This was worse to me than all the licks. Sometimes when he called me to wash him I would not come, my eyes were so full of shame. . . . He struck me so severely for this, that at last I de-fended myself, for I thought it was high time to do so. I then told him I could no longer live with him, for he was a very indecent man – very spiteful, and too indecent; with no shame for his servants, no shame for his own flesh."[31] This episode is one of the most marked scenes of resistance in Prince's text. It culminates in an act of verbal self-defense ("I then told him . . . he was a very indecent man – very spiteful, and too indecent") as well as one of physical self-defense, her flight from Mr. D's house. At the same time, read as a story of resistance to sexual abuse, it also emerges as one of the narrative's least materially descriptive scenes. Coerced sex work is never named – only suggested metonymically by Mr. D's nudity and metaphorically by the association between water and forced labor established in earlier episodes. This abstraction does not read as Prince's "choice." This slave narrative, dictated and transcribed by white English writers and *not* in Prince's own hand, poses problems of voice – and particularly, of what the woman of color can and will say of her sexualized body – that Capécia's novel shares. By narrating water as a space that crosses physical, emotional, and sexual abuse, as well as between literal and figurative denunciations of slave owners' actions, Prince develops the materially informed metaphor as a strategy of subaltern (or better, *submarine*) speech. This strategy allows the Caribbean woman to make a partial account of her sexualized body and, as Anne B. Dalton writes of Harriet Jacobs's metaphoric descriptions of sexual abuse, "render the material relating to sexual exploitation in a 'delicate' manner, so that she would not alienate her audience from listening, while still being graphic enough to be persuasive." [32] Prince's repetition of the verb *wash* becomes such a "delicate" metaphorical description of coerced sex work. This verb, used elsewhere to describe her labor, now takes on a second meaning, echoed by the also repeated *indecent*. Both terms suggest that though she may have much to say of her abuse and in her defense, the vocabulary that she is allowed to employ for the English reading public remains restricted to metaphors and abstractions.

But Prince's complex material and metaphoric representation of the laundress as working *and* speaking subject is drowned out in late nineteenth-century Caribbean literature. The *blanchisseuse* emerged as a recurring figure in Haitian Romantic poetry, which, from 1860 forward, enunciated a nationalist poetics allegorizing the unique beauty of Haitianness in the local color of its landscape and its women. Imaginarily severed from the community of female workers to which Prince belonged, the washerwoman entered this poetry as a beautiful, eroticized figure blending into equally beautiful landscapes. She appears as such in Oswald Durand's "La laveuse de Mando" and Alcibiade Fleury Battier's "La blanchisseuse," both of which narrate a male speaker's erotically charged appreciation of the spectacle of a washerwoman in the river cheerfully performing her very wet labor. [33] Using a similar romanticization and hyperheterosexualization for *anti*nationalist political ends, nineteenth-century travelogues aestheticized the *blanchisseuse* to stand in for the exotic, erotic, and passive colony. Lafcadio Hearn's "Martinique Sketches" of 1890 figure her as an anachronism in need of benevolent protection: "It has a curious interest, this spectacle of primitive toil: the deep channel of the Roxelane winding under the palm-crowned heights of the Fort; the blinding whiteness of linen laid out to bleach for miles upon the huge bowlders of porphyry and prismatic basalt; and the dark bronze-limbed women, with faces hidden under immense straw hats, and knees in the rushing torrent – all form a scene that makes one think of the earliest civilizations." [34] Unlike Durand or Fleury Battier, Hearn does not elide the details of the washerwoman's work. His sketch "Les Blanchisseuses" meticulously describes processes of *frotté* (rubbing), *fessé* (beating), *pouèmiè lablanie* (bleaching), and *coulé* (steeping in lye). He notes that it is taxing work and that "the trade is said to kill all who continue at it beyond a certain number of years – 'Nou ka mò toutt dleau' (we all die of the water), one told me." [35] But he attributes the continuance of this "savage style of washing" to Martinicans' premodern predispositions. "There is a local prejudice against new methods, new inventions, new ideas. . . . The public were quite contented with the old ways of laundrying and saw no benefits to be gained by forsaking them," he explains. [36]

Hearn also maintains that natural physical strength makes women of "black or of that dark copper-red race" overrepresented in this dangerous trade. He rationalizes that it "requires a skin insensible to sun as well as the toughest of constitutions to be a blanchisseuse." Even this demanding labor, then, supposedly cannot wear away the thick skins and solid bodies of dark-skinned women. [37] The racial metaphor built into the verb *blanchir* (whiten) seems to surface in his assumption that black women can never whiten too much and are dark enough to be able to continually work in others' dirt. By the end of the sketch, Hearn succeeds in introducing the material impact of *blanchissage* only to deny this materiality. The Roxelane becomes abstract space in which both water and women are beyond the ravages of time. "The great voice of the Roxelane . . . will sing on when the city itself shall have ceased to be, just as it sang one hundred thousand years ago," he reflects. "In all seasons, while youth and strength stay with them, [*blanchisseuses*] work on in wind and sun, mist and rain, washing the linen of the living and the dead ." [38] The singing river, the aestheticized landscape, obscures the hard, gendered, and racialized toil that goes on here. The implication is that both Martinique and Martinican women – hopelessly primitive and yet endlessly cheerful – are naturally made to work for more modern French employers, the bodies and rivers of the island content to eternally do the mother country's laundry.

Hearn does not deny the intense, intriguing homosociality of women working waist-deep in water together. He notes folklorically: "It is one of the sights of St. Pierre, – this daily scene at the River of Washerwomen: everybody likes to watch it; – the men, because among the blanchisseuses there are not a few decidedly handsome girls; the women probably because a woman feels always interested in women's work. . . . every bonne on her way to and from the market stops a moment to observe or to greet those blanchisseuses whom she knows. Then one hears such a calling and clamoring – and such an intercrossing of cries from the bridge to the river, and from the river to the bridge. . . . 'Ouill! Noémi!' . . . 'Comment ou yé, chè?' . . . 'Eh! Pascaline!' . . . 'Bonjou,' Youtte! – Dédé!-Fifi – Herillia!' . . .'Coument ou kallé, Cyrillia?' . . 'Toutt douce, chè! et Ti Mémé?'" [39] The scene is dominated by women's gazes directed at other "decidedly handsome" women and their voices creating a network ("an intercrossing of cries") of greetings, recognition, and intimacies. The narrator associates women's work with a community of speaking subjects, and the interplay between work and voice builds to an orgasmic pitch of excitement – of "calling and clamoring," shouting out – that eroticizes the washerwomen's river.

Yet even as he describes this excitement between women, Hearn works to narrate it away. Here again fluid sexuality works in a problematic way, imagining that non-normative eroticism can be washed away by imperial desires. He does this, first, by creating a nonerotic reason for the gaze. He states that men watch out of desire for the *blanchisseuses*, while women do so "probably because a woman always feels interested in women's work." For men women are *only* potential sexual partners, while for women they are *only* potential coworkers. At the same time, the description of the bridge from which the men watch the washerwoman interposes a male gaze dominating the scene of female eroticism below. Throughout the sketch, Hearn periodically reminds the reader that what proves the interest of this working intimacy between the women in water is men's fascination with the spectacle and that this masculine presence has power over the scene beneath it. At the end of the sketch, for example, he returns to his interrupted description of the bridge: "Idle men stare at some pretty washer, till she points at them and cries: – '*Gadé Missié-à ka guetté-nou! – anh!-anh!-anh!*' And all the others look up and repeat the groan – '*anh!-anh-anh!*'" [40] Just as Hearn simultaneously evokes and denies the materiality of the overworked black woman, so the heterosexualizing male gaze from the bridge at once makes visible and eclipses the gynoeroticism of a river scene of "joy for the washers."[41] In his exoticized, eroticized portraits of the washerwoman, Hearn, like the Haitian Romantics, assumes that woman's contiguity to nature means that she is naturally accessible to the men above her. In both visions of the washerwoman's river, compulsory heterosexuality is the hallmark of a properly ordered Caribbean environment. The pain of work and the eroticism of female company are equally washed away.

The trope of the *blanchisseuse,* then, constitutes a fraught topos for Capécia to enter, but not for the reasons that Fanon assumes. If Hearn posits that washerwomen are a spectacle that women like to watch "because a woman feels always interested in woman's work," Capécia begins her novel by asking: What if this is *not* why these women watch each other? What happens when a woman takes on the erotic gaze of the male speaker? What *does* the spring of her look open onto? In imagining this look, Capécia opens space for the kind of play with clichéd images that Mary Poovey describes as potentially subversive. She reminds us that though overused tropes can be reductive, "because metaphors are neither subject to precise control nor assimilable to a single set of connotations, figures of speech also introduce semantic play into the lived experience of the material world" and "open possibilities for the symbolic appropriation of physical space" that "can lay the groundwork of material alterations of that space."[42] Capécia's imaginative appropriation of woman-as-water metaphors functions much like her claiming of an imaginary name: both explore possibilities for reinventing the material and social locations of Caribbean women's working and erotic bodies. The next section explores how Capécia's entry into the washerwoman trope and its equation of woman and water is—and is not—able to reclaim the physical and social landscape of Martinique. Her washerwomen speak to the possibilities and limits of fluid erotic identities in the Caribbean and to crosscurrents of complexities that make the *blanchisseuse* publishing in French necessarily a *lamayòteuse.*

The Prettiest Washerwoman and the Slipperiest Mermaid:
Glimpses of Sexual Fluidity

"When we were little," *I Am a Martinican Woman* opens ticklishly, "my twin sister and I, we looked so much alike that our mother had to make us laugh to tell us apart."[43] Bypassing the protagonist's birth—a classic autobiographical moment of individuation – the novel instead starts with an identity-blurring twinning of Martiniquaises, the subject a feminine first-person plural whose splitting only comes as part of a laughable joke. Yet as soon as this *we* is evoked, the girls' likeness is undercut. Mayotte continues, "But we're very different in our tastes and character. Me, for example, I was never very gifted and learned to walk much later than Francette. My mother dangled a bunch of bananas in front of my mouth so I'd try to catch them, since I adored them" (7).[44] As the girls are differentiated, *we* becoming *me*, bananas dangle as foreshadowing – a ripe cluster of phallic symbols Mother coaxes Mayotte to follow so she can mature "properly." In some ways the rest of the novel cycles through this pattern, evoking female solidarity only to show it complicated by the pursuit of compulsory heterosexuality. Yet in others it complicates that pattern, walking toward alternative uses of the banana and all stock images of Caribbean sexuality.

Mother knows she craves bananas, but young Mayotte also seems to want some things she cannot quite name. Her favorite play spot is the Cambeille River, whose powerful wetness thrills her to bursting: "This river, about eight meters wide, could transform itself into a furious torrent from one moment to the next. As if a dyke had burst, a flood of water then rushed with a rumbling like that of an eruption" (10).[45] Unafraid of this orgasmic flow, women and girls gather daily at the river bank. Here Mayotte watches *blanchisseuses* cheerfully performing their work:

> They greeted the women arriving, carrying their wash on their heads the way we do in our country:
> "*Bonjou Fifi! Comment ou yé, ché? . . .*"
> "*Toute douce, ché, et té, Youte? . . .*"
> "*Tu vini poend ou bain? . . .*"
> The bravest women set themselves up on the rocks in the middle of the river, the more timid staying on shore. In Martinique laundry isn't done the way it is in France. No need to boil linens in our country – the sun takes care of everything. For bleach and perfume, women rinse with warm water they've mixed with charcoal ash and orange peel.
> After their work, the youngest bathed unselfconsciously in the river. (10–11)[46]

Splashing about in a river where they have just washed clothes – water softened by warmth and sweet, cunnic oranges – these laundresses call to each other and wash themselves along with their laundry. As they do, their shouted names and soaking bodies remain between women even if the product of their labor (the wash on their heads) does not. In "Commodities among Themselves," Luce Irigaray imagines that patriarchal heterosexuality functions as "nothing but assignment of economic roles" where men become traders, women commodities. But a feminine economy of desire – of "commodities among themselves" – would circulate with no fixed roles or functions; erotic, as well as economic, activity would be fluid and uncapturable, "a river which does not empty into any sea."[47] Capécia's Cambeille looks like a culturally specific, Caribbean version of this utopian Irigarayan river – the working and desiring of *blanchisseuses* among themselves.

The Caribbeanness of this river shows not only in its tropicalness or its washerwomen but also in the character Capécia peoples it with: *la guiablesse* (literally, "she-devil"), a roaming spirit who seduces and tricks passersby. "*La guiablesse,*" the narrator confides, "wanders roads and isolated plantations, looking like a pretty young girl, and you never see the men who follow her again. But us, we weren't afraid of *guiablesses*" (11).[48] Her deceptively ingenuous sexuality is a dangerous *lamayòt* to men, but something that washerwomen and their playmates – all part of *la guiablesse*'s river economy – never fear. In fact, the tricky spirit that shares Mayotte's childhood river seems to offer a clue about the "pretty young" sexuality the adult protagonist will present to men. Namely, such sexuality can be a mask that spirits power away from roving male desire, allowing its femme wearer to navigate a feminized landscape without danger. The she-devil's alluring heterosexuality is a strategically fabricated illusion that veils what Sylvia Wynter, in her groundbreaking "Beyond Miranda's Meanings," names "demonic ground" – "an alternative sexual-erotic model of desire" in which the Caribbean woman's eroticism refuses to be fixed on one "appropriate" object but instead circulates as endlessly as Capécia's Cambeille, creating a black feminine subject who threatens to reveal desires as numerous and dangerous as snakes on a Gorgon's head.[49] Or put another way, females like Mayotte and *la guiablesse* may seem to want just one thing (a man); but really, from their road-wandering, racialized, gendered, sexualized, and classed positions, they desire so many things and people that to speak them all would explode the patriarch's text.

This spirit's presence also alerts readers to something else: Capécia deliberately spins folktales, and readers need to beware what they accept as "reality." Take her description of washerwomen's work, a deliberate misrepresentation of her own labor. Accurate in stating that "in Martinique laundry isn't done like it is in France," she is purposefully misleading in implying the labor's lightness. Her cheery assertion that "the sun takes care of everything" magically omits scrubbing and ironing, turns the taxing *fessé* into a game, and expressly denies bleaching or steeping in lye. Given the text's hybrid authorship, it is difficult to attribute too much agency to Capécia as tale teller. Her elisions may be based in editors' choices and her own commercial aspirations: *lamayòtaj* is first and foremost a means for the *lamayòteur* or *lamayòteuse* to earn a living, and the peeks he or she offers inside the box are not just a game but an activity attracting paying customers. Whether intentional or not, Capécia's misrepresentations become double-voiced discourse, offering different meanings to different publics. For French readers, the sanitation and sexualization of laundry fits the smiling, seductive images used to market the novel: the scantily clad, madras-coiffed woman on the cover could hardly be pleasantly imagined ruining her legs, back, and eyes in the water. But for Caribbean readers the gaps serve another purpose; the egregious omissions hint that from the outset the novel engages in the *lamayòtaj* of offering incomplete glimpses of the Martinican woman's reality. *I Am a Martinican Woman* becomes what Mae Henderson calls a "spookerly text": one whose black queerness is not an expression of "identity" but a writerly praxis, a subversion of realist narrative techniques that signals haunting presences of race, class, and sexuality while refusing to transparently represent their experience.[50] Writing this scene under the sign of *la guiablesse* suggests that the narrator's account of laundry is neither a betrayal of truth, as a too-literal reading might posit, nor a betrayal of race, as Fanon's too-figurative reading posits. It is not about sexualized "fidelity" to concepts like *truth* and *race* at all, but about fluid (non)identity that allows the speaking "I" to keep her textual-sexual autonomy and use it strategically, as *la guiablesse* uses both her pretty face and hidden claws.

The most sustained *lamayòt* under the mask of docile heterosexuality comes just after *la guiablesse*'s appearance. Watching the washerwomen bathe, Mayotte becomes fascinated by the youngest and most appealing of them, her beautiful friend Loulouze: "Loulouze was the prettiest and gayest [of the washerwomen] and, despite the difference in our ages, we were real friends [*de vraies amies*]. . . . Loulouze's movements brought a new kind of feeling to me. At times, she also bathed with us. She had golden skin with traces of orange and banana, long black hair which she rolled in braids and which was only frizzy at the roots, a nose that was rather flat and thick lips, but a face whose shape showed she must have white ancestry not too far removed. I looked at her chest with desire [*envie*], me, who was still flat chested" (12–13).[51] The prettiest and gayest, indeed. A *lamayòt* gynoeroticism begins here with the evocation of an unnameable new "feeling" that Loulouze, naked and frolicking in the water, rouses in Mayotte. Next follows a description that compares the older girl's skin to tropical fruit, oranges and bananas that invite oral incorporation. Oranges are the cunnic fruit, well-known for their juiciness, that washerwomen bring to the river, and bananas the fruit that we know Mayotte loved to eat and chased with her mouth watering. Further layers of eroticism emerge when we look at the nuances of the original French – especially the noun *envie*, or desire, used in relationship to Loulouze's beautiful breasts, and the phrase "real friends," *vraies amies*. Beginning with this reference to Mayotte and Loulouze, Capécia inscribes an echo of the Creolisms *fe zanmi*, to have female-female sex, and *vré zanmi*, real girlfriends, women who love each other. In interpreting these echoes, the fact that her original spellings were largely phonetic takes on added significance. Was Capécia writing/saying *vraies amies*, *fe zanmi*, or both? Are we meant to slip and slide between the two interpretations?

Much as this Creole word hovers under the written text, another Martinican figure glimmers under the surface of Loulouze's description: the *manman dlo* (mother of waters), a mermaid who lives in the rivers and lakes of Martinique, Guadeloupe, Haiti, Trinidad, and Grenada and often emerges with messages for passersby. With the top half of her body rising out of the water, Loulouze looks like tales of this hybrid creatures. Her visible *métissage* echoes the *manman dlo*'s fair, smooth skin, her hair recalls the mermaid's famously long, black tresses, and Mayotte's fascination with her large breasts evoke the generous chest the *manman* (like the related *orishá* Yemaya) is gifted with. And as Mayotte follows her through the river, Loulouze seems poised to act like this figure, who spirits young women underwater, where they may be permanently turned into shrimp or temporarily turned into mermaids. A character who bridges rivers and seas, the *manman dlo* is a creature of figurative as well as literal crosscurrents. As Patrick Chamoiseau notes, she emerges from a *métissage* of myths of feminine power: "In a Manman Dlo," he explains, "you have African aquatic divinities who meet those of the Native Americans, who add themselves to European mermaids."[52] Some stories suggest her form is borrowed from the carved mermaids on slave ships' bows.[53] If so, *manman dlo* are at once shipbound mermaids released back into the water and the drowned of the Middle Passage now equipped with the wooden figures' fins, buoying them to the surface. The water mother swims in Martinican rivers as a historically sedimented imagination of how Caribbean womanhood has been both molded through violent globalization and transculturated to imagine physical and psychic survival; like the novel's title character, she tells a complicated story of what it means to navigate being Martiniquaise.

But the *mannman dlo* is not just racially *métisse*; the representatively watery Martinican is also sexually fluid. She most directly descends from the gold-wearing West African spirit Mami Wata who, feminine from the waist up, is more ambiguous below the water. She/he is often said not to have human genitalia but a fluid body that can both penetrate and be penetrated by the human lovers she chooses, who may be either striking males or beautiful females.[54] Similarly, the always feminine Haitian water mother still has both a male (Agwé) and a female (La Baleine) consort.[55] And throughout the Caribbean, while the *manman dlo* snatches men who disrespect her to discipline them, she spirits women and girls underwater for days at a time to keep her company and share her knowledge. Sometimes implicitly sexual, these watery sojourns are always erotic, a time-space in which a woman is loved and nurtured by another female. Stories of women's encounters with the *manman dlo* repeat the same pattern: walking alone they are embraced and taken underwater by this woman-from-the-waist-up, and at the bottom of the river the land dweller temporarily becomes a mermaid while she undergoes an (erotic?) initiation whose contents are never revealed. She returns to land with fairer skin and straighter hair, temporarily able only to speak a mermaid's language of clicks but having acquired a sacred knowledge that is recognized by the community and allows her to work as a priest.[56] Erotic power in the mermaid's river is not only about sexual pleasure but also about empowering women to take care of all their bodies' needs: far from being purely otherworldly, this jewelry-laden mermaid promises earthly abundance to those who follow her and become her priests. Calling up a *manman dlo*, then, Capécia taps into childhood stories that, like women's kinship networks, naturalize female subjects sharing both affective and material power, one "woman" loving another and disclosing what she needs to know to live more comfortably after they part. Back on land, the *manman dlo*'s companion benefits from knowing a Caribbean feminine topos of power and desire but keeps its secrets out of common parlance—just as Capécia's river scenes suggest hidden eroticism but keep its secrets out of the text. As with *mati*, the very wordlessness of the feminized erotic suggests its power. Karen McCarthy Brown remarks evocatively, "She is a fleeting presence, never fully seen, hinting at something monumental – huge, deep, sudden, and powerful."[57]

But the undercurrent of "fleeting" manman dlo tales in Capécia's Cambeille also foreshadows that Mayotte and Loulouze's time-space of female erotic primacy will only prove an interlude. One of the laughing wishes Loulouze shares with Mayotte as they bathe is her desire to acquire the gold jewelry often associated with manman dlo; but she can only get a gold bracelet through her white male lover, the single character who has the resources to buy such a thing. (The one he gives her, she later discovers, is fake.) While female subjects' learning the material power of eroticism in this Martinican river hints at something "huge, deep," the problem that emerges on land is that the erotic remains the only power they have to navigate a patriarchal colonial world. Relying on her sexuality to earn her gold, the Martiniquaise becomes much like a Martinique haunted by monoculture, trapped in the decidedly unfluid state of having only one resource worth cultivating. At the time the novel is set, that resource was an agricultural product associated with both Mayotte and Loulouze – the banana. Claudie Beauvue-Fougeyrollas calls the postwar period "the age of the banana" since, after the decline of rum, Martinican landowners replaced the earlier export commodity with banana production and small farmers were encouraged by the government to make the transition from subsistence to banana farming. With the vast majority of Martinican agricultural products grown for export and the majority of food consumed now imported from the metropole, Beauvue-Fougerollas concludes, "Never had Guadeloupe and Martinique been so colonially dominated and subjugated as in this banana economy."[58] And Loulouze's maturation into a banana-like sexuality similarly locks her into colonial and feminized subjugation: her eroticized body will be shipped out to serve interests other than her own, and the gold she's given in exchange for her sexual companionship will be worthless.

This shipping occurs at the end of the chapter, when Loulouze's father throws her out for becoming pregnant by her white "fiancé" and she leaves town – and Mayotte – for Fort-de-France where she can earn more money. Mayotte finds her just before she leaves, staring into the Cambeille: "She was sitting on a rock and looking fixedly at the current that washed along pieces of wood like after a storm" (18).[59] She tells Mayotte that she's imagining herself drifting off on the current too. When Capécia shows Loulouze carried downriver by a current stronger than her desires, the novel insinuates the problems of imagining that two women who will be employed by békés throughout their adult life can live

and love as freely as mermaids.[60] Washerwomen cannot build a river community of *blanchisseuses* among themselves as long as colonial economies channel
them into working and birthing for someone else. Loulouze leaves Mayotte
with a discolored vision of her beautiful laundress: "Her beautiful orange color
had become muddy," she notices, as if the fair skin associated with the *manman
dlo*'s tutelage had worn off, the orange of her dreamy cunnic power brought
down to earth (19).[61] She also leaves her with a resounding warning on the
inevitability of the woman of color's entry into an exploitative material and
sexual economy: "Life is difficult for a woman, you'll see, Mayotte, especially for
a woman of color" (20).[62] This sparse sentence becomes the initiatory *manman
dlo* knowledge that Loulouze gives Mayotte to take back into the world and into
the rest of the novel.

Capécia's river of washerwomen proves Fanon wrong about the presence of
same-sex eroticism in the West Indies. Martinique can have, the scene at the
Cambeille suggests, *zanmi* or gynoerotic space in which desire between women
emerges as uniquely Caribbean as a *manman dlo* and as homegrown (the literal
meaning of *criollo*/Creole) as the oranges sprinkled on the wash. At the same
time, this scene's conclusion suggests that in some other way Fanon is right.
Same-sex eroticism cannot maintain a safe or sustained place in colonial, patriarchal economies of work and desire in which mermaids remain fictions and
oranges are muddied by earthly pressures.[63] Even as Mayotte imagines her body
and Loulouze's meeting in the river, these fluid bodies are already no longer
theirs; they are intended to be commodities in this other economy. Fanon cites
the lack of an Oedipus complex as the reason why homosexuality fades out in
Martinique, but the problem that emerges in Capécia's novel is much more
concrete. Why stay with *zanmi* at the Cambeille when washerwomen make
more money in the capital? Why would Loulouze partner for the long term
with Mayotte or any other female when they would never earn more than
women of color's salaries together? While women embracing dual sexual systems like the *mati*'s may understand that the emotional benefits of partnership
are strongest between women, they also remain clear that the economic benefits of partnership are strongest with men. And so for working-class women
looking for a way out of an economy of subsistence, female partners may at
once be the most painful to lose – "you don't just lose a sexual partner, you lose
a lifeline," as Carol Thames writes of Jamaican women's relationships – and the
most economically necessary to deprioritize for those who, like Capécia, want
to cross to the middle class.[64] Powerful as the *manman dlo* suggests Caribbean

womanhood could be, her shimmer in the water does not erase the historical limitations of what this womanhood is offered in interwar Martinique. Danticat tells us, "A too short rendezvous with one's lover was a *lamayòt*, as was a false personal or political promise."[65] So, too, is the fluid desire of the mermaid and the *Martiniquaise*, their sexual openness a *lamayòt* that appears in the text only long enough to make its presence known – then slipping underwater so Loulouze and Mayotte can make their living downstream.

A Deep Blue Harbor Hemmed in by the Hills:
Imperial Flows of Desire

Life is difficult for Capécia's woman of color, and the novel's second part goes on to show this difficulty powered by colonial as much as hetero-patriarchy. Irigaray imagines the desires of commodities among themselves as a river that empties into no known sea. But in *I Am a Martinican Woman*, the *blanchisseuses'* river runs into a very real sea – the policed bay of Fort-de-France during World War II. In chapter 1 of part 2, the interrupted erotic scene between the two women is rescripted between an adult Mayotte and her white male lover, the French sailor André, in the latter's bedroom overlooking the coastline. As the carefree Cambeille is overlain with images of the occupied bay, the metaphorics of Caribbean women's sexuality are inserted into a symbolic system of imperial desire and domination that, like the harbor, hems in their waters.

Before entering this scene, I want to consider how "devilishly" Capécia transitions from part 1, whose stories are (partially) her own, to part 2, rewritten from André's manuscript. When she moves to Fort-de-France, Mayotte initially shares her living space and a bed with a newly single Loulouze, sleeping on her pillow and contemplating "her voluminous chest, which I took pleasure in comparing to my small breasts" (118).[66] Yet shortly thereafter, she finds her own apartment, and when she does so, the unplagiarized portion of the novel quickly draws to a close. Part 1's last chapter is a description of Carnival, where, still flirting with sexual fluidity, Mayotte dresses as a man to pursue erotic adventures with a man dressed as a woman, whom she leads in several biguines before discovering a male voice behind the mask (126–27). Drawing a narrative loop back to the Cambeille, this cross-dressing takes place the day after Mardi Gras, which is, the narrator tells us, "the day of *la guiablesse*," Carnival's last day of singing, shouting, dancing, and sex (128).[67] At the close of *la guiablesse's* day, the cross-dressed Mayotte falls into a deep sleep, fighting a nightmare filled with feisty devils. The part of the novel composed by Capécia ends with the narrator dreaming fitfully, a state that prepares the transition from her lived experience to the alienating realm of another's imagination. Perhaps not coincidentally, sailors – André's comrades – also appear as Carnival characters; the entry of Mayotte's marvelous sailor, then, is set up as part of a tradition of masquerade and disruption. In effect, Mayotte shows herself entering André's high-flown, oneiric portrait of the Martinican woman in disguise. Following her lover's manuscript, Capécia's text acts like the masked man-dressed-as-woman who follows cross-dressed Mayotte; rather than showing a "true" auto-biographical self, the novel's second part performs *en travesti*, speaking from a disguised masculine subject position rather than the feminized "I" written into the title.

Much of the "dream sequence" of Mayotte's early encounters with the sea-man is lifted verbatim from André's manuscript, and her description of their first meeting takes entire sentences and paragraphs from his. Capécia's appro-priations include a paragraph evoking "the harbor [that] glittered softly under the light breeze," the lovers' waiting out a storm in the Pavillon du Tourisme, their conversation about André's Algerian love, and his bungled attempt to kiss Mayotte (133).[68] The chapter also includes a conversation about the difficulties of their liaison – where he self-importantly muses that "on the earthly level . . . our union must only be fleeting," then realizes he has spoken in terms too complex for her – reproduced almost word for word (137).[69] As significant as what Capécia includes from his memoir, however, is what she omits and adds, revisions that effect a *lamayòtaj* of her lover's narrative. Refusing to wander in the abstract space André describes as the only one in which their love can sur-vive, Capécia cuts short his frequent philosophical asides. For example, André describes their repose in the Pavillon du Tourisme with this complex sentence: "The idea came to them to sit and, finding no seat, they thought it picturesque to perch at the edge of the sidewalk: they had already long broken with con-ventions and acted on their first whim."[70] Capécia reproduces the first half but elides his postcolon commentary, resisting any suggestion of the transgressive nature of a coupling that places a brown woman at the feet of passersby. Con-versely, much of what she adds are concrete details of her woman of color's body: how flattering her blue dress is, how André's touch feels – notably, how she flinches at his first kiss and then slips her arm around his neck to initiate a kiss with him instead. Like the portrait of laundry, these descriptions seem double-voiced. On the one hand, representing herself as the initiator of sexual contact with André plays on the exotic figure of the *doudou*, the woman of color uncontrollably propelled by desire for white men – a French fantasy not only of the colonial woman but also of a feminized colony who gives herself freely and expects nothing in return.[71] At the same time, Mayotte's pursuit of André reclaims the power of the *Martiniquaise*'s active desire by echoing her pursuit of the "woman" who followed her in her Carnival suit. André's manuscript opens with his memory that, arriving in Martinique, he was determined to find a car, a house, a dog, and a woman. But Capécia's rewrite suggests that the *doudou* he finds is only (like *la guiablesse*) wearing a disguise of submissive femininity, and in fact he himself may be in the position of the woman (or dog) he came in search of. *La Martiniqu(ais)e* has more agency than the occupier fantasizes, Mayotte's kiss hints.

Capécia makes another significant addition. She scripts an opening scene, set on the morning after the lovers' first night together, that becomes the starting point for her "romantic" flashbacks. This opening reprises – and reconfigures – the watery eroticism of the Cambeille, as we find Mayotte's gazing onto Fort-de-France's bay after a night with her "marvelous lover":

> I came out onto the balcony. I needed to be alone for a moment because I was too happy.
>
> We had gotten up late and the sun was already high. André's house overlooked the vast harbor of Fort-de-France. At my feet, through the rustling foliage of a badly trimmed hedge, I made out the fine silhouette of the Émile Bertin, the ship that had brought to Martinique the gold from the Bank of France. A marsh bordered by coconut trees extended along the other side of the Tourelles bay, and the airplane hangar threw a dark shape onto the brilliant surface of the cement terreplein ...
>
> But mostly I looked at the deep blue harbor, crossed by the white sails of yachts, which looked like a vast lake hemmed in by the hills. I gazed at it as if it were the image of my happiness. (129–30)[72]

In these blue waters, the *manman dlo* is eclipsed by the *Émile Bertin*. That is, the mythic power of fluid Creole eroticism is overshadowed by the historical supremacy of France's maritime force. If motion dominated the portrait of the Cambeille, restraint dominates the portrait of the Fort-de-France harbor. Where the river description began with storms that blurred divisions between land, water, and sky, the bay's description opens with the brusque emergence of vertical spatialization. Gazing from André's house onto the French fleet in the bay, Mayotte is now aligned with an authority from "above" that marks her life in a very different way from the mermaid's submerged power. She has just moved into the bedroom view of an imperial force whose policing of the colony is simultaneously based in its fleet and in its domestic arrangements. Domestic and military power literally occupy the same space in this scene, as the house that André shares with Mayotte stands in the position of a maritime fortress whose unseen military gaze prefigures Michel Foucault's Panopticon. Mayotte's balcony becomes where Ann Laura Stoler's "empire of the night" – domestic arrangements between European men and "native" women that sexualize and reinscribe colonial "arrangements" between Europe and the Global South – meets an empire of the morning, the revelation of military and political domination that inflects the daily realities and choices of Caribbean women.[73] Life is hard for the woman of color not because of who she "is" or who she beds, but because of the imperial, patriarchal conditions under which she lives.

Where her portrait of the Cambeille and its washerwomen among themselves is set in the fluid, unmeasureable time of myth, the sketch of the harbor begins with the immediate entry of women's eroticism into a historical scene and, specifically, into the history of World War II in Martinique. "At my feet," Mayotte notes in her description of the view, "through the rustling leaves of a badly trimmed hedge, I made out the fine silhouette of the *Émile Bertin*, the ship that had brought the gold of the Bank of France to Martinique." The *Émile Bertin*, Admiral Georges Robert's chief charge as Vichy's representative in the French Antilles, surfaces as a material representation of the military and ideological importance of keeping Martinique and France – like Mayotte and André – "intimate allies" during World War II. The chainlike link between landscape, domestic space, and military force becomes clear in the sentence that begins with Mayotte's gaze moving her window through the rustling foliage and wild hedge only to be stopped by the *Émile Bertin*, carrying the gold of the Bank of France. As the sentence ends here, the gold folklorically possessed by the *manman dlo* and sought by Loulouze finally materializes as property historically claimed and guarded by a male-named war ship. With water and happiness "crossed by the white sails of yachts ... hemmed in by the hills," the fluid possibilities of the Cambeille and its sexual and textual model of Caribbean womanhood become stagnant, trapped in a harbor dominated by both the fort and André's house. The compulsorily heterosexualized Caribbean woman and the battleship become two vessels conscripted by Vichy's colonial order, both no longer free to move or desire autonomously despite their "natural" connection to water.

Where the last section excavated myths floating beneath the surface of Capécia's novel, I now want to look at the history that also subtends her text. Vichy's sexual politics in Martinique, and especially its restraints on Martinican women, remain scantily recorded history. On the rare occasions when the story of World War II in the tropics is told, West Indian scholars and novelists focus on its impact on male bodies and masculinist nationalisms.[74] As the colonies are marginalized in the European historiography of the great wars, so women are marginalized in their postcolonial chronicles. Yet Robert's export of Vichy to the West Indies relied heavily on the militarization of women like Mayotte: soldiers' lovers, baby mothers, washerwomen, seamstresses, cooks, servers, and nurses. Capécia's example of Mayotte's tripled reproductive work for André – as washerwoman, partner, and (eventually) the mother of his son – suggests much about why Vichy needed Caribbean women to labor and launder for them. On the literal level, the sailor needed the laundress to bleach his uniform to be suitable for a Vichy representative. Cynthia Enloe documents laundresses as key female figures in military history, encouraged along with cooks, nurses, and prostitutes to accompany armies as a pool of inexpensive labor.[75] Grouped as "camp followers," these women are neither peripheral to war efforts nor passive hangers-on as their name suggests. Rather, they are mobilized as a workforce essential to meeting troops' physical and emotional needs; and aware of the (slight) power that being needed by the army affords them, they use this to what advantage they can. As Enloe notes, when working-class women like Mayotte capitalize on military presence to earn more for reproductive labor from laundry (whitening the clothes) to childbearing (lightening the race) than they would in peace time, these *lamayòteuses* maneuver in their own individualistic strategies to get something out of war. At times these power plays move from the individual to the collective. During World War I, Puerto Rican laundresses disrupted the army's reliance on their labor by striking to protest the war and demanding their sons be returned home. The military panicked and negotiated in earnest.[76]

But Mayotte stands on André's water-dominating balcony only as a guest. And as her position makes clear, André's need for her to wash his sheets and sleep between them gives her some power – but nothing like the state-sanctioned authority that commands the ships and planes darkening her view of the bay. In fact, her very necessity also works to disempower her, motivating André to control her movements outside his house (limiting who she dances with) and the Vichy government to control how sexualized bodies moved during wartime (limiting how eroticism can be expressed). "The militarization of women," Enloe stipulates, "has been so pervasive because so many military officials have presumed that they need to control not only women, but the very idea of 'femininity'"—and, I would add, sexuality.[77] This control became juridical in wartime Martinique, surfacing in laws that curtailed the rights of women and people with same-sex partners. The historian Eric Jennings notes that laws limiting women's and gays' access to jobs were more stringently enforced in the West Indies than in the Hexagon; here prostitutes, abortionists, career women, and "sodomites" were identified and targeted by government policies as enemies of "normal" gender roles and so of the state.[78] The military needed clean women—washerwomen, hetero-lovers, mothers—to attend to sailors; resisters to this order, like those who attempted to cross the water to join the Resistance, were made examples of.

Vichy desired women like Mayotte, then, both as Martinican workers and as Martinican symbols. As he and his navy need her on a material level, on a symbolic level, too, André needs Mayotte to bleach his dirty laundry: to legitimize his power over her labor and land by being "voluntarily" seduced by a French baby father, so willingly washing out an erotic history with women of color to lighten the race. Placing the *manman dlo*'s habitat—water and its feminized crosscurrents—under symbolic attack, Vichy's ideology in the tropics was propagated around a rhetoric of *return to the earth*. This valorization of the fictively solid, unchanging, and so wholesome grounds of Frenchness attempted to reduce all forms of earth to the same thing, the hallowed land of the *mère patrie*. The quintessential moment of this reduction came in 1942, when Robert arranged for a sample of the earth from each commune of Martinique to be sent to Gergovie, "where, from all corners of the Empire, there will arrive similar parcels containing earth from each village in France, from this metropolitan and colonial France whose indivisible unity is admired the world over!"[79] This mythic return to the earth was paired with a *return to the family*—but not, of course, just any family. Marginalizing flexible, gynocentric family models symbolized by the *manman dlo*'s river and actualized in kinship networks, tropical Vichy glorified the patriarchal nuclear family and identified its order with the ultimate patriarch, Marshal Pétain. As Richard Burton documents, wartime Martinique propagated a romance of the patriarchal overtaking the matriarchal that was also a romance of Vichy overtaking Martinique; and hailing his fictive omnipotence and omnipresence, "every parade, demonstration or ceremony – whether the consecration of Bishop Varin de la Brunière in January 1942, the annual celebration of Joan of Arc, or a simple distribution of scholastic prizes – becomes an occasion to celebrate the saving and healing powers of the totemic Great Father."[80] The mother of water's healing powers are eclipsed by those of Father Pétain, the figure whose mythic representation Martinicans are now urged to put their faith in. In this urging, Martinique is propagandized to love its submission to French penetration as faithfully as a woman loves the father of her children; if she does, material rewards follow for loyal Caribbean colonies as for loyal Caribbean consorts.

Capécia's balcony scene at once reflects and critiques this sexualized symbolic order. As the morning continues, Mayotte cultivates the illusion that André gives Martinique to her as a gift. When he names the bodies of water visible from the balcony, she raves: "It seemed to me that everything he named belonged to me" (137).[81] On the one hand, as Mayotte plays on André's patriarchal fantasies of being the provider for a house, woman, and dog by letting him "give" her all she views, she puts herself in the position of a military strategist taking over the waters in her line of vision. Loulouze had no place to offer Mayotte, not even a spare room. But because the patriarch in training André needs a woman in his bed- and laundry room, his house becomes a position from which Mayotte can maneuver – if only in her imagination, if only for a morning – to regain control over water that she had stopped splashing freely in when Loulouze left the Cambeille. At the same time, however, this gift recalls the counterfeit gold bracelet that Loulouze received from her own white male lover; it immediately announces itself as a lure, a false promise. Over the course of the novel André gives Mayotte no property, no steady income, and little concrete besides a child, so that his enactment of the Great Father role benefits Mayotte as little as Pétain's fathering benefitted Martinique. Patriarchal protectorship gives Martinique and Martiniquaises an illusion ("it seemed to me") of participation in power while real gold and authority remain locked onboard the Émile Bertin. In this view from André's house, scripts of compulsory heterosexuality and benevolent patriarchy – rather than of "passive" homosexuality (as chez Fanon) – surface as the tricky imperial desire that screws the Antilles.

Finally, unlike the mati's ecology, Bliss's wide open sea, or Faubert's Haiti of the imagination, the fluid universe of I Am a Martinican Woman leaves little physical or discursive space for the Caribbean woman to maneuver. The washerwomen's Cambeille runs into the policed bay; Capécia's narrative runs into

André's. While the novel begins with the possibility of swimming with women of color's fluidly desiring bodies, the move from myth to history proves a slippery and dangerous enterprise for Martinican women and waters. Again and again, the *manman dlo*'s obscured, potentially disruptive desire is unrelentingly undermined by the "somber mass" of a militarily buttressed colonial machine. Only in the gaps — *lamayòts* — that Capécia succeeds in breaking into André's narrative, in the short but powerful "storms" that disrupt the text's flow, does a narrow space open to imagine an/other's mermaidlike desire. The harbor at the end of the passage reads as a powerful metaphor for this space. Even from André's house, the grammatically and metaphorically feminized "deep blue harbor [*la rade*]" — water now without Loulouze's body as a focal point — remains the site to which Mayotte's gaze gravitates, moving past the grammatically and symbolically masculine *Émile Bertin*. Here she looks for "the image of my happiness" only to find her sexual autonomy "hemmed in by the hills": the deep blue of eroticism remembered from other waters secretly remains in Mayotte's psychic landscape even in André's bedroom, but it never finds its own place. The *Martiniquaise*'s harbor is always hemmed in by other structures; and yet, like the promised eruption of storms and mermaids, always threatening to disrupt calm meanings and configurations of the seemingly placid view and the seemingly unthreatening text. When Fanon professed to know nothing about the woman of color's sexuality, perhaps this was why: how could he locate such a *lamayòt*-like, fleeting thing? In Capécia's Martinique the possibilities for a "real" emergence of brown women's eroticism seem like those sea-threatened atolls that surface and disappear again as tides fall and rise, fall and rise.

*   *   *

> There are, layered up against the islands, the beautiful green
> waves of water and silence. . . . We can only guess about the easy
> love of fish. They make the water move, which amicably winks at
> the clipper's porthole. . . . And as for the hummingbird-women,
> the tropical flower-women, the women of four races and dozens
> of bloodlines, they are no longer there.
> — Suzanne Césaire, "The Great Camouflage"

One of the most memorable, painfully beautiful texts written by a Martinican woman during World War II, Suzanne Césaire's "Great Camouflage" (1945) opens with a surrealist subversion of the arriving tourist's gaze on Martinique — a gaze she pushes to look beyond "perfect colors and forms" and see "the plot of unsatisfied desires [that] has ensnared the Antilles."[82] The endlessly troubling, anti-imperial, antisexist Caribbean Sea that she paints haunts me for many reasons, not the least of which is how rich an image it offers for the unsatisfied Martinican woman's desires that ensnare Capécia's work. Mayotte's sexual fluidity moves through the novel not as the turquoise flow of freedom and cash that Olivia advertises, but as green waves of water and silence that reflect great camouflage and lamayòtaj. As for the easy love of fish, readers are left only able to guess about the love of washerwomen; but we know that the exotic stereotypes that pin Capécia in—the orange- and banana-woman living in a free love zone that northern lesbians dream of visiting—must be washed away, no longer there. In these West Indian "specks of dust," as Charles de Gaulle imagined them, motion from shore to shore, lover to lover is not necessarily or simply a libratory practice. It can be libratory when la guiablesse and Loulouze navigate the Cambeille. At the same time, when rivers run to the sea and the Émile Bertin oversees the harbor, it can also emerge as a product of colonial histories, one that can be redirected to serve imperial needs just as Mayotte flows into André's arms. I Am a Martinican Woman paints concrete examples of why transnational queer travelers and thinkers approaching the Caribbean need to come ready to complicate fluidity and other conceptual geographies, and to look for all the crossings of washerwomen and warships that make the Fort-de-France bay what it is for Mayotte. Traveling to expanded, historically specific queer oceanographies means looking not only elsewhere but otherwise; it means plotting how sexuality, class, and imperialism mix into and wash through each other in slippery, opaque ways in Caribbean rivers and bays, expanding and limiting what Martinican women can want and have in the wake of battle- and cruise ships.

five

Transforming Sugar, Transitioning Revolution

Male Womanhood and Lesbian Eroticism
in Michelle Cliff's No Telephone to Heaven

Transgendered individuals (especially men to women) maintain
a very low public profile due to the overwhelmingly negative
attitudes toward them, and are therefore not commonly subject
to public scrutiny.

—Anthony Hron, *Report on Persecution of Sexual Minorities in Jamaica*

And so it came to pass that upon that time, not so long ago,
in that part of the world, there lived a child who dreamt.
I am not so sure even now as to the definitive facial features
of that child, but I am fairly certain, having myself wandered
through various dreams that became stories that were told
and did not fade over time, that the child was both female and
male—a common enough occurrence in that place of the child's
origin at that time, as, contrary to numerous prevailing opinions,
happens frequently today.

—Thomas Glave, "Whose Caribbean? An Allegory, in Part"

"Between you and me, it's over with now."[1] So pronounced Jowelle De Souza, answering a reporter's questions in her San Fernando, Trinidad, beauty salon wearing a sea blue dress that caught her interviewer's eye.[2] Born Joel, De Souza underwent surgical sex reassignment at nineteen and made history in 2001 by becoming the first transsexual Trinidadian to sue the state for a violation of constitutional rights and win. Charged with assault in 1997 for pushing a photographer shooting unauthorized pictures, she was hauled to a police station where officers harassed her for hours about her gender and (perceived) sexuality. They finally forced an unwarranted strip search to determine her sex — "even though," the reporter notes, "her identification and appearance indicated that she was a woman."[3] Four years later, outstandingly represented by the attorney general's wife Lynette Maharaj, De Souza won $5,000 in damages and logged an important public opinion victory as, the New York-based Trinidadian activist Colin Robinson notes, press reports routinely waxed sympathetic to her case.[4] Whether or not De Souza was "really" a woman did not become the issue here, and reporters commented admiringly on her beauty, grace, and dresses. This intelligent beauty went on to become one of the region's most prominent LGBT rights activists, advocating for the legal protection of transsexuals, lesbians, and gays — even if regional gay rights advocates have not, in response, expanded their platforms to deal specifically with transsexual and transgender issues. The first Caribbean nation to outlaw sex between females in 1986, De Souza's Trinidad currently criminalizes all same-sex sexuality and prohibits gay immigration. However, De Souza firmly believes this situation will change soon. "I'm quite confident that the Equal Opportunity Bill [for LGBT rights] will be implemented. We have our people on both the Opposition and government sides, they are there," she told a reporter in 2005. "I know them and you know them too, and they are looking out for us . . . soon something will happen for us." The reporter goes on to note: "Some years ago, Jowelle, formerly a male named Joel, publicly declared a sex-change. And now the sexy socialite keeps heads turning anywhere she goes."[5] The stories the press tells of the "sexy socialite" are sympathetic, indeed — and flirtatious in ways that are simultaneously exoticizing, patronizing, supportive, and appreciative.

Such press coverage mythifies De Souza's moral strength and beauty, accompanying her David-and-Goliath legal story with glamorous head shots that highlight silky tresses in the manner of manman dlo. And it publicizes that — despite what Anthony Hron reports, and in line with what Thomas Glave poeticizes — recognizable public spaces supporting gender complexity do currently exist in the Caribbean. These may be the beauty shop that De Souza owns, government offices where she projects her hopes, and now, as Robinson notes, local and international media. In the case of the latter, the supportiveness of its discursive space is architectured by showily inserting De Souza into heterosexual scripts. The abusive police officers thought they were taunting a gay man, articles suggest, and they should never have done that – not necessarily because taunting gays is wrong but because De Souza is "actually" a heterosexual woman, so much so that male reporters and the head-turning public cannot help but be charmed by her. Reporters' flirtatious documentation of their own response to her heterosexual desirability collaborates with their descriptions of her female-imprinted identification to build proof that she is, indeed, a real woman. Even as they report these nearly queer ideas of who Caribbeans look at as a beautiful woman, the heterosexual clichés through which they frame her coquettish portrait bold-print a lack of imagination around this woman's sexual possibilities. What if De Souza were both a "real woman" and "gay" – if she both became a woman and desired to turn the heads of other women passing by? To be both/and rather than either-or hovers as an impossible story to narrate even in this putatively supportive framework, a story with no readily formed language or neatly turned phrases to sell to readers.

Tracking the both/and as black feminist praxis, this chapter asks what it might mean for a nonbiological woman to love another woman in the Caribbean – how such a configuration of desires pressures narratives of gender, sexuality, race, nationality, and class in ways that both are and are not like other stories of female same-sex relationships.[6] This inquiry is framed through a reading of the second novel published by the Jamaican writer whose question I echo again here, Michelle Cliff's *No Telephone to Heaven* (1987). Cliff's first novel, *Abeng* (1983), spins a subtext of female same-sex desire between the preteen protagonist Clare Savage and her playmate Zoe as the girls explore Clare's grandmother's land and river side by side in rural Jamaica. Its sequel, *No Telephone to Heaven*, pushes more openly against narratives of sexual and gender normativity by rescripting these erotic journeys with Zoe between Clare and the novel's male woman character, Harry/Harriet, who lovingly survey Jamaica and each other in more sexually and politically adult ways. The scenes that Cliff scripts between the two are unique in Caribbean literature not because they feature a gender-complex character but because they imagine this character loving her own kind (as Harry/Harriet puts it) – that is, loving another Afro-Caribbean woman.[7] As these women travel Caribbean back roads together, they open space for readers to question what intersections between male woman-ness and lesbianism, gender and sexual complexity do, and do not, make black feminist sense in this regional and historical context. De Souza's press coverage, as well as her activism, point to reasons why the two should not be summarily divorced; such separations risk reinforcing heterosexual scripts, on the one hand, and justifying gay rights' groups' continual marginalization of trans-gender issues, on the other. At the same time, neither should the two be con-flated, as groundbreaking transsexual and transgender scholars of the Global North, including Jay Prosser and Viviane Namaste, have strongly argued; such conflation once again renders invisible the specificities of gender-complex experiences and politics, reinforcing trans-ignorance and homonormativity.[8] Traveling precariously between these two poles, Cliff's love story between a male woman and a latent lesbian charts intersections that open new erotic and social directions for both characters – but also bumps into rougher junctures that, either by overlooking or forcing connections between the two women's situations, narrow the roads she looks to open.

Before I follow these travels, let me open a brief note on terminology. Navi-gating a variety of fictional, biographical, philosophical, psychological, and theoretical texts that thematize male femininity in the Caribbean, I avoid using the terms transgender or transsexual, common in the Global North, to refer to such formations "in general." While these terms do important social and critical work, they are neither the only nor the most prominent ones in this context. [9] Instead, I move between various noun phrases suggested by the texts themselves – macommère, girlfriend, male woman – to reflect the multiplicity and nonfixity of genders that circulate in and around the Carib-bean. For an umbrella term, I follow Randy Conner's use of the phrase gender complexity, which, referencing Edgar Morin, he employs to connote "a kind of thinking that, instead of isolating the object being studied, considers it in and through its . . . relation to its cultural, social, economic, political, and natu-ral environment."[10] To speak of desire between gender-complex women and other women I draw on Cliff's own term for Harry/Harriet and other women who love women, the previously backgrounded lesbian. When nouns become pronouns in my discussion of No Telephone to Heaven, I again take Cliff's lead in sometimes using the split s/he and her/him and at others simply her to refer to Harry/Harriet (later Harriet), depending on how the character frames her (or her/his) experience in the scenes in question. Like the multiplied nouns, the splitting and changing pronouns may at times be jarring or confusing – but in ways intended to be meaningful. As Kate More and Stephen Whittle explain their own split pronouns in a note to the typesetter included in *Reclaiming Genders*: "h/is, h/er, s/he, f/h-email: This strange set of constructions, where an oblique stroke is used to introduce an approximate break in the subject between the signifier/signified, sex/gender is deliberate."[11] The instability and mutability of my nouns and pronouns here speak to an ongoing exploration of how language constantly attempts and reattempts to define, undefine, and redefine imaginations of the racialized genders that Caribbeans can live out and desire: how the watery images that sirenize De Souza dissolve and reconstitute themselves to mythologize Harry/Harriet, how the landscape metaphors that naturalize Clare's racial hybridity spill over into Harry/Harriet's gender complexity, and how these mobile figures trace and trouble ever-changing "natures" of gender and sexuality in the neocolonial West Indies.

Who Wants to Be a Woman and Loves Women?: Harry/Harriet's Impossible Desires

In her *New York Times* review of *No Telephone to Heaven*, Michiko Kakutani praises the lyrical, uncompromising prose with which Cliff continues the story of *Abeng* protagonist Clare Savage, the light-skinned, green-eyed mulatta who returns as a now adult "spiritual exile, a wanderer between cultures." She notes less enthusiastically the introduction of another mixed-race character who becomes Clare's intimate friend, "a hermaphrodite named Harry/Harriet" whom Kakutani reads as an "awkward, heavy-handed" representation of "the divided psyche of many Jamaicans."[12] But in an interview with Meryl Schwarz conducted in 1992, Cliff paints an almost diametrically opposed picture of this character, explaining that s/he was conceived as the ideally integrated Jamaican subject—"female and male, black and white" and able "to deal with it, to say 'this is who I am. Even if I'm the only one in the world, this is who I am.'"[13] For Cliff, Harry/Harriet is the novel's "most complete character" and its "hero/heroine," a foil for Clare's unresolved racial and sexual fragmentation.[14] When Schwarz comments on Clare's inability to act on same-sex desire, Cliff reorients this reading and points to the character's romantic interlude with Harry/Harriet: "Her love for Harry/Harriet is a step towards herself. And if she wasn't killed she probably would have gone the whole way. Harry/Harriet is the novel's lesbian in a sense; he's a man who wants to be a woman, and he loves women, which is complicated."[15] Later she explains that it is with this mulatta, woman-loving, feminine male character that she – as a mixed-race female Jamaican lesbian – identifies, rather than with Clare.[16] Yet as clear as this identification is for Cliff, for early readers like Kakutani and Schwarz, the unexpected choice of a male woman to represent not only the author's most complete vision of Jamaica but her most decolonized vision of Jamaican lesbianism – her own answer to what it means "for a woman to love another woman in the Caribbean" – emerges as an unmistakably charged metaphor for something that remains confusingly opaque, not easily translated via familiar tropes of race, nation, or same-gender desire.

If Harry/Harriet's desire to "be a woman, and love women" evokes perplexity, this certainly is not because male gender complexity was previously unimagined in the Caribbean. Easily locatable in certain districts of late twentieth-century capitals like Santo Domingo and Port-of-Spain, the visible presence of male women in the region had in fact been documented for centuries when No Telephone was published. Enslaved male women's relationships with men on sugar plantations were recorded not only by Méderic Moreau de St. Méry in eighteenth-century Haiti (as noted in chapter 1) but also by Esteban Montejo in his memories of nineteenth-century Cuba. Montejo remembers that despite "effeminacy"'s stigma in Fidel Castro's Cuba, men's partnerships with male wives were common and accepted during slavery: "Many men . . . had sex with each other and didn't want anything to do with women. . . . Those men washed clothes, and if they had a husband, they also cooked for him. They were good workers and were busy tending their conucos. They gave the produce to their husbands to sell to the guajiros. And the word effeminate came about after slavery because that situation continued on."[17] This testimony offers an important addition to colonial chronicles' notes on enslaved females' self-decoration with flowers, head wraps, and other expressions of reclaimed femininity. It suggests that the work of thiefing and transculturating femininity – a gender that chattel slavery attempted to systematically disallow enslaved Africans – was undertaken not only by females but also by woman-identified males: that while racialized colonial gender systems insisted that not even African females could be "real" women, the enslaved developed gender systems in which not even males could be denied this possibility by material bondage. At the same time, in Montejo's memory as in the mati's, this reclaiming of femininity did not constitute luxury but work. Good wives were "good workers" who used plantation land to grow and sell their own produce; their gender complexity –

like Montejo's maroonage – was not merely "about" individual self-expression but about configuring relationships that literally and figuratively worked for cane workers rather than plantation owners.

And as Montejo notes, this division of gender and labor did not end with slavery. Such continuing situations generated a spectrum of Creolized names beyond effeminate to designate culturally specific formations of male femininity – including Suriname's male mati, Caribbean Spanish travestí, and the French/Kreyòl masisi and macommère. These male women are routinely understood as "natural" parts of the Caribbean cultural landscape and occupy recognized places in their communities; every Haitian has a masisi in their hometown, one native of Grand-Anse assured me.[18] Like same-sex-loving female women, male mati and masisi often play important roles in Afro-Caribbean spiritual communities as devotees of and mediums for Oshún, Ezili, and related spirits of sweet water and femininity, those figures of the divine, endlessly drinkable creativity of feminine sexuality in its myriad forms. The problem in making sense of Harry/Harriet, then, stems less from the absence of a regional frame of reference for male womanishness as a longtime part of Caribbean super/nature than from a disconnect around imagining feminine males literally and metaphorically tending gardens not for male husbands but for lesbian lovers – in imagining male macommères not in competition with female commères but in pursuit of such women as same-gender sexual interests. Yes, of course, a male might "want to be a woman" in the Caribbean. But for a male woman to want a woman still lurks in the realm of what Gayatri Gopinath calls "impossible desires": those desires that remain illegible, invisible, or nonsensical to dominant discourses, including hegemonic feminisms and postcolonial nationalisms.[19] While Gopinath focuses on how queer female and feminine desires lurk in the margins of South Asian nationalist imaginations, Cliff's male mulatta's love for her own, mulatta kind fleshes out transgressive possibilities yet to be conceptualized by the lesbian feminisms and West Indian postcolonialisms circulating in the 1980s Americas.

Certainly, in the garden-positive Massachusetts and California feminist communities where Cliff and her partner Adrienne Rich lived in the 1970s and 1980s, the possibility of male lesbianism remained – at best – a thorny, unresolved controversy. Both Cliff and Rich found their names loosely tied to this controversy in the peritext of Janice Raymond's infamous lesbian feminist manifesto against gender complexity, *The Transsexual Empire*, published in 1979. The acknowledgments thank Rich profusely but nod more reservedly to Cliff

for her publishing advice and for having "encouraged, in many ways, the publication of this book" – though in other ways she was apparently not so encouraging.[20] Raymond starts her polemic by finding fault with transsexual women
for their excessive femininity in relationships with biological men. Transwom-
en's (Oshún-like?) embrace of cosmetics, frilly clothes, and cooking and ironing
for boyfriends and husbands, she seethes, represents a harsh setback to feminism's rethinking of gender roles. But when in the chapter "Sappho by Sur-
gery" the subject turns to transwomen's sexual relationships with biological
women, she now accuses these "transsexually constructed lesbian feminists"
of excessive masculinity – of treating biological women with the entitlement
and possessiveness characteristic (Raymond believes) of all patriarchs.[21] Disguised heterosexuals and "synthetic hybrids" who act out the worst of both
masculinity and femininity, trans lesbians are, she virulently argues, nothing
less than boundary violators who "not only violate the boundaries of women's
bodies but of our minds and spirits . . . our boundaries of self-definition," trespassing on women's physical and psychic spaces.[22] In her worldview, then,
male women can never tend female lesbians' gardens; they can only invade
and overrun them. This stunning, purportedly feminist defense of transphobia
seethes with an unquestioned fear of an omnipotent masculinity that inevitably overwhelms both male femininity and feminist empowerment, keeping
females rooted as heterosexual sex objects while males gallivant through any
number of gender and sexual configurations. But however they present themselves, Raymond insists, transsexuals can never become "real" lesbians, only
interlopers.

   Much less vocally but equally tenaciously, prominent Caribbean postcolonial thinkers – inspired in the 1980s by the masculinist figure of the maroon,
not the maroon's male wife – also remained impervious and resistant to the
possibility of male women's desire for women. One of the most notable and
bizarre proclamations on interactions between male and female women in the
Caribbean comes in Frantz Fanon's Black Skin, White Masks, rereleased on the
twenty-fifth anniversary of his death the year before No Telephone's publication. While Fanon differs radically from Raymond in his understanding of empire and/as sexuality, their analyses converge on one point: on the exceptional
occasion when male femininity is considered in relationship to bio-women,
the macommères who might appear so decidedly not-men beside heterosexual
male masculinity are suddenly imagined acting just like men toward female
femininity. But for Fanon, this is a sign of Caribbean sexual health. His in-

famous footnote on the absence of homosexuality in the Antilles continues
ever more problematically, first conflating sexual and gender non-normativity,
then proudly denying that the latter implies the former. After proclaiming the
nonexistence of Caribbean homosexuals, he concedes: "We should not overlook,
however, the existence of what are called there 'men dressed like women' or
'god-mothers' ("Ma Commères" in the original French text). Generally they
wear shirts and skirts. But I am convinced that they lead normal sex lives ... they
are not impervious to the allures of women – fish and vegetable merchants."[23]
Not impervious could, of course, mean many things. But assuming that it suggests sexual-erotic contact, market women seem very iffy figures for proving
macommères' disinterest in non-normative sex. In fact, female merchants had
long been known to maintain relationships with women in the Francophone
Caribbean. In the early twentieth century, partnerships between madan sara
(female traveling vendors) and other women were commonplace as communities recognized these itinerant workers' need for a wife to perform the kind of
domestic labor that Montejo remembers male wives providing.[24] Madan saras'
homo-seductions were in fact so commonplace, Havelock Ellis reports, that
European women travelers were shocked by the openness of French Caribbean
market women's advances.[25] Quite possibly, then, the fish vendors that Fanon
evokes might be flirting with macommères as women desiring women. Nonetheless, Fanon insists that this interaction proves macommères' preference for
"normal" sex, which – his chapter on sexual pathology makes clear – he limits
to heterosexual encounters whose main event is penis-vagina intercourse.

What else could market women and macommères do in bed together, and
how else might they understand, touch each other's skirt-covered bodies besides as male men meeting female women? Édouard Glissant, in his watershed *Caribbean Discourse*, offers a brief but evocative suggestion regarding why
these questions can be neither asked nor answered in prominent Caribbean
thinkers' texts – why, as he puts it, so little variation in sexual practice can
be imagined as "possible desires" in the region. For him it is not a problem of
male sexuality programmed for invasion but of Caribbean sexuality reduced to
little more than evasion, snatched on the run and never developed in all its possibilities. In "Pleasure and Jouissance," Glissant contends that to understand
Martinican sexuality one must take a historical view, and he takes as his "point
zero" cane fields in which slaves' hidden sexual encounters – acts completed
almost literally in flight, as male slaves grab and penetrate females while both
move through the cane – momentarily nullified slavery's systematic reification

of their bodies, thiefing sugar in a brutally abrupt way. But far from finding space to explore the multiple possibilities of bodily pleasure, Glissant concludes that "this clandestine jouissance, these orgasms snatched under cover create a hunger for and an obsession with orgasm, a violent and uncontrollable desire to move immediately to the definitive impunity of the act, which sums up and annihilates the pleasure of orgasm."[26] So he finds Martinicans caught in a "short circuited" heterosexuality stolen from under the masters' gaze, a frenetic insertion of penis into vagina evacuated of all variation or eroticism.[27]

This leads, on the one hand, to a cultural understanding of the penetrating penis as a dangerous tool-cum-weapon, a redeployed machete that simultaneously steals the master's property and subjugates the penetrated partner to create a fleeting sense of power. Glissant supports this by noting the "mutilating transitivity" of Kreyòl phrases that denote penis-vagina sex—"coupé famm' la, batt famm'là, raché famm' la," cut a woman, beat a woman, hack off a woman.[28] On the other hand, the penetrated orifice becomes an abject site of powerlessness and degradation, a sticky object of revulsion entered and exited as quickly as possible, while its possessor, "the most extreme victim" in Glissant's sexual universe, lies immobilized by "sexual indifference."[29] This is why virtually no Martinican male, Glissant posits, desires to pleasure a woman; and why absolutely no Martinican male would desire to be a woman, so thrusting her/himself into a victimhood that postslavery Caribbeans burned to leave behind. A Caribbean male cannot, would not, be a woman tending another woman's garden in Glissant's landscape, then, because all garden space—all space for feminine eroticism—is choked out by the shadows of violent cane fields.

I rehearse Glissant's unfinished Caribbean sexual geography here not, of course, to second his mappings. On the contrary, *Thiefing Sugar* starts from a similar point zero to move into an opposite direction, tracing the continually opening, never short-circuited possibilities that Caribbean women imagine for their erotic journeys through many land- and seascapes. Rather, my interest in Glissant's sketchy analysis is the window it offers into the Caribbean construction of what Marlon Bailey and Matt Richardson have insightfully discussed as a culturally specific black queer gender phobia in the (post)slavery Americas.[30] The queer gender phobia of black masculinist intellectuals, Bailey and Richardson posit, cannot be understood as "the same" construction as the transphobia of white feminists like Raymond. Instead, to unravel the former one must, like Glissant, return to the gendered particularities violently enunciated by slavery and its aftermath.

Following Fanon, they argue that as the Other, black males (like white women) have been barred from phallic power from the moment they became property. As chattel, rather than having the phallus – Jacques Lacan's precondition for manhood – they are the eternally erect penis that negrophobes simultaneously fear and desire, big black dicks whose frightening potency justifies brutality to their bodies and psyches. Black nationalist discourse, in turn, responds to this violent shadow of the black as biological/sex by investing genitalia with particular, slavery-haunted roles in power struggles. Like Glissant's male slaves with their machete-penises, black males are charged with reclaiming that frustrated potency by using the penis to fight for access to phallic power, staking a claim to "real manhood" through their hyperperformance as masterful heterosexual lovers, husbands, and fathers. In turn, black females, like the slaves on their backs in the cane, are charged with opening their vaginas as vehicles through which black men stake a claim to phallic masculinity, becoming "their" heterosexual sex objects, spouses, and baby mothers. The reverse side of this fetishization of normative gender roles tied to stark division between two (and only two) sexes is a phobia of blacks who trouble these uses of the body. This phobia is no individual neurosis but a matter of official discourse: for while black friends, families, and communities may often accept sissies and masisi as one of many kinds of people they live, work, and recreate with, the self-consciously representative texts of black masculinist leaders never can. Those who have a penis but do not use it to penetrate, those who do not have a penis but do not want to be penetrated, those with a penis who do not want to be black men, those with a vagina who do not want to be black men's women: in the discourses of ministers, politicians, and public intellectuals, all routinely become objects of a black queer gender phobia that fears not so much these individuals per se but the possibility they represent. Namely, that blacks may never be men and women – that is, fully human – in the way that whites are; that blacks may never master hegemonic gender in the way that whites once mastered blacks.

So the macommère who loves the madan sara, the male woman who loves female women, becomes an impossible subject in black masculinist landscapes like Fanon's marketplace and Glissant's cane field because she doubly, volatilely activates black queer gender phobia. As someone with a penis who at once refuses to chase phallic power and lets herself be chased by a woman who will be penetrated by no man while they are together, she doubly pressures the fragile, cherished fiction of powerfully hypernormative black male masculinity – and so cannot be imagined within such black masculinist discourse without exploding it. At the same, time, however, when she raises herself out of the shadow of the cane field, this figure stands to doubly dismantle the psycho-sexual enslavement that short-circuits eroticism in Glissant's Caribbean. If those who have penises do not have to use them as the machetes that slavery constrained them to do, they can develop not only different kinds of eroticism but also different vehicles of resistance; they can decolonize gender and sexuality otherwise. And if feminine sexuality does not have to play victim to a masculinity unimaginatively frozen as always already violent, it can become something that both females and males can claim and celebrate as women and with women; they can gender and eroticize postcoloniality otherwise.

Harry/Harriet is at once difficult for 1980s feminist or postcolonial critics to decipher and (in the novelist's own opinion) Cliff's most radical vision of decolonized gender and sexuality because s/he is imagined as the ideal, meta-phorically perfect figure of this Caribbean otherwise. Her/his integration of "female and male, black and white," works through an alternative vision of wholeness that counters black masculinism's pursuit of white masculine phallic power. And her/his role as sexual, emotional, and political guide for the wandering, almost-tragic mulatta Clare traces an alternative mapping of male femininity's journey that moves against Raymond's fear of invasion or Glissant's curse of evasion. Instead, her guided tours through a rural Jamaica unknown to Clare and her lessons in finding beaches and mangroves, histories and politics models a revolutionary pleasure in free-floating, transversal con-nections between West Indians and the flora, fauna, men, women, and poten-tialities around them. As s/he leads Clare to new Caribbean landscapes and desires, s/he indeed becomes the male woman who tends another woman's garden, helping Clare come to the decision to reclaim and cultivate maternal lands gone to ruin in postcolonial Jamaica. And when Clare and Harriet return to the fields of St. Elizabeth not as cane workers but as landowners, they grow crops not to sustain themselves as individuals but to finance a group revolu-tionary action. This constellation of ideally integrated, politically radical char-acteristics united in Harry/Harriet create a Jamaican male lesbian figure whose metaphoric import is indeed unmissable but whose believability as a realistic character is consistently strained by her perfection as a symbol. Harry/Harriet makes sense not as an "accurate" representation of the psychological and cul-tural complexities lived by male Caribbean women who love women but as a mythic character constructed to counter a composite of myths about male femininity and desire that loom as huge and violent as the cane field.

Wonderful Adventures of a Male Mrs. Seacole:
Trans-ing Black Women's History

Yet unlike the more realistically drawn Clare, whose name echoes that of the fictional protagonist of Nella Larsen's *Passing*, Harry/Harriet is a myth who builds on "real life" black women's history. Her name and travels repeat those of another revolutionary who chose the same first name, Harriet (née Araminta Ross) Tubman; and her work as healer puts her in a similar red-caped costume and community-building role as the "yellow doctress" Mary Seacole, the famous Jamaican to whom Cliff compares her more than once. Marking Harry/Harriet as an imaginative extension of these two figures – whose (auto)biographies received a flurry of attention in 1980s feminist media and scholarship, heralded as rediscovered "mother's gardens" of history – Cliff locates her character not as part of an eccentric or queer past but as one in a powerful, celebrated line of women of African descent applauded for their literal boundary crossings.[31] Born into slave societies, these black and brown women traveled across national borders rather than remaining supine in the fields, and their travels were neither invasion nor evasion but a passage to new narratives of racialized gender.

While both were memorialized as examples of conventionally upstanding womanhood (Tubman's name graced a black branch of the Women's Christian Temperance Union, Seacole's the headquarters of the Jamaican General Trained Nurses' Association), Cliff's linkage between these figures and an unconventional male woman expands on an infrequently noted aspect of their (auto)biographies. On their travels to emancipation and healing, "the Moses of her People" (Tubman) and "the female Ulysses" (Seacole) come across – and at times become – female men, men in dresses, and travelers whose genders change as they move. That is, they enter what Clare Sears, in her research on California gold rush migrations, calls the "spaces of possibility for male femininities and female masculinities" enabled by migratory movements.[32] Offering a corrective to unidimensional, invasion-versus-evasion analyses of gender complexity and/as movement, Sears's work outlines the importance of trans-ing histories of migration: that is, of opening intersectional – literally trans – analyses of how sex, gender, sexuality, class, race, and nationality pressure each other in the cross-gender practices that occur during relocation. And indeed, Cliff's portrait of Harry/Harriet in many ways reads as a trans-ing of the migration stories told by Tubman and Seacole. Jarring but frequently uncommented moments of cross-gender practice in their narratives underscore that blacks' gender non-normativity has long formed part of the celebrated journey to freedom; and that seeds of the myth of Harry/Harriet's transcendent gender complexity had long lain dormant in canonical imaginings of African diaspora femininity.

Reflecting on Tubman as portrayed in the 1978 miniseries *A Woman Called Moses*, Cliff, in an article published in *Sinister Wisdom* in 1982, offers her as a self-motivated feminist role model who first connects to and transforms herself to be powerfully able to connect to and transform the conditions of her fellow enslaved.[33] Indeed, Sarah Bradford's classic biography *Harriet Tubman: The Moses of Her People* (1886)—based on extensive interviews and testimonies echoed in the series—shows Tubman with remarkable confidence in her ability to transform the restrictive, supposedly natural properties of the world she navigates from bondage to freedom. For Tubman, the landscape itself can and must be remade to enable passage. The biography repeats this incident twice: on a journey north, Tubman's party comes to a stream that the men with her were afraid to cross—but Tubman insists that if she calls for divine intervention, God will calm the stream to allow them to cross. She plunges in and finds "de water never came above my chin; when we thought surely we were all going under, it became shallower and shallower, and we came out safe on the odder side," so that Bradford concludes: "To her was literally fulfilled the promise: 'When through the deep waters I cause thee to go / The rivers of sorrow shall not overflow.'"[34] While this stream may simply be one that rapidly rises from deep to shallow, neither Tubman nor Bradford consider this explanation. Instead, both emphasize the power of language—Harriet's divinely charged language first in entreating God, then in reporting the incident as a small miracle—to reshape southern landscapes in which enslavement had been naturalized, opening paths for black bodies to cross "the magic line" to emancipation.[35]

And as the woman called Moses leads parties northward, natural and unnatural genders—particularly black female masculinities—also, like landscape, can and must be remade. Sometimes cross-gendering serves as a temporary disguise for Underground Railroad travelers, as when the mulatta Catherine dons a suit to pass as a "darkey boy," rather than be the brown woman her master is hunting.[36] Yet more extensively and consistently, the narrative depicts Harriet herself/himself performing masculinity as part of freedom fighting— and doing so more convincingly than the males around her/him. Throughout the biography Bradford and her informants emphasize that Harriet "did all the work of a man" and traveled longer and more bravely than any, and that "powerful men often stood astonished to see this woman perform feats of strength from which they shrunk incapable."[37] But the most celebratory testament to Tubman's masculine valor comes from John Brown, who considered the comrade he named General Tubman to be one of his men. Bradford cites a letter in which Brown refers to Harriet entirely in the masculine: "He (Harriet) is the most of a man naturally that I ever met with. There is abundant material here and of the right quality."[38] Brown's language here, like Tubman's earlier, forcefully rescripts the "nature" of the antebellum South: in this terrain of struggle, female manness manifests itself most naturally and springs from the richest raw materials. Of course, blacks' notable, natural propensity for female masculinity was a long entrenched theme in racist fictions of Africans' social and biological underdevelopment; like the (probable) steep rise to the stream Tubman fords, this rhetoric had existed in the South for a long time. But Brown and Bradford, describing Harriet's awe-inspiring crossed gender, radically reorient these meanings of black female masculinity. Borne on Tubman's capable shoulders, this female masculinity signifies that just as blacks need not be classified as lesser humans than whites, females need not live as lesser physical or moral forces than males – that rather than lying in fields as receptacles for phallic power, they, like (and more bravely than) males, can flee fields altogether.

In Tubman, then, Cliff taps into an underexplored black history of heroic gender crossing; but where is a history of the heroic femininity that Harry/ Harriet also exemplifies? Such bonneted, womanly valor suffuses the *Wonderful Adventures of Mrs. Seacole*, the autobiography, published in 1857, of a freeborn Jamaican widow celebrated for her voyage to nurse British soldiers in the Crimea. Forgotten after brief postwar celebrity, Seacole's memory was revived by Jamaicans and black Britons after the accidental rediscovery of her grave led to a memorial for the centenary of her death in 1981 and the republication of her long out-of-print *Adventures* in 1984. Celebrating this reprint, the Kingston *Sunday Gleaner Magazine* proclaimed Seacole "nothing short of a Jamaican heroine" whose "statue should be today in Heroes' Park."[39] Her status as national heroine seems warranted by the widow's insistent combination of dangerous overseas exploits with a conscious upholding (or so she writes) of norms of respectable, bourgeois womanhood. Stressing her ability to recreate home in the battlefield with the nurturing power of "a woman's voice and a woman's care,"

Seacole directs the British public to read her trek as a traveling version of Victorian domesticity, an angel in the house going abroad.[40] But despite Seacole's care to write herself into Victorian mores, the femininity she sutures together throughout her adventures ends up quite a bit queerer than the normative ladylikeness she pays lip service to.

While Seacole became famous for her Crimean nursing, her *Adventures* begin in Panama. Here she opens the British Hotel, a lodging house for migrants come to build the world's first transcontinental railroad. Unlike ragged fellow travelers she arrives by sea "with that due regard to personal appearance, which I have always deemed a duty as well as a pleasure to study . . . in a delicate light blue dress, a white bonnet prettily trimmed, and an equally chaste shawl."[41] But the land she disembarks on is literally too slippery to sustain this Victorian-style femininity. Caught in a relentless downpour — and, unlike Tubman, unable to will water to recede — she finds herself forced to climb a soggy bank of red clay; steady slippage washes away borders between land and water, between rough nature and nurtured femininity as her pretty dress becomes so clayey it turns completely red. Finally arrived in town, she is surprised to see numerous other females arriving from gold rush California, and more surprised still at how their travel outfits differ from hers. Many, she writes, were "clothed as the men were, in flannel shirt and boots; and rode their mules in unfeminine fashion, but with much ease and courage; and in their conversation successfully rivaled the coarseness of their lords. I think, on the whole, that those French lady writers who desire to enjoy the privileges of men, with the irresponsibility of the other sex, would have been delighted with the disciples who were carrying their principles into practice."[42] Seeing the boundary between the sexes as forcefully washed away as that between land and water, Seacole waxes ambivalent about the female masculinity surging in this construction zone — her descriptions disapproving but grudgingly appreciative, acknowledging why educated European ladies would cheer such cross-gendering but refraining from agreeing. And she consistently depicts herself as avoiding dressing, riding, or sleeping around "like a man"; the only vaguely phallic thing she takes up is her brother's gun, brandished at a thief making off with her dress (money in its pocket). As in this scene, Seacole defends women's pursuit of physical and economic mobility conventionally denied feminine subjects, as well as their ability to protect the bodies and earnings that they move into traditionally masculine territory. At the same time, she also stakes femininity itself — the fine dress she proudly arrives in, the everyday one she snatches back — as something worth fighting for, worth trying to simultaneously preserve and recon-figure in this new territory. Seacole never states why this fight might be par-ticularly charged for her as a woman of color. But her sympathetic account of an enslaved mother's choice between freedom in Panama and reunification with a child in Louisiana shows this mulatta keenly aware of why sheltered femininity never came easily for travelers of African descent, why it might need and merit a strong defense.

After surviving nursing through a cholera epidemic and wading through floods, Seacole, "tired to death of life in Panama," turns her hotel over to her brother and leaves for London intent on joining Florence Nightingale's nursing brigade in the Crimea.[43] When her application meets with racist rejection, she determines to travel there independently and open another British Hotel to nurse, feed, and house the wounded. Unlike her trip to Panama, the ostensibly more dangerous voyage to Constantinople is literally, remarkably smooth sail-ing: "The weather, although cold, was fine, and the sea good-humouredly calm, and I enjoyed the voyage amazingly."[44] Here, surrounded by males and militar-ism, Seacole depicts herself settling much more comfortably into her nurtur-ing femininity than among female migrants in the Americas. Proudly remem-bering how soldiers responded to her ministrations by calling her "Mother," she paints wartime nursing as work that allows her to develop a nonconjugal domesticity and a nonbiological maternity that moves the yellow "doctress" to the temporary status of feminine archetype. At the silent touch of her hand a blinded soldier cries, "Ha! This is surely a woman's hand," then whispers: "God bless you, woman — whoever you are, God bless you!"[45]

At the same time, Seacole's nursing and mothering is work that makes the soldiers she cares for more womanly themselves — opening space for rough-and-tumble men to express vulnerability and compassion on the sidelines of war. Rather than recounting soldiers' bravery in battle or stoicism in injury, she remembers them sighing, plaintive, and teary-eyed; she reports that "rough-bearded men stand by and cry like the softest-hearted women" and particu-larly lauds the sensitivity of a Major R, "a brave and experienced officer, but the scenes on the sick-warf unmanned him often."[46] When such "unmanned" soldiers tearfully call Seacole "Mother," she seems to respond to them as boys, yes, but also as male daughters whom she encourages to mirror back what she sees as feminine tenderheartedness. As she mothers this sensitivity, the gen-dered battle she wins in the Crimea seems the negative image of what Tubman accomplishes on the Underground Railroad. Rather than reclaiming the power of black female masculinity, she nurses and nurtures the femininity of two kinds of subjects – females of color and white males – who, in an imperial logic that needed both inexhaustible slaves and soldiers, were never supposed to be so soft.

The pièce de resistance in her feminine artistry comes after victory at Sebastopol, when soldiers celebrate by putting on skits, masquerades, and races. Declining to perform, she instead takes charge of the womanliness that male actors sashay across stage: "I lent them plenty of dresses; indeed, it was the only airing which a great many gay-coloured muslins had in the Crimea. ... And in addition to this, I found it necessary to convert my kitchen into a temporary green-room, where, to the wonderment, and perhaps scandal, of the black cook, the ladies of the company of the 1st Royals were taught to manage their petticoats with becoming grace."[47] After stopping one man from stealing a dress at gunpoint, she now delights in lending her boys more beautiful muslins and directing their borrowed femininity in a "gay-coloured" performance that couples the public pleasure of displaying her fine gowns with behind-the-scenes play with protégés' petticoats. Her mention of the black cook watching with "wonderment, and perhaps scandal," suggests that she takes up this cross-dressing as an unconventional, transgressive pastime – even as the cook's marginality points to ways in which these soldiers' gender play is not so transgressive at all. The recreational space open for white males to experiment with womanness for their own amusement – and at a celebration of military dominance, no less – bespeaks a racial and sexual privilege enjoyed by neither Seacole nor the black male cook, who share backstage. And the fact that Seacole happily lends dresses to soldiers but never shares admittedly excess clothing with females or blacks, in the Crimea or in Panama, insinuates that her attention to building up white male femininity comes at the expense of rethinking gender in collaboration with those who share her sex and/or race – especially with the women of color who, for this proud servant of the queen's army, often remain minor characters. In the end, the cross-dressing cooked up in her kitchen exemplifies the complexities that Sears notes in California migrants' temporary cross-gender practices: for while migrations create new space for males to try on femininity in dress, work, and recreation, these tryings-on have "contradictory effects" that underscore "the need to distinguish carefully between cross-gender practices that challenge racialized gender normativity and those that shore it up."[48]

While heroizing female masculinity formed part of the work that Tubman performed as the Moses of her people, providing (problematically) heroic males with access to femininity formed part of the work that Seacole undertook as an emissary of Queen Victoria. Both black hero/heroines traveled as gender transgressors in ways that neither icon has often been recognized for, but that Harry/Harriet's characterization calls on provocatively; at the same time, both figures' gender transgressions leave gaps for the revolutionary brand of black womanhood Cliff wants to imagine. If Tubman offers no model for resistant femininity, the insistently feminine Seacole stops her woman of color's adventures short of claims against empire or in favor of sustained cross-gender living, of supporting any trans-ing that goes beyond temporary heart-softening or dress-wearing to "challenge racialized gender normativity." Much as Harry/Harriet serves as Cliff's bridge between black and white, male and female, s/he also moves between the possibilities and limitations of the black Moses and the female Ulysses: exploring freeing paths through her native landscape while also fighting for a reconfigured, non-normative Afro-femininity, mothering her own nonbiological black womanliness as well as green-eyed Clare's. A mode of travel that is neither exodus nor adventure, Harry/Harriet's journey offers no opening into the genre that Prosser calls the transsexual travelogue – an autobiography that foregrounds a narrator's voyage to surgical transition from male to female (or more rarely, female to male).[49] Instead, the transition that Harry/Harriet represents is a nonphysical one between black women's rewritten history and their revolutionary future, between smooth sailing to the Crimea and a bumpy ride on the truck called No *Telephone to Heaven*.

Trespassing, Transforming Sugar:
Harry/Harriet, Clare, and a Journey across Lines

No *Telephone to Heaven* opens en route, in the middle of the eponymous truck's climb through Cockpit Country and in the thick of a boundary-flooding rainstorm that slicks mountain roads. In the back ride twenty-odd Jamaicans – including Harriet and Clare – in army fatigues that add "a touch of realism, cinematic verité" and make "them feel like real freedom-fighters" as they guard a stash of guns to carry into revolutionary action (7). The novel proceeds as a series of flashbacks motivated by this bumpy truck ride, vignettes of earlier journeys that interrupt and inform the final drive: Clare's migration to New York, her unfinished studies in London, a Christmas holiday in Kingston, months drifting through Europe, an eventual return to her family's land. These travels are recounted as fragmentary and fragmenting, told with no clear beginning or end in disconnected, antichronological episodes that disrupt any linear narrative. Unlike Tubman's or Seacole's many voyages, Clare's proliferating journeys – even on the No Telephone to Heaven – are neither hopeful nor empowering, never successfully moving her to freedom or to healing. Instead, this alienated Jamaican's travels recapitulate the neocolonial cycles that Cliff sees transitioning, colonial-to-postcolonial Jamaica caught in: "So lickle movement in this place. From this place. Only back and forth, back and forth, over and again, over and again – for centuries" (16).

The one exception to this endless zigzagging is Harry/Harriet. The first character named in the novel, she is the only one on the No Telephone to Heaven who has a jacket – and so an identity – of her own. And in truck-jostled flashbacks to Clare's Christmas return trip, readers learn that s/he is also the only character to guide Clare across the island and lovingly explain its history, beauty, and need for revolution, the only one to help her chart their native land otherwise than as a place of transit. Clare meets Harry/Harriet at a Christmas pool party where the latter is clad in a tiny bikini, a "boy-girl . . . that nature did not claim" and that the outsider Clare quickly befriends (21). After this memorable meeting and a night of drinking and confidences, Harry/Harriet leads Clare on a day trip that becomes the novel's most erotic and postcolonial journey. The two drive up the coast to an unenclosed beach that Harry/Harriet praises as Jamaica's most beautiful and secluded, one where s/he and Clare "could swim as girlfriends" (130). In her/his guidance to girlfriend space, Harry/Harriet deliberately defies boundaries (as Raymond warns that male lesbians are wont to do), "trespassing determinedly" through a cane field to reach the endless openness of the beach (130). Cliff marks their cutting across the cane as a reclaiming that is both justified and natural, the girlfriends sharing "their short trek with lizards and songbirds" as bush and cane trash gives way for them without struggle (130). So, as in Tubman's crossings, a potentially dangerous path readily softens and opens for their passage. Once arrived at the shore, these only human occupants mix effortlessly and pleasurably with the landscape around them, eating, drinking, swimming, and covering their skins in a mixture of coconut water, golden rum, mango juice, sea water, and spicy oil. "All the ingredients of Jamaica" come together in this salty-sweet mix: those, like golden rum, reclaimed from cane plantations, and those, like mangoes and coconuts, that resist capture by plantocrats (25). Leading Clare on this coconut-and-sea-water swim, Harry/Harriet introduces her to an erotic association with the landscape she has been separated from – the girlfriends drinking and wave-riding their way to a pleasurably polymorphous connection to Jamaican lands and waters, one as infused with physical, emotional, and cultural expansiveness as their mangoed skin.

And covered in juices, the erotic connection to the landscape segues into an erotic connection between Clare and Harry/Harriet. Lying on the beach, the girlfriends' bodies mix equally effortlessly and pleasurably with each other: "Touching gently, kissing, tongues entwined, coming to, laughing" (130). This interlude unfolds in stark contrast to Clare's mechanical poolside sex with a male landowner at the party at which she meets her girlfriend; that short-circuited penis-vagina sex by chlorinated water seems rinsed away by Clare and Harry/Harriet's slow, horizontal touch of skins, their mutually penetrating tongues, and the natural body of water splashing behind them. These two figures of racially, sexually complex Afro-Jamaican femininity wash together here like the sweet and saltwater on their bodies, different forms of a common element whose embrace seems to embody not only Caribbean women loving each other but the Caribbean loving itself and its own multiplicity. The pair end their day naked and catching oysters in that particularity of tropical geographies in which saltwater blends with fresh, the mangrove swamp – "water lapping softly against them . . . mix of salt and sweet" (132). This bio-rich swamp is space that, in the years before and after *No Telephone*, Glissant's *Caribbean Discourse* and Jean Bernabé's, Patrick Chamoiseau's, and Raphaël Confiant's *Éloge de la créolité* theorize as a paradigmatically Caribbean space of transversal, rhizomatic connections.[50] Departing from their gender-normative versions of this metaphor as determinedly as Harry/Harriet turns through the cane field to get to the beach, Clare and Harry/Harriet's erotic movement through the mangrove traces this transversality as an image of how both racial complexity – embodied in the fair mulatta – and gender complexity – embodied in her male girlfriend – "naturally" belong and come together in Cliff's postcolonial geography of rhizomatic expansiveness. Concluding Clare's memory of the day, this meeting of mangrove and human, mulatta and male woman is cast not as a single erotic encounter but as the protagonist's first deep connection with the "beauty, the wildness of this New World – her point of origin" (132).

Unlike Clare's ever-present wrestling with her racial métissage, Harry/Harriet's gender complexity seems magically unproblematic in this embrace.

Even with makeup washed away and clothes shed, the character's confidence in her girlfriendness shows no fissures; and while Cliff narrates her/him integrated with nature, this incredible ease in at once displaying a penis and remaining womanly seems close to supernatural – the divine, unshakeable integration of the gynandrous Fon deity Mawu-Lisa to whom s/he is later compared (171). But Harry/Harriet does express a limit even to her/his miraculous gender malleability when, in the thick of their kissing, s/he asks: "Girlfriend, tell me something. Do you find me strange?" When Clare hesitantly answers, "No stranger . . . no stranger than I find myself. For we are neither one thing nor the other," Harry/ Harriet corrects her: "For the moment, darling, only at the moment. . . . the time will come for both of us to choose. For we will have to make the choice. Cast our lot. Cyaan live split. Not in this world" (131). These short statements reverberate with provocatively wide-reaching implications. In the mangrove-complex racial and gender landscape of the Caribbean, they suggest, female as well as male women are made by transitioning, by choosing and learning black Jamaican womanhood. The usually inquisitive Clare does not ask why such a choice – such an endpoint to their travels between white-skinned and African, male and woman – is necessary, but Harry/Harriet's next speech traces an indirect explanation. While Bailey and Richardson evoke the figurative ghosts of slavery that complicate black gender queers' situations, Harry/ Harriet, gesturing to the "canefield right behind . . . our blessed bodies," points to literal ghosts of the enslaved that may be sharing the beach with their pleasure: "T'ink of de duppy in such a place, eh? . . . Were we to sleep on this beach we might hear more than the breeze rattling the stalks, and singing through the blades" (131). Even when no one else is present, their potential rattling pressures and momentarily interrupts the girlfriends' erotic reclining on the beach.

The seaside transition from kisses to duppies (ghosts) initially reads almost as a non sequitur. But as Avery Gordon writes, ghost stories – which, she theorizes, are never merely stories about dead or missing individuals, but about how systemic hauntings produce material effects – in fact serve to join what seems disjointed: "In haunting, organized forces and systemic structures that appear removed from us make their impact felt in everyday life in a way that confounds our analytic separations and confounds the social separations themselves."[51] What seems difficult for Clare to connect in this scene is the complex humanity of the girlfriends' bodies loving each other and its coexistence, in time and space, with the aftereffects of a chattel slavery system that reduced

African-descended bodies to things. One cane-rattling ghost that this system produces, and that Harry/Harriet's supernatural eyes seem to see that afternoon, is a fear of Afro-Caribbean bodies that are not hegemonically legible as human – including, as Bailey and Richardson show, gender non-normative bodies. In this world, a world of cane duppies and the specters of slavery's deformation of racialized, gendered, and sexualized bodies, Harry/Harriet insists that s/he and Clare cannot live "split" – fragmented, broken like ancestors under forced labor, lashes, and sexual violence.

This ghost that disrupts the kissing on the beach will later return as a haunting that moves Harry/Harriet to transition from a woman who claims maleness to one who no longer does, renaming herself Harriet and passing for female to join No Telephone to Heaven's revolutionary action with acceptance from fellow guerillas. Harry/Harriet finally transitions so that she can become the contemporary Harriet Tubman – the woman leading her people to freedom – that her name promises. Speaking of this choice in an interview with Opal Palmer Adisa, Cliff frames it as motivated simultaneously by Jamaicans' queer gender phobia and Harriet's own commitment to help liberate the people of the island on which she trespasses beautifully, loves unconventionally, and fights for social change: "I wanted to portray a character who would be the most despised character in Jamaica, and show how heroic he [sic] is. . . . Anyway, he really loves his people. He is there helping, yet if they knew what he really was, they would kill him."[52] While this last statement risks reinforcing the rhetoric of Jamaica's savage intolerance of queers, Cliff goes on to complicate her point. She speculates that this potential violence against non-normative gender stems from another kind of brutality – slavery's sexual violence against feminine males. She repeats this question as if it haunts her: "Does it go back to slavery? Is it something that has its roots in slavery? Were the slaves used in that way?"[53] Cliff's questions and answers are at once rich and problematic. Her evocation of African slavery and contemporary non-LGBT social justice movements in relation to Harriet's transition speaks to the importance of engaging culturally and historically specific politics around gender complexity, which may not always be about "liberation" (just) from transphobia but from racism, economic injustice, and neoimperialism. But providing a ghost story of slavery's continued hauntings as the only reason for Harriet's transition flips Raymond's transphobic narrative of trans-ness as oppression without opening room for any more nuanced imagination of what passing for female might mean to an Afro-Caribbean male woman. Cliff's elision not only becomes a stumbling block in the mangrove-expansive, postcolonial path *No Telephone to Heaven* desires to trace for male femininity. Setting up a roadblock in the trans-ing of Tubman's and Seacole's travel narratives, it obstructs a more complex imagination of how non-normative gender has historically, and could potentially, move through the African Americas to intersect with other resistant femininities.

The beach interlude with Clare, however, unfolds at once as a prelude to Harriet's later service to her people and as a counterpoint to it. This secluded afternoon is a moment when s/he makes an intimate connection to one Jamaican whom s/he can love and help lead to freedom while embracing both women's full complexity, and so opens the novel's only lesbian scene and a unique imagination of the erotics of decolonizing gender and sexuality otherwise. But Harry/ Harriet's continual support of Clare – her/his continual tending of the landowning woman's gardens, explaining their fruits to her – raises its own questions. In her innovative analysis of trans characters in Caribbean fiction, Rosamond King critiques Cliff's portrait of Harry/Harriet as an angel always ready to help guide wayward Clare and never expressing needs or contradictions of her/his own.[54] And indeed, the list of things Harry/Harriet helps Clare with in this scene alone includes driving her through the island, explaining its history and landscape, opening her to a lesbian eroticism she has been afraid to explore, and, perhaps most important, validating and loving green-eyed Clare's often unseen black womanness. When the two call each other "girl-friend," Clare not only speaks intimacy with another complex woman. She fulfills a wish made by her late mother in New York: that black women around her would call her girl as they do each other, seeing and expressing solidarity with her differently colored African diaspora femininity. Loving Clare as her/his black girlfriend, this male Harriet Tubman indeed helps her cross many geographic, racial, and cultural lines, continuously adding to her/his sheen as a Jamaican heroine.

But as Harry/Harriet leads up to the beach's ghost story, readers momentarily glimpse how Clare's embrace may help heal her/him too. When s/he asks her/his girlfriend if she finds her/him strange, the former's brown eyes are met by the latter's, "naked, green as the cane behind them" (131). Clare's eyes betray her own continued, embodied link to slavery – but to landowner ancestors, those who held possession of both the green cane that colors her eyes and the brown human chattel reflected in her interlocutor's. What might it mean for this dark-skinned male mulatta to gaze with mutual love at a female mulatta who could pass for white but desires to pass for black; at someone who has access to the only kind of femininity that plantocratic rhetorics recognized as "real" – that is, fair-skinned and female – but who embraces the visibly African, visibly male femininity she is supposed to negate? In this moment, not only the beach duppies stand poised to rattle and sing through the sugar stalks: as s/he moves cane-green Clare, Harry/Harriet also moves cane and the shadows it casts on people like her/him. This is not thiefing sugar, reappropriating Clare's model of femininity; rather, it is transforming sugar, reforming plantations' yield so their formations of racialized gender no longer cut her/him. I use the verb transform in the sense employed by Gordon, as the transition from being troubled by systemic hauntings to an embodied, impassioned effort to confront and reconfigure social formations and "underground historic fault lines" that rock individual and collective experiences of race, gender, sexuality, class.[55] And being haunted by cane or other ghosts always, Gordon concludes, presents an opportunity to change individually and systemically that which comes to haunt: "Because ultimately haunting is about how to transform a shadow of a life into an undiminished life whose shadows touch softly in the spirit of a peaceful reconciliation."[56] Clare and Harry/Harriet "touching gently, kissing, tongues entwined, coming to, laughing," look a lot like Gordon's "shadows touching softly in the spirit of a peaceful reconciliation." This small movement is one of the few in the novel that, rather than initiating extended wandering, brings characters to a personally and culturally meaningful stopping point – the beautiful complexity of the mangrove. It is one of the few moments in which a frozen social script seems poised to move, when green- and brown-eyed, gender-normative and gender-complex people look at each other differently in Cliff's Jamaican landscape. And it is a movement and a moment, certainly, that Glissant's static vision of the cane field's gendered and sexual violence would never have allowed. The erotic trek Harry/Harriet leads across the beach is not the Underground Railroad; but it is another attempt to shepherd her/himself and others beyond the grips of slavery.

Sweet Water, Real Revolutionaries:
Harriet's Path to Loving Change

After her Christmas visit ends, a mango-hued Clare returns to London where, discontent, she impulsively leaves her graduate studies to drift through Europe.

Feeling "like a shadow . . . like a ghost," she travels still without destination—but, as she says, with "persistence in drifting to the wrong side . . . what most of my family would consider the wrong side" (152). She finds a travel companion and lover in a wounded African American Vietnam veteran and deserter, becomes pregnant by him, and miscarries. The deserter soon deserts her, and Clare, unmoored again, books passage to Jamaica. There she lands in Kingston Hospital with a uterine infection and wakes to a ribbon-capped visitor who calls herself "Harriet, now, girlfriend . . . finally" (168). In her hospital bed Clare learns, first, that Harriet has nonsurgically transitioned ("Castration ain't de main t'ing . . . not a-tall, a-tall"), then, that she herself is now sterile; so the girlfriends add to their bond a commonly nonchildbearing womanhood (168). In other ways, however, their paths have diverged radically. While Clare has been (in Harriet's words) "dragging her ass through parts unknown" to care for one man, Harriet, studying healing practices at the university and with traditional Afro-Jamaican women doctors, has trekked through Kingston's urban landscape to treat downtown's sick and wounded (171). Cliff narrates Harriet's journey to "her true vocation" as an explicit decolonization and re-patriation of Seacole's wonderful adventures: "Harriet traveled through the yards of downtown, in her uniform and carrying her bag, sometimes wearing a red cape, a dashing figure even in the heat, like Mary Seacole, crossing open drains and bending her height into dark interiors. But this was not Scutari, and these were not the Queen's cavalries" (171). Taking her yellow doctress's healing powers out of the service of the imperial army and returning them to Jamaica's subalterns, Cliff positions post-Harry Harriet not only as a national heroine but as a nationalist one. Her commitment to recreating home manifests not in performing and teaching Victorian domesticity abroad but in healing her homeland—in donning Seacole's dramatic feminine healer's dress to carry her doctress's bag downtown.

The one-page trans-ing and decolonization of Seacole that describes Harriet's nursing is the only passage in the novel in which she is centered acting on her love for "her people" by herself, no Clare in the picture. But immediately after this vignette, the narrative focus shifts again to imagine Harriet using her healing powers to repatriate her girlfriend, suggesting and accompanying her on a trip to visit the land she inherited from her mother and the river where she played with Zoe as a girl. The cure that she seeks for Clare here seems not primarily from the European miscarriage but from the split that led to her ghostly, transcontinental wandering in the first place—extending Seacole's healing from white men to women of color, from physical to psychological battle scars. The women's riverside trek initially reads as a reprise of their beach trespassing, as they cut through the overgrown land's "chaos of green" to arrive at cascading fresh water – the "sweet on an island surrounded by salt" whose importance Clare has almost forgotten – where they once again swim together (172). But as Clare immerses herself in this water, something shifts from the earlier encounter. For the first time, in an internal monologue that she finds herself incapable of sharing with her confidante, the green-eyed wanderer expresses a deep connection to place – a deeply green place of red, yellow, and purple intergrowth that she feels not only belonged to, but *is* her mother in all her racial and emotional complexity. As this feeling develops and Harriet remains silent and unseen beside her, the eroticism that unfolds is not between the two women but simply between Clare and the river itself: "She shut her eyes and let the cool of it wash over her naked body, reaching into her as she opened her legs" (172). And the closer Clare moves physically and emotionally to the Jamaican countryside, the more distant she seems from Harriet. "After their bath," instead of kissing and talking as before, "they lay together on the rocks, and Clare let herself drift further," tracing in her memory the bends and complex history of the river while momentarily leaving the complexities of her sweet, watery girlfriend untraced (172).

Despite the running water's penetration of Clare, the riverine eroticism here is in many ways more muted (and at times disappointing) than the beach embrace. Even as Clare's racial split begins to ease, the water itself is split – fresh from salt – and the polymorphous perversity of the girlfriends' simultaneous bath in mangoes, rums, oils, waters, and each other seems to split and dilute too. Now that both characters have begun to transition fully to black Jamaican womanhood, the eroticism between them risks appearing transitional – no longer necessary to either in this scene in which the green of Clare's eyes takes on a different, postcolonial meaning, and in which the presence of the black feminine dead (Clare's mother) is comforting rather than ominous. The remainder of the novel does not foreclose the possibility of eroticism between the two girlfriends, who go on to live together in Kingston; but neither does it thematize their lesbianism again, so leaving it possible for readers to see transitioned Harriet as the kind of desexualized caretaker that Seacole also (strategically) painted herself to be. But another, more engaging reading of the erotic shift also presents itself here, bolstered by the increasingly explicit political narratives accompanying the women's encounters. Rather than merely transitional, the eroticism shared by Harriet and Clare might, like them, be entering into transition at this moment in the text—a transition from their secluded beach dialogue to another, more expansive form that Chela Sandoval calls the "neorhetoric of love in the postmodern world." An agent of social rather than personal change, this love is not a private feeling shared by individuals but the linguistic and cultural work of forging transformative connections; it is a "methodology of the oppressed" meant to transform the "colonizations of gender, sex, race, class, or any social identity or styles of analysis" that confront Clare and Harriet as they move through Jamaica.[57] Tracing ways to interface across and against those multiple colonizations, Sandoval's neorhetoric "generates a differential form of social movement that is bent on coalition between subordinated constituencies, and capable of transforming the politics of power."[58] Yes, it is like the love that Harry/Harriet and Clare shared on the beach, the intimate solidarity between sexually, racially marginal figures—but widened from two characters isolated on their deserted island-like beach to embrace the collectively "subordinated constituencies" of the Jamaica they travel through to get there.

And in the novel's last sections, the potential explored by the male woman and the green-eyed mulatta is their ability to make nonconventional, loving connections with communities around them. Harriet, of course, has been working on a neorhetoric of healing with downtown yard dwellers. Now having been a recipient of her companion's healing and able to move to her own solidarity-building work, Clare leads Harriet on a walk directly after the river bath to reconnect with inhabitants and hear their stories of food shortages, rising prices, and the International Monetary Fund's (IMF) squeeze on the nation's resources. (Later she will distribute food surpluses to them when she, Harriet, and other revolutionaries return to tend her long-overgrown family land.) After this transitional riverside trip, Harriet no longer leads Clare on treks to beautiful bodies of water, and the women no longer join in metaphorically projecting their desire for a multiply postcolonial Jamaica onto a multiply eroticized natural landscape. Instead, Harriet leads her to a small room in downtown Kingston to meet a leader of the revolutionary cell in which the two women work across race, class, and gender lines at "making something new" for Jamaica's political, economic, and cultural landscapes (5). As part of this cell she and Harriet return to live and prepare for action on her family land, communally cultivating ganja ("last natural resource left to them") to trade for weapons and food to eat and share. Finally, then, under Harriet's guidance,

Clare has paused her nomadic journeys to tend her garden, collectively and revolutionarily (15). Finally, too, this light-skinned Jamaican – who, rather than falling in love with a farmer, becomes one herself – learns the lesson that Bliss's white Jamaican sails away from: that meaningful identification with blackness, "claiming an identity they taught me to despise" (as Cliff puts it elsewhere), is not about individual feeling but about social, economic, and political commitments.[59]

The novel's conclusion returns readers to where they started, to the action that the No Telephone to Heaven has been heading toward throughout the text. Now Cliff reveals that this action is aimed not at political but at media representations of the Caribbean: the truck is barreling through mountains to attack the set of an American-British film dramatizing and romanticizing the life of the Windward Maroon leader Nanny. No Telephone to Heaven's destination finally revealed, readers see Harriet, Clare, and their companions taking up arms in struggle over something that has haunted the novel from start to finish – what black femininity can and should look like as it continually resists slavery. After the text's extended wrestling with cane field ghosts and late mothers, however, No Telephone to Heaven's guerillas are swiftly and easily defeated, helicopters immediately descending and gunfire spraying the bushes in which they hide. As Clare dies, language itself jarringly splits apart and dissolves, and the novel closes with staccato, gunfire-like lines of repeating syllables: hoo hoo . . . be be . . . kut ktu . . . cwa cwa. Speaking with Cliff about an ending that has often frustrated critics, Schwarz offers: "What I like to do with it is to argue that the ending leaves readers with a sense of incompletion that may motivate them to continue the struggle in which Clare was engaged." And Cliff adds: "Yes, that's good. Also, we don't know that Harry/Harriet dies, so there is always a possibility that he's [sic] going to go on. He's [sic] the real revolutionary in the book."[60]

Cliff's observation here reads as a layered, engaging, but unsettling postscript to the myth of postcolonial black male femininity that her novel spins around (Harry)/Harriet. Offering her/him as the "real" revolutionary in a novel so caught up with the dangers and possibilities of passing, she positions this character's complexity and integration as a way of connecting that Jamaica must learn to embrace to move from neocolonialism and neoslavery to a neo-rhetoric of love. But why is this revolutionary hailed not as a heroine or even a hero/heroine, but as a he? Even as Cliff praises the radical nature of the male lesbian's move beyond either-or gender and sexuality, her language falls short of reflecting this complexity. Her oddly misgendered statements leave readers to question the use of masculine pronouns and the split name Harry/Harriet to speak of the character at a time in the novel when she not only has proclaimed that "Harriet live and Harry be no more" but has done so to go forward with her revolutionary healing.

The delesbianized river scene and grammatically masculinized quote both point to a common sticking point in the mythically smooth trans-ed national heroine that Cliff sets out to write. Although explicitly committed to representing and exploring impossible desires between Harriet and Clare – a West Indian male's desires to be a woman, and love women – she herself seems to have trouble holding on to the gendered and sexualized language of their possibility, at times effacing either Harriet's womanness or her woman-loving. Like the ghost-story explanation of Harriet's transition, such erasure shows Cliff's myth stopping short of developing mangrove-complex narrative strategies for representing gender complexity. At the same time, the author's occasional haziness around (Harry) Harriet's possibly impossible desires often seems to stem less from latent queer gender phobia than from internalized homophobia. That is, Cliff's problems saying that Harriet is a woman come when she also says that Harriet loves women. As the clarity of Harriet's transition to womanhood grows, the shadowiness of her erotic love for the other woman does so as well; and at times, as in the above discussion in which Cliff also talks about Harriet's love for Clare, the reverse occurs as well. Indeed, in this interview Cliff also explicitly states that while writing No Telephone she was wrestling with sometimes anguished discomfort around representing any kind of lesbianism. Commenting on the near absence of woman-to-woman sexuality in her writing, she squarely claims that "part of it is self censorship. I have to be honest. I think it is. And I think it's having grown up in a society that is enormously homophobic," which she says led her to decades of sexual silence.[61] So the extreme boundary-challenging form of lesbianism that she undertakes to write between Clare and (Harry)/Harriet seems narratively and linguistically challenging for the author herself to hold onto as she, too, writes in the cane fields' shadows. Even as she metaphorically trespasses through these fields, their sugar is not yet completely transformed. Finally, Harriet's revolutionary male lesbianism slides in and out of Cliff's novel and her own discussion of it much as the river slides in and out of Clare's consciousness: its importance can only be fully grasped at certain incandescent moments, but moments that promise the beginning of healing and revolution.

*   *   *

> To write as a complete Caribbean woman, or man for that
> matter, demands of us . . . reclaiming as our own, and as our
> subject, a history sunk under the sea, or scattered as potash
> in the canefields, or gone to bush. . . . It means realizing our
> knowledge will always be wanting.
> —Michelle Cliff, preface to *The Land of Look Behind*

Barreling through Jamaica and centuries of colonial history sedimented in its mountains, *No Telephone to Heaven* refuses to deliver a story of successful revolution—even after a novel of truck-bound flashbacks led readers imagine Clare and Harriet on such a path. And never returning to the mangrove's erotic idyll, it also stops short of developing a story of sexual partnership between a male woman and another woman—even after a glimmer of that possibility glances across Jamaican waters. As far as the No Telephone to Heaven travels, Cliff still finds her text not quite able to *go there*, still finds that when and where she writes—from within, not beyond, colonialism and black queer gender phobia—the words and imagination to construct another Jamaica and another gender "will always be wanting." The work of her second novel is neither crossing a magic line nor arriving at an ideal destination. Instead, arduously, it is the work of dredging the sea before diving into the wreck, trespassing through cane fields to speak back to ghosts, clearing bush that still chokes out space for new geographies of gender complexity, same-gender eroticism, and meaningful postcolonialism. (Harry)/Harriet moves through this novel as a mythic figure whose vocation is to be not only a healer but also a path clearer, flushing out imaginative blocks against new, revolutionary formations of Afro-Jamaican womanness without a machete. Or, to put it another way, this character's work is to open space for readers to ask (signifying on Cliff's much-quoted question): What would it mean to *trans* artistic, academic, and activist visions *in the Caribbean*—not "in a room in the Mediterranean, not in a Paris bar, not on an estate in England"?[62]

    Certainly, as Sears posits for North American scholarship, the ebb and flow of desire between Clare and Harriet suggests that trans-ing Caribbean journeys will mean looking for where imaginations and enactments of gender crossing undermine racism and homophobia—and where, even unwillingly and even in the work of queers of color, racial and sexual norms are reinforced while gender is disrupted. Even more powerfully, though, the new body that Harriet gives to women of the African Americas' past, and her embrace of black womanness in the canefield and seaside space in which she knows they lived and died, communicate that trans-ing the Caribbean will mean cultivating an intimate knowledge of its specific, slavery-haunted history. This will be a past, as Cliff writes above, sunk under the sea and gone to bush but that must be rediscovered and touched as closely as Clare and Harriet caress Jamaica's waters and overgrown landscapes. The histories that Cliff pushes readers to become intimate with here are equally of hallowed names like Tubman and Seacole and of nameless workers like those who haunt the cane – that is, histories of individuals and collectivities, of resistance and oppression alike. What possibilities such excavation will suggest for love between male women and other women, No Telephone remains uncertain of. But the novel's bumpy journey does seem directed by the belief that it is only after this excavation that we can enunciate how, as Cliff once lyricized, "Love in the Third World can be just as powerful / complicated / multileveled / varied / long-standing/ As in the First or Second Worlds – maybe more so."[63] This sustained, deepened, multileveled Caribbean male lesbian love story will have to come in yet another sequel – if not literally in Cliff's oeuvre, then in another Caribbean text. So too will a thorough mapping of the mangrove-like convergences and divergences possible between gender-complex and lesbian poetics and politics in this slavery-haunted, (post-?)postmodern archipelago in which sugar is still being transformed.

six

Breaking Hard against Things

Crossing between Sexual and Revolutionary Politics
in Dionne Brand's *No Language Is Neutral*

breaking hard against things, turning to burning reason
this is you girl, this is the poem no woman
ever write for a woman because she 'fraid to touch
this river boiling like a woman in she sleep

— Dionne Brand, "hard against the soul"

My concern, then, is a passionate one, for the literature of people
who are not in power has always been in danger of extinction or
co-optation, not because we do not theorize, but because what
we can even imagine, is constantly limited by societal structures.

— Barbara Christian, "The Race for Theory"

"Castro champions gay rights in Cuba: There is a Castro who is fighting to introduce radical changes," a BBC headline proclaimed in the serious, bold sans serif gray font of its "One-Minute World News" for the Americas on 27 March 2008.[1] No, the writer Michael Voss quickly went on to explain, this Castro is neither Fidel nor the new president Raúl, but the latter's forward-thinking daughter, Mariela Castro Espín. Offset by a light background with a hint of green foliage, her image met readers with a thoughtful expression, her youthful face framed by flowing chestnut hair and a red beaded necklace sitting slightly askew on her neck, shifted to the left as if by her continual movement to disrupt straightness. Castro's national and transnational work in support of LGBT rights has, indeed, been prolific and ongoing. As the head of the Cuban National Center for Sex Education (CENESEX), she has campaigned for HIV prevention and treatment, acted as the president of the National Commission for Treatment of Disturbances of Gender Identity, and served as the director of the journal *Sexología y sociedad*. And in 2005, she began work to pass what Voss describes as one of "the most liberal gay and transsexual rights laws in Latin America" through the Cuban National Assembly.[2] This legislation proposes the recognition of same-sex unions and inheritance rights, as well as state sponsorship of free sex-reassignment surgeries for qualifying individuals and provisions to change gender on identification cards. State support and funding of such surgeries became the first part of the proposal passed into law on 7 June 2008. This legislative success is not an isolated event, Castro trusts, but part of a larger movement toward openness to LGBTs in postrevolutionary Cuba. "In the early years of the revolution much of the world was homophobic. It was the same here in Cuba and led to acts which I consider unjust," she explains. "What I see now is that both Cuban society and the government have realised that these were mistakes. There is also the desire to take initiatives which would prevent such things happening again."[3]

Castro's rhetoric and activism on Caribbean LGBT rights is engaging and innovative in many ways. The daughter of the transnational feminist Vilma Espín insists that LGBT rights, like women's rights, are a natural extension of the revolution begun in 1959. As part of this argument, she also insists that Cuba and the Caribbean are not the rampantly homophobic places they are so often defamed as—but, in fact, are more tolerant than much of the Global North. "I would say that in Cuba there's a soft, unaggressive homophobia; gays aren't beaten or killed as happens in Europe or the United States," she clarified in an April 2008 interview with Alessandra Coppola. "It's true that there was a difficult period during the sixties and seventies, but homosexuality was not accepted anywhere in the world at that time. Later, thanks to work that had been done on women's rights, differing sexual orientations came to be recognized as well."[4] At the same time, this presidential daughter's enunciation of a rights platform in the style of the Global North poses its own problems for many same-sex loving Cubans. Continuing her conversation with Coppola, Castro noted that her father had advised her that the most effective way to pursue political goals was "to do things like my mother did, carefully, with respect, with sensitivity. Without breaking things. And so I have."[5] But as her "carefully" worded legislative proposals stop short of calling for adoption, same-sex marriage, or other more controversial reforms, she acknowledges that her incremental, "without breaking things" strategy to secure rights bit by bit has met with significant resistance from more radical activists and citizens. This resistance has continually come not merely around homonormative desires for marriage but around more expansive social issues. Voss's BBC article includes a photograph of a blonde, gold-earringed, white male-to-female transsexual who expresses her appreciation of CENESEX's work: a snapshot that might serve as emblematic of the populations – white, monied, and male (-born) – that many see Castro's activism to be most responsive to. As Tanya Saunders's work on Afro-Cuban lesbians suggests, CENESEX's innovations may mean little change in the lives of same-sex loving, poor, black females whose chief concerns are neither inheritances nor medical models of transition.[6]

At those political intersections at which her work bumps up against – and sometimes continues with – the racial, economic, and sexual inequalities that the revolution has not (yet) dismantled, this famously unconventional Castro still seems hindered by the kind of societal structures that Barbara Christian sees limiting "what we can even imagine" in the way of change. But, if not the child of revolution and feminism, who and what would it take to delimit such imagination? And if not legislative reform, what kind of language could chart a meaningfully revolutionary politics of same-sex desire that taps into what Audre Lorde theorizes as not the liberal but the *transformative* power of the erotic?[7] What things might Caribbean women need to break, or at least *break hard against*, to imagine more imaginatively? Taking seriously Christian's privileging of figurative language as a space to conceptualize power differently, this final chapter traces answers to these questions through a reading of the first erotic text published by a writer who, like Mariela Castro, grew up captivated by an uncle (a much less famous one) who participated in the Cuban

Revolution – a leftist writer well known in Canada and the Caribbean during the 1970s and 1980s as a revolutionary Marxist poet. This writer is Trinidad-born, Toronto-resident Dionne Brand, and the text her collection of poetry published in 1990, *No Language Is Neutral*, a finalist for the Governor General's Award. Describing Trinidadian beaches on which black women's desire for each other revolutionizes the lay of the land and the water around them, *No Language* not only imagines a sexual politics as West Indian as the Caribbean Sea but also charts complex relationships between eroticism, colonialism, militarism, resistance, revolution, poverty, despair, fullness, and hope that explore the pliability necessary to imagine Caribbean same-sex loving politics differently, postcolonially.

Myriam Chancy, in the first study of Brand's poetry, writes her artistic vision as a rescripting of traditional *poetics* into *poelitics*: "A fusion of politics and poetry that recalls Lorde, who once wrote of the transformative power of poetry as 'a revelatory distillation of experience' and as an act of fusion between 'true knowledge' and 'lasting action.'"[8] Brand vocalizes quite lucidly the threat that this infusion of politics into poetics poses to both revolutionary and neo-colonial Caribbean thinkers: "To dream about a Black woman, even an old Black woman, is dangerous even in a Black dream, an old dream, a Black woman's dream, even in a dream where you are the dreamer," she writes of reactions to her black lesbian feminist revolutionary artistic work by Marxists and conservatives alike. "Even in a Black dream, where I, too, am a dreamer, a lesbian is suspect; a woman is suspect even to other women, especially if she dreams of women."[9] And, she predicts, "I will pay for this fearlessness."[10] Yet it is only in such an unprotected, multiply exposed imagination that Caribbean same-sex loving landscapes move toward – without necessarily reaching – a cartography of decolonization, one in which so many things are broken, yes, but also finally reconfigured.

As I mention above and explore below, *No Language* marks a new crossing in Brand's art. In this text her focus shifts from talking back to official politics to speaking more intimately to a feminized and eroticized addressee, from remaking the world through political intervention to remaking it through intersubjective engagements. This expansive eroticism gives voice to the complex ways in which radical black feminism is not something *out there* but *in here*, a set of praxes and ways of knowing woven into Afro-Caribbean women's daily interactions with themselves and others. Responding to Brand's movement (as if, I sometimes feel, I am following her lead in a dance), my writerly praxis shifts here too. In the first chapter, I explained my move to explore an intertextuality that reaches eclectically outward to bring together sources and voices that are "supposed" to be kept apart. And while this final chapter does not leave behind this kind of motion, I also privilege a different intertextual reading practice here: one that reaches more deeply into Brand's own writerly corpus, taking care to draw out the echoes and variations between her many kinds of political and artistic work. As I do, I hope to follow Brand's lyrical suggestion to think through a black feminist epistemology that, through a radical work of introspection – through piecing together (but never fixing) fragments of a voice dispersed in many places, thoughts, politics, and desires – traces a path that arrives at social, political, economic, and scholarly inquiries *another way*. This other way sometimes leaves me feeling more vulnerable as I end this book than when I opened it. More vulnerable, certainly, because I cite with more focus, without such a varied shield of sources. But more vulnerable, too, because this close attention to Brand's words is my own desiring, black femme reading practice. "Writing is an act of desire, as is reading," Brand offers, and these readings of her work are my expression of the feeling, charged, intimately engaged way I pore through her many texts, my expression of how the (never easy) pleasure they evoke becomes at once an erotics and a politics that changes how I see.[11] Finally, as I break hard against Brand's body of work, I hope to offer this chapter as a quieter kind of meditation on the Caribbean, eroticism, and change – quieter, certainly, than any of Castro's impassioned speeches, and quieter than the way my thiefing sugar began.

Relief from the Enclosure of the Door of No Return:
Dionne Brand's Caribbean Crossings

On an embattled shoreline, bomber-crossed:

> this surf, this night
> of american warships in barbados . . . this night of tension
> and utterly huge ocean
> I see orion like an imperialist
> straddle the half sky

Mapping an oceanography of anticolonial struggle, Brand's beachscapes – like this scene of a speaker awaiting the U.S. invasion of Grenadan shores in

Chronicles of the Hostile Sun – emerge as painfully evocative, relentlessly political sites in her work prior to *No Language Is Neutral*.[12] The uncompromising
poetic craft with which she voices radical politics was what she was known for
in the 1980s Toronto literary scene, and what she wanted to be known for. "I
find nothing shameful about being a leftist, and I want to state explicitly that
my work is leftist work and that I've always seen my work as leftist work," she
affirmed in an interview with Makeda Silvera conducted in 1994.[13] This work
was already prolific when she sat for the interview and consistently defied a
separation between its social justice and literary currents. Her debut poetry
collection, *Fore Day Morning*, appeared in 1978; in the following twelve years
she published seven books of poetry and short stories, made documentary films
on black women in Canada, and worked as an activist and educator on behalf
of youth, immigrants, trade unions, and domestic violence survivors. In 1983,
she joined what Jacqui Alexander describes as "droves of women who left the
Caribbean and the metropolis with equal discontent to build the revolution in
Grenada" and went to work for Maurice Bishop's People's Revolutionary Government (PRG) as an information officer for the People's Development Agency.[14]
There, continuing her writing, she authored reports on agency activities and
published a newsletter. Brand spent nine months in a PRG office overlooking
St. George's harbor and the Caribbean Sea – water that flowed directly to the
north shore of her neighboring native Trinidad and that, she remembers, remained "its usual blue" the day U.S. warships' attack led to the death of PRG
leaders and Brand's colleagues.[15] After this experience of revolution and reinva-
sion, she wrote, "of course nothing was the same."[16] Brand's time at St. George's
harbor informed her literary-political work for decades to come – thematically,
yes, as in *Chronicles of the Hostile Sun*, but also in more layered and complex ways
that wash through *No Language*.

No Language marks the beginning of Brand's navigation between Standard
English and Creole, "the language [she] grew up in."[17] Before this, she explained
to Silvera, "I never wanted to write in so-called dialect – certainly not without
first appreciating what I was doing, and that had a lot to do with finding myself
in a country like Canada where everything can be turned exotic."[18] Her appreciation seems to have been fed in the year during which she did *not* find herself
in Canada, during which she was living in as close proximity to the highly
publicized language politics of the PRG as she was to the harbor. Reclaiming
Grenada's linguistic plurality was a central element of PRG cultural politics
and the Freiran pedagogy of the oppressed enacted by its Centre for Popular

Education (CPE). The minister of education, Jacqueline Creft, proclaimed to the volunteer tutors who would help bring half of Grenada's illiterate adults to basic literacy in six months: "We cannot stress enough the need to master *language*. . . . Since our revolution is a revolution in ways of communicating, consulting, organising, criticising and planning, the Language Arts that we learn must give us the capacity to master all those aspects."[19] Developing the symbolic and practical importance of maneuvering beyond an entrenched Creole-English binary proved crucial to this communication revolution. Bishop and the CPE promoted not diglossia or code switching but creative movement along the English-Creole continuum as a goal for *all* citizens, including leaders themselves. Bishop's talks moved famously between Standard English and Creole: his celebrated "yard fowl" speech in response to the actions of the Barbadian prime minister Tom Adams veers from a formal "Let me summarize, comrades, by repeating what our position is" to explaining this position in nation language. "You know," he continued, "that America has this backyard policy, of believing that we is she backyard and when they spit we must open we mouth and collect it. And you know we in Grenada say we is part of nobody back yard. But . . . any time there is a backyard there must be a yard fowl in it."[20] Bishop's proof that he was no yard fowl came not only in what he said but also in how he said it—in a mix of authoritative English and resistant, richly metaphoric Creole that refused to sound like Ronald Reagan, let alone act like him. Even as Bishop demonstrated the political possibilities of linguistic mobility, the CPE developed innovative literacy projects to simultaneously teach Creole speakers to read, write, and speak Standard English and provide classroom space and literary events promoting Creole linguistic arts. "Every Grenadian needs to be bilingual," the educator Chris "Kojo" De Riggs insisted. [21] That is, every Grenadian deserved the possibility of flourishing in her or his own yard's language while also being able to speak (back) to hegemonic English speakers across the waters.

When Brand wrote *No Language* not in English or in Creole but between the two, her verse seemed to fulfill De Riggs's revolutionary promise. Yet what she lyricizes between languages, what the collection became most famous for, is something the PRG never opened linguistic space for—her love and desire for women. "Yes . . . ," Brand explained in an interview with Frank Birbalsingh, "In *No Language Is Neutral* I am also trying to be explicit about my sexuality. Just like writing in Creole, I thought that it had to wait until I could do it really well, because lesbian sexuality is either not represented at all, or badly represented by heterosexuals. I wanted to express how tender and gentle it was, but I had to wait until I had the words to do it with."[22] This other language she grew up in – not as a child, but as a young woman maturing in other ways – was hardly speakable in the political movements she joined in the 1970s and 1980s. Profoundly committed to PRG land and language reforms, Brand nonetheless found herself deeply disturbed by the sexual politics of Caribbean and Caribbean-Canadian activist organizations, by their insistent masculinization and heterosexualization of the movement. Preaching an end to deadly black economic marginalization, race *men* entrenched their own positions as central revolutionary figures, with women standing backstage as adjuncts, sexual partners, and/or assistants. As the fellow poet-activist Merle Collins writes, for women who were scripted to be caretakers, the language of revolution remained only partially accessible:

Wid a lesson
like dat
1979 revolution talk
not no easy ting
But de strength was dey
De weakness imposed.[23]

Like Collins, Brand, "seeing the sexual capital of the radical men played out in the subjugation of women," held in the movement "despite the uneasy feeling that Black women's experiences were secondary and that men exemplified the voice, the life, the physical body and the spiritual breath of the movement. And even more, one had a sense that male power over women was a prerequisite and a condition of the movement. The movement did not examine patriarchy. It examined white patriarchy, but only as something that white men did to Black men, not as something that men did to women, and in this it deserted its highest goals: freedom from all exploitation and expression."[24]

Despite myriad linkages between the "natures" of colonialism and heteropatriarchy, Brand's searing prose charges, the anticolonial movements that followed Frantz Fanon's call for revolution rarely linked fighting the former to dismantling the latter – and instead actively worked to reinvent heteropatriarchy in black and brown, in Creole. This discursively and materially violent work is a process that Alexander discusses as the region's "heteropatriarchal recolonization": a system of ideological and material limitations imposed on (particularly women's) erotic autonomy that became an ingrained feature not only of masculinist revolutionary discourse but of Caribbean "post" colonial nationalisms in general.[25] Alexander's close readings of official discourses – particularly laws that criminalize same-sex sexuality in the name of protecting fledgling island nations – demonstrates that while nominally postcolonial politics pays lip service to broadening Afro- and Indo-Caribbean heteropatriarchs' involvement in the nation, it actively excludes other West Indians from full political participation on the basis of their sexuality. Analyzing the Bahamas' Sexual Offences and Domestic Violence Act (1991), she argues that even as politicians speak on behalf of "this independent state of ours,"[26] their homophobic rhetoric "forges continuity between white imperial heteropatriarchy – the white European heterosexual inheritance – and black heteropatriarchy," so that the "ideal typical citizen is still premised within heterosexuality and maleness and this, for women, prostitutes, lesbians, gay men . . . poses a profound dilemma."[27] As long as this dilemma remains unaddressed, she notes pointedly, decolonization will remain a failure. Caribbean states – revolutionary (Bishop's Grenada, Fidel Castro's Cuba, Michael Manley's Jamaica) and "yard fowl" (Puerto Rico, the Cayman Islands, the Bahamas) alike – will continue in collusion with neocolonial sexual politics that they refuse to recognize as such, "delivering criminality instead of citizenship."[28] Decolonizing this recolonization necessitates "crafting interstitial spaces beyond the hegemonic where feminism and popular mobilization can reside," where "women can love themselves, love women, and transform the nation simultaneously."[29]

Alexander's first monograph gives a watery name and fluid shape to these interstices: not pedagogies of the (undifferentiated) oppressed but *pedagogies of Crossing*. Crossing, here, is figurative – the work of thinking intersectionality, of recognizing (as June Jordan writes) why freedom is indivisible and how parsing national from sexual, racialized from gendered, linguistic from same-sex loving politics continues imperial ways of knowing.[30] Instead, those in search of radical change "would need to adopt, as daily practice, ways of being and of relating, modes of analyzing, and strategies of organizing in which we constantly mobilize identification and solidarity, across all borders," whether linguistic, national, racial, sexual, or other.[31] But the Crossing that Alexander calls on to excavate submerged epistemologies is also a specific, historical crosscurrents – "the tidal currents of the Middle Passage."[32] These currents mark colonialism's emergence not only because they captured the colonies' labor force but also because the violence to personhood enacted here provided the epistemic underpinnings for empire: the deep brutality of this crossing was the uncrossing of the linguistic, spiritual, ethnic, gendered, and sexualized threads that held people together as sentient beings. Alexander's pedagogies of Crossing thus start not by enunciating well-delineated platforms like those Brand encountered in her early Canadian and Caribbean activism, but by "literally unearthing and piecing together the fragmented members of existence" that the multiple violences of colonization have left to re-member.[33] In the evocative and beautiful language she weaves to describe her complexly signifying Crossings, Alexander resists offering formulas or definitions for what their lessons might entail. Instead, generalizing only that they are "premised within a solidarity that is fundamentally intersubjective: any dis-ease of one is a dis-ease of the collectivity; any alienation from self is alienation from the collectivity," she gestures open-endedly toward wave after wave of ways to rethink relationships of self to other, self to collectivity.[34] These include "the desire to forge structures of engagement, which embrace that fragile, delicate understanding of revealing the beloved to herself and to one another, which James Baldwin sees as the work of the artist. 'The artist does at [her] best what lovers do, which is to reveal the beloved to [herself] and with that revelation make freedom real.'"[35]

This is the work that Brand undertakes in *No Language*. Her own creative prose on the Middle Passage, *A Map to the Door of No Return*, charts her migration to Grenada as a search to move beyond that Crossing: "I had come here in search of a thought, how to be human, how to live without historical pain. It seemed to me then that a revolution would do it . . . I wanted to be free. I wanted to feel as if history was not destiny. I wanted some relief from the enclosure of the Door of No Return."[36] When internal contradictions and external attacks violently revealed that this kind of revolution would not "do it," she boarded a plane back to Canada, unable (she narrates) to re-member herself—to recognize her own arms and legs—or to reconnect to her former political vision. Instead, arriving in Toronto with a deep sense that another direction for change was imperative, she spent years tracing a conceptual map of what direction this might be—a map "to places you don't even know exist—to a new place."[37] And her recolored and reconfigured oceanography for this map begins with the opening lines of *No Language*. Here, as the speaker looks at Trinidad's north coast and tenderly writes to her female lover, "This is you, girl," an equally recolonized Caribbean landscape and Caribbean same-sex desire return to sentience and meaningfulness, *unearthed* and *pieced back together* (to use Alexander's verbs) as they become *yous* to address lovingly. The speaker's branching into nation language will immediately be a branching into erotic language, discovering what Brand calls "a woman's tongue so like a culture" to reveal a beloved and a beachscape "to herself and one another."[38] Following up on her question about what it would mean for a woman to love another woman in the Caribbean, Michelle Cliff cites No Language as the text that represents a lesbian eroticism she herself was not ready to voice, making the jump to speak desire between women not in another place but here.[39] At the same time, the route to this place also remaps the gun-ringed beaches of Chronicles of the Hostile Sun and recasts its struggles in different terms. For as Brand makes clear in discussing No Language: "When I started to write I thought that writing was action and I still do . . . I put [my poems] forward as weapons."[40] Weapons to decolonize many kinds of difference.

The Unsoundable Mysteries of the Sea:
Failures of Caribbean Water and Desire

"Love, we are both shorelines," Lorde calls in "Bridge through My Windows."[41] And as this line suggests, in the decade during which Brand composed No Language, beachscapes were not only being mapped as sites of invasion and resistance; Caribbean women who loved women were also writing and reflecting the many possible erotic contours of this quintessentially West Indian topos. These include Cliff, of course, as well as two other writers whose texts from the 1980s emerge as intertexts for Brand's: Lydia Cabrera's Yemayá y Ochún and Lorde's Zami. But, like Cliff's No Telephone to Heaven, both begin a map to a new erotics of Caribbean shorelines that they never quite finish. Cabrera's tales of feminine water spirits and Lorde's imaginary, idyllic shores of Carriacou gesture toward beachscapes as a possible crosscurrents in which to imagine sexual complexity and decolonized Caribbeanness at a conflux, only to end by not being able to carry this possibility through—by leaving this space as myth rather than reality. Or, to use Brand's own language toward the end of No Language, this conflux hovers as "the peace of another life that didn't happen and / couldn't happen in my flesh and wasn't peace but / flight into old woman, prayer, to the saints of my/ ancestry" (47).

Just after her harrowing account of leaving Grenada, Brand narrates a peaceful return to another Caribbean beach: "I have awakened to go to the jetty to reason with Yemaya, the goddess of the ocean, to entreat her to help me . . . I am not religious, but this I do every time I am at the ocean."[42] Beyond this, the author does not explain who Yemayá is. But her own answer may come partly from stories gathered by one Santería's most famous chroniclers, Cabrera. In 1980, while living in Miami with her partner María Teresa de Rojas, Cabrera published a book-length study of Afro-Cuban water spirits titled *Yemayá y Ochún: Kariocha, iyalorichas y olorichas.* Like all her later work, the study draws on fieldwork undertaken before she left Cuba definitively in 1960 in opposition to Castro's revolution. This dense, heterogeneous text's opacity begins with its subtitle, three untranslated Yoruba words linked by the Spanish conjunction *y.* Divided into neatly labeled chapters, *Yemayá y Ochún* manages to spill messily outside the content any section title suggests. The chapter on Yemayá poses as its title the seemingly straightforward question, "Quién es Yemayá?," or "Who is Yemayá?," and then spirals through stories that may or may not clarify this query. Concrete blocks to transparency mark the chapter's pages in the form of italicized, rarely glossed Yoruba words, phrases, and sentences. This opacity continues on a thematic level as Cabrera gives multiple, contradictory stories about the deity's origin and interactions with other spirits, all laced with stories of other *orishá,* always without reducing these to a coherent thread or providing interpretation for her enigmatic tales. She also spends several pages detailing Yemayá's many paths—as motherly, warriorly, feminine, masculine, indulgent, vengeful, stormy, calm—without explaining the *logique métisse* behind such plurality. Instead, she leaves readers to puzzle out why the answer to "Quién es Yemayá?" becomes asking, *Quiénes son Yemayá?,* in the plural

Her braid of answers includes three stories relating Yemayá to same-sex loving. The first is a description of the path of Yemayá Okuté, whom Cabrera calls *la amazona* and links to female same-sex eroticism.[43] The second, as if a counterpoint to the first, same-sex positive story, is an account that Yemayá left her husband Orula because she found out he was an *adodí* or "reversed"— that is, feminine and man-loving—male. (This despite the fact that Cabrera cites Yemayá as a patron of *adodís* in *El Monte.*) The third comes directly after: a *pataki,* or sacred story, of Yemayá's affair with Inle, the voiceless, androgynous *orishá* who, Cabrera also notes in *El Monte,* acted as patron of a prerevolutionary Cuban society of same-sex loving and cross-gendered daughters who honored her/him with a spectacular procession each 24 October. "Lesbians also abound in Ocha," she relates, "where yesteryear the patron saint was Inle." [44] Cabrera, who never openly acknowledged her own lesbianism and eligibility for Inle's protection, narrates the story behind the patron saint's speechlessness this way: "Yemayá was madly in love with an androgyn, the fantastically beautiful Inle. To satisfy the passion the young deity inspired in her, she kidnapped him, carried him to the bottom of the sea, and had him there until, sated beyond all appetite, she grew tired of her lover and desired to go back to the world, to the company of other Orishá and of men. Inle had seen what no other divine or human creature ever had. The unsoundable mystery of the sea, what it hides in its deepest recesses. And so that Inle would not tell this to anyone, before undertaking the return to earth Yemayá cut out his tongue."[45] Forever after, Cabrera concludes, Inle could only speak through Yemayá in divination.

Cabrera is one of few Santería chroniclers to narrate this fluid, non-normative sexual encounter, and the only one to do so after having named Inle the patron saint of lesbians and male women.[46] This "fantastically beautiful" spirit's striking, prominent appearance in Cabrera's work, where she/he seems to captivate Cabrera almost as forcefully as Yemayá, suggests that Inle represents more for her than for some other scholars of the religion. Certainly, this androgyn that loves (in) the sea's deepest recesses reflects a non-normative sexuality that Cabrera – like Inle – voices only indirectly, encoded in the complex textual maneuvers of Yemayá's stories. More broadly, the gender- and element-crossing deity of fishing and hunting, the dweller in both waters and forests, femininity and masculinity alike, takes on importance as the *orishá* of liminality: she/he who bridges male/female, straight/same-sex loving, earth/land, in one's element/out of one's element, at home/in exile. But by the time this *pataki* is over, Inle's watery multiplicity is a thing of the past; the final, violent amputation of her/his tongue cuts out both a sexual organ and his/her vehicle for speaking gender, sexual, and geographical complexity aboveground. As Cabrera specifically calls Inle the patron saint of lesbians and male women *before* the revolution, this tale of violence seems to reflect how the author saw Fidel Castro's government treating the same-sex loving and gender transgressive: what happens to lesbians and *adodís* after the revolution resembles what happens to their patron after returning to land. Indeed, *Yemayá y Ochún* appeared the same year in which the Mariel boatlift transported thousands of same-sex loving Cubans (particularly feminine males) across the Florida Straits to Cabrera's Miami, arriving with the stated intention of leaving behind the state's repressive policies toward "homosexuals."[47]

But Cabrera presents this *pataki* not to explain who Inle is, but to answer "quién es Yemayá?" Introduced as the patron saint of capitol city Havana, this water deity seems to reflect, in her relationship with Inle, Cuba's changing relationship to sexual complexity as Cabrera saw it in her lifetime: an initial promise of complete integration into the revolution – the dream of melting together under the sea – that gives way to severance and betrayal. As important as this historically informed reading is, however, a move deeper into Inle's West African back story suggests that Yemayá also stands in here for something that reaches back much further than 1959 – that this *pataki* names her as a metonym for the tidal currents of the Middle Passage, a trauma that other stories narrate as that which first cut out Inle's tongue. For the Yoruba Inle is Erinle, an elephant spirit who can indeed speak; and as Eric Lerner writes in "Olokun and the Art of Suppression," Erinle loses a syllable of her/his name and his/her tongue only in the slave trade.[48] What or who is it, then, that cuts out the tongue of Cuban lesbians' and *locas'* patron saint and makes her/him unable to speak? Is it a Yemayá who channels Fidel's Havana, water colored with the revolution's homophobia, water that washes *locas* into the Mariel boatlift; or is it a Yemayá who channels the Crossing, the currents of slavery's sexual and social violence, currents that still rock "revolutionary" gender and sexual politics? Cabrera's opaque tale makes a single answer to this question unworkable, leaving these strands of violence impossible to untangle from each other; and perhaps Brand might call for Yemayá's help not as a deity but as a figure for the irreducible complexity of where heterosexism in revolutionary movements comes from and where it resides. But unlike the mapmaker Brand, Cabrera – who never returned to Cuba or imagined another story for Inle – offers no way out of the liaison between Caribbean revolution and homophobia, no space in which the androgyn and the sea goddess can live together lovingly across the Florida Straits.

But Brand's memories of the Grenadan revolution gesture to another intertext for *No Language* that blooms as romantically optimistic about this space as Cabrera's is pessimistic. On the morning on which U.S. troops stormed St. George's harbor, Brand remembers that it was a friend she calls only "the woman from Cariacou" who saved her life by leading her away from the beach.[49] This path-altering *woman from Cariacou* calls up the pathbreaking work of one of that island's most celebrated mythologizers, the black lesbian feminist poet warrior Lorde. Lorde's expansive corpus of work broached many subjects that intersect with Cabrera's and Brand's work, including the love of the *orishá* and the U.S. invasion of Grenada. But her imagination of shorelines where women love each other in the Caribbean emerges fully only in her biomythography *Zami*, published in 1982. Like the rest of her work, this "autobiographical manifesto" (to use Sidonie Smith's phrase) looks to imagine somewhere that a black lesbian feminist could find the beyond-binaries on-land space Inle never reached, somewhere she/he could keep her tongue to speak and love.[50] Two images of this on-land space prevail in Zami. Appearing at the biomythography's beginning and end, enfolding the text like a mother's arms, the first of these is her mother's homeland, Carriacou. The first chapter reenters her mother's childhood tales of "the sweet place, back *home*": "Here Aunt Anni lived among the other women who saw their men off on the sailing vessels, then tended the goats and the groundnuts, planted grain and poured rum upon the earth to strengthen the corn's growing, built their women's houses and the rainwater catchments, harvested the limes, wove their lives and the lives of their children together. Women who survived the absence of their sea-faring men easily, because they came to love each other, past the men's returning. *Madivine. Friending. Zami. How Carriacou women love each other is legend in Grenada, and so is their strength and their beauty.*"[51]

This meeting of sea and earth takes men and heterosexuality to a faraway place and leaves women-loving women on land, occupying the terrestrial space that sexually and gender complex figures could not reach whole in Cabrera's *patakí*. Since Zami's prologue begins with Lorde expressing her desire to be with women sexually as the desire to "be both man and woman . . . to share valleys and mountains upon my body the way the earth does in hills and peaks," the zami home of Carriacou reads as the island on which androgyny and same-sex loving both become the lay of the land.[52] This island is a utopia of sunny similarity: a country of "women's houses" where there are no other racial, gender, or sexual identities and so no need for a black lesbian feminist to be a warrior. Instead, women "wove their lives and the lives of their children together" until they, like Yemayá and Inle, were inseparable. This weave is constructive and protective rather than exposing, as zami build women's houses and rainwater catchments. Not sterile but fruitful, it provides sustenance for the body rather than cutting it away as the women tend groundnuts, plant grain, and harvest limes. Even from afar, its very name offers sweetness and nourishment that wraps around, embraces delicious browns: "Carriacou, a magic name like cinnamon, nutmeg, mace, the delectable little squares of guava jelly each lovingly wrapped in wrappers, the long sticks of dried vanilla and the sweet-smelling tonka bean, chalky brown nuggets of pressed chocolate for cocoa-tea, all set on a bed of wild bay laurel leaves, arriving every Christmas time in a well-wrapped tin."[53] As it touches the sea and sends its fruits across the water, Carriacou reverses the violent fragmentation of the Middle Passage that haunts Cabrera's *patakí* and Brand's work in neighboring Grenada. Here, women who "walk like Africans" stay planted on earth rather than going out to sea, and they water the ground with rum for ancestors as they would in Yorubaland.[54] As a result of this they have language, affirmative Creole names for their connections: *madivine* to evoke another model of divinity, *friending* or *zami* to speak their intimacy as support rather than shame that needs silencing.

But of course *Zami*'s narrator does not live in Carriacou, any more than Inle lives at the bottom of the sea. In fact, the first chapter tells us she cannot even find the island on a map, so that "home was still a sweet place somewhere else which they had not managed to capture yet on paper, nor to throttle and bind up between the pages of a schoolbook."[55] The beyond-binaries space that the narrator can and does inhabit, that she finally recognizes as a here-and-now home, is the second on-land space that *Zami* imagines for the black woman who loves women: the famous "house of difference," Lorde's imagination of the diversity of her social spaces as a black lesbian in 1950s New York. As she remembers of the many gendered, sexual, racial, and other communities she navigated there: "Being women together was not enough. We were different. Being gay-girls was not enough. We were different. Being Black together was not enough. We were different. Being Black women together was not enough. We were different. Being Black dykes together was not enough. We were different. . . . It was a while before we came to realize that our place was the very house of difference rather than one particular difference."[56] Unlike Inle on land, the narrator will speak in New York and will speak in many tongues – as gay girl, black, woman, bringing together multiple identity formations in ways that proved challenging for both Cabrera in Castro's Cuba and Brand in Caribbean revolutionary movements. But she will never find these many tongues in Carriacou. The epilogue returns to close the text with a second description of the island of women and makes clear: "Once home was a long way off, a place I had never been to but knew out of my mother's mouth. I only discovered its latitudes when Carriacou was no longer my home."[57] So when she returns to the imagination of her mother's island at the end of the text, she no longer calls it *home* because she has come "to realize that our place was the very house of difference" rather than a predifferential, black woman-loving woman island. Carriacou serves *Zami*'s narrator as a myth that helps her have a sense of herself as whole, floating the idea that elsewhere there existed a space in which she could be the same as everyone else, farmer and lover rather than warrior or victim. While this sense helps her claim and speak her different identities in a lesbian North America, *zami* Carriacou can only continue to exist for her as a mythic, faraway place whose Creole she does not speak.

But what about women who love women in the real, rather than the mythic, West Indies? Can they speak? Can they have a house of difference there, while still nurturing similarities? Finally, the question of how to imagine a woman who loves women *in* and not *from* Caribbean islands and seas remains, as Juana Rodríguez writes of *Zami*, unresolved.[58] Or, like Inle's voice, such desire remains placeless, sustained neither in water nor on land and lost at the meeting of the two. Brand does not *resolve* such an imagination; this is not the verb for the complexity and opacity with which she moves through this shoreline topos. Rather, building on the problems of same-sex loving and Caribbeanness, erotics and revolution that these earlier writers lay out, her poetry writes the voice of a Caribbean woman who loves women arriving not in Miami or New York but on West Indian shores. And while Cabrera finds landless Inle fantastically beautiful and Lorde finds faraway Carriacou magically sweet, Brand imagines this beachscape on which she arrives as an on-land Caribbean space where "to be awake is /more lovely than dreams" (4).

This Cut of Road up to Blanchicheuse:
Brand's New Maps to Desire

On another shoreline, desire-crossed and many-blued:

> this is you girl, this cut of road up
> to Blanchicheuse, this every turn a piece
> of blue and earth carrying on, beating, rock and
> ocean this wearing away, smoothing the insides
> pearl of shell and coral
> this is you girl, this is you all sides of me
> hill road and dip through the coconut at Manzanilla
> this sea breeze shaped forest of sand and lanky palm
> this wanting to fall, hanging, greening
> quenching the road
> this is you girl, even though you never see it
> the drop before Timberline, that daub of black shine

sea bush on smoke land, that pulse of the heart
that stretches up to Maracas, La Fillette bay never know
you but you make it wash up from the rocks. (3)

No language is neutral, indeed. Titled "hard against the soul," these are the first stanzas of Brand's collection and the start of her map to a new place. "This is you girl, this cut of road up / to Blanchicheuse": from its opening cut of road, *No Language*'s shoreline geography/oceanography traces Caribbean space in which desire between women is not only part of a return to the poet's native land, but *is* the way through Trinidad. And "this is you girl, this is you all sides of me": repeated at the beginning of each the stanza, the opening, feminized, and eroticized words become a refrain that rhythms the poem, connects its disparate landscape images, and continually foregrounds the powerful presence of the addressee—a same-sex lover and listener whose invocation is written across sea and land, bush and bay. But this *girl* is not Brand's only rewriting of Trinidad's map in these first lines. The roads she traces here connect on no road atlas but hers; the speaker's journey winds elliptically and nonlinearly through the island from stanza to stanza, beginning on the North Coast Road, shifting without transition to the East Coast's Manzanilla Road, then returning farther west on the north coast to stretch to Maracas and La Fillette bays. So this map makes its own geography—one that brings side by side Caribbean and Atlantic coasts, rain forests and swamps, fishing villages and coconut plantations, a north to which Afro-Trinidadians flocked after emancipation and an east where slaves worked the fields, a road that leads to the remaining Carib population and another that leads to the center of the South Asian population.[59] Openly speaking same-sex desire and imagining the Caribbean beyond its usual divisions immediately occupy the same place and proceed through the same figures of speech here, as the speaker's voice continually travels between so much that is supposed to remain separate to connect with and touch *you, girl*, again and again.

Let us stop a moment at the town where the opening lines tell readers the speaker and her desire are directed, Blanchisseuse. This site indeed calls for a different kind of journey and map. In the years in which Brand wrote *No Language* (and until the present day), the north coast's paved road ends here and becomes a mountain trace; so to move farther along the Caribbean shore, travelers must leave cars behind and proceed on foot or by boat. But in the colonial period the town got its name as the site where European ships' paths ended and where

black women began. That is, the name *Blanchisseuse* — "washerwoman" – comes
from the group of laundresses who worked where the town now sits, where the
Marianne River meets the Caribbean Sea. Sailors headed toward the island used
their presence as a landmark, knowing that where they saw the washerwomen
was where they wanted to land.[60] In fact, a sixteenth-century Spanish map on
display in Port-of-Spain's National Museum prominently marks the "Punto de
las Blanquisales" and shows a full-masted ship sailing toward it.[61] (Changed to
Blanchisseuse during French colonization, the name is now pronounced *Blanchicheuse* in Trinidadian Creole.)

Opening en route to this washerwomen's spot speaks a lot about what and
how Brand looks to map here. Blanchisseuse is a Caribbean site named from the
point of view not of the land but of the sea – not, certainly, the way cartography
usually works. As Brand writes in her novel *At the Full and Change of the Moon*, a
conventional map "can only describe the will of estate owners and governors. . . .
This map cannot note the great fluidity of maps, which is like the fluidity of
air. Paper rarely contains – even its latitudinal and longitudinal lines gesture
continuations. Paper does not halt land any more than it can halt thoughts.
Or rain showers, for that matter. The best cartographer is only trying to hold
water."[62] But Blanchisseuse – a town first charted from the water – seems positioned to trace that great fluidity of beachscape and thought that colonial maps
silence, and the speaker's journey toward it moves with Trinidad's waters (*ocean*
and *sea breeze*, Manzanilla, Maracas, and La Fillette bays) rather than trying to
hold them. As it does, this poem charts an anti-imperial epistemology, a way
of knowing Trinidad that defies the will to divide all fluidity exercised in the
maps of "estate owners and governors." At the same time, moving toward the
gynoerotic space of washerwomen's wet work makes this decolonizing map
equally a lesbian map, a coming (out) to *you, girl,* and *you, blanchisseuses*. Here is
a feminine speaker's route to land in women of color: a course to somewhere
named for no European conquistador or neocolonial governor but for working
black women who, even enslaved, never lost the connections to one another
that were so visible they could be seen from the sea's distance. As the speaker's
cartographic and erotic desires announce themselves on this watery cut of road,
the coming to Blanchisseuse segues into becoming a *blanchisseuse*. That is, the
poet's work begins to parallel the laundress's: a scrubbing and rinsing of the
buildup of the old (language) to make room for her new map, one on which
epistemological and erotic decolonization coincide. Here, without the underwater hide-and-seek of Capécia's Cambeille, the washerwoman/poet turns her

gaze and her words to *you, girl,* to trace the spring of *her* look – what Caribbean waters might look like narrated in another, woman-loving West Indian tongue.

And indeed, this map experiments with a linguistic fluidity new to Brand's published poetry. Acting on the transgressive promise of its title, *No Language Is Neutral*'s opening poem is written neither entirely in Standard English nor in Creole – but rather, porous as a shoreline, opens to Creolisms that enter more visibly and frequently as the poem progresses. Traces of nation language first appear in the opening line, as the spoken-language invocation *girl* immediately points to an oral language (Creole *gal*) backgrounding the written text. The poem's feminizing of language-blending continues as the next two Creolisms come around feminized geographic names: *Blanchicheuse,* the Creole rendering of *Blanchisseuse,* and the phrase "La Fillette bay never know," where the verb remains uninflected as in Creole. Working with and multiplying beyond twos, the second pair of Creolisms come two stanzas later around feminized human subjects, *she's.* The fifth stanza beings: "this is you girl, this is the poem no woman / ever write for a woman because she 'fraid to touch / this river boiling in she sleep" (4). The verbs here, uninflected *write* and elided *is* (optional in Creole), along with the modifiers *'fraid* and *she* as possessive adjective, make this most explicitly lesbian verse also the most explicitly Creolized. So readers see Creole and Standard English joining at the points at which geography and gender, Caribbeanness and woman loving mark the text – charting a meeting of Creole and English that serves the meeting of woman speaker, woman addressee, and feminized landscape, never separating lesbian from nation language as had been Brand's experience in other Caribbean poetics or politics.

In this new language, the opening poem – even as it thematizes and Creolizes writing "queer," unexpected connections between women and waters – also experiments with writing "queer," unpredictable junctures at the level of form. The poem builds on frequent enjambments, sentences and phrases spilling between lines and sliding fluidly around fragmentation. In fact, the first two lines put forth an enjambment that thematizes its image, cutting up a sentence that curves over to the next line like the curving road it describes as a "cut of road up." Like this road, enjambment becomes paradigmatic of the poem's work. That is, it concretizes connection across the "cut" – complex connection that, never giving way to flatness, traces a path to join hills and drops, hard-breaking sea and resistant rock. But without end rhymes and with enjambment breaking up parallel grammatical structures, how the poem builds across-the-cut junctures takes unpredictable, shifting forms from stanza to stanza. In the first, lines link across enjambments by a string of commas that draw together words before each pause. *Girl* (feminized human) answers to *Blanchicheuse* (feminized Caribbean geography), while both answer to seemingly contradictory verbs *carrying on, beating, wearing away*, whose internal grammatical rhyme helps gel a cohesive rhythm for the stanza. But the second stanza progresses with a slightly different work of linkage. As commas disappear, the stanza is instead held together sonorically, by the repetition of *this* (reaching back to the poem's first word); and visually, by the superimposition of water imagery onto the landscape ("sea breeze shaped forest," "quenching the road"). A trace of the previous linkage scheme remains in the comma-offset *hanging, greening, quenching* of the last two lines. In turn, in the third stanza, *this* disappears after the first line and *that* — slipping from demonstrative to relative pronoun — becomes the stanza's connecting particle.

In the poem's very structure, then, in a concatenation that refuses to settle into one pattern yet builds on patterns that came before, Brand creates space for a complex schema of connection, one in which configuration becomes constant reconfiguration, in which linkages remain mobile and creative. The significance of these mobile junctures goes beyond a display of poetic craft (though this craft makes clear why the collection was nominated for the Governor General's Award). Their multiple strategies for reaching across the cut are also political work, a formal example of how Brand's poems become weapons. Her connecting structures reflect the politics of change that she desires post Grenada, a change that never entirely breaks with its former directions yet also never leaves behind a constant movement to rework and reimagine its own visions and goals, what it wants to connect its work to and how. Bringing together phrases that never become complete sentences in a single line, Brand's junctures enact this change in a syntactic version of Alexander's pedagogy of Crossing: a formal piecing together of what has been fragmented, from the "rock and / ocean" divided in the interest of landowners and governors to desires for "you, girl," recolonized in the interest of heteropatriarchial nationalism. Embedding this piecing together not only at the level of content but also of form crystallizes the brilliance of the poem's decolonizing work — its map to break down and "cut . . . up" imperial desires for containment at the level not only of rhetoric but also of deep linguistic and psychic structures. Finally, *No Language* suggests, these structures are something the poet can work with and against; they are where she can rewrite even revolution's need for a (gendered, sexualized) other, one whose break from the self is unbridgeable.

But just as significant as how Brand connects across the cut is what she connects. Woven together over enjambments, winding through the poem like the North Coast Road, a chain of figures of comparison bridges not only land and sea but Brand's thematic and formal remappings of the postcolonial Caribbean's possible oceanographies and geographies. The poem opens with a classically phrased metaphor — "this is you girl, this cut of road up / to Blanchicheusse" — that sets readers up to trace, in the lines that follow, an image of what an openly gynoeroticized Trinidad would look like. But refusing to keep figures of comparison "straight," the metaphoric vehicle — the road — immediately also becomes a metonymic vehicle, one that works through an ongoing relationship between the land and the ocean it touches on either side. "This every turn a piece / of blue and earth carrying on, beating": if this is a map to where a Caribbean meeting of erotic (blue) and anticolonial (earth) politics takes the speaker, it is a very charged, hard-breaking course indeed. On this path, water and land flow in and out of each other, the dirt of the road dissolving into the blue of the sea before being brought back to "earth." Yet the present participles maintain a structural ambiguity that guards distance between these elements. Is every turn a piece of blue while earth carries on, or do the two carry on together? Does *beating* modify water (a cognitive match) or earth (its closest antecedent), or both? Lexical ambiguity further complicates the journey. Does *carrying on* mean fighting, bickering, as it would in Creole; or does it mean continuing together, moving toward the future? In the phrase *this wearing away*, is the ocean (the element of the *blanchisseuses*, of erotic decolonization) wearing away the rock (the element of Grenada's land reform, of political decolonization), or is the ocean itself wearing away? And is the wearing action a loss, a defeat of the earth by the ocean — or is it a smoothing, a softening that needs to happen, as suggested by the stanza's next phrase?

The encounter of rock and water is at once a carrying on and a breaking down in both senses of both words. Its contestation, erosion, and softening are at once of rock, of expected images, and of language itself, so that readers' concepts of blue and earth, Creole and English, broken and whole, eroticism and Caribbean must fight and continue on, conflict and come together before the path to the Trinidad of *you, girl*, can continue. In this encounter earth will not be passive nor ocean pacific. The process and products of the meeting of water and earth — as that between erotically and politically decolonized Trinidad — is mapped as a network of possible relationships, a set of tensions but also of softenings and alliances. Not just a breaking down, "this wearing away" is also a "smoothing the insides / pearl of shell and coral." The new, third substance created from the meeting – pearl of shell and coral – makes for a cunnic image from the seascape that outlines pearl like clitoris, shell like labia, and coral the color of both. This image, centered as its own line and the only line with no enjambment, occupies a position of power in Brand's poetic structure. This power is amplified by the multiple associations of the feminized shell – identified with *conch* in Caribbean writing, and especially in predecessor Cliff's novel *Abeng* – that is equally an image of a call to uprising (another echo embedded in "cut . . . up") and revolution. Caribbean earth (sand that becomes pearl), Caribbean sea (shell), and Caribbean woman lover connect again here, and the image of their connection is underlain with tones of forceful, revolutionary, and loving change, spoken through textual gestures toward women's erotic empowerment.

But all these parts, blue and earth, lover and seascape, eroticism and revolution, refuse to congeal into a stable whole. Immediately after this image of pearl of shell and coral, the poem segues from metonymy back to its guiding metaphor: "this is you girl, this is you all sides of me." But even as *you, girl*, shifts its positions in this poetic landscape to appear *all sides*, the girl's body is not yet *any* side – not there for readerly consumption as an image of the new Trinidad. "This is you girl, even though you never see it," the third stanza opens, situating this observation at the poem's very middle. So halfway up the road and at the midpoint of the poem, we learn that *you, girl*, are the road to Blanchicheuse and yet are not that road; *you* are not even on that road and have never been, have always been somewhere else in the world. This exaphoric deixis, pointing readers outside the poem and outside the edges of its map, marks the impossibility of conflating landscape with the female beloved's body. Her body is *like* land and sea, yet we are reminded that that body cannot be comprehended only by looking at land and sea; it exists elsewhere in its own space. Or, as a character in Brand's novel *In Another Place, Not Here* says to a female lover who engages her with a water metaphor: "See me beyond rock and beyond water as something human that need to eat and can die, even as you dive into me today like a fish."[63] This beyond-water vision is also called forth by a pedagogy of Crossing, by an ongoing commitment to reverse the imperial empirics that could not see black females as *something human that need to eat and can die*. To learn from that Crossing, the black female beloved cannot be captured or contained to represent something other than herself – even in a black poem, a woman's poem, a black lesbian poem. Uncontainably elusive, "wanting to fall, hanging, greening," she cannot be reduced to a symbol for a new politics of erotic decolonization either on Carriacou or Trinidad's blue and green northern coast. To map from the point of view of the sea must, instead, mean always giving the water and the *blanchisseuse* room to move somewhere else, to carry on to a La Fillette bay that does not know her yet.

A Map to the Tough Geography of Trenches, Quarrels, Placards: Remembering Other Beaches and Battles

Beginning on Trinidad's coastal roads, "hard against the soul" continues to wrap its way through No *Language* until, written across the "cuts" of other interspersed poems and its own internal breaks, it becomes a ten-part poem that both opens and concludes the collection. Throughout, these parts move from beach to beach, theme to theme, while continuing their charged, erotic address to a female beloved who, herself fluid, seems to become different women from poem to poem. But at the very center of this complex love song, part 6 interrupts the speaker's second-person, intimate invocations to challenge an interlocutor who is at once the lover and the reader:

> listen, just because I've spent these
> last few verses fingering this register of the heart,
> clapping life, as a woman on a noisy beach,
> calling blood into veins as dry as sand,
> do not think that things escape me,
> this drawn skin of hunger twanging as a bow,
> this shiver whistling into the white face of capital, a
> shadow traipsing, icy veined and bloodless through
> city alleys of wet light, the police bullet glistening
> through a black woman's spine in November, against
> red pools of democracy bursting the hemisphere's
> seams, the heart sinks, and sinks like a moon. (41)

Listen, *just because*: shifting abruptly from erotic lyricism to angry response, this single stanza makes up the entirety of part 6. And while the opening of "hard against the soul" charts a watery map to a new place, its center traces a new map to a repeatedly trodden watery place – Grenada's beaches during the U.S. military invasion. Unlike *you, girl*'s beachscape, lovingly marked with feminized place names, this map to what Brand calls earlier in the poem "the tough geography / of trenches, quarrels, placards, barricades," withholds all explicit place markers, the poet unwilling, it seems, to reproduce those names that appeared on military attack plans (39). But both the opening beach image and the final bloody explosion put readers in dialogue with her earlier poetic documentation of Grenada's revolution and invasion, particularly with the beach-haunted *Chronicles of the Hostile Sun*. In *Chronicles*' "October 25, 1983," the arrival of "america . . . to restore *democracy*" and the hunger the invaders' import echo the "red pools of democracy" and "hunger twanging like a bow" here, while the description of Bloody Wednesday – the day Bishop and key members of the PRG were executed – in "October 19, 1983," prefigures this poem's imagery of blood-bursting hopes for political change in the hemisphere.[64] Quite explicitly, the speaker's interjection from a "noisy beach" – a beach ringing with the noises of many histories and struggles – reminds readers that the shoreline is never marked as a site *either* of erotic reclaiming *or* of material struggle on the fluid maps of *No Language* but is always already both. While my reading of the opening poem searched out how writing at this juncture creates a newly eroticized map for the place where the poet was born, I now want to follow Brand's call to *listen* by hearing how its center creates a differently politicized cartography for the place where her comrades died.

From the woman on a noisy beach onward, continuities echo like claps between the *you, girl*–Blanchicheuse imagery of the beginning and the unaddressed women and unnamed shorelines here. Initially, Brand's heart imagery in this central poem remaps the opening's play of water and earth onto a metaphoric human body. Imagining the rhythm-creating poet/woman's clapping at the meeting of sea and land as "calling blood into veins," the poet simultaneously maps the internal flow of blood onto the outdoor scene of a noisy beach and, in the simile "veins dry as sand," maps the beach as part of the human body's inner geography. This coming together of blood and vein, sea and sand visualizes creative rebirth through wet/dry, fluid/earth exchange – "calling blood into veins as dry as sand" – that rushes through the poem in concert with the poet's speech to her lover, a "fingering this register of the heart" that evokes a physical and verbal caress of the beloved's now-flowing circulation. But while in the opening "that pulse of the heart" beats continually in the (not, of course, pacific) register of erotic love, here Brand abruptly superimposes the skin of a body dying of hunger onto the suddenly pumping heart—as "fingering the register of the heart" jarringly meets the disturbing tones of "this drawn skin of hunger twanging like a bow." The "white face of capital" further disrupts Brand's body drawings, the first lines' reanimated body now hauntingly transformed into the colorless "shadow traipsing" at the stanza's midpoint. The pattern of line breaks—each line to this point ending with a comma—is disrupted from the appearance of the word *capital* on, all lines afterward ending in enjambments. Thematizing this change of rhythm, the traces of music that began as "clapping life" wrench into sounds of pain and protest, "hunger twanging like a bow" and a "shiver whistling into the face of white capital." The heart imagery, equally disturbed and pained, sees the white face of capital fall into the line like a snowstorm to chill Brand's circulatory images from sandy veins to "icy veined and bloodless." And the sexual penetration suggested by *fingering* violently transforms into the penetration of "the police bullet glistening / through a black woman's spine" toward her heart, bringing her to literal death. Like and unlike the beloved who became *all sides of* Trinidad, this murdered black woman's body then becomes the entire region, her exploded heart bursting into "red pools of democracy bursting the hemisphere's / seams" as "the heart sinks, and sinks like a moon."

Yes, the opening road to Blanchicheuse and the beloved traces one innovative imagination of Caribbean women's body politics, a refusal to open space where a reclaimed landscape can be severed from a reclaimed gynoeroticism. But the heart bursting the hemisphere's seams traces another, equally pressing imagination, an imperatively phrased (*listen*) guard against any divorce between erotic decolonization and resistance to deadly neoimperialism. This moment of re-membering the region's violence reminds readers that the black woman's heart is not merely a sentimental cliché, but flesh and blood that can be spilled in the Global North's economic and political invasions. This second heart visualizes the distinction that Lizbeth Paravisini-Gebert draws between European feminists' search for a new metaphorics of women's bodies and Caribbean women writers' more concrete body concerns: "The flesh-and-blood quality of women [characters] must be remembered when reading how Caribbean women writers—and indeed most Third World women writers—'read' and 'write' the female body. Their depictions of the 'body-as-metaphor' must be seen in the context of political systems where women's bodies have been subject to abuse, rape, torture, and dismemberment precisely because this very treatment, through its interpretation as a symbolic construct, has been an effective method of political control. Their reading of the body thus emerges from an ever-present threat to their own vulnerable flesh and blood, and the resulting symbolism is too close to the material body to allow for the comfort of seeing this danger merely as metaphor."[65] Unlike the Caribbean texts Paravisini-Gebert cites, "hard against the soul" metaphorizes a desiring female body that continually marks the poem even as it refuses reduction to a mere "symbolic construct." But buried at its center like a heart, the evocation of a bleeding black female body pulses unexpectedly to remind readers how this other body politics informs the first. As the black woman's heart – rather than becoming sentimentalized, internalized, and individualized – becomes politicized, externalized, and regionalized in the final, explosive outrage, no wonder it "sinks like a moon": a moon, a figure of eroticized femininity that in this stanza sinks the way the woman's body does under political violence.

As the speaker voices her commitment to hearing hunger's twang, capital's shiver, and the bullet through the black woman's spine in the same space in which she "fingers the registers of the heart," Brand's beachscapes – repeated with a difference between opening and center – bring disparate topoi together at once fluidly and explosively. Superimposing the two enunciations of woman and/as beach, readers find an interaction of elements (water, earth, blood, veins), identities (Caribbean, woman, lesbian, revolutionary), and voices (lover, protester) that weave in and out of each other as complexly as blue and earth, touching, pressuring, and transforming without any term overpowering the others. This interaction "claps life" into – that is, offers a creative poetic rendering of – what Alexander imagines "a feminist emancipatory project in which women can love themselves, love women, and transform the nation simultaneously" would entail. Namely, she writes, "This would mean building ... new landmarks for the transformative power of the erotic, a meeting place where our deepest yearnings for different kinds of freedom can take shape and find rest."[66] In Brand's maps, this meeting place emerges when she repeatedly landmarks beachscapes as those spaces that neither revolutionaries (where the hemisphere bursts) nor women-loving women (on the road to Blanchicheuse) were meant to occupy but that both reclaim in "hard against the soul" – that is, where guerillas and lovers stand positioned as participants in a common struggle for an autonomous Caribbean space in which deep yearnings for freedom might take shape. These yearnings might be less for "freed" sexual love than for what Colin Robinson meant when he originally called for *imagining Caribbean queer politics imaginatively*: for conceptual tools to trace those inti-

macies that clarify common causes between feminist, same-sex loving, environmental, and anticapitalist movements struggling without widespread bases
for support but crucial for the region's broader well-being – for its unburst
heart.[67]

Imagining imaginatively, indeed, is the work of No Language. In its beginning, middle, and end, this volume is not about describing a lived past of
Caribbeanness, politics, and identity in Grenada and Canada as Brand's earlier
collections are. While continually touching this personal and regional history, the poet's pedagogy of Crossing is ultimately about writing a complex,
feeling-restoring future out of a fragmented, often violent past. As she charts
this pedagogy, her work shifts to imagine yet unrealized, potential junctures
between Caribbean erotic and political landscapes and desires, those desires
she imagined when working as a revolutionary in Grenada as "making yourself
for the future, and you do not even know the extent of it when you begin but
you have a hint, a taste in your throat of the warm elixir of the possible."[68] In
another poem from No Language, she distills this work in these terms:

> In another place, not here, a woman might touch
> something between beauty and nowhere, back there
> and here, might pass hand over hand her own
> trembling life, but I have tried to imagine a sea not
> bleeding, a girl's glance full as a verse . . .
>   . . . Each sentence realised or
> dreamed jumps like a pulse with history and takes a
> side. What I say in any language is told . . . not in
> words and in words and in words learned by heart,
> told in secret and not in secret, and listen, does not
> burn out or waste and is plenty and pitiless and loves. (31)

So Brand voices the very language in which her maps are "told" as a system of
communication completely across the cut, completely beyond those overdeter-
mined lesbian binaries of in words/in silence, in secret/not in secret. Beyond
these isolating frameworks for categorizing women's eroticized speech to one
another, innovative, layered ways of figuring the transformative power of the
erotic emerge. Loves comes only as, but does become the last word: not a priva-
tized or "in secret" feeling, but the culmination both of a work of imagination
that heals landscape and woman together – "a sea not bleeding, a girl's glance
full" – and a complex, material history that makes dreams jump like a pulse.

This glance-full stanza explicates the title and the work of *No Language*. Its first line will become the title of Brand's first novel, *In Another Place, Not Here*, a lyrical, nonlinear story of two Caribbean women's love affair in motion between Grenada, Trinidad, and Toronto. Coming full circle in the writing of this book, then, I want to end my consideration of Brand by turning to the opening of the novel, looking at how we get from beachscape to thiefing sugar.

*   *   *

grace, you see, come as a surprise and nothing till
now knock on my teeming skull, then, these warm
watery syllables, a woman's tongue so like a culture,
plunging toward stones not yet formed into flesh,
language not yet made . . .
— Dionne Brand, "hard against the soul"

Claiming languages that have never been neutral, *In Another Place, Not Here* opens in Creole and in desire, with a lyric evocation of the cane cutter Elizete's thirst for the activist Verlia. In the field one day, Elizete sees the revolution-preaching woman who will become her lover walk across the cane toward her. And she thinks: "Grace. Is grace, yes. And I take it, quiet, quiet, like thiefing sugar. From the word she speak to me and the sweat running down she in that sun. . . . That woman like a drink of cool water."[69] Dipping sugar into the water of Brand's earlier poetry, this opening metaphor distills the semiotics of transformative desire that develops throughout Brand's work. The phrase *thiefing sugar* speaks transgression (*thiefing*) but also the pleasure or sweetness of *sugar*, and by bridging these registers Brand transforms both terms — wetting sugar and sugaring water, so to speak. *Thiefing* speaks in doubled language. A common Creole verb (synonymous with the Standard English *stealing*, which is not used in Creole), for Anglophone audiences it also reads as a verbalization of the noun *thief*. In Standard English this *thiefing* claims radical power by slipping away from the canonical *thieving* (an adjective with disparaging connotations) yet retaining the criminal, transgressive image of the thief, in effect stealing language itself. Sugar becomes the metonymic object of action of this thiefing, as well as its accomplice. The pleasure of sweetness, colonized in the Caribbean since the advent of the plantation system, is now linked to black women taking themselves for themselves. Coining this verb phrase as an image of desire between Caribbean women, Brand continues her search for "language not yet made" through an erotic metaphor: a figure of connection that imagines transformative contact – between thiefing and sugar, woman and water, action and the material world – as pleasure (grace, sugar) that intersects and transforms violence. This image of same-sex desire is also queer praxis: a use of speech that, bridging transgressive, erotic, and active verbs, brings together the politics of language, desire, and radical transformation. As it untangles in her thick, joyful, and painful prose, this kind of speaking sounds like a juncture of same-sex loving and Caribbean that is "*neither/nor, but kind of both, not quite either*," as Maria Lugones describes the *mestiza*'s messy consciousness.[70]

What interests me in this verb phrase is not just its meaning, though, but its tense (or lack thereof), and what this suggests about the work of imagining desire between women both in Brand's literary texts and in my own critical praxis. The comparison of verb phrases in mismatched tenses here – *take it* and *thiefing sugar* – takes us back to the poetry of the *mati*, where *teki* (take) is the verb women use to express their desire for other women and where food, especially birthday party sweets, are something women share. And the practice of thiefing sugar, like that of storming the beach, is about reclaiming a Caribbean and same-sex loving past like the *mati*'s: something that, like sugar – originally cultivated in North Africa and Asia – has been reappropriated and boiled down to serve European imperial desiring machines. At the same time, thiefing sugar is also about claiming a present that remains as blurry, colonized, and resistant as the obscured past. This is a present that can only be enunciated by thiefing sweet (or bittersweet) parts of different languages – by *going a piece of the way*, to use Carole Boyce Davies's felicitous phrase, with lesbian, gay rights, black feminist, revolutionary discourses.[71] This *thiefing* and *going a piece* is the movement of Brand's poetics and politics; and it is also the movement of the critical *métissage* I have sought in this study as I maneuver between Caribbean, queer, and feminist theory, as well as between literary studies, history, anthropology, and linguistics. Never simple, it is a complex, composite present, situated at a crossroads of political, historical, linguistic, and artistic circumstances as historically grounded and shifting as cane fields: circumstances that, like Brand's women lovers and their cane field, are both reflected and transformed by the texts of Caribbean women who love women. In both erotic and literary senses, a woman-loving woman's tongue is "so like a culture," carrying and manipulating all the contradictions of the day-to-day of the worlds that *mati*, *femmes*, *lamayòteuses*, and girlfriends enter.

But like the "language not yet made" that Brand goes in search of, *thiefing sugar* also reaches for a future tense. This is the tense of a still sugary, sticky, and murky future that can only be imagined by piecing together parts of the past and present and bringing them to a crosscurrents – pieces that stick to its fingers and its fingering the register of the heart. Brand's beachscapes, like the *mati*'s roses, Faubert's garden, and Capécia's waters, continue to direct readers' attention outward: to other unmapped geographies in Caribbean and same-sex loving writing and activism, where new, more mobile gazes are still needed to drive backgrounded landscapes into future foregrounds. Gay rights, feminism, decolonization theory, historiography, immigration studies, linguistics: the landscape metaphors that emerge from Suriname to Trinidad imagine concrete spaces where, complicatedly, the need for these fields to listen differently – queerly – is voiced without being defined or fixed. The work of *thiefing sugar* is *breaking hard against things*: not fencing in new hegemonic definitions of same-sex desire, but questioning and transforming them from stanza to stanza, moment to moment, as they wash up on the beach. Sexuality as stable, balkanized identity does not, Brand's ever-breaking beachscapes suggest, emerge as a useful tool for political organization or intellectual analysis. It is only with a consideration of sexuality's shifts and overlaps with many shores – with many kinds of lived experience – that can it become effectively politicized and theorized. That sea sky and sea floor, future and past, desire and revolution can begin "plunging toward stones not yet formed into flesh."

Notes

Introduction: The Spring of Her Look

1. Lucie Thésée, "Beautiful as . . . ," in Rosemont, *Surrealist Women*, 147.

2. Roumain, *Gouverneurs de la rosée*, 26; translation mine. The original French reads, "Si l'on est d'un pays, si l'on y est né, comme qui dirait: natif-natal, eh bien, on l'a dans les yeux, la peau, les mains, avec la chevelure des arbres, la chair de sa terre, les os de ses pierres, le sang de ses rivières, son ciel, sa saveur, ses hommes et ses femmes: c'est une présence, dans le coeur, ineffaçable, comme une fille qu'on aime: on connaît la source de son regard, le fruit de sa bouche, les collines de ses seins, ses mains qui se défendent et se rendent, ses genoux sans mystères, sa force et sa faiblesse, sa voix et son silence."

3. Franco, *Plotting Women*, xi, xxiii.

4. See the anonymous *Code noir*. Article 18 prohibits cane sales while Articles 44 to 50 explain slaves' status as *meubles*, or movable property. The code is available online at http://www.tlfq.ulaval.ca/axl/amsudant/guyanefr1685.htm.

5. See Audre Lorde's "The Uses of the Erotic: The Erotic as Power" in her *Sister Outsider*, 53–59; and Frantz Fanon's "De la violence" in *Les damnés de la terre*, 5–52.

6. Bench trails are unpaved, winding paths originally cut for mules in Trinidad.

7. I am signifying here on Epeli Hau'ofa's brilliant rethinking of the geography of archipelagos in "Our Sea of Islands" in Waddell, Naidu, and Hau'ofa, *A New Oceania*, 2–16.

8. De Lauretis, "Queer Theory," iv–v.

9. See Manalansan, *Global Divas*; Sinnott, *Toms and Dees*; Gopinath, *Impossible Desires*; and Joseph A. Massad, *Desiring Arabs*.

10. See Glave, *Words to Our Now*, 245.

11. Johnson, "'Quare' Studies," 125.

12. The second edition of the *Oxford English Dictionary* notes the first use of *lesbianism* to denote female homosexuality occurring in 1870, while *lesbian* appears as an adjective in a medical dictionary in 1890.

13. On this history, see Price and Price, *Two Evenings in Saramaka*; and Wekker, *Ik ben een gouden munt*.

14. Edwards, *The History, Civil and Commercial, of the British West Indies*, 2:94.

15. Wekker, "What's Identity Got to Do With It?," 124.

16. While the phrase *woman-loving woman* circulated in North American feminist circles in the 1970s – as witnessed by Teresa Trull's 1977 song "Woman-Loving Women" – my use of the phrase "women who love women" is not meant to reprise this idealistic vision of same-sex desire. The phrase has since come to be used in a variety of contexts that have taken it away from its 1970s iteration.

17. Walcott, "Outside in Black Studies," 95.

18. See Judith Butler, "Subjects of Sex/Gender/Desire," in her *Gender Trouble*, 4.

19. *Obinrin* is a Yoruba feminine gender often translated as "woman." Oyěwùumí powerfully argues in *The Invention of Women* that these two terms are not the same and that *woman* is a construct brought to Nigeria only with colonization.

20. *Mannengre meid* (Suriname) and *man royal* (Jamaica) name masculine females; *masisi* and *makoumè* (Haiti, Guadeloupe, Martinique) name feminine males.

21. Spillers, "Mama's Baby, Papa's Maybe," 72.

22. See Reddock, "Women and Slavery in the Caribbean," 66.

23. Quoted in Bush, *Slave Women in Caribbean Society*, 14, 15.

24. See Reddock, "Women and Slavery in the Caribbean," 72.

25. Quoted in Williams, *Capitalism and Slavery*, 198.

26. See the second edition of the *Oxford English Dictionary* for the queer history of *Amazon*.

27. Quoted in Edwards, *The History, Civil and Commercial, of the British West Indies*, 2: 32.

28. Quoted ibid., 2:96.

29. Shepherd, *Women in Caribbean History*, 67.

30. On colonial laws targeting free women of color, see ibid.; Hoogbergen and Theye, "Surinaamse Vvrouwen in de slavernij," 126-51; and Dayan, *Haiti, History, and the Gods*, 180-81. On these pages, Dayan also cites Leonora Sansay's assessment of the sexual power of mulattas in her *Secret History; or, The Horrors of St. Domingo, in a Series of Letters, Written by a Lady* . . . (Philadelphia: Bradford and Inskeep, 1808), 78.

31. Edwards, *The History, Civil and Commercial, of the British West Indies*, 2: 98.

32. Oshun, the beautiful, generously erotic Yoruba-Caribbean *orishá* of sexuality, femininity, fresh water, and sweetness syncretized with the Nuestra Señora de la Caridad del Cobre, has often been evoked by scholars and poets as a model for a uniquely creolized Caribbean femininity. See, for example, Antonio Benítez-Rojo's introduction to his *The Repeating Island*, 12-15.

33. Brand, *No Language Is Neutral*, 38.

34. *Macha* is used in the Spanish-speaking Caribbean to refer to masculine females.

35. Shango is the Yoruba-Caribbean divinity of lightning, warfare, dance, and social jus-

tice. On the gender and sexually complex roles of Shango, see Conner, Sparks, and Sparks, *Cassell's Encyclopedia of Queer Myth, Symbol, and Spirit*, 304.

36. Raiskin, "The Art of History," 69.

37. A *hounfort* is a compound where Vodoun ceremonies take place.

38. Cassid, *Sowing Empire*, 191.

39. Quoted in Sheller, *Consuming the Caribbean*, 6.

40. See Beckles, *Centering Woman*.

41. Lorde, "The Uses of the Erotic," 53–59.

42. Luce Irigaray, "Commodities among Themselves," in *This Sex Which Is Not One*, 195–204.

43. For an interesting discussion of these names for female genitalia, see Dayan, *Haiti, History, and the Gods*, 134–35.

44. See Javier Arnaldo's discussion of the abolitionist uses of Brunias's work in his online catalogue entry http://www.museothyssen.org/thyssen/ficha_obra/1006.

45. Alejo Carpentier, "On the Marvelous Real in America," in Zamora and Faris, *Magical Realism*, 85.

46. Velma Pollard quoted in Cooper, *Noises in the Blood*, 38–39.

47. Neijhorst, *Bigisma taki*, 322; translation mine.

48. Ibid., 65.

49. See Bernabé, Chamoiseau, and Confiant, *Éloge de la créolité*, 28.

50. See Glissant, *Caribbean Discourse*, 139.

51. See Glissant, *Poétique de la relation*, 72. Here Glissant proclaims feminism a luxury indulged in by Western women; and Bernabé, Chamoiseau, and Confiant, *Éloge de la créolité*.

52. Bernabé, Chamoiseau, and Confiant, *Éloge de la créolité*, 28.

53. Ibid., 29.

54. See Sedgwick, *Epistemology of the Closet*. Recently, several studies have emerged that question the urban bias of earlier queer studies, including Halberstam, *In A Queer Time and Place*.

55. See, for example, Terry Castle, *The Apparitional Lesbian*.

56. Sedgwick, *Epistemology of the Closet*, 70–71.

57. See King, "Remixing the Closet."

58. I am grateful to Siobhan Craig for pointing out that closets are in fact distinctly North American architectural features and that much of Europe, as well, counts closets as a rarity. So more than anything else, then, the exportation of the closet as a dominant metaphor seems to speak of the cultural hegemony of the United States.

59. See Johnson and Henderson, *Black Queer Studies*. The symposium celebrating the book's publication, titled "Black Queer Studies: A Symposium," was held at Northwestern University, 20 January 2006.

60. Robinson, "Toward a Strategy of Imagination."

61. Christian, "The Race for Theory," 336.

Chapter 1: "Rose is my mama, *stanfaste* is my papa"

1. Ruben Gowricharn reports these facts on immigration in his keynote address to the symposium "Immigration and Multiculturalism on Aruba," organized by the Fundacion Estudionan Social Cristian, Aruba, on 15 May 2004. The speech is archived at http://www.forum.nl/pdf/aruba.pdf.
2. Prengaman, "Lesbian Couple Caught in Aruba-Netherlands Rift."
3. Quoted ibid.
4. Ibid.
5. See "Court: Aruba Must Recognize Dutch Same-Sex Marriages," Nationalgaynews .com, 14 April, http://nationalgaynews.com.
6. Quoted in Clemencia, "Women Who Love Women in Curaçao," 82.
7. Quoted ibid., 82.
8. I take this phrase from Michelle Cliff's poem, also entitled "Love in the Third World," in *The Land of Look Behind*, 77–79.
9. This definition of theorizing is taken from standard English dictionary definitions of theory as an "analysis of a set of facts in their relation to one another" (http://www .merriam-webster.com, accessed 19 January 2007).
10. Hiss, *Netherlands America*, 27.
11. Herskovits and Herskovits, *Suriname Folk-Lore*, 9.
12. On Paramaribo yard dwellings in the eighteenth and nineteenth centuries, see Hoefte, "The Development of a Multiethnic Plantation Economy," 11.
13. On trees, snakes, and the importance of yard flora in the Afro-Surinamese religion Winti, see Stephen, *Winti*, 43–44, 116–17.
14. In the context of Suriname, *Creole* is used to refer to people of African descent who are descendants of slaves, in contradistinction to Maroons. When I employ *Creole* as an ethnic designation, it is thus in line with this use.
15. Wekker, *Ik ben een gouden munt*, 144.
16. J. van Donselaar, *Woordenboek van Het Surinaams-Nederlands*, 248–49.
17. Mintz and Price, *The Birth of Afro-American Culture*, 44.
18. Glissant, *Le discourse antillais*, 297. The original French speaks of an "inappréciable avantage" – "au débarquer sur la terre nouvelle, elle connaît déjà le maître"; translation mine.
19. Quoted in Wekker, *The Politics of Passion*, 210.
20. Th. A. C. Comvalius briefly describes these police interventions in his article on *lobisingi*, "Een der vormen van de Surinaamsche lied na 1863," 358.
21. Quoted in Wekker, *Ik ben een gouden munt*, 146. The original Dutch reads, "geslachtelijke gemeenschap tusschen vrouwen onderling (het matispelen)."Translation mine.
22. McCook, *States of Nature*, 139–40.

23. Quoted in Wekker, *Ik ben een gouden munt*, 146.

24. These household manuals, widely distributed to Indonesian colonists, are fascinating documents whose in-depth analysis unfortunately falls outside the scope of this study. On this subject, see Ann Laura Stoler's detailed exploration in *Carnal Knowledge and Imperial Power*, 70–72; or an introduction to the topic in Locher-Scholten, "So Close and Yet So Far."

25. Wekker puts forward this important relationship premise in her discussion of *kamra prekti* in *Ik ben een gouden munt*, 127–28.

26. Quoted ibid., 147.

27. Hannau and Garrard, *Flowers of the Caribbean*, 8.

28. See ibid.

29. Moreau de St. Méry, *Description de la partie française de l'isle de St. Domingue*, 1022. The original reads, "à coté de cette preuve d'aridité, sont des plantes auxquelles l'arrosement donne la plus brillante vegetation. On a ainsi le contraste de la nature abandonnée à elle-même ou secondée par l'industrie de l'homme"; all translations mine.

30. Ibid., 1073.

31. The subjects of Enlightenment botanical gardens in general, and the history of such catalogued gardens in the Caribbean in particular, are fascinating ones that are unfortunately beyond the scope of this study. For an important analysis of the former, see Michel Foucault's "Classifying" in his *The Order of Things*, 136–79. For a groundbreaking analysis of the latter, see Cassid, *Sowing Empire*.

32. See Hulme, "Polytropic Man." In fact, as Shaden Tageldin has pointed out in our conversations, compasses were not European inventions at all, though European colonizers were responsible for turning them into a magic technology.

33. Stedman, *Narrative of a Five Years' Expedition against the Revolted Negroes of Suriname*, 80.

34. Edward Long, quoted in Edwards, *The History, Civil and Commercial, of the British West Indies*, 540.

35. Bush, *Slave Women in Caribbean Society*, 110–11.

36. Condé, *En attendant le bonheur (Heremakhonon)*, 189.

37. See Long, *The History of Jamaica*, 2:356–64.

38. Moreau de St. Méry, *Description de la partie française de l'isle de St. Domingue*, 109. The original reads: "Les mulatresses sont femmes qui aiment les fleurs avec passion, qui s'en parent, qui en jonchent leurs lits et leurs armoires, et qui, sachant bien que leur parfum éveille la volupté, ont un grand plaisir à en former des bouquets pour l'objet qui leur est cher."

39. Ibid., 104. The original reads: "Charmer tous les sens, les livrer aux plus délicieuses extases" and "éveillent la volupté."

40. See de Man, "Epistemologies of Metaphor," 11–28.

41. See the introduction to Benítez-Rojo, *The Repeating Island*, 1–30.

42. Moreau de St. Méry, *Description de la partie française de l'isle de St. Domingue*, 1070.

43. Dayan, *Haiti, History, and the Gods*, 191.

44. Moreau de St. Méry, *Description de la partie française de l'isle de St. Domingue*, 106.

45. Quoted in Williams, *Capitalism and Slavery*, 198.

46. Stedman, *Narrative of a Five Years' Expedition against the Revolted Negroes of Suriname*, 112.

47. Moreau de St. Méry, *Description de la partie française de l'isle de St. Domingue*, 54. The original reads: "Déjà malheureux par une complexion faible, beaucoup d'entr'eux le sont encore par l'effet d'une pratique révoltante (dont d'autres Africains offrent aussi quelquefois des preuves aux îles), et qui leur enlève le titre d'homme en leur laissant la vie"; translation mine.

48. Ibid., 77. The original reads: "Un grand plaisir pour elles, c'est de faire ce qu'elles appellent l'assortiment; c'est à dire, qu'à certaines fêtes solennelles, elles s'habillent plusiers d'une manière absolument uniforme, pour aller se promener ou danser. On fait plus fréquemment l'assortiment avec une bonne amie qui est la confidente, celle dont on ne peut se passer. Cet attachement [est] extrêmement vif"; translation mine.

49. See Lilian Faderman's chapter "The 'Fashion' of Romantic Friendship in the Eighteenth Century" in her *Surpassing the Love of Men*, 74–84.

50. Moreau de St. Méry, *Description de la partie française de l'isle de St. Domingue*, 108. The original reads "remarquable . . . fidelité." Stedman, *Narrative of a Five Years' Expedition against the Revolted Negroes of Suriname*, 80.

51. See McLeod, *De vrije negerin Elisabeth*, 41.

52. Details of this case are recounted by Michiel van Kempen in his *Een geschiedenis van de Surinaamse literatuur*, Deel 3, 35–36; as well as by McLeod, *De vrije negerin Elisabeth*, 42.

53. Quoted in Dayan, *Haiti, History, and the Gods*, 191.

54. Hannau and Garrard, *Flowers of the Caribbean*, 6.

55. See Hoogbergen and Theye, "Surinaamse vrouwen in de slavernij," 142.

56. Wekker, *Ik ben een gouden munt*, 80.

57. Here I am expanding Ann McClintock's ideas about the interplay between colonial and sexual ideas of the fetish. McClintock's idea of the fetish revises competing psychoanalytic, Marxist, and colonial ideas of this concept to posit that the fetish is a "displacement onto an object (or person) of contradictions that the individual cannot resolve at a personal level. These contradictions may originate as social contradictions but are lived with profound intensity in the imagination and the flesh." McClintock, *Imperial Leather*, 184.

58. Cosentino, "On Looking at a Vodou Altar," 67.

59. See Hoogbergen and Theye, "Surinaamse Vrouwen in de slavernij," 142; and Clemencia, "Women Who Love Women in Curaçao," 82–83.

60. See Herskovits and Herskovits, *Trinidad Village*, 128.

61. Herskovits and Herskovits, *Suriname Folk-Lore*, 32–33.

62. Gloria Wekker, personal communication, August 2001.

63. Quoted in Neijhorst, *Bigisma taki*, 307.

64. Mbembe, *On the Postcolony*, 6.

65. Wekker, "'Girl, It's Boobies You're Getting, No?,'" 45.

66. See Bernabé, Chamoiseau, and Confiant, *Éloge de la créolité*, 28.

67. On sexual and gender complexity among Afro-Caribbean spirits, see Conner with Sparks, *Queering Creole Spiritual Traditions*, 51–87.

68. On the predominance of same-sex relationships in Afro-Caribbean religion, see ibid., 89–112.

69. See Van Wetering, "Polyvocality and Constructions of Syncretism in *Winti*," 183–200.

70. Thompson, *Face of the Gods*, 110.

71. See ibid., 109.

72. Jet is quoted by Rudolf van Lier in his study of *mati* undertaken in the 1940s but not published until the 1980s, titled *Tropische Ttribaden*, 49.

73. Ibid., 49.

74. Herskovits and Herskovits, *Suriname Folk-Lore*, 33.

75. See Glissant, *Poétique de la relation*, 40.

76. Wieringa, "Desiring Bodies or Defiant Cultures," 212.

77. Herskovits and Herskovits, *Suriname Folk-Lore*, 31.

78. Neijhorst, *Bigisma taki*, 76. The original reads: "Zelf gecomponeerde lobisingi (vaak hekeldichten over rivalen van in gevoelens gekrente vrouw) wereden in die tijd in de open lucht gezongen, waarbij de dames dan hun (lesbische) liefde met veel fanfare (koperen blaasorkest) declameerde"; translation mine.

79. Wekker, *The Politics of Passion*, 202.

80. On the presence of male *mati*, see ibid., 115.

81. Comvalius, "Een der vormen van de Surinaamsche lied na 1863," 355. The original reads: "Overgansvorm van het Negerlied . . . dat naar den vorm tusschen het Afrikaansche and het Europeesche lied staat." My translation.

82. The Herskovitses quote this text (29) in *Suriname Folk-lore*, as do Jan Voorhoeve and Ursy Lichtveld in *Creole Drum: An Anthology of Creole Literature in Suriname*, 48. This version comes from a generous personal communication with Gloria Wekker, August 2001.

83. Neijhorst, *Bigisma taki*, 76.

84. Wekker, "Of mimic men and unruly women," 188.

85. Neijhorst, *Bigisma taki*, 327.

86. Ibid., 324. The original reads: "Fosi yu ben de mi rosu na tapu tafra, di yu komopo fu drape, yuk on tron stanfaste na ini mi ati"; my translation.

87. Wekker, *Ik ben een gouden munt*, 62. The original reads: "Roos e flaw a de fadon, ma stanfaste dat e tan sidon"; my translation.

88. McCook, *States of Nature*, 81.

89. Quoted in van Lier, *Tropische Ttribaden*, 49. The original reads: "Ti toe soema di mattie, dan na wan di pree foe man"; my translation.

90. See Wekker, *Ik ben een gouden munt*, 163.

91. See ibid. Wekker also notes that females cross-dress in public much less frequently than males (Wekker, *The Politics of Passion*, 116).

92. Quoted in van Lier, *Tropische tribaden*, 48. The original reads: "Mattie diesie na wan sanie foe sosso oema-soema"; my translation. Wekker notes the term *uma wroko* (*The Politics of Passion*, 41).

93. Keeling, *The Witch's Flight*, 84.

94. See Wekker, *The Politics of Passion*, 103.

95. On the humanization of flowers as well as the composite parts of the Afro-Surinamese self, see Charles J. Wooding's classic article, "Traditional Healing and Medicine in Winti." See also Wekker, "What's Identity Got to Do with It?," 132–33.

96. Quoted in Wekker, *Ik ben een gouden munt*, 165. The original reads: "Mi yeye no ben wan' de ondro man'. . . . Sommige vrouwen zijn so. . . . Het is je ziel dat je zo maakt. Mijn ziel wilde met een vrouw zijn"; my translation.

97. For a thorough and very helpful introduction to the history of *na* and *de* and the linguistic controversies around them, see Migge, "The origin of the copulas *d/n/a* and *de* in the Eastern Maroon Creole."

98. For interesting discussions of dynamics between Surinamese and Dutch women who love women in Amsterdam, see Marie-José Janssens and Wilhelmina van Wetering, "Mati en lesbiennes, homoseksualiteit en etnische identiteit bij Creools-Surinaamse vrouwen in Nederland"; as well as Wekker, "Sexuality on the Move," in *The Politics of Passion*, 223–57.

Chapter 2: Darkening the Lily

1. Quoted in Hari, "Murder Music in Jamaica."

2. Buju Banton, *Boom Bye Bye* (New York: VP Records, 1992).

3. Quoted in Chin in "'Bullers' and 'Battymen,'" 127.

4. Powell with Stephens, "A Culture of Intolerance."

5. Quoted in White, "Rhythm of Hatred."

6. Cooper, *Sound Clash*, 154.

7. Chin, "Staceyann Chin."

8. Powell with Stephens, "A Culture of Intolerance."

9. Beenie Man, "Damn!!," on Various Artists, *Real Sex 2000* (New York: VP Records, 2000).

10. Chrisman, "The Imperial Unconscious?," 38, 41.

11. O'Callaghan, *Women Writing the West Indies, 1804–1939*, 85.

12. On the power of the imperial gaze scanning mountainscapes, see Pratt, *Imperial Eyes*, 59–60.

13. O'Callaghan, *Women Writing the West Indies, 1804–1939*, 85.

14. Albinia Catherine Hutton, "Up among the Mountain Passes," in Mitchell, *Voices of Summerland*, 99.

15. Wolcott, *The Island of Sunshine*, 53.

16. Henderson, *Jamaica*, 158.

17. Ibid., 158.

18. Besson, *Martha Brae's Two Histories*, 41.

19. See Henriques, *Family and Colour in Jamaica*, 42.

20. See ibid., 152–59, a chapter titled "The Upper Class Family."

21. Stokes, *The Color of Sex*, 17.

22. See ibid., 21.

23. Kent, *Making Girls into Women*, 71.

24. Ibid., 46.

25. Ibid.

26. I am referring here to Louise Bennett's famous poem "Colonisation in Reverse," reprinted in Fenwick, *Sisters of Caliban*, 37–38.

27. Adisa, "Three Landscapes," 213.

28. Nugent, *Lady Nugent's Jamaica Journal*, 76.

29. Bush, *Slave Women in Caribbean Society*, 23.

30. Bush, "'Sable Venus,' 'She Devil,' or 'Drudge'?," 775.

31. Nugent, *Lady Nugent's Jamaica Journal*, 179.

32. Ibid., 65.

33. Ibid., 98.

34. Quoted in D'Costa and Lalla, *Voices in Exile*, 16.

35. Long, *The History of Jamaica*, 2:279.

36. Lugones, "Purity, Impurity, and Separation," 280.

37. Long, *The History of Jamaica*, 2: 278, 276.

38. The sable handmaids serve a function similar to that of the black woman servant in Édouard Manet's *Olympia*: their presence signifies sexuality lurking in the background. On the black female figure in *Olympia*, see Gilman, *Difference and Pathology*, 99.

39. Long, *The History of Jamaica*, 2: 280.

40. Ibid., 2: 279–80.

41. Lugones, "Purity, Impurity, and Separation," 275–76. Emphasis in original.

42. This information on population comes from Blackburn, *The Making of New World Slavery*, 441.

43. Bliss, *Luminous Isle*, 3. All further references to this text will be made parenthetically in the running text.

44. A range of early twentieth-century elite Jamaican women's poetry is assembled in one of the island's first poetry anthologies, Mitchell, *Voices from Summerland*. It includes poems by Constance Hollar, Albinia Catherine Hutton, Lena Kent, Phyllis May Myers, Eva Nicholas, Nellie Olson, the Ormsby sisters (Eileen and Stephanie), and Tropica (Mary Adela Wolcott), many of whom were members of the elite literary group called the Jamaica Women's Poetry Circle and whose work remained unpublished elsewhere. The women's poems collected here are almost exclusively landscape pieces with titles such as "Purple Grapes," "Tree of Silence," and "Flaming June" by Hollar, "Up among the Mountain Passes" by Hutton, "The Hills of St. Andrew" and "Violets" by Kent, "A Country Idyll" by Nicholas, and "Kingston Buttercups" by Stephanie Ormsby, all describing high-flown sentiments surrounding the Jamaican landscape. The poems I quote from are Eileen Ormsby's "The Hills at Sunrise" (237) and "Unrest" (239), and Hollar's "Purple Grapes" (79).

45. Dionne Brand, "This Body for Itself," in *Bread Out of Stone*, 33–34.

46. Ginger lilies come in other colors, notably pinks and yellows, but in Bliss's novel they are always (tellingly) white.

47. Butler, *The Psychic Life of Power*, 135.

48. Burton, *Afro-Creole*, 44.

49. Butler, *The Psychic Life of Power*, 190.

50. For more on this definition of anger, see Deirdre Lashgari's introduction to the volume she edited titled *Violence, Silence, and Anger*, 9.

51. Quoted in Lionnet, *Autobiographical Voices*, 173.

52. Chin, "Neighbors."

Chapter 3: Blue Countries, Dark Beauty

1. HGLA Web site, http://www.haitiangaysandlesbiansalliance.org, accessed 29 December 2007.

2. Ibid.

3. Pineau, "Gisèle Pineau, mémoire vive," 7. The original French reads: "On cache la chose. On ne veut pas voir ni croire"; translation mine.

4. See the HGLA Web site, http://www.haitiangaysandlesbiansalliance.org.

5. Santos-Febres, *Sirena Selena vestida de pena*, 190; written in English in the original Spanish text.

6. See Édouard Glissant, "Transparency and Opacity," in *Poetics of Relation*, 111–20.

7. Byron Williams, "Silence about 'Down Low' Culture Reflects Black History."

8. Gopinath, *Impossible Desires*, 153.

9. See Métraux, "L'honneur des makoumès." The original French reads: "De plus en plus de jeunes gays . . . découvrent le sens du mot 'visibilité'"; translation mine.

10. Vilaire in Berrou and Pompilus, *Histoire de la littérature haïtienne, illustrée par les textes,*

139. The original French reads: "L'avènement d'une élite haïtienne dans l'histoire littéraire de la France"; my translation.

11. See Bouchereau, *Haïti et ses femmes*, 170.

12. Marty, *Haïti en littérature*, 75. The original French reads: "On note un progrès de plus dans l'acceptation des réalités locales: c'est d'avoir permis à quelques femmes de s'exprimer... Mlle Liane, dans *La Ronde* du mai 5 1898, écrit une lettre assez ambiguë qui tient d'un discours à la fois très conforme aux préjugés de l'homme traditionnel et modulé par des accents de révolte féministe. . . . En 1907, une conférence pose la question de savoir si le féminisme existe en Haïti (cf. *Haïti littéraire et sociale* du 5 juillet 1907) tandis que le même périodique, le 5 septembre 1906, par la voix de Dora, met au point les revendications féministes dans le monde. . . . Enfin, dans *Les Variétés* du 20 janvier 1906, Yvette parle du féminisme associé à la réhabilitation des noirs aux Etats Unis, elle évoque la solidarité des femmes noires contre les hommes blancs"; my translation.

13. Mme. Virgile Valcin (Cléanthe Desgraves), "Les quelques fleurs du Cercle Fémina," in *Fleurs et Pleurs*, 66. The original French reads: "Je connais un 'Parterre' où d'admirables plantes / Se cachent pour fleurir et fleurissent toujours"; translation mine.

14. Ibid., 66–67.

15. Laleau, "Ida Faubert," 247. The original French reads: "Une grande dame de la haute société de Port-au-Prince"; my translation.

16. Ibid., 247. The original French reads: "Elle allait d'un cocktail à un té, à une sauterie. Que ce fût à pied, le visage auréolé de son ombrelle aux teintes égayantes et tournantes; que ce fût dans sa voiture tirée par cet allègre cheval souris qui, à la promener, semblait au comble de la fierté; toujours sa grace aduste et tropicale laissait auprès elle, telle la traîne d'une robe de cour, un long sillage de frémissante admiration"; my translation.

17. Gardiner, *Sonate pour Ida*, 24. The original French reads: "Le liberalisme, l'indépendance de caractère d'Ida ont du mal à supporter l'étroitesse des cadres et des idées de sa Patrie... elle se sent étrangère dans ce pays où elle n'a aucune amie véritable, aucune attache"; my translation.

18. On Anna de Noailles's nickname and sexual escapades, see Casselaer, *Lot's Wife*, 63.

19. Gardiner, *Sonate pour Ida*, 27. The original French reads: "Ida admire beaucoup la poétesse qu'elle aura l'occasion de fréquenter et dont l'influence s'est certainement fait sentir dans l'oeuvre de notre héroïne"; my translation.

20. Berrou and Pompilus, *Histoire de la littérature haïtienne, illustrée par les textes*, 309.

21. Gouraige, *Histoire de la littérature haïtienne (de l'indépendance à nos jours)*, 219. The original French reads, incredibly: "Renée Vivien dont pourtant Ida Faubert . . . a suivi à demi le chemin des amours perverses et équivoques"; my translation.

22. Laleau, "Ida Faubert," 247. The original French reads: "Toilette dernier cri, signées des couturiers parisiens fameux et . . . des bijoux qui . . . avant d'étoiler les lobes de

ses oreilles, le geste de ses mains ou la chaude carnation de son décolleté, avaient constellé certaines vitrines de la rue de la Paix"; my translation.

23. Keeling, *The Witch's Flight*, 143.

24. Gardiner, *Sonate pour Ida*, 18. The original French reads: "Cocotiers à la longue chevelure peignée par le vent, bananiers balançant leurs larges éventails, amandiers chargés de fruits à la pulpe charnue, quénépiers aux grappes smaragdines, manguiers aux senteurs de resine"; translation mine.

25. Roland Bonaparte, ["Three Unidentified Women in the Jardin Zoologique d'Acclimatation at the Exposition Universelle"], reprinted in Willis and Williams, *The Black Female Body*, 68.

26. Pollock, "Missing Women," 236.

27. Ibid.

28. As Ellen Messer Davidow generously pointed out to me, both the subject matter (female nudes) and the poses of the photographic technique (the straight-on angle, the centering of women) of this image code it as geared toward male, presumably heterosexual viewers. It would have been coded as improper for nineteenth-century European "ladies," who presumably would have felt embarrassment at such a display.

29. See Willis and Williams, *The Black Female Body*, 67–69.

30. See Chevalier, *Inversion sexuelle*.

31. Ibid., 231.

32. See H. Hildebrandt, *Die Krankheiten der äusseren weiblichen Genitalian, Handbuch der Frauenkrankheiten*, vol. 2, ed. Theodor Bilroth (Stuttgart: Enke, 1877), quoted in Gilman, *Difference and Pathology*, 89; and Perry M. Lichtenstein, "The 'Fairy' and the Lady Lover," *Medical Review of Reviews*, no. 27 (1921), 372, quoted in Somerville, *Queering the Color Line*, 27.

33. Chevalier, *Inversion sexuelle*, 248, 223, 227, 224. The original French speaks of "pretresses de ce nouveau culte"; translation mine.

34. Ibid., 246.

35. Ibid., 240.

36. Bard, *Les garçonnes, fantasmes et modes des années folles*, 7, 98. The original reads: "La visibilité lesbienne devient éclatante dans les années vingt" and "le lesbianisme a une visibilité qui lui donne une certaine légitimité – on parle alors de mode saphique"; my translation.

37. For a thorough discussion of the specificities and varieties of the *garçonne*, see ibid.

38. Halberstam, *In a Queer Time and Place*, 51.

39. On Lady Una Troubridge's monocle and its reproductions in art and Parisian lesbian fashion, see Latimer, *Women Together, Women Apart*, 23–24.

40. Chevalier, *Inversion sexuelle*, 34, quoted and translated in Frank Proschan, "Eunuch Mandarins, *Soldats Mamzelles*, Effeminate Boys, and Graceless Women," 443; see also Ellis, *Sexual Inversion*, 87–88.

41. Brassaï, *The Secret Paris of the 30's*, 157, 4.

42. Keeling, *The Witch's Flight*, 143.

43. Faubert, *Coeur des îles*, front pages. The French reads: "Madame Amy NICOLET, l'incomparable interprète 'sans qui mes vers ne seraient que ce qu'ils sont', avec toute mon affection"; my translation.

44. Ibid., 10–11. The original reads: "On sera surpris en lisant des poèmes tels . . . d'apprendre que l'auteur appartient à une vieille race africaine, tant il y a de grâce, de subtilité et de mesure dans ses vers. L'amour, chez elle, ne prend pas une forme sauvage ni farouche, il est au contraire plein de réserve, à la fois secret et pathétique"; my translation.

45. Ibid., 33–34.

46. Keeling, *The Witch's Flight*, 143.

47. For a discussion of the dominant floral-vaginal imagery in turn-of-the-century lesbian poetry, see Casselaer's *Lot's Wife*, 142–43. For a particularly striking example, consider Renée Vivien's "Fleurs orgiaques" in *Oeuvre poétique complète de Renée Vivien*, 473.

48. Many thanks to Christophe Wall-Romana for first pointing out the *genoux/je-nous* wordplay.

49. Faubert, *Coeur des îles*, 10. The original reads: "La douceur et le charme qui eminent de cette poésie écrite ou plutôt rêvée par cette femme originaire de la vieille île de Saint-Domingue"; my translation.

50. J. A. Cuddon, *The Penguin Dictionary of Literary Terms and Literary Theory* (New York: Penguin, 1999), 772.

51. Faubert, *Coeur des îles*, 84.

52. Pierre Dominique, preface to Faubert, *Sous le ciel Caraïbe*, 9. The original has "baignés d'une lumière iréelle"; translation mine.

53. See Guy de Maupassant, "L'oiseleur," in *Des vers*, 73–75.

54. Faubert, *Sous le ciel Caraïbe*, 15. The original reads: "Ce bleu implacable des pays chauds"; my translation.

55. See Marc Allégret's film starring Baker, *Zouzou* (France, 1934). "Haiti" is included on the Baker collection *Exotique* (Sussex: Pearl Records, 1992). My translation.

56. Jane Nardal, "Exotic Puppets," in Sharpley-Whiting, *Negritude Women*, 109.

57. On Baker's famous female lovers, see the biography by Jean-Claude Baker and Chris Chase, *Josephine*, 120, 145.

58. See Price-Mars, *Ainsi parla l'oncle*, 8.

59. Nardal quoted in Sharpley-Whiting, *Negritude Women*, 109.

60. Keeling, *The Witch's Flight*, 137.

61. Ida Faubert, "Une histoire étrange," in *Sous le ciel Caraïbe*, 121–32. All translations of the story are mine.

62. Ibid., 131–32. The original reads: "Une femme? Non. Une forme étrange . . . ces yeux enfocés et sans flame."

63. Ibid., 132. The original reads: "Lélia, levant la tête, rencontra fixes sur elle, deux prunelles fulgurantes qui s'éteignirent aussitôt."

64. Malevolent supernatural dealings are known as "working with the left hand," while benevolent workings are "working with the right hand."

65. Price-Mars's defense of Vodoun runs throughout *Ainsi parla l'oncle.*

66. On the queer paths of Ezili, see Conner with Sparks, *Queering Creole Spiritual Traditions,* 58–62.

67. See the definition of *bull* and *bulldagger* compiled in Conner, Sparks, and Sparks, *Cassell's Encyclopedia of Queer Myth, Symbol, and Spirit,* 98.

68. See the documentary by Anne Lescot and Laurence Magloire, *Des hommes et dieux* (Haiti, 2002).

69. See Conner with Sparks, *Queering Creole Spritual Traditions,* 57–58.

70. *Vèvès* are elaborate cornmeal drawings used to invoke *lwas* during Vodoun ceremonies.

71. See the HGLA Web site, http://www.haitiangaysandlesbiansalliance.org.

Chapter 4: At the River of Washerwomen

1. See these and other cruises at http://www.olivia.com (accessed 12 August 2009).

2. See Kiesnoski, "Charting the Caribbean."

3. Puar, "Circuits of Queer Mobility," 105.

4. Olivia Web site, http://www.olivia.com.

5. Ibid.

6. On these and the other environmental hazards of cruise ships, see Klein, *Cruise Ship Squeeze,* 137.

7. Pate, *West of Rehoboth,* 84.

8. Announcements of these and other Martinican LGBT get-togethers can be found on the Web site of the French Caribbean gay and lesbian rights group An Nou Allé, http://annoualle.france.qrd.org.

9. See the Olivia Web site, http://www.olivia.com.

10. Fajardo, "Filipino Cross Currents."

11. See Makward, *Mayotte Capécia ou L'aliénation selon Fanon,* 97.

12. McClintock, *Imperial Leather,* 170.

13. All biographical information, unless otherwise noted, comes from Makward's pioneering study and excavation of Capécia's history, *Mayotte Capécia ou L'aliénation selon Fanon,* to which I am much indebted. Her research, along with Beatrice Stith Clark's introduction to the English translation of *I Am a Martinican Woman,* provided the ground that has allowed critics to rethink Fanon's class assumptions about Capécia.

14. Ibid., 218.

15. The original French reads: "A Lucette en témoignage de notre amour divin." Quoted ibid., 117.

16. See Beauvue-Fougeyrollas, *Les femmes antillaises*, 56–57.

17. See Édouard Glissant, "L'étendue et la filiation," in *Poétique de la relation*, 47–62.

18. Quoted in Makward, *Mayotte Capécia ou L'aliénation selon Fanon*, 29. The original French reads: "Mayotte Capécia est Martiniquaise, je dirais bien qu'elle en a la couleur, celle du moins que nous prêtons aux charmantes Martiniquaises – un très joli café au lait. C'est la première fois que nous avons une romancière de couleur"; my translation.

19. Danticat, *After the Dance*, 99–100.

20. See Fanon, *Black Skin, White Masks*, 41–62.

21. Ibid., 42.

22. Ibid..

23. On the same page as the footnote discussed below, Fanon writes: "Those who grant our conclusions on the psychosexuality of the white woman may ask what we have to say about the woman of color. I know nothing about her." Ibid., 179–80.

24. See ibid., 180.

25. I am signifying here on the title of Grace Nichols's collection of poetry, *I Is a Long-Memoried Woman*.

26. Mascia-Lees and Sharpe, "Locked in or Locked out or Holding Both Ends of a Slippery Pole," 234.

27. Prince, *The History of Mary Prince*, 192.

28. Ibid., 198.

29. By "saltwater slavery," I mean at once to reflect the element in which Prince worked in the salt ponds and to evoke Stephanie Smallwood's idea of a system of enslavement that began not on land but at sea, in the transnational passage. See Smallwood, *Saltwater Slavery*.

30. Prince, *The History of Mary Prince*, 199.

31. Ibid., 202–3.

32. Dalton, "The Devil and the Virgin," 39.

33. See Oswald Durand, "La laveuse de Mando," and Alcibiade Fleury Battier, "La blanchisseuse," in St. Louis and Lubin, *Panorama de la poésie haïtienne*, 91, 109; my translations.

34. Hearn, *Two Years in the French West Indies*, 253.

35. Ibid., 254.

36. Ibid., 252–53.

37. Ibid., 254.

38. Ibid., 263.

39. Ibid., 253.

40. Ibid., 259.

41. Ibid.

42. Poovey, "The Production of Abstract Space," 81.

43. Capécia, *Je suis Martiniquaise*, 7. The original French reads: "Lorsque nous étions petites, ma soeur jumelle et moi, nous nous ressemblions tellement que notre mère devait nous faire rire pour nous reconnaître." All further references to this work will be made parenthetically in the running text; translations of Capécia are my own.

44. The original French reads: "Pourtant, nous sommes très différentes de gouts et de caractère. Moi, par exemple, je n'ai jamais été très douée, j'appris à marcher beaucoup plus tard que Francette. Ma mère suspendait devant ma bouche un régime de bananes. Je cherchais alors à les attraper, car je les adorais."

45. The original French reads: "Cette rivière, d'environ huit mètres de large, pouvait d'un instant à l'autre se transformer en torrent furieux. Comme si une digue s'était rompue, un flot d'eau se précipitait alors avec un grondement qui ressemblait à celui d'une éruption."

46. The original French reads: "Elles saluaient celles qui arrivaient, portant leur linge sur la tête, à la mode du pays:

'Bonjou Fifi! Comment ou yé, ché? . . .'

'Toute douce, ché, et té, Youte? . . .'

'Tu vini poend ou bain? . . .'

  Les courageuses s'installaient sur les pierres au milieu de la rivière, les timorées restaient sur la rive. La lessive à la Martinique ne se passe pas comme en France. Chez nous, point besoin n'est de faire bouillir le linge, le soleil se charge de tout. Pour le blanchir et le parfumer, les femmes l'arrosent avec de l'eau tiédie dans laquelle elles ont mis de la cendre de charbon de bois et des pelures d'oranges.

  Après leur travail, les plus jeunes se baignaient sans façon dans la rivière."

47. Irigaray, *This Sex Which Is Not One*, 209.

48. The original French reads: "La guiablesse se promène ainsi sur les routes et dans les plantations isolées, sous les traits d'une jolie jeune fille et l'on revoit jamais les hommes qui la suivent. Mais nous, nous n'avions pas peur des guiablesses."

49. Wynter, "Beyond Miranda's Meanings," 360, 363.

50. Mae Henderson, "Opening Remarks," delivered at "Black Queer Studies: A Symposium," Northwestern University, Chicago, 20 January, 2006. She is, of course, innovatively signifying on and quaring Henry Louis Gates's famous discussion of the speakerly text.

51. The original French reads: "Loulouze était la plus belle et la plus gaie et, malgré notre différence d'âge, nous étions de vraies amies. . . . Les mouvements de Loulouze me causait une sorte d'émotion. Parfois aussi, elle se baignait avec nous. Elle avait une peau dorée qui tenait de l'orange et de la banane, de longs cheveux noirs qu'elle roulait en tresses et qui n'étaient crépus qu'à la base, un nez assez épaté et des lèvres épaisses, mais le visage d'une forme telle qu'elle devait avoir des blancs assez proches dans son ascendance. Je regardais sa poitrine avec envie, moi qui était tout plate."

52. Patrick Chamoiseau, "Dans la Pierre-Monde," reproduced at http://www.potomitan
.info/divers/pierre.php#top (accessed 12 August 2009). The original French reads:
"Dans une Manman Dlo, il y a les divinités aquatiques africaines qui rencontrent
celles des amérindiens, lesquelles viennent s'ajouter aux sirènes occidentales"; my
translation.

53. Brown, *Mama Lola*, 223.

54. See, for example, the anthropologist Misty Bastian's work, reproduced online at
http://www.mamiwata.com/mami%20wata.html. While this fluidity of genitalia
does not seem to have transculturated to Caribbean *manman dlo*, the earlier double
sexing seems an interesting palimpsest perhaps layered into the figure's complex
sexuality.

55. See Conner, Sparks, and Sparks, *Cassell's Encyclopedia of Queer Myth, Symbol, and Spirit*,
306.

56. See Brown's discussion of these stories in her *Mama Lola*, 220.

57. Ibid., 221.

58. Beauvue-Fougeyrollas, *Les femmes antillaises*, 17. The original French reads: "Jamais la
Guadeloupe et la Martinique n'avaient été aussi colonialement dominées et asservies
que sur la base de cette économie bananière"; my translation.

59. The original French: "elle était assise sur une pierre et regardait fixement le courant
qui charriait du bois comme après un orage."

60. *Beké* (like the Jamaican *backra*) is a term for elite Caribbean whites.

61. The original French reads: "Son beau teint d'orange était devenu terreux."

62. The original French reads: "La vie est difficile pou' une femme, tu ve'as, Mayotte,
s'tout pou' une femme de couleu'."

63. I mean "place" here in the way discussed by Michel de Certeau in *The Practice of Everyday Life*, 117–19.

64. Carol Thames, "Two Happy People in the World," in Elwin, *Tongues on Fire*, 29.

65. Danticat, *After the Dance*, 100.

66. The original French reads: "Poitrine volumineuse à laquelle je pris plaisir à comparer
mes petits seins."

67. The original French reads: "Le jour de la guiablesse."

68. The original French reads: "La rade [qui] scintiallaient doucement sous la brise légère,
éclairée vaguement par la lune."

69. The original French reads: "S]ur le plan terrestre . . . notre union doit rester fugi-
tive."

70. Reproduced in Makward, *Mayotte Capécia ou L'aliénation selon Fanon*, 162. The original
French reads: "L'idée leur vint de s'asseoir et, ne voyant aucun siège, ils trouvèrent
pittoresque de s'installer au bord du trottoir: depuis longtemps déjà ils avaient
rompu avec les conventions, et la première fantaisie de leur esprit avait été mise à
exécution"; my translation.

71. See Burton, *La famille coloniale*, 133–37.

72. The original French reads: "Je sortis sur le balcon. J'avais besoin d'être seule un moment, parce que j'étais trop heureuse.

  Nous nous étions levés tard et le soleil était déjà haut. La maison d'André dominait la vaste rade de Fort-de France. A mes pieds, à travers le feuillage agité de la haie mal taillée, je distinguais la fine silhouette de l'*Emile Bertin*, qui avait apporté à la Martinique l'or de la Banque de France. De l'autre côté de la baie des Tourelles, s'étendait un marécage bordé par une rangée de cocotiers et le hangar de l'aviation jetait une masse sombre sur la surface éclatante du terre-plein de ciment. . . .

  Mais je regardais surtout la rade d'un bleu profond que parcouraient les voiles blanches des yachts et qui semblait un vaste lac fermé par les collines. Je la regardais comme si elle était l'image de mon bonheur."

73. Stoler, *Carnal Knowledge and Imperial Power*, 112.

74. Examples of this include the war novels penned by *créolité*'s founding fathers: Raphaël Confiant's *Le nègre et l'amiral* and *La lessive du diable*, as well as Chamoiseau's *Chronique des sept misères* and *Texaco*, the latter of which, despite its female protagonist, recounts little of Vichy's gender politics.

75. See Enloe, *Maneuvers*, 48.

76. On this strike, see Morales, *Remedios*, 172–73.

77. Enloe, *Maneuvers*, 36.

78. See Jennings, *Vichy in the Tropics*, 97–104.

79. Quoted in Burton, *La famille coloniale*, 151. The original French reads: "Où, de tous les coins de l'Empire, arriveront des sachets semblables renfermant de la terre prise dans chaque village de la France, de cette France métropolitaine et coloniale dont l'indissouluble unité a fait l'admiration du monde!"; my translation.

80. Ibid., 152. The original French reads: "Chaque défilé, manifestation ou cérémonie qu'il s'agisse du sacre de l'Archevêque Varin de la Brunière en janvier 1942, de la fête annuelle de Jennne d'Arc ou d'une simple distribution de prix scolaires, devient une occasion de célébrer les vertus salvatrices et guérisseuses du Grand-Père totémique"; my translation.

81. The original French reads: "Il me semblait que tout ce qu'il nommait m'appartenait."

82. Suzanne Césaire, "The Great Camouflage," in Sharpley-Whiting, *Negritude Women*, 136.

Chapter 5: Transforming Sugar, Transitioning Revolution

1. Quoted in "In Conservative Caribbean, Transsexuals Fight for Rights."

2. Many thanks to Lawrence La Fountain Stokes for reminding me of de Souza's case and so sparking this discussion.

3. "In Conservative Caribbean, Transsexuals Fight for Rights."

4. Quoted ibid.

5. "We Want Equal Rights!," TNTmirror.com, 20 March 2005, http://www.tntmirror.com.

6. On the importance of inclusive, both/and thinking as black feminist praxis, see Patricia Hill Collins's famous passage in her *Black Feminist Thought*, 221-22.

7. Cliff, *No Telephone to Heaven*, 122. All further references to this work will be made parenthetically in the running text.

8. See Prosser, *Second Skins*; and Namaste, *Invisible Lives*.

9. See, for example, Kale Fajardo's discussion of the work that *transgender* can do in dialogue with Tagalog *tomboy* to think through female masculinity in a transnational context in "Transportation."

10. Edgar Morin quoted in Conner with Sparks, *Queering Creole Spiritual Traditions*, 17.

11. Kate More, "Introduction 1," in More and Whittle, *Reclaiming Genders*, 1.

12. All quotes from Kakutani, "Books of the Times."

13. Schwarz, "An Interview with Michelle Cliff," 614.

14. Ibid., 601.

15. Ibid., 601.

16. See also Cliff's 2002 interview with Jim Clawson, "Re-visioning Our History."

17. Barnet with Montejo, *Biography of a Runaway Slave*, 40.

18. Personal communication with informant, Port-au-Prince, July 2002.

19. See Gopinath, *Impossible Desires*, 18-19.

20. Raymond, *The Transsexual Empire*, x.

21. Ibid., 102.

22. Ibid., 109.

23. Fanon, *Black Skin, White Masks*, 181.

24. I first received this information on the *madan sara* from VèVè A. Clark, personal communication, September 1997. I thank her for suggesting this direction for further research.

25. See Havelock Ellis, "Sexual Inversion in Women," in *Studies in the Psychology of Sex*, 207. Ellis here refers to Dr. A. Corre's *Crime en Pays Créoles* (1889) for his information on inversion among black and mulatta women.

26. Glissant, *Le discours antillais*, 295. The original French reads: "Le dérobé de la jouissance détermine alors un appétit ou une obsession de la jouissance, un violent et incontrôlable besoin d'aller immédiatement à l'impunité résolutive de l'acte, qui résume et annihile le plaisir de la jouissance." The translation here is mine; and because of the difficulty of rendering *jouissance* in English, I have translated it liberally to try to retain some of the connotations of the original French.

27. Ibid., 295; my translation.

28. Ibid., 299.

29. Ibid., 298. The original phrases read "la victime la plus extreme" and "indifférence sexuelle"; my translation.

30. Bailey and Richardson, "Black Queer Gender Phobia." All references to Bailey and Richardson's theorizing are taken from this paper.

31. My reference here it to Alice Walker's influential collection of essays *In Search of Our Mothers' Gardens*, which discusses the recovery of forgotten black women's history — that of Zora Neale Hurston, Phillis Wheatley, and other ancestors.

32. Sears, "All That Glitters," 398.

33. Cliff, "Making Soul, Creating Alchemy," 30–31. The miniseries in question, directed by Paul Wendkos and starring Cicely Tyson, aired on NBC.

34. Bradford, *Harriet Tubman*, 74.

35. Ibid., 30.

36. Ibid., 73.

37. Ibid., 110, 22.

38. Ibid., 96.

39. Kingston *Sunday Gleaner Magazine*, 1 April 1984, quoted in Sarah Salih, introduction to Seacole, *Wonderful Adventures of Mrs. Seacole in Many Lands*, xliii.

40. Seacole, *Wonderful Adventures of Mrs. Seacole in Many Lands*, 112.

41. Ibid., 20.

42. Ibid., 26.

43. Ibid., 55.

44. Ibid., 76.

45. Ibid., 88.

46. Ibid., 88, 90.

47. Ibid., 155.

48. Ibid., 398.

49. See Prosser, "Exceptional Locations," 83–114.

50. See Glissant, *Caribbean Discourse*, 67; and Bernabé, Chamoiseau, and Confiant, *Eloge de la créolité*, 28.

51. Gordon, *Ghostly Matters*, 19.

52. Adisa, "Journey into Speech," 276.

53. Ibid.

54. King, "Re/Presenting Self and Other." *Trans* is the umbrella term that King uses for non-normatively gendered subjects, also in contradistinction to the global northern terms *transgender* and *transsexual*.

55. Gordon, *Ghostly Matters*, 202.

56. Ibid., 208.

57. Sandoval, *Methodology of the Oppressed*, 130.

58. Ibid.

59. My reference here it to the title of Cliff's first collection of poetry, *Claiming an Identity They Taught Me to Despise*.

60. Schwarz, "An Interview with Michelle Cliff," 602.

61. Ibid., 604.

62. Raiskin, "The Art of History," 69.

63. Michelle Cliff, "Love in the Third World," in *The Land of Look Behind*, 102.

Chapter 6: Breaking Hard against Things

1. Voss, "Castro Champions Gay Rights in Cuba."

2. Ibid.

3. Ibid.

4. Castro, "Memo to Europe from Mariela Castro."

5. Ibid.

6. Tanya Saunders discussed Castro's lack of impact on black lesbians in her presentation "Where Are All the (Black) Women?"

7. See Audre Lorde, "The Uses of the Erotic: The Erotic as Power" in *Sister Outsider*, 53–59.

8. Chancy, *Searching for Safe Spaces*, 119.

9. Dionne Brand, "Bread Out of Stone," in *Bread Out of Stone*, 14.

10. Ibid., 17.

11. Brand, *A Map to the Door of No Return*, 192.

12. Brand, *Chronicles of the Hostile Sun*, 7.

13. Silvera, "In the Company of My Work," 356.

14. Alexander, *Pedagogies of Crossing*, 259.

15. Brand, *A Map to the Door of No Return*, 159.

16. Ibid., 168.

17. Silvera, "In the Company of My Work," 366.

18. Ibid., 367.

19. Quoted in Searle, *Words Unchained*, 70.

20. Quoted ibid., 111.

21. Quoted ibid., 24.

22. Birbalsingh, "No Language Is Neutral," 135.

23. Merle Collins, "Butterfly Born," in Fenwick, *Sisters of Caliban*, 79.

24. Brand, *Bread Out of Stone*, 136–37.

25. Alexander, *Pedagogies of Crossing*, 25–26.

26. Bahamian parliamentarians quoted ibid., 45.

27. Ibid., 25, 62.

28. Ibid., 61.

29. Ibid., 65.

30. See June Jordan, "A New Politics of Sexuality," in *Some of Us Did Not Die*, 133.

31. Alexander, *Pedagogies of Crossing*, 265.

32. Ibid., 6.

33. Ibid., 279.

34. Ibid., 18.
35. Ibid.
36. Brand, *A Map to the Door of No Return*, 168.
37. Brand, "Opening the Door."
38. Brand, *No Language Is Neutral*, 35. All further references to this work will be made in parenthetically the running text.
39. See Raiskin, "The Art of History," 69.
40. Brand with Birbalsingh, "No Language Is Neutral," 129.
41. Audre Lorde, "Bridge through My Windows," in *The Collected Poems of Audre Lorde*, 9.
42. Brand, *A Map to the Door of No Return*, 172.
43. Cabrera, *Yemayá y Ochún*, 29.
44. See Cabrera, *El Monte*, 59–60.
45. Cabrera, *Yemayá y Ochún*, 45. The original Spanish reads: "Yemayá amó locamente a un andrógino, el bellísimo Inle. Para satisfacer la pasión que el joven dios le inspiraba, lo raptó, lo llevó al fondo del mar y allí lo tuvó hasta que, saciado del todo su apetito, se aburrió de su amante y deseó regresar al mundo, a la compañía de los demás Orichas y de los hombres.

    Inle había visto lo que ninguna criatura divina o humana. El misterio insondable del mar, lo que oculta en lo más profundo. Y Yemayá, para que Inle a nadie lo contara, antes de emprender el retorno a la tierra, le cortó la lengua"; my translation.
46. On Cabrera's uniqueness in narrating Inle's affair with Yemayá and naming him/her the protector of lesbians and the gender complex, see Rodríguez-Mangual, *Lydia Cabrera and the Construction of an Afro-Cuban Cultural Identity*, 91–92.
47. On the complexities of how men were allowed to leave Cuba during the Mariel boat-lift by declaring and proving themselves homosexuals, as well as on their problematic reception in the United States, see Peña, "'Obvious Gays' and the State Gaze."
48. See Lerner, "Olokun and the Art of Suppression."
49. See Brand, *A Map to the Door of No Return*, 159–64.
50. See Sidonie Smith, "Autobiographical Manifestos," in Smith and Watson, *Women, Autobiography, Theory*, 434–37.
51. Lorde, *Zami*, 13–14.
52. Ibid., 7.
53. Ibid., 14.
54. Ibid., 9.
55. Ibid., 14.
56. Ibid., 226.
57. Ibid., 256.
58. Rodríguez, "'From the House of Yemanjá.'"
59. While the north coast has a fishing and small farming economy, eastern and central Trinidad contain its expanses of cane and coconut plantations. The Blanchisseuse-

Arima road leads to the Cleaver Woods Amerindian museum and Trinidad's Carib community, while the central stretch of the island (including Manzanilla) constitutes the heart of the Indo-Trinidadian population.

60. I want to offer heartfelt thanks to many residents of Blanchisseuse, including Tanti Joyce Chin, Tanti Bertha Jones, and Mrs. Holder, for their hospitality and generosity in sharing what they knew of the history of the town and its name. Their stories led me to the history archived in the museum.

61. A reproduction of this map is on display at the National Museum at Fort San Andres, Port of Spain, Trinidad.

62. Brand, *At the Full and Change of the Moon*, 52.

63. Brand, *In Another Place, Not Here*, 7.

64. Brand, *Chronicles of the Hostile Sun*, 40–43.

65. Paravisini-Gebert, "Decolonizing Feminism," 8.

66. Alexander, *Pedagogies of Crossing*, 65.

67. Robinson, "Toward a Strategy of Imagination."

68. Brand, *Bread Out of Stone*, 138.

69. Brand, *In Another Place, Not Here*, 5.

70. Lugones, "Purity, Impurity, and Separation," 275–76.

71. Carol Boyce Davies addresses the problematic position of black feminist scholars who find that neither masculinist Africana theorists nor Eurocentric feminist theorists provide adequate tools for analysis. To engage these without either completely following or turning away from them, Boyce Davies suggests we follow the model that Zora Neale Hurston gives in a story of walking the road in rural Florida where she was from. There, when she encountered someone she knew, she went a "piece of the way" in the friend or relative's direction, the distance traveled with them depending on the closeness of the relation. This, Boyce Davies concludes, is how the black woman writer, critic, and activist can find agency in negotiating between her many different identities without either trying to be the same as black nationalists or completely other than white feminists. See Boyce Davies, *Black Women, Writing, and Identity*, 47.

Bibliography

Adisa, Opal Palmer. "Journey into Speech: A Writer between Two Worlds; An Interview with Michelle Cliff." *African American Review* 28, no. 2 (1994): 273–81.
———. "Three Landscapes: Jamaican Women Writers at Home and in the Diaspora." PhD diss., University of California, 1992.

Alexander, M. Jacqui. *Pedagogies of Crossing: Meditations on Feminism, Sexual Politics, Memory, and the Sacred.* Durham: Duke University Press, 2005.

Anonymous. *Le Code noir ou Recueil d'édits, Déclarations et arrêts concernant les esclaves nègres de l'Amérique.*Versailles, 1685.

Bailey, Marlon M., and Mattie Richardson. "Black Queer Gender Phobia." Paper presented at "Race, Sex, Power: New Movements in Black and Latina/o Sexualities," University of Illinois, Chicago, 12 April 2008.

Baker, Jean-Claude, and Chris Chase. *Josephine: The Hungry Heart.* New York: Random House, 1993.

Bard, Christine. *Les garçonnes: Fantasmes et modes des années folles.* Paris: Flammarion, 1998.

Barnet, Miguel, with Esteban Montejo. *Biography of a Runaway Slave.* Trans. W. Nick Hill. Willimantic, Conn.: Curbstone, 1994.

Beauvue-Fougeyrollas, Claudie. *Les femmes antillaises.* Paris: L'Harmattan, 1985.

Beckles, Hilary McD. *Centering Woman: Gender Discourses in Caribbean Slave Society.* Kingston: Ian Randle, 1999.

Benítez-Rojo, Antonio. *The Repeating Island: The Caribbean and the Postmodern Perspective.* Trans. James E. Maraniss. 2nd edn. Durham: Duke University Press, 1996.

Bernabé, Jean, Patrick Chamoiseau, and Rafaël Confiant. *Eloge de la créolité: Édition bilingue français/anglais.* Trans. M. B. Taleb-Khyar. Paris: Gallimard, 1993.

Berrou, Raphaël, and Pradel Pompilus. *Histoire de la littérature haïtienne, illustrée par les textes.* Vol. 2. Port-au-Prince: Éditions Caraïbes, 1975.

Besson, Jean. *Martha Brae's Two Histories: European Expansion and Caribbean Culture-Building in Jamaica.* Chapel Hill: University of North Carolina Press, 2002.

Birbalsingh, Frank. "Dionne Brand: No Language Is Neutral." *Frontiers of Caribbean Literature in English,* ed. Birbalsingh, 120–37. New York: St. Martin's, 1996.

Blackburn, Robin. *The Making of New World Slavery: From the Baroque to the Modern, 1492–1800*. London: Verso, 1997.

Bliss, Eliot. *Luminous Isle*. 1934. London: Virago, 1984.

Bouchereau, Madeleine Sylvain. *Haïti et ses femmes: Une étude d'évolution culturelle* Port-au-Prince: Presses Libres, 1957.

Boyce Davies, Carol. *Black Women, Writing, and Identity: Migrations of the Subject*. London: Routledge, 1994.

Bradford, Sarah. *Harriet Tubman: The Moses of Her People* [1886]. Bedford, Mass.: Applewood, 1993.

Brand, Dionne. *At the Full and Change of the Moon*. New York: Grove, 1999.

———. *Bread Out of Stone*. Toronto: Coach House, 1994.

———. *Chronicles of the Hostile Sun*. Toronto: Williams-Wallace, 1984.

———. *In Another Place, Not Here*. New York: Grove, 1996.

———. *A Map to the Door of No Return: Notes to Belonging*. Toronto: Doubleday, 2001.

———. *No Language Is Neutral*. 1990. Toronto: McClelland and Stewart, 1998.

———. "Opening the Door: An Interview by Maya Mavjee." *Read Magazine* 2, no. 2 (2001), http://www.randomhouse.ca/readmag.

Brassaï. *The Secret Paris of the 30's*. Trans. Richard Miller. New York: Pantheon, 1976.

Brown, Karen McCarthy. *Mama Lola: A Vodou Priestess in Brooklyn*. Berkeley: University of California Press, 1991.

Burton, Richard. *Afro-Creole: Power, Opposition, and Play in the Caribbean*. Ithaca: Cornell University Press, 1997.

———. *La famille coloniale: La Martinique et la mère patrie*. Paris: Harmattan, 1994.

Bush, Barbara. "'Sable Venus,' 'She Devil,' or 'Drudge'? British Slavery and the 'Fabulous Fiction' of Black Women's Identities, c. 1650–1838." *Women's History Review* 9, no. 4 (2000): 761–89.

———. *Slave Women in Caribbean Society*. Bloomington: University of Indiana Press, 1990.

Butler, Judith. *Gender Trouble: Feminism and the Subversion of Identity*. New York: Routledge, 1990.

———. *The Psychic Life of Power: Theories in Subjection*. Stanford: Stanford University Press, 1997.

Cabrera, Lydia. *El Monte*. 1968. Miami: Colección del Chicherekú, 2000.

———. *Yemayá y Ochún: Kariocha, iyalorichas y olorichas*. 1980. Miami: Universal, 1996.

Capécia, Mayotte. *I Am a Martinican Woman*. Trans. Beatrice Stith Clark. Pueblo: Passeggiata, 1998.

———. *Je suis Martiniquaise*. Paris: Corréa, 1948.

Casselaer, Catherine van. *Lot's Wife: Lesbian Paris, 1890–1914*. Liverpool: Janus, 1986.

Cassid, Jill. *Sowing Empire: Landscape and Colonization*. Minneapolis: University of Minnesota Press, 2005.

Castle, Terry. *The Apparitional Lesbian*. New York: Columbia University Press, 1993.

Castro, Mariela. "Memo to Europe from Mariela Castro." *Machetera*, 1 April 2008, http:// machetera.wordpress.com.

Certeau, Michel de. *The Practice of Everyday Life.* Trans. Stephen Rendall. Berkeley: University of California Press, 2002.

Chamoiseau, Patrick. *Chronique des sept misères.* Paris: Gallimard, 1986.

———. *Écrire en pays dominé.* Paris: Gallimard, 1997.

———. *Texaco.* Paris: Gallimard, 1992.

Chancy, Myriam J. A. *Searching for Safe Spaces: Afro-Caribbean Women Writers in Exile.* Philadelphia: Temple University Press, 1994.

Chevalier, Julien. *Inversion sexuelle.* Paris: Masson, 1893.

Chin, Staceyann. "Neighbors: For Centuries." Staceyann Chin, http://www .staceyannchin.com (accessed 17 August 2009).

———. "Staceyann Chin: Interviewed by Maya Trotz." Jouvay, 9 November 2004, www .jouvay.com/interviews.

Chin, Timothy S. "'Bullers' and 'Battymen': Contesting Homophobia in Black Popular Culture and Contemporary Caribbean Literature." *Callaloo* 20, no. 1 (1997): 127–41.

Chrisman, Laura. "The Imperial Unconscious? Representations of Imperial Discourse." *Critical Quarterly* 32, no. 3 (1990): 38–58.

Christian, Barbara. "The Race for Theory." *Making Face, Making Soul / Haciendo Caras: Creative and Critical Perspectives by Women of Color,* ed. Gloria Anzaldúa, 335–45. San Francisco: Aunt Lute, 1990.

Clawson, Jim. "Re-visioning Our History: An Interview with Michelle Cliff." *Nidus,* no. 2 (2002), http://www.pitt.edu/nidus/archives.

Clemencia, Joceline. "Women Who Love Women in Curaçao: From *Cachapera* to Open Throats; A Commentary in Collage." *Feminist Studies* 22, no. 1 (1996): 81–88.

Cliff, Michelle. *Claiming an Identity They Taught Me to Despise.* Watertown, Mass.: Persephone, 1980.

———. *The Land of Look Behind.* Ithaca, N.Y.: Firebrand, 1985.

———. "Making Soul, Creating Alchemy." *Sinister Wisdom* 19 (1982): 26–31.

———. *No Telephone to Heaven.* 1987. New York: Plume Penguin, 1996.

Collins, Patricia Hill. *Black Feminist Thought: Knowledge, Consciousness, and the Politics of Empowerment.* Boston: Unwin Hyman, 1990.

Comvalius, Th. A. C. "Een der vormen van de Surinaamsche lied na 1863." *De West Indische Gids* 20, no. 21 (1939): 355–60.

Condé, Maryse. *En attendant le bonheur (Heremakhonon).* Paris: Seghers, 1988.

Confiant, Raphaël. *La lessive du diable.* Paris: Serpent à Plumes, 2003.

———. *Le nègre et l'amiral.* Paris: Grasset, 1988.

Conner, Randy P., with David Hatfield Sparks, *Queering Creole Spiritual Traditions: Lesbian, Gay, Bisexual, and Transgender Participation in African-Inspired Traditions in the Americas.* New York: Harrington Park, 2004.

Conner, Randy P., David Hatfield Sparks, and Mariya Sparks. *Cassell's Encyclopedia of Queer Myth, Symbol, and Spirit.* London: Cassell, 1997.

Cooper, Carolyn. *Noises in the Blood: Orality, Gender, and the "Vulgar" Body of Jamaican Popular Culture.* Durham: Duke University Press, 1995.

———. *Sound Clash: Jamaican Dancehall Culture at Large.* New York: Palgrave Macmillan, 2004.

Cosentino, Daniel. "On Looking at a Vodou Altar." *African Arts* 29, no. 2 (1996): 67–70.

Dalton, Ann B. "The Devil and the Virgin: Writing Sexual Abuse in *Incidents in the Life of a Slave Girl.*" *Violence, Silence, and Anger: Women's Writing as Transgression,* ed. Deirdre Lashgari, 38–61. Charlottesville: University of Virginia Press, 1995.

Danticat, Edwidge. *After the Dance.* New York: Alfred A. Knopf, 2002.

Dayan, Joan. *Haiti, History, and the Gods.* Berkeley: University of California Press, 1995.

D'Costa, Jean, and Barbara Lalla, eds. *Voices in Exile: Jamaican Texts of the Eighteenth and Nineteenth Centuries.* Tuscaloosa: University of Alabama Press, 1989.

De Lauretis, Teresa. "Queer Theory: Gay and Lesbian Sexualities." *differences* 3, no. 2 (1991): iii–vviii.

De Man, Paul. "Epistemologies of Metaphor." *On Metaphor,* ed. Sheldon Sacks, 11–28. Chicago: University of Chicago Press, 1979.

Donselaar, J. van. *Woordenboek van Het Surinaams-Nederland.* Muiderberg: Coutinho, 1989.

Edwards, Bryan. *The History, Civil and Commercial, of the British West Indies,* vols. 1–2 [1794]. New York: AMS, 1966.

Ellis, Havelock. *Sexual Inversion.* London: Wilson and MacMillan, 1897.

———. *Studies in the Psychology of Sex.* New York: Random House, 1905.

Elwin, Rosamund, ed. *Tongues on Fire: Caribbean Lesbian Lives and Stories.* Toronto: Women's Press, 1997.

Enloe, Cynthia. *Maneuvers: The International Politics of Militarizing Women's Lives.* Berkeley: University of California Press, 2000.

Faderman, Lilian. *Surpassing the Love of Men: Romantic Friendship and Love between Women from the Renaissance to the Present.* New York: William Morrow, 1981.

Fajardo, Kale Bantigue. "Filipino Cross Currents: Histories of Filipino Seafaring: Asia and the Americas." Paper delivered at the University of Minnesota, Twin Cities, 14 February 2005.

———. "Transportation: Translating Filipino and Filipino American Tomboy Masculinities through Global Migration and Seafaring." *GLQ* 14, nos. 2–3 (2008): 403–24.

Fanon, Frantz. *Black Skin, White Masks.* Trans. Charles Lam Markmann. New York: Grove, 1967.

———. *Les damnés de la terre.* Paris: Maspero, 1961.

Faubert, Ida. *Coeur des îles.* Paris: René Debresse, 1939.

———. *Sous le ciel caraïbe: Histoires d'Haïti et d'ailleurs.* Paris: O.L.B, 1959.

Fenwick, MJ, ed. *Sisters of Caliban: Contemporary Women Poets of the Caribbean; A Multilingual Anthology*. Falls Church, Va.: Azul, 1996.

Foucault, Michel. *The Order of Things: An Archaeology of the Human Sciences*. London: Routledge 2002.

Franco, Jean. *Plotting Women: Gender and Representation in Mexico*. New York: Columbia University Press, 1989.

Gardiner, Madeleine. *Sonate pour Ida*. Port-au-Prince: Henri Deschamps, 1984.

Gilman, Sander L. *Difference and Pathology: Stereotypes of Sexuality, Race, and Madness*. Ithaca: Cornell University Press, 1985.

Glave, Thomas. "Whose Caribbean? An Allegory, in Part." *Callaloo* 27, no. 3 (2004): 671–81.

———. *Words to Our Now: Imagination and Dissent*. Minneapolis: University of Minnesota Press, 2005.

Glissant, Édouard. *Caribbean Discourse*. Trans. Michael Dash. Charlottesville: University of Virginia Press, 1999.

———. *Le discourse antillais*. Paris: Gallimard, 1981.

———. *Poetics of Relation*. Trans. Betsy Wing. Ann Arbor: University of Michigan Press, 1997.

———. *Poétique de la relation*. Paris: Gallimard, 1997.

Goodison, Lorna. *To Us, All Flowers Are Roses*. Urbana: University of Illinois Press, 1995.

Gopinath, Gayatri. *Impossible Desires: Queer Diasporas and South Asian Public Cultures*. Durham: Duke University Press, 2005.

Gordon, Avery. *Ghostly Matters: Haunting and the Sociological Imagination*. Minneapolis: University of Minnesota Press, 1997.

Gouraige, Ghislain. *Histoire de la littérature haïtienne (de l'indépendance à nos jours)*. Port-au-Prince: Action Sociale, 1982.

Halberstam, Judith. *In a Queer Time and Place: Transgender Bodies, Subcultural Lives*. New York: New York University Press, 2005.

Hannau, Hans W., and Jeanne Garrard. *Flowers of the Caribbean*. Miami: Argos, 1986.

Hari, Johann. "Murder Music in Jamaica: The Campaign to Stigmatize Anti-gay Hate Music." Johann Hari, http://www.johannhari.com/archive (accessed 17 August 2009).

Hearn, Lafcadio. *Two Years in the French West Indies*. New York: Harper, 1890.

Henderson, John. *Jamaica*. London: Adam and Charles Black, 1906.

Henderson, Mae. "Opening Remarks." Presented at "Black Queer Studies: A Symposium," Northwestern University, Evanston, Ill., 20 January 2006.

Henriques, Fernando. *Family and Colour in Jamaica*. London: Eyre and Spottiswood, 1953.

Herskovits, Melville J., and Frances S. Herskovits. *Suriname Folk-Lore*. New York: Columbia University Press, 1936.

———. *Trinidad Village*. New York: Columbia University Press, 1947.

Hiss, Philip Hanson. *Netherlands America: The Dutch Territories in the West*. New York: Duell, Sloane, and Pearce, 1943.

Hoefte, Rosemarijne. "The Development of a Multiethnic Plantation Economy." *Twentieth-Century Suriname: Continuities and Discontinuities in a New World Society*, ed. Hoefte and Peter Meel, 1–22. Kingston: Ian Randle, 2001.

Hoogbergen, Wim, and Marjo de Theye. "Surinaamse Vrouwen in de slavernij." *Vrouwen in de Nederlandse Koloniën*, ed. Jeske Reijs, 126–51. Nijmegen: Sun, 1986.

Hron, Anthony. *Report on the Persecution of Sexual Minorities in Jamaica*. Kingston: Jamaica Forum of Lesbians, All-Sexuals, and Gays, 2003.

Hulme, Peter. "Polytropic Man: Tropes of Sexuality and Mobility in Early Colonial Discourse." *Europe and Its Others: Proceedings of the Essex Conference on the Sociology of Literature*, vol. 2, ed. Francis Barker et al., 17–32. Colchester: University of Essex, 1985.

"In Conservative Caribbean, Transsexuals Fight for Rights." Courtroom Television Network, 14 May 2001, http://www.courttv.com.

Irigaray, Luce. *This Sex Which Is Not One*. Trans. Catherine Porter. Ithaca: Cornell University Press, 1985.

Janssens, Marie-José, and Wilhelmina van Wetering. "Mati en lesbiennes, homoseksualiteit en ethnische identiteit bij Creools-Surinaamse vrouwen in Nederland." *Sociologische Gids* 32, nos. 5–6 (1985): 394–415.

Jennings, Eric T. *Vichy in the Tropics: Pétain's National Revolution in Madagaskar, Guadaloupe, and Indochina, 1940–1944*. Stanford: Stanford University Press, 2001.

Johnson, E. Patrick. "'Quare' Studies, or Almost Everything I Know about Queer Studies I Learned from my Grandmother." *Black Queer Studies: A Critical Anthology*, ed. Johnson and Mae G. Henderson, 124–60. Durham: Duke University Press, 2005.

Johnson, E. Patrick, and Mae G. Henderson, eds. *Black Queer Studies: A Critical Anthology*. Durham: Duke University Press, 2005.

Jordan, June. *Some of Us Did Not Die: New and Selected Essays*. New York: Civitas, 2002.

Kakutani, Michiko. "Books of the Times: No Telephone to Heaven." *New York Times*, 15 July 1987.

Keeling, Kara. *The Witch's Flight: The Cinematic, the Black Femme, and the Image of Common Sense*. Durham: Duke University Press, 2007.

Kempen, Michiel van. *Een geschiedenis van de Surinaamse literatuur, Deel 3*. Digitale Bibliotheek voor Nederlandse Letteren. http://www.dbnl.org/tekst/ kemp009gesc03_01/kemp009gesc03_01_0008.htm. Accessed 15 September 2009.

Kent, Kathryn. *Making Girls into Women: American Women's Writing and the Rise of Lesbian Identity*. Durham: Duke University Press, 2003.

Kiesnoski, Kenneth. "Charting the Caribbean: Which Islands Are Gay-Friendly, Which Aren't?" Gay.com, http://www.gay.com/travel (accessed 17 August 2009).

King, Jason. "Remixing the Closet: The Down-Low Way of Knowledge." *Village Voice*, 24 June 2003.

King, Rosamond S. "Re/Presenting Self and Other: Trans Deliverance in Caribbean Texts." *Callaloo* 31, no. 2 (2008): 581–99.

Klein, Ross A. *Cruise Ship Squeeze: The New Pirates of the Seven Seas*. Gabriola Island, B.C.: New Society, 2005.

Laleau, Léon. "Ida Faubert." *Femmes haïtiennes*, ed. Ligue Féminine d'Action Sociale, 247–52. Port-au-Prince: Henri Deschamps, 1954.

Lashgari, Deirdre, ed. *Violence, Silence, and Anger: Women's Writing as Transgression*. Charlottesville: University of Virginia Press, 1995.

Latimer, Tirza True. *Women Together, Women Apart: Portraits of Lesbian Paris*. New Brunswick: Rutgers University Press, 2005.

Lerner, Eric. "Olokun and the Art of Suppression." *Oya N'Soro*, May 2005, http://www.oyansoro.com.

Lier, Rudolph van. *Tropische tribaden*. Dordrecht: Foris, 1986.

Lionnet, Françoise. *Autobiographical Voices: Race, Gender, Self-Portraiture*. Ithaca: Cornell University Press, 1989.

Locher-Scholten, Elsbeth. "So Close and Yet So Far: The Ambivalence of Dutch Colonial Rhetoric on Javanese Servants in Indonesia, 1900–1942." *Domesticating the Empire: Race, Gender, and Family Life in French and Dutch Colonialism*, ed. Julia Clancy-Smith and Frances Gouda, 131–53. Charlottesville: University of Virginia Press, 1998.

Long, Edward. *The History of Jamaica*, vols. 1–3 [1774]. New York: Arno, 1972.

Lorde, Audre. *The Collected Poems of Audre Lorde*. New York: W. W. Norton, 1997.

———. *Sister Outsider*. Freedom, Calif.: Crossing Press, 1984.

———. *Zami: A New Spelling of My Name*. Freedom, Calif.: Crossing Press, 1982.

Lugones, María. "Purity, Impurity and Separation." *The Second Signs Reader*, ed. Ruth-Ellen B. Joers and Barbara Laslett, 275–96. Chicago: University of Chicago Press, 1996.

Makward, Christiane. *Mayotte Capécia ou l"aliénation selon Fanon*. Paris: Karthala, 1999.

Manalansan, Martin. *Global Divas: Filipino Gay Men in New York City*. Durham: Duke University Press, 2003.

Marty, Ann. *Haïti en littérature*. Paris: La Flèche du Temps, Maisonneuve et Larose, 2000.

Mascia-Lees, Frances E., and Patricia Sharpe, "Locked in or Locked Out or Holding Both Ends of a Slippery Pole: Confusion of Metaphors, Collaborations, and Intellectual Travesties." *Making Worlds: Gender, Metaphor, Materiality*, ed. Susan Aiken et al., 227–42. Tucson: University of Arizona Press, 1998.

Massad, Joseph A. *Desiring Arabs*. Chicago: University of Chicago Press, 2007.

Maupassant, Guy de. *Des vers*. Paris: G. Charpentier, 1880.

Mbembe, Achille. *On the Postcolony*. Berkeley: University of California Press, 2001.

McClintock, Ann. *Imperial Leather: Race, Gender, and Sexuality in the Colonial Contest*. New York: Routledge, 1995.

McCook, Stuart. *States of Nature: Science, Agriculture, and Environment in the Spanish Caribbean, 1760–1940*. Austin: University of Texas Press, 2002.

McLeod, Cynthia. *De vrije negerin Elisabeth: Het historische verhaal van een vrijgebochten zwarte vrouw in het Suriname van de achttiende eeuw*. Amsterdam: Zilver Pockets, 2000.

Métraux, Joël. "L'honneur des makoumès" *Têtu*, no. 37 (1999): 7–8.

Migge, Bettina. "The Origin of the Copulas d/n/a and de in the Eastern Maroon Creole." *Diachronica* 19, no. 1 (2002): 81–133.

Mintz, Sidney, and Richard Price. *The Birth of Afro-American Culture: An Anthropological Perspective.* 1976. Boston: Beacon, 1992.

Mitchell, David, ed. *Voices of Summerland: An Anthology of Jamaican Poetry.* London: Fowler Wright, 1929.

Morales, Aurora Levins. *Remedios: Stories of Earth and Iron from the History of the Puertorriqueñas.* Cambridge, Mass.: South End, 2001.

More, Kate, and Stephen Whittle, eds. *Reclaiming Genders: Transsexual Grammars at the Fin de Siècle.* London: Cassell, 1999.

Moreau de St. Méry, Médéric. *Description de la partie française de l'isle de St. Domingue.* 1797. Paris: Société de l'Histoire des Colonies Françaises, 1955.

Namaste, Viviane. *Invisible Lives: The Erasure of Transsexual and Transgender People.* Chicago: University of Chicago Press, 2000.

Neijhorst, Julian H. A. *Bigisma taki . . . Herkomst en betekenis van meer dan 3000 Surinaamse spreekwoorden (odo's) en uitdrukkingen.* Paramaribo, Surinam, 2002.

Nichols, Grace. *I Is a Long-Memoried Woman.* 1983. London: Karnak House, 1990.

Nugent, Maria. *Lady Nugent's Jamaica Journal.* Ed. Philip Wright. Kingston: Institute of Jamaica, 1966.

O'Callaghan, Evelyn. *Women Writing the West Indies, 1804–1939: "A Hot Place, Belonging to Us."* London: Routledge, 2004.

Oyěwùmí, Oyèrónke. *The Invention of Women: Making an African Sense of Western Gender.* Minneapolis: University of Minnesota Press, 1997.

Paravisini-Gebert, Lizbeth. "Decolonizing Feminism." *Daughters of Caliban: Caribbean Women in the Twentieth Century,* ed. Consuelo López Springfield, 3–17. Bloomington: University of Indiana Press, 1997.

Pate, Alexs. *West of Rehoboth.* New York: Perennial, 2001.

Peña, Susana. "'Obvious Gays' and the State Gaze: Cuban Gay Visibility and U.S. Immigration Policy during the 1980 Mariel Boatlift." *Journal of the History of Sexuality* 16, no. 3 (2007): 482–514.

Pineau, Gisèle. "Gisèle Pineau, mémoire vive." *Têtu,* no. 37 (1999): 8.

Pollock, Griselda. "Missing Women: Rethinking Early Thoughts on Images of Women." *Over Exposed: Essays on Contemporary Photography,* ed. Carol Squiers, 38–66. New York: New Press, 1999.

Poovey, Mary. "The Production of Abstract Space." *Making Worlds: Gender, Metaphor, Materiality,* ed. Susan Aiken et al., 69–89. Tucson: University of Arizona Press, 1998.

Pratt, Mary Louise. *Imperial Eyes: Studies in Travel Writing and Transculturation.* New York: Routledge, 1992.

Prengaman, Peter. "Lesbian Couple Caught in Aruba-Netherlands Rift." *Seattle Times*, 21 August 2005.

Price, Richard, and Sally Price. *Two Evenings in Saramaka*. Chicago: University of Chicago Press, 1991.

Price-Mars, Jean. *Ainsi parla l'oncle*. Ed. Robert Cornevin. New edn. Ottawa: Leméac, 1973.

Prince, Mary. *The History of Mary Prince*. 1837. *The Classic Slave Narratives*, ed. Henry Louis Gates Jr., 183–238. New York: Mentor Penguin, 1987.

Proschan, Frank. "Eunuch Mandarins, *Soldats Mamzelles*, Effeminate Boys, and Graceless Women: French Colonial Constructions of Vietnamese Genders." GLQ 8, no. 4 (2002): 435–67.

Prosser, Jay. "Exceptional Locations: Transsexual Travelogues." *Reclaiming Genders: Transsexual Grammars at the Fin de Siècle*, ed. Kate More and Stephen Whittle, 83–114. London: Cassell, 1999.

———. *Second Skins: The Body Narratives of Transsexuality*. New York: Columbia University Press, 1998.

Puar, Jasbir K. "Circuits of Queer Mobility." GLQ 8, nos. 1–2 (2002): 101–37.

Raiskin, Judith. "The Art of History: An Interview with Michelle Cliff." *Kenyon Review* 15, no. 1 (1993): 57–71.

Raymond, Janice. *The Transsexual Empire: The Making of the She-Male*. Boston: Beacon, 1979.

Reddock, Rhoda. "Women and Slavery in the Caribbean: A Feminist Perspective." *Latin American Perspectives* 12, no. 1 (1985): 63–80.

Robinson, Colin. "Toward a Strategy of Imagination." Paper presented at "Queer Islands?" University of Chicago, 16 April 2005.

Rodríguez, Juana. " 'From the House of Yemanjá': Mother, Myth, and Sexuality in Audre Lorde's Zami: A New Spelling of My Name." *Let Go My Mouth: Breaking Silences in African Diaspora Studies*. Berkeley: African American Studies Department, University of California, 1992.

Rodríguez-Mangual, Edna M. *Lydia Cabrera and the Construction of an Afro-Cuban Cultural Identity*. Chapel Hill: University of North Carolina Press, 2004.

Rosemont, Penelope, ed. *Surrealist Women: An International Anthology*. Austin: University of Texas Press, 1998.

Roumain, Jacques. *Gouverneurs de la rosée*. Paris: Messidor, 1946.

St. Louis, Carlos, and Maurice A. Lubin, eds. *Panorama de la poésie haïtienne*. Port-au-Prince: Henri Deschamps, 1950.

Sandoval, Chela. *Methodology of the Oppressed*. Minneapolis: University of Minnesota Press, 2000.

Santos-Febres, Mayra. *Sirena Selena vestida de pena*. Barcelona: Mondadori, 2000.

Saunders, Tanya. "Where Are All the (Black) Women? Thinking Race and Gender in

Cuba's Underground Lesbian Scene." Paper presented at "Race, Sex, Power: New Movements in Black and Latina/o Sexualities," University of Illinois, Chicago, 12 April 2008.

Schwarz, Meryl. "An Interview with Michelle Cliff." *Contemporary Literature* 34, no. 4 (1993): 595–619.

Seacole, Mary. *Wonderful Adventures of Mrs. Seacole in Many Lands.* Ed. Sarah Salih. London: Penguin, 2005.

Searle, Chris. *Words Unchained: Language and Revolution in Grenada.* London: Zed, 1984.

Sears, Clare. "All That Glitters: Trans-ing California's Gold Rush Migrations." GLQ 14, nos. 2–3 (2008): 383–402.

Sedgwick, Eve Kosofsky. *Epistemology of the Closet.* Berkeley: University of California Press, 1990.

Sharpley-Whiting, T. Denean. *Negritude Women.* Minneapolis: University of Minnesota Press, 2002.

Sheller, Mimi. *Consuming the Caribbean: From Arawaks to Zombies.* London: Routledge, 2003.

Shepherd, Verene. *Women in Caribbean History.* Kingston: Ian Randle, 1999.

Silvera, Makeda. "In the Company of My Work." *The Other Woman: Women of Colour in Contemporary Canadian Literature,* ed. Silvera, 365–80. Toronto: Sister Vision, 1994.

———. "Man Royals and Sodomites: Some Thoughts on the Invisibility of Afro-Caribbean Lesbians." *Piece of My Heart: A Lesbian of Colour Anthology,* ed. Silvera, 14–26. Toronto: Sister Vision, 1991.

Sinnott, Megan. *Toms and Dees: Transgender Identity and Female Same-Sex Relationships in Thailand.* Honolulu: University of Hawai'i Press, 2004.

Smallwood, Stephanie. *Saltwater Slavery: A Middle Passage from Africa to the American Diaspora.* Cambridge: Harvard University Press, 2007.

Smith, Sidonie, and Julia Watson, eds. *Women, Autobiography, Theory: A Reader.* Madison: University of Wisconsin Press, 1998.

Somerville, Siobhan S. *Queering the Color Line: Race and the Invention of Homosexuality in America.* Durham: Duke University Press, 2000.

Spillers, Hortense. "Mama's Baby, Papa's Maybe: An American Grammar Book." *Diacritics* 17, no. 2 (1987): 65–81.

Stedman, John Gabriel. *Narrative of a Five Years' Expedition against the Revolted Negroes of Suriname.* 1796. Baltimore: Johns Hopkins University Press, 1988.

Stephen, Henri J. M. *Winti: Afro-Surinaamse religie en magische rituelen in Suriname en Nederland.* Amsterdam: Karnak, 1985.

Stephens, Gregory. "A Culture of Intolerance: Insights on the Chi Chi Man Craze and Jamaican Gender Relations with Julius Powell of JFLAG." Jahworks.org, spring 2002, http://www. jahworks.org. music.

Stokes, Mason. *The Color of Sex: Whiteness, Heterosexuality, and the Fictions of White Supremacy.* Durham: Duke University Press, 2001.

Stoler, Ann Laura. *Carnal Knowledge and Imperial Power: Race and the Intimate in Colonial Rule*. Berkeley: University of California Press, 2002.

Thompson, Robert Farris. *Face of the Gods: Art and Altars of Africa and the African Americas*. New York: Museum for African Art, 1993.

Valcin, Mme Virgile [Cléanthe Desgraves]. *Fleurs et pleurs*. Port-au-Prince: Haïti, Imprimerie de l'État, 1924.

Vivien, Renée. *Oeuvre poétique complète*. Paris: Régie Deforges, 1986.

Voorhoeve, Jan, and Ursy Lichtveld. *Creole Drum: An Anthology of Creole Literature in Suriname*. New Haven: Yale University Press, 1970.

Voss, Michael. "Castro Champions Gay Rights in Cuba." BBC News Online, 27 March 2008, http://news.bbc.co.uk.

Waddell, Eric, Vijay Naidu, and Epeli Hau'ofa. *A New Oceania: Rediscovering Our Sea of Islands*. Suva, Fiji: School of Social and Economic Development, University of the South Pacific, in association with Beake House, 1993.

Walcott, Rinaldo. "Outside in Black Studies: Reading from a Queer Place in the Diaspora." In *Black Queer Studies: A Critical Anthology*, ed. E. Patrick Johnson and Mae G. Henderson, 90–105. Durham: Duke University Press, 2005.

Walker, Alice. *In Search of Our Mothers' Gardens: Womanist Prose*. San Diego: Harcourt Brace Jovanovich, 1984.

"We Want Equal Rights!" TNTmirror.com, 20 March 2005, http://www.tntmirror.com.

Wekker, Gloria. "'Girl, It's Boobies You're Getting, No?': Creole Women in Suriname and Erotic Relationships with Children and Adolescents." *Paidika: The Journal of Paedophilia* Vol. 2 No.4 (1992): 43–48.

———. *Ik ben een gouden munt: subjectiviteit en seksualiteit van Creoolse volksklasse vrouwen in Paramaribo*. Amsterdam: VITA, 1994.

———. "Of mimic men and unruly women. Social relations in twentieth century Suriname." *Suriname in the Twentieth Century*, ed. Rosemarijn Hoefte and Peter Meel, 174–97 Leiden and Kingston: KITLV Press and Ian Randle, 2001.

———. *The Politics of Passion: Women's Sexual Culture in the Afro-Surinamese Diaspora*. New York: Columbia University Press, 2006.

———. "What's Identity Got to Do With It?" *Female Desires: Same-Sex Relations and Transgender Practices across Cultures*, ed. Evelyn Blackwood and Saskia E. Wieringa, 119–38. New York: Columbia University Press, 1999.

Wetering, Ineke van. "Polyvocality and Constructions of Syncretism in Winti." *Reinventing Religions: Syncretism and Transformation in Africa and the Americas*, ed. Sidney Greenfield and Andre Droogers, 183–200. Lanham, Md.: Rowman and Littlefield, 2001.

White, Nicole. "Rhythm of Hatred: Anti-gay Lyrics Reflect an Island's Intolerance." *Miami Herald*, 5 August 2001.

Wieringa, Saskia E. "Desiring Bodies or Defiant Cultures: Butch-Femme Lesbians in

Jakarta and Lima." *Female Desires: Same-Sex Relations and Transgender Practices across Cultures*, ed. Evelyn Blackwood and Wieringa, 206–29. New York: Columbia University Press, 1999.

Williams, Byron. "Silence about 'Down Low' Culture Reflects Black History." *Oakland Tribune*, 15 July 2004.

Williams, Eric. *Capitalism and Slavery*. Chapel Hill: University of North Carolina Press, 1944.

Willis, Deborah, and Carla Williams. *The Black Female Body: A Photographic History*. Philadelphia: Temple University Press, 2002.

Wolcott, Mary Adela [Tropica]. *The Island of Sunshine*. New York: Knickerbocker, 1904.

Wooding, Charles J. "Traditional Healing and Medicine in Winti: A Sociological Interpretation." *Issue: A Quarterly Journal of Africanist Opinion* 9, no. 3 (1979): 35–40.

Wynter, Sylvia. "Beyond Miranda's Meanings: Un/silencing the 'Demonic Ground' of 'Caliban's Woman.'" *Out of the Kumbla: Caribbean Women ad Literature*, ed. Carol Boyce Davies and Elaine Savory Fido, 355–72. Trenton, N.J.: Africa World, 1990.

Zamora, Lois P. and Wendy B. Faris, ed. *Magical Realism: Theory, History, Community*. Durham: Duke University Press, 1995.

Index

Omise'eke Natasha Tinsley is an assistant professor
of English at the University of Minnesota.

Library of Congress Cataloging-in-Publication Data
Tinsley, Omise'eke Natasha, 1971–
Theifing sugar : eroticism between women in Caribbean
literature / Omise'eke Natasha Tinsley.
    p. cm. – (Perverse modernities)
Includes bibliographical references and index.
ISBN 978-0-8223-4756-9 (cloth : alk. paper)
ISBN 978-0-8223-4777-4 (pbk. : alk. paper)
1. Caribbean literature – 20th century – History and criticism.
2. Lesbianism in literature. I. Title. II. Series: Peverse modernities.
PN 849.C3T56 2010
809′.933526643098611 – dc22   2010004456